The Progress of a Gardener

by Barbara Hyde

Design, Layout & Illustrations by Daina D. Penn
& Illustrator Cristi Schmich

Barbara J. Hyde, Inc.
2431 W. Peakview Ct.
Littleton, CO 80120
(303) 794-7088

Introduction

G ardeners are open channels for information regarding the craft, but they want it on their own terms. Whether it be a long winter's read before the fire, or a quick riffle through an index with muddy fingers to find a needed bit of information that will mend a troubled plant, the gardener will always rely on a book or two that will fill the need of the moment. Written for the eight mountain western states, this book brings forward the amateur gardener of Volume 1 into the world of slightly rarer air, but with no aspirations toward the professional horticulturist. Leave the propagation chapter till last if you are reader that begins at the beginning and reads straight through. If you are a dabbler, do the same. Your increasing skills in the world of horticulture will gradually whet your appetite to try your hand at some propagation procedures.

This volume is dedicated to
Daina, Marge, Jeanne, and Marie
We're a team!

© 1995 by Barbara Hyde
First edition, first printing January 1995
First edition, second printing December 1997

Design, Layout & Ilustrations by Daina D. Penn
Cover photograph of author's garden by Robert Pollack

Libarary of Congress 92-094319
Hyde, Barbara
The Progress of a Gardener — 1st edition
Includes bibliographical reference and index.
ISBN 0-9635224-0-8

Copy Editors:
Marie Orlin
Book Nook • Silverthorne, Colorado

Jeanne Collins
WordsWorth • (303) 355-5038

Printed In the United States of America by
Associated Printers
P.O. Box 8115
Longmont, Colorado 80501

Acknowledgements

Paula Boyle
Lois Clark
Marlene Cowdery
Dr..Whitney Cranshaw
Shirley Ela
Steve Ela
William Ela
Dr. Harrison Hughes

David Leatherman
Dr. Samuel Litzenberger
Don and Carroll McCallister
Isadore Million
Ila Sheehan
Dorothy Wallace
Gayle Weinstein
Gayle Zweck

Table of Contents

Vegetables

S ince the early 1970's, gardening polls have consistently shown that beginning gardeners grow vegetables. Some continue to develop their ability by increasing the number of species until they have reached the entire gamut of the vegetables. Others zero in on refining the design and efficiency of very small plots. Still others aim toward bringing supreme quality to their vegetables without ever branching out into other fields of horticulture. Yet statistics show that many vegetable gardeners quickly abandon vegetables after a year or two to become experts in another aspect of gardening.

This chapter will introduce vegetable gardening to the beginner as well as delve into some of the finer points of culture for the advanced vegetable grower.

Site

Because we live in the Mountain West we can be more flexible in our choice of a site for a vegetable garden. Only 6 hours of sunlight are required for a good garden. The quality of light at our average altitude gives us an advantage over the low-landers who must have 8 to 12 hours of sun.

An almost level site with no competition from tree roots will give the best results. The height of nearby deciduous or evergreen trees will affect the number of sunlight hours. Before choosing a site, consider the sunlight at all seasons,

■ *Before choosing a site, consider the sunlight at all seasons.*

especially the low angle of the sun in early spring and fall, as well as in midsummer at summer solstice, June 21.

Hillside sites away from the direction of the prevailing wind are not to be dismissed. Building up raised beds to accomodate the site make them the first to drain and warm in spring. South-facing hillside sites are especially desirable in the high country.

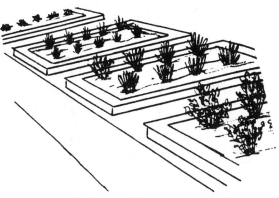

Raised beds on a hillside site in the high country.

Soil

Almost any soil can be improved. Poor soil is a handicap, but with diligence even junkyard soil can be reclaimed to improve the structure for tilth and fertility so that the soil will retain moisture and nutrients, yet provide aeration for plant roots. Mountain West soils have the advantage of our Eastern and Coastal West soils by having all the needed minerals necessary for good plant growth. In the East minerals have been leached away by 40 inches of precipitation annually. The only ingredient our soils lack is organic matter which is easily added in the form of homemade compost, sphagnum peatmoss, or weathered manure, preferably rabbit manure (See Vol I, p.38). With annual additions of organic matter, you will soon have a soil that crumbles in

your fingers like chocolate cake.

If It Doesn't Grow Good Weeds, Watch Out!

The exception to the statement above "almost any soil..." are the 2 contingencies known as the saline and the sodic soils. The saline soil contains an excess of water-soluble salts. The sodic soil contains an excess of exchangeable sodium. To complicate matters, there can be a combination soil that has both soluble saline salts and exchangeable sodium.

The saline soil inhibits seed germination and plant growth. It is easily recognized by the patchy white crust on top of the soil, though water intake is usually satisfactory. In the Mountain West this soil is known also as "alkali," and there are many small towns throughout the Mountain West with a seamy section known as "Alkali Flats."

The sodium soils occur in heavy clay with a high pH, usually above 9.0. Cations are positively charged atoms. The good-guy cations in a sodium soil are calcium, magnesium, potassium, and ammonium. Clay particles attract and hold cations, but if more than 15% of the bad-guy sodium cations are attracted to the clay particles, the soil is a sodium or sodic soil. Sodium soils are hard and cloddy when dry, and crust badly after wetting. Water intake is poor.

Both the saline and the sodium soil are often the results of being irrigated with poor quality water. If you plan to use river, creek, or well water, have it tested for mineral content before you plant.

Reclamation of the saline/sodium soils can be a lengthy procedure involving leaching the offending salts away with the use of 6 inches of good quality water all at one time. It also involves digging drainage ditches so that the water, now salt-laden, can be drained into a harmless sump. Adequate drainage prevents salts leached from the surface by irrigation from returning to the plant root zone by upward capillary action. The white, crusty alkali patches are usually found on high spots or in a swale. Land leveling and heavy additions of organic matter to the patches will often eliminate the problem, but if the area is low, drain ditches are imperative or the organic matter will tie up with the offending minerals to compound the problem. With the sodium soil, the bad-guy cations of sodium can be replaced on the clay particles with gypsum, which is calcium sulfate. It is a mined product. If a soil test conducted at the soil laboratory of your state university shows results are a saline/sodium soil, there will be recommendations for the amount of gypsum to add to the soil. If not, contact your Cooperative Extension Service for direction in applying gypsum.

Clay, Silt, and Sand Plus OM Leads to Loam

Pick up a handful of soil in the proposed vegetable garden site. Moisten it slightly if it is dry; then squeeze the handful and open your hand. If there is a tight sticky, shiny lump with the imprints of your fingers, it is a clay. Use your thumb and forefinger to press it into a ribbon. Sticking together in a ribbon that can stand alone is another signal that you have a heavy clay.

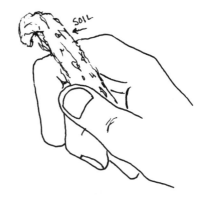

Ribboning a soil for clay, silt, and sand content.

If your ribbon has deep indentations (known as "teeth") along the edges, then pick up a dry handful of the same soil. If it feels silky and smooth like talcum, you have a silt soil. If the ball of soil is gritty and crumbles and falls apart without making any semblence of a ball, it is a sandy soil. If you have a reasonably good loam, it will form a ball and a ribbon, but will quickly fall apart without keeping its shape. If you can see organic matter (OM) in this soil — bits of root hairs, leaves, etc.— you have a loam soil. It is the ultimate goal of every gardener.

Soil Testing

If you want to check your assessment of your soil texture, send a sample to your state university soil testing laboratory for confirmation. The test will also give you the organic matter percentage, and parts per million of each mineral considered to be a plant nutrient with recommendations for amendments. One pound (approximately 2 cups) of air-dried soil taken from different sites throughout the proposed area then mixed together will be necessary for testing. Sending soil to a private soil-testing laboratory is seldom a risk, but there are a few laboratories that will make recommendations for unnecessary fertilizers in order to receive kick-back from unscrupulous fertilizer manufacturers.

Solarizing the Soil

In some soils weed seeds are in the gazillion range. To avoid the back-breaking toil of weeding week after week in the years to come, consider solarizing the soil by covering it for a growing season with clear plastic. Securing the edges of the plastic is an absolute necessity to prevent billowing air from inflating the sheet and blowing it away. Digging a trench beside the edge, inserting the edge of the plastic, and filling and tamping the trench will secure the plastic, but a few rocks or bricks here and there won't hurt. Moisten the soil before installing the plastic. Once installed, the weed seeds will germinate, but soon cook in the excessive heat and lack of air regime under the plastic.

Adding Organic Matter and Phosphorous

If you have not had a soil test and the site you have selected seems to grow a *moderate* amount of weeds, chances are strong that you can grow good vegetables. A general recommendation for an annual addition of organic matter is **1 pound per square foot**. This amount will depend upon the moisture in the organic matter when you weigh it, but a little more or less is not of extreme importance. At the same time weigh up a **pound of triple superphosphate (0-45-0) to add to each 100 square feet of your site.** This is a very small amount, but too often phosphorous is not present in sufficient quantity at the root level. Since this element does not move readily in the soil, it is necessary to add this small amount each year to till in at the same time as you till in the annual dollop of organic matter. See

Raised Beds. A word here about the use of rock phosphate. Organic gardening information sources state that to be "organic," the source of phosphorous must be rock phosphate, which is a mined product. Soil scientists in the Mountain West tell us that when rock phosphate is used, it may be 200 years before it is broken down sufficiently for plant use. The organic acids, such as carbonic, are too weak to do the job. Superphosphate is rock phosphate treated with sulfuric acid. It is available to the plant immediately.

Double-Digging - NOT!

In the early seventies a sleeping giant awakened that was not favorable to soil fertility in the Mountain West. Bright, young new gardeners, highly trained in such fields as astro-physics or other complex fields of science but untrained in the field of agronomy or horticulture awakened to the joys of gardening and began reading trestises from previous centuries that told of the farmer who lovingly (and back-breakingly) dug his spade into the soil 2 feet deep, lifted the load, and tossed it aside. He continued this laborious task in rows, tossing his load into the previously dug trench until he reached the last row of his plot. He then filled the last trench with the soil dug from the first row. This is double-digging.

The reasoning behind this gargantuan endeavor was to bring up soil nutrients long since buried by previous weather events, human incidents, and horticultural happenings. Well and good in the East where the soil profile contains a wide B horizon of an accumulation of leached organic matter and mineral nutrients at about the 2 foot depth. Double digging brings up this rich source of plant nutrients to the root level of future carrots, giant rutabagas, etc. In the Mountain West the soil profile is limited to a thin skin of sparse organic matter on top. Below this is a rich mineral subsoil completely devoid of organic matter. The double-digging results in burying the little dab of organic matter 2 feet deep, out of reach of the roots of a carrot. If copious amounts of organic matter are incorporated during the double-digging, there might be some slight advantage, but not enough to overcome the disadvantage of bringing up to sunlight and water the weed seeds buried by centuries of wind-blown, water-borne dust in the process of parent material weathering and soil-making. And who needs more weeds? Save your back and shake the notion that every organic information source is gospel. In the Mountain West there are many weather/water/soil relationships that make charting new ground your responsibility as you learn how to deal with your own piece of real estate.

Raised Beds

Spring is a sometime thing in these parts. It is never the calm, sweet unfolding of poetry and song. Wild wind, late snows, and deadly frosts are more the norm. To encourage the soil to thaw and warm requires a technique of building a stable bed of soil above the surface. The raised bed will drain and warm faster than a deep planting furrow. If a dump trunk releases a load of soil, the pile forms in a conical shape with a constant angle of 37°. This is known as *the angle of repose*. It is very stable. If you pile more soil on top of the cone at a steeper angle, soil will begin to trickle down until the angle of repose is once again reached. If you take away soil from the pile to make the angle less steep, it begins to break down into a shapeless,

irregular form. Therefore, we try for the 37° angle when we make a raised bed.

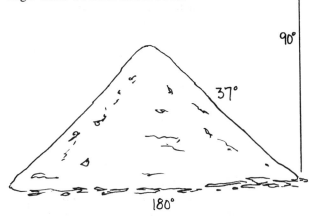

Angle of repose on a pile of soil.

Your objective is to form raised beds that will be 12 inches wide. Before you begin, consider the lay of the land. Making rows of raised beds from north to south or east to west is not nearly as important as considering the force of gravity. Water does not run uphill. Even though you may be planning a drip system, make sure your rows run with the lay of the land so that the irrigation system will function.

Spade in the measured amounts of organic matter and superphosphate as described above. Go back with a bow rake to break up clods until the soil particles are the size of peas. Using a small 2-stroke, gasoline-powered tiller will also give good results. Go back once again to begin to form the raised bed at the 37° angle. With practice your eye will guide your hands. As a final procedure, use the back of the rake to make the top of the bed flat.

The beds should be about 2 to 3 feet apart. Use your wheelbarrow or cart to determine the width. This portion will be the path and will become compacted with foot and wheeled traffic and you will not cultivate it. **EVER!** The compaction of this soil will prevent weeds from growing. Wide-spreading crops, such as cucumbers and squash will range over the paths, making foot and wheeled traffic impossible, but not impeding harvesting.

Raised Beds Not Recommended in New Mexico, Nevada, S. Utah

The varied altitudes and southern latitudes of the Mountain West make necessary different methods of culture. Long, hot summers, with low humidity and little rain are normal. Instead of raised beds, lowered beds are more efficient. Beds 4 feet wide (the reach of your arm plus your hoe handle) are dug with the same incorporation of organic matter as recommended above so that 6 inches of water can be applied all at one time. You can install a drip system if you wish, but flood irrigation is also very efficient with this type of garden. This is also a good method if your soil is somewhat sandy. See Vol. I, p. 73.

Lowered bed more efficient in southern Mountain West.

End Row Flowers for Beauty and Pollination

The Fetzer Gardens of Hopland, California, have demonstrated the art of raised bed gardening, as well as the technique of adding a half-moon shaped flower garden at the end of each row. Beauty and fragrance are of importance, but the more lasting value is the pollination potential. The honeybees and other insects are drawn to the flowers, and stay around to pollinate the vegetables. Good flower choices are those with fragrance and all-season bloom characteristics.

Half circles of flowers at ends of vegetable rows add beauty and attractants to pollinating insects.

Box Gardening

For some gardeners, a different kind of raised bed is necessary. If you must garden on a steep slope, or if you are handicapped and need planting areas at wheelchair-arm height, you will like the idea of growing vegetables in a box. The construction of permanent beds is expensive, but long-lasting, and will add to the value of the property if you wish to sell. Make them within close view of the house and close to a water source that can be piped underground to a stand pipe in each bed.

"Big Box Gardens"

shaped flower bed where low-growing, fragrant flowers are planted. Cap the lines and fasten down with U-pins. If you remove the caps and drain the lines each fall, you should not have to take up and store the system unless you are bothered by rodents that chew into the tough plastic. In this event, give them a 10 foot length of telephone cable all their very own, and they may leave your drip system alone.

Trellis Construction

With the box bed the construction of trellises is not difficult. Unlike that of wire, PVC gives climbing crops a cool surface upon which to climb. If you are using the raised bed construction, use the same or additional 2x4's with drilled holes in which to fit a PVC trellis. Crops that sprawl unless caged, such as tomatoes, can be allowed a controlled sprawl, keeping the shoot growth direction *within* the bed, or they can be caged in sturdy cages.

Installation of the Drip System

The purchase of a drip irrigation system is routine nowadays in this area. It is the only truly efficient means of delivering water to plantings in the greater Mountain West. (See Vol. I, p. 72). Two lines of drip hose are run down each of the raised beds. This may seem excessive, but will save time and money on water over the long run. You can plant seeds, alternately, on either side of a single, center-positioned line, but the root systems are never as good, nor the plants as thrifty as when they don't have to reach for water. At the end of each row, continue the lines to water the half-moon

Drip system lines running down raised beds; half-moon of flower beds at ends aid pollination of vegetables.

Installing Protection

The use of floating row cover[1] and clear plastic protection from frost, hail, and snow will be necessary from time to time. Purchase flawed 8-foot lengths of 2x4 at sale prices. Line them up adjacent to each other. Use an electric drill to drill in each support identical holes in each large enough to accomodate lengths of PVC or #9 wire. Place these 2x4's on either side of a row to form supports for floating row cover or plastic row protection. With the addition of a center spine of PVC or wire, the covers

7

are held down at intervals with bricks, stones,or additional 2x4's which are easily set aside so that the covers can be lifted to tend or harvest the plants beneath.

Planting in Cold Soil and Winter Planting

There are times when it is wise to plant early — even during winter - and there are times when early planting in cold soil results in aberrations of seedlings that lead to failure. For example, in planting beans early before the soil temperature reaches 60°F, the result is *ballheads,* a stem emerging with no seed leaves attached. They have been destroyed by the corn-seed maggot which attacks seeds of corn, peas, beans, and seed potatoes. The adult resembles a small house fly. If you plant early, establish a raised bed where soil will be warm, planting seed only l inch deep. Replant at once if ballheads appear.

Winter planting can be a risk, but if you win, you have crops that are far ahead of spring-planted ones and you have a leisurely spring watching them grow! Seeds do not rot in the seed row as they do in the East and other wet climates. After you have spaded the soil in fall, choose a sunny day in November or January to take the risk of opening trenches 8 inches deep to plant peas, spinach, leaf lettuce, radish, and any other cool season crop you favor. Cover with only the amount of soil recommended on the packet. Water thoroughly. The depth of the trench will protect the emerging seedlings from wind and dessication. The warm, spring sun, beginning in February, will radiate warmth back across the sides of the trench. Frequent snows will melt to water the seedlings, but they won't show much growth until late March. Seed is cheap. Take a chance!

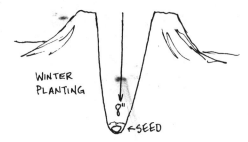

WINTER PLANTING

8"

←SEED

If You Live at High Altitude

If you live at high altitude or at a northern latitude, do as Alaskans[2] do — plant germintaed seeds in a jelly of cooked cornstarch. Add 1 tablespoon of cornstarch to 1 cup of cold water, stirring until starch is dissolved. Cook over low heat, stirring constantly until the mixture is clear and thick. Cool. Pour 1/2 cup into a zip-lock bag and slide **germinated** seeds into the gel and stir very gently; close and store if it's a bad day for planting. When planting, open a seed row in a raised bed. Cut off a corner of the bag and squeeze a ribbon of the starch/ seed mixture down the row. Sprouted seed will grow in cooler soil than unsprouted. If you're planting sprouted beans, squeeze a ribbon of starch into the furrow, then press each sprouted seed with the eye down into the gel. Cover with another light coating of the starch. Then cover with 1 inch of soil. Water lightly by sprinkling. Install a row cover of clear plastic with ends that can be opened in warm daytime temperatures. Usually, no more watering is necessary before germination takes place. This

[1] *See Glossary*
[2] *This planting method was gleaned from a lecture by Lenore Hedla of Alaska at the Master Gardener's convention in Portland OR, October, 1987.*

method is good for areas where it is impossible to plant vegetables until late June.

To germinate seeds for the above procedure, see Chapter 8, Propagation, Seeds.

The Cutworm Collar

The cutworm lies, C-shaped, just under the surface of the soil by day, then roams about at night cutting soft stems of seedlings at the soil line, but not eating them. No one knows why. Prevent the damage by surrounding the seedling stems with a collar made from a strip of waxed milk carton. A kitchen match stuck next to the seedling and snugged up against the stem will also protect it.

MILK CARTON COLLAR

Cutworm collar.

As we begin to explore the different vegetables, culture of each will be included.

■ ARTICHOKE, GLOBE

The possibility of growing gourmet globe artichokes in the Mountain West never occurred to anyone until Dr. Harry Mack of Oregon State University began trials in 1980. Grown as an annual, they are on the high-dollar end of commercial production. As a backyard garden novelty the harvest will be small compared to the amount of space they will occupy, but they will make you proud and prove oneupmanship.

Seed planting in a greenhouse should begin in late February to mid-March in individual 3 inch pots, hardened off and planted out 6 to 8 weeks later. Space the transplants 24 inches apart in rows 3 feet apart. If you grow organically, one shovelful of fresh chicken manure worked into the soil at planting time should suffice for the season. Use 14-14-14 Osmacote if you prefer chemical fertilizer. Harvest the globes before they start to open as flowers.

To try to winter-over the plants: Cull the plants so that only the best remain, leaving one plant for every 4 feet of row. In late October, cut off plants about 6 inches above ground, cover with a straw mound, and insert moth balls to ward off mice. Cover the straw mound with clear plastic to keep the stump from freezing. Uncover in early April. Survival rate is about 35%.

Cultivar

'AR100 Green Globe'- Available from Territorial Seed Co., 20 Palmer Ave., Cottage Grove OR 97424. Catalog free.

'Grand Beurre' - Very prickly, said to be hardier.

'Purple Globe' - From Italy.
Troubles

This crop is too new in the Mountain West to see any established pest and disease problems.

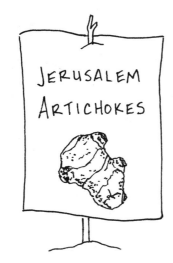

■ *Helianthus tuberosus*
ARTICHOKE, JERUSELEM

A perennial of the *Composite* family, the Jeruselem artichoke resembles several of the roadside daisy-type wildflowers, and vigorous 8 foot clumps of it can be seen surviving with no care on the banks of irrigation canals throughout the Mountain West. Dried stalks are often used for kindling. It is grown for the tuberous root, which tastes a little like water chestnut and can be either eaten raw or cooked like potatoes. It has a nut-like flavor and is very low in calories. It is often recommended to those who suffer from Diabetes mellitus. Begin digging the tubers after frost has killed the tops in early winter. Store in plastic bags in the refrigerator.
Cultivar
'Stampede' - Available from Johnny's Seeds, Foss Hill Rd. Albion, ME 04910-

9731. Catalog free.
Troubles
Aphid
Grasshoppers

■ ARUGULA

In the "what-is-it category, arugula is a cool-season gourmet green with a robust, peppery flavor. It is used as an accent in salads. Also called 'Roquette,' it is planted in early spring or the middle of August, except in areas of high altitude, where it can be grown throughout the summer. Harvest when the leaves are the size of dandelion leaves, cutting with scissors at the base. More leaves will spring up from within the rosette.
Troubles
See Chapter 4 Insects, Chapter 5, Diseases
    Aphid
    Leafminer

Asparagus planting is a once-only endeavor.

■ ASPARAGUS

The first vegetable of the spring season is the most welcome. We plant asparagus to last a generation of the family, for the crowns are long-lived if planted correctly. Plan for 10 plants for each member of the family. Four feet between rows is standard procedure, for the fern growth in summer is wide-spreading. Prepare the soil by removing the soil from a trench 2 feet deep and 1 foot wide and incorporating weathered manure in the bottom of the trench along with 1 foot of the soil removed. Plant the crowns so that the roots are spread over a slight mound. Deep planting is necessary because asparagus roots migrate in the soil. Cover the crowns, tamp down slightly and water well. Incorporate more weathered manure into the remaining backfill, but leave it set aside. The crowns will begin to grow as soon as spring sun warms the trench. As the sprouts grow, fill in the trench with the remaining backfill until the level grade is reached. Install the drip lines.

As the summer progresses, the plants will put up ferns that may need shoring up by means of hilling up around the stems. If you wish to be very selective, dig and destroy all female plants, identifiable by their red berries. Male plants produce more stalks. Harvesting does not take place until the third spring unless you are planting one of the new varieties (see below). Each spring for each 5 plants, broadcast 1 quart of an all purpose fertilizer such as 8-10-8 for 6-inches on each side of the crown growth.

In the third season and thereafter harvest the stalks by cutting at the soil level with a sharp knife. Breaking will leave a ragged tip open to disease and insects. Harvest every few days, but never harvest a stalk smaller than the diameter of your thumb. Leave the ferns standing in the fall until about March 1. Then cut them off cleanly at ground level.

Cultivars

The following are all male crosses from research conducted at Rutgers University, University of California and research institutions in Germany. They are said to withstand harvesting in the second year without harm to future growth.

'Greenwich'

'Jersey Giant'

'Jersey Knight'

'Jersey Prince'

'Lucellus'

'UC-72'

'Mary Washington' - The old standard variety is still good.

Troubles

See Chapter 4 Insects & Chapter 5 Diseases

INSECTS	DISEASES
Asparagus aphid	Asparagus rust
Asparagus beetles (2 species)	

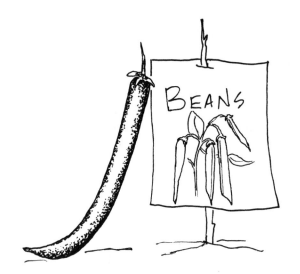

■ BEANS

The staff of life among vegetables, high protein, vitamin-rich beans are satisfied with moderately rich soil. If you add organic matter and phosphorous in the amounts recommended on p. 4, no further fertilization will be necessary. Keep soil moist, but just barely. Lima beans will need slightly more water. Follow a strict 3-year rotation in growing beans. Two bean diseases are prevalent throughout the Mountain West, but will seldom strike if you follow a 3-year rotation.

The genus *Phaseolus* is divided into 4 categories: *P. acutifolius* is the tepary bean; *P. coccineus* is the scarlet runner bean; *P. lunatus* is the lima bean; *P.vulgaris* is the common bean into which are dumped all the rest - such as kidney, snap, haricot, French horticultural, Italian flat green, etc. Many cultivars of each are available as both bush and pole climbers.

Any bean grown to the point where the seed swells in the pod is a "shell bean." You may find them called "shelly beans" in cans at the grocery. If beans are dried, they may be referred to as "shell" or "dried."

Planting with the Eye Down at Correct Temperature, Spacing

The yield of any type of bean will be increased if the seeds are planted so that the indentation or "eye" is down and in contact with the soil beneath it.

The soil temperature should be 60°F. or slightly above. The spacing should be 4 to 5 inches apart. For pole beans, plant 6 around the base of each pole and thin to the 3 strongest. For bush beans, planting distance is the same, but row culture is preferred.

Using an Inoculant

The nitrogen-fixing bacteria *Rhizobium phaseoli* in the soil may not be present in sufficient quantity to assure a good crop of beans or any other legume. You may improve the crop yield by sprinkling the dry powdered bacterial inoculast over the planted seed just before you close the row with your hoe. This inoculant enables the bean plants to convert the gaseous soil nitrogen between the soil particles to a form they can use. It is sold in small quantities for the backyard gardener at most garden centers.

Succession Cropping

Almost every cultivar of bush bean can be planted successively, a row at a time every 2 weeks, until August 1. The last row will require a row cover (see "Installing Protection") to mature properly. When the beans are swelling in the pod, pull the entire row and drag the plants to a shady spot where you can pull the pods from the vine from the comfort of a chair. Be sure to put on some nice music. The harvested vines make excellent compost.

If the cultivar is to be grown for dried beans, allow them to remain on the vines as long as possible, but when pods split, the beans are scattered, so don't wait too long. If you can leave a dent in the bean with your fingernail, it is not dry enough to store well. It's not always easy to determine the best time to pull the vines and proceed as above. After pulling the pods from the vines, place them in a cloth bag or old pillow case and stomp on them several times. Set up a fan and blow the chaff from the beans. Dried beans should be spread in a cookie sheet and heated through in an oven set at 130°F. for 30 minutes to kill any corn seed maggot eggs that might be present. Though beans won't freeze, they store easily in glass or plastic in the freezer.

■ POLE BEANS

Pole beans have the advantage of a longer season of production, and can be harvested once a week all summer. Poles are set up in a variety of ways. For the apartment dweller, use a large wooden tub for a bean tower of strings attached to a metal pole, which is attached to hoops at top and bottom. This device is author-tested and available in many nursery catalogs.

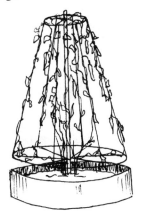

Bean tower for growing pole beans.

Cultivars
■ BUSH BEANS
Extra early
  'Strike'
  'Earliserve'
  'Spring Green'
  'Improved Tendergreen'
  'Tenderlake'
Early
  'Provider'
  'Green Lantern'
Main Season
  'Derby'
  'E-Z-Pick'
  'Bush Blue Lake'
  'Bush Kentucky Wonder'
Flat Green Beans
  '23 Greencrop'
  'Bush Romano'
  'Fava'
Bush Wax Beans
  '8 Cherokee Wax'
  'Golden Rod'
  'Sungold'
Bush Lima Beans
  'Fordhook 242' - the All America Winner

Cultivars
■ POLE BEANS
Burpee's 'Fordhook Lima' - A packet will plant 10 poles 2 to 3-feet apart.

'Kentucky Wonder' - An old stand-by.

'Blue Lake'- Of superior flavor.

'Scarlet Runner' - Good fresh or dried; hummingbirds swarm to the attractive flowers.

■ SOYBEANS
'Hodgson'[1] - Considered the best variety. Harvest when pods begin to yellow. Blanch pods 2-3 minutes, cool and shuck. Each pod contains 3 beans. Do not eat raw.

[1] *Available at Seed Savers Exchange, 3076 N. Winn Rd., Decorah IA 52101.*

◼ NOVELTY GREEN BEANS AND DRIED BEANS

'Anasazi' - To preserve our cultural heritage, Mountain Westerners should grow this every year. Requires growing season of 100 days. Sweet, nutty.

'Black Turtle Beans' - The basis for many Mexican dishes.

'French Horticultural'- Delicious shelled or dried.

'Flageolet' - A French shell bean as tasty as a lima, and MUCH easier to grow!

'Haricot Verts' (filet beans) - Slender pods of rich flavor distince from ordinary beans. 'Triumph de Farcy' should be cooked to crunchy stage; bears heavily very early. Harvest the pods as they ripen, thus encouraging the plants to continue bearing.

'Hutterite Soup Bean' - Soup beans make a gravy as they cook.

'Jacob's Cattle' - A standard baking bean from Maine.

'Navy' - The Boston baked bean; makes a gravy.

'Red Mexican' - Better than the Kidney; shorter growing season.

'Royal Burgundy'- Long straight purple pods that turn green after 2 minutes of cooking. Good for freezing.

'Taos Pueblo Red' - For high altitude growing.

◼ ENGLISH RUNNER BEANS

The cultivars grown in England before and during World War II are seldom available in North America. If you are travelling in England or have access to English nursery catalogs, purchase one or more of these to perpetuate in your own garden: 'White Princeps,' 'Springbok,' 'Scarlet Ornamental.' They are said to be far superior to our runner beans.

Troubles

See Chapter 4 Insects, Chapter 5, Diseases

INSECTS	DISEASES
aphids	blights
bean weevil	powdery mildew
blister beetle	
corn seed maggot	
cutworm	
flea beetle	
leafhopper	
leafminer	
Mexican bean beetle	
spider mites	

◼ BEETS

Beets do best in well-drained, friable soils. They are ideally suited to the Mountain West in raised bed culture. They prefer an alkaline soil, easily provided in this area.

Plant seed 1 inch deep in rows as soon as the frost is out of the ground. Seeds require 10-14 days to germinate; thus the seed bed must be kept moist (not soggy) to insure prompt emergence. A thin layer of straw, or cardboard placed over the planted rows aids germination. Remove cardboard just as seedlings emerge. Thin to 2 inches. An early July planting will mature for fall and winter use.

Beet greens, lightly steamed, make possible 2 palatable dishes for the table. Beets are easily baked, microwaved, or boiled. Cut the foliage an inch above the top of the beet to avoid excessive "bleeding" when boiling. The skin will slip away when they are fork-tender.

Cultivars

Baby Beets
'Little Mini Ball' - About the size of a silver dollar. 54 days.

'Little Ball' - A gourmet treat, prolific.
Early Beets
'Stokes Special Early' - Round; dark red flesh.

Main Crop
'34A Detroit Supreme' - An improvement over an old variety.

'Detroit Dark Red Short Top' - 63 days.

Troubles

See Chapter 4 Insects, Chapter 5 Diseases

INSECTS	DISEASES
aphid	beet curlytop
beet armyworm	leafspot
blister beetle	
cutworm	
leafhopper	
leaf miner	

■ BROCCOLI

Seed may be sown indoors in March. Harden off transplants before planting out about April 15. Use a hotcap or row cover to protect from freezing and *buttoning*, a condition of premature formation of small button-like heads that are inedible. Broccoli is a good crop to follow peas as a succession crop. Seed may be sown outdoors about April 10, 1 inch deep. Thin to 12 inches apart. The harvest is of the developing flowers, when heads are firm and while still green. Any sign of yellowing means the blooms are too far along. Practice 3-year rotation with crops other than crucifers (brocolli, cabbage, etc.).Broccoli is frost tolerant and can usually withstand the first few freezing nights in fall without harm.

Cultivars

'Green Goliath'- Bred especially for home gardens to give an early and extended harvest.

'Romanesco' - A regional variant from Rome with the flavor of broccoli and cauliflower; especially popular with those of Italian heritage. Needs side-dressing fertilization every 3 weeks. Transplant early using plastic protective cover. After danger of heavy frost, replace plastic with floating row cover to prevent insect invasion. Grows 4 feet in height before beginning production which continues into November.

'Premium Crop' - A standard commercial variety, but still one of the best; central head harvesting followed by months of harvest of lateral heads.

Troubles

See Chapter 4 Insects, Chapter 5 Diseases

INSECTS	DISEASE
aphids	black leg
cabbage loopers	black rot
cabbage worms	buttoning
cutworms	cabbage yellows
harlequin bug	
root maggot	

■ BRUSSELS SPROUTS

A long season crop not appreciated by many. Plant young transplants in early May, spacing 12 inches apart. Fertilize with soluble liquid fertilizer monthly. In late September, pinch out the growing tip, and begin clipping off the yellowing lower leaves as they occur. When sprouts are golf-ball size and still very firm, begin harvesting from the bottom upward. Extremely hardy into the fall, frost improves flavor. Plants can be harvested gradually up until heavy snows break them down.

Cultivars

'Jade Cross E Hybrid' - An improved cultivar from an old favorite.

'Queen Marvel Hybrid' - A late variety useful only in the southern range of this volume.

'Rubine' - An early variety that produces red leaves and red sprouts.

Troubles

See Chapter 4, Insects, Chapter 5 Diseases
See Broccoli

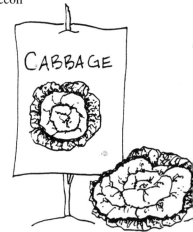

■ CABBAGE

Cabbage and broccoli cultural requirements are about the same, except that cabbage plants should be spaced 18 inches apart. As heads become solid, they are ready for harvest. If left too long, the heads split. Heavy rain following prolonged drought will also cause splitting. If you wish to prevent the splitting, grasp the plant at the base, brace your feet, pull until you hear the roots begin to pop. Don't pull too hard or the roots will be pulled out of the ground. Frost-tolerant to 27° F.; cabbage flavor is improved by frost.

Cultivars

Early
 'Golden Acre'
 'Little Rock'
 'Stokes Early 711'

Midseason
 'Centron'
 'Roundup' YR
 (meaning yellows and rot resistant)

Late
 'King Cole'
 'Late Flat Dutch'
 'Red Acre'
 'Savoy Salarite'
 'Savoy Ace'
 'Tenacity' (for sandy soils)

Troubles
See Chapter 4 Insects, Chapter 5 Diseases
See Broccoli

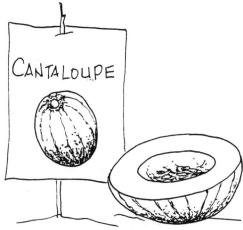

■ CANTALOUPE (Muskmelon)

The term *muskmelon* refers to all types of melons except watermelon. The following cultural procedures are for the so-called *winter* melons, meaning those that mature in late summer. They are: casaba,

¹ See Glossary

crenshaw, honeydew, Persian, and cantaloupe, though the true cantaloupe is not grown in North America.

Growing melons is a challenge in the northern sections of the Mountain West; however, there are cultivars and cultural techniques that will make them succeed. Plant seeds indoors in peat pots or styrofoam drink cups with drainage holes in early March. Give bottom heat to insure germination. After emergence, keep the seedlings at 72°F. day temperature in full sun or 16 hours of florescent light. Night temperature is 68°F.

Transplant to permanent position when the plants begin to topple over (about 4 inches). Sink a 3 pound coffee can that has been perforated at 2 inch intervals all over the sides, with 3 or 4 punctures on the bottom. Fill the can with fresh cow, horse or rabbit manure. Plant 3 seedlings (or seeds if you live in a long growing-season area) *in the open ground* around the rim of the can. Mulch the area 2 feet around each planting with clear plastic until soil is very warm, then remove it and spread a light-colored bark chip mulch. Black plastic covering the soil over the area of vining will prevent powdery mildew. Protection may also be necessary with hotcaps, plastic and/or floating row cover. Fill the manure-filled can with water as needed to seep outward to feed and water the plants at the same time. As fruits begin to form, set them atop a tuna can to prevent chewing insect damage and to keep them warm and dry. As ripening approaches, withhold water until a slight amount of leaf wilting is apparent. Harvest when netting pattern is going from green to yellow, when the "slip" (stem end) is beginning to soften and shrivel and when thumb pressure on the bottom elicits a slight softening. A ripe melon scent is strong with some varieties.

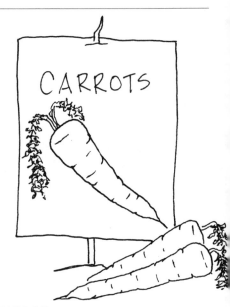

Melon seedlings nestle around their source of food and water - a manure-filled coffee can, punctured and sunk rim deep into the soil.

Cultivars

'Ambrosia' - An old award-winning variety still well-worth growing. Wait to harvest until almost yellow.

'Lucious Plus Hybrid' - Hybrid vigor gives it heavy production and resistence to Powdery Mildew.

'Honeydew Orange Flesh' - Taste-tested at Fetzer gardens

'Earli-dew' - Small but early; green-fleshed.

Troubles

See Chapter 4 Insects, Chapter 5 Diseases

INSECTS	DISEASE
aphids	leaf spot
cutworms	angular leaf spot
cucumber beetles	powdery mildew
leafhoppers	Mosaic
leaf miners	seedling decay
mites	and blight
thrips	root rot
wireworms	fusarium wilt

■ CARROT

Thorough soil preparation to particles no larger than 1/8 inch pays off with long, smooth carrots. Skimp on the soil prep and you get forked, knobby carrots. The annual application of organic matter is all that's required, for average fertility is their preference. Don't think you're doing them a favor by applying manure.

Sow seed shallowly from March to the end of May, depending on your latitude and altitude. Seeds are slow to germinate, often with a 3-week wait for the first sprout. Some gardeners sow radishes along with the carrot seed as a "breaker" crop to break through the soil's crust where carrot seed has been planted. The radishes will be up and harvested before the carrots know they were there! Plant 1 radish seed per inch of row. Pull all the radishes 3 weeks later, even though they may be too small to be edible. Thin seedlings to stand 4 inches apart; thin again if you notice the roots are touching. Root length of a carrot is determined within 2 weeks of germination. If the root runs into hardpan or a bad weather scene during that time, it's a root problem from that point forward. If the root may encounter rocks or tough clay, choose a variety that is short and blunt. When a variety has reached the mature size of its heredity, wait a little before harvesting. Check the 'days to maturity' on the seed packet. However, the best test is a taste test. Usually a week is sufficient, but some cultivars will keep a good quality for a month or more. Carrots that are not ready to harvest will have a harsh, bitter taste.

Cultivars

'Planet' - A baby carrot mature at an inch in diameter.

'Thumbelina' - A baby carrot good for children's gardens.

'Amsterdam Forcing' - Early maturing 4-6 inch length.

'A-Plus - Bred to have high level of beta-carotene, the building block of vitamin A.

'Bolero'

'Goldinhart'

'Minicor'

'Nanco'- Early maturing hybrid; slim, tapering.

'Primo'

'Rhumba'

'Touchon'

'Red-cored Chantenay' - Best storage carrot.

'Royal Chantenay'

'Improved Imperator' - Best for eating raw as a snack

Troubles

See Chapter 4, Insects, Chapter 5, Diseases

INSECTS	DISEASES
alfalfa webworm	yellows
carrot aphid	

carrot rust fly
climbing cutworm
lesser bulb fly
parsleyworm

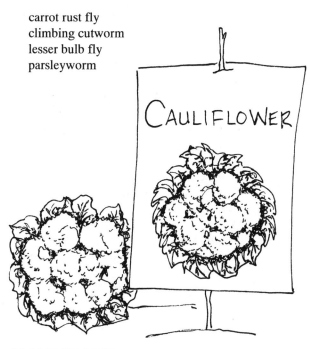

■ CAULIFLOWER

Cauliflower grows best in cool, moist, weather and, unlike cabbage, will not withstand severe freezing or extreme heat. It is important that the plants are not checked in growth at any time. If growth is not steady and vigorous, resulting heads will be small and grainy. Luck, more than any other factor, grows good cauliflower. Soil, planting and cultural requirements are the same as for broccoli, except that seed planting is best in Jiffy-7's to avoid shock when planting out. Reject seedlings with a bluish tint. They produce only small curds. Transplanting may be extended to July 1. The second application of fertilizer (10-10-10) should be applied when the tiny heads are golf-ball size. Only about 10 days elapse from the beginning formation of the head (called a curd) until harvest time. When heads are tennis-ball size, use soft twine to tie adjoining leaves over the top of the head to shade and blanch[1] it until harvest. Don't fret if the midribs of the leaves break as you bend them over the curd. Check each day by pressing your fingers against the curd. When it is fully formed, it will be rock-hard and six or more inches in diameter. Cut at the base and compost the plant, as it will not produce again, but it will attract insects if left in the ground.

Cultivars

'Snow Crown - Early.

'White Queen' - Midseason

'White Sails' - Late

'Yukon' - Very large, late.

Troubles

See Chapter 4 Insects, Chapter 5 Diseases see Broccoli

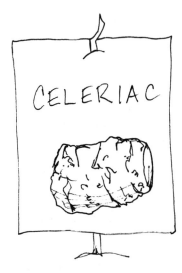

■ CELERIAC

This ugly brown, hairy, baseball-size root has the same flavor as celery, doesn't need blanching, and is a good winter-keeper. It's requirement of 100-120 growing days makes it a candidate for protection with a plastic frame or floating row cover toward the end of the growing season. Start seeds indoors in late February, presoaking

overnight. To avoid transplant shock, use Jiffy 7's or peat pots. Seeds may take 3 weeks to germinate at 70 F°. Transplant out when night temperatures are above 45°F. Deep rich soil is required with plenty of moisture. Fertilize lightly at weekly intervals. Mulch lightly through midsummer. Trim off most of the lateral roots at the soil surface when bulbs start to form. Hill up as needed. Mulch heavily with straw to winter over.

Cultivars

'Alabaster'

'Globus'

'Marble Ball'

'Jose'

Troubles

leaf tier

■ CELERY

Market gardeners around Denver once grew many acres of celery on native sandy loam and on muck soils of their own making. Pascal celery was often shipped as Christmas gifts to Eastern gentry and was also featured on the menu of the railway dining cars early in the twentieth century. Today it is grown in the backyard gardens of those willing to cater to its sometimes fickle ways.

Soil temperature is critical with celery. Set out purchased transplants or those you have grown indoors from seed 18 inches apart about June 1, when soil temperature is above 55°F. Roots are shallow and must be kept moist and below 85°F. Mulch with straw or dried grass clippings. Celery is a heavy feeder. Fertilize once with a slow-release, such as 14-14-14, or weekly with a weak soluble solution, such as RaPidGro.

When height is above that of a 2 quart milk carton, slip a bottomless carton over each plant so that foliage reaches above. This protection will blanch the stalks. When top growth slows, harvest stalks as needed or the whole bunch. Wash each bunch thoroughly with a strong stream of water. Leave roots intact and clean before slipping into a plastic bag. The bag your newspaper arrives in on a stormy day is ideal. Bunches will keep in the refrigerator past the holiday season.

Cultivars
'CL340 Utah 5270 Improved' - Thick, green stalks

'CL342 Hercules' - Early.

Troubles
See Chapter 4 Insects, Chapter 5 Diseases

INSECT
leaf tier

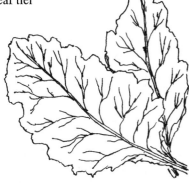

■ CHARD, SWISS
A single planting of Swiss chard will provide you with enough greens for the entire growing season. Make sure, however, that you like its flavor before planting. Unlike spinach, it will continue to produce tender, succulent leaves during the heat of summer. Cultural practice is the same as for beet, to which it is related. Thin plants to 3 inches apart; then to 9 inches apart. Harvest outer leaves by snapping off at the base. Young leaves will continue to form in the center.

Cultivars
'Argentata' - A highly rated Italian import.

'Lucullus' - A green chard with white midribs.

'Rhubarb' - A red chard with deep red midribs.

Troubles
See Chapter 4, Insects, Chapter 5, Diseases

INSECTS	DISEASES
aphid	leafspot
leafhopper	seed decay
leaf miner	
spider mites	
tarnished plant bug	

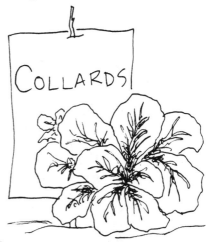

■ COLLARDS
Transplanted Southerners long for this non-heading cabbage-like plant. Lightly

steamed and dressed with vinegar and a little bacon fat, collard greens are a treat they value from their homeland. Seed it directly into prepared soil early in the season. It will germinate at soil temperatures above 40°F. Because it has a large leaf surface, it does not tolerate wilting and must be kept reasonably moist. Harvest outer leaves before they toughen.

Cultivar

'Vates Non-heading' - Tolerant of clay soil.

See Chapter 4, Insects, Chapter 5, Diseases
See Cabbage

■ CORN

This vegetable is the reason many gardeners have a garden. The flavor of hot, freshly steamed ears is unbeatable and will quickly make your reputation as a vegetable gardener.

Corn requires a well-drained soil, rich in organic matter as well as nutrients. Work in 5 pounds of 10-10-10 per 100 square feet of row before planting. This is one crop that does not do well in raised beds. Plan the plantings, a block planted every 2 weeks, on the north or west side of the

garden so that the plants will not shade other crops. Block planting also allows for its pollination by the wind. When soil temperature is 75°F. (about May 1), make furrows 2 inches deep and rows 36 inches apart. Sow seeds, 2 at a time, 1 foot apart; cover to the soil level. If both seeds germinate, thin to the 1 that is most vigorous. If neither germinates, replant. Corn does not transplant well, so you can't move seedlings about. Hill up plants twice, when plants are 4 inches tall and again at 18 inches.

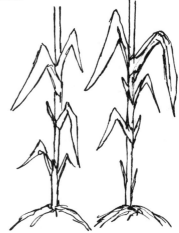

Hilling up corn plants assists brace-roots.

The Scarecrow

When the first corn seed is planted, it is time to set up the scarecrow. Nothing is so tasty to the Red-Winged Blackbird, the Common Grackle, or the Common Crow as corn seed. The birds march up and down rows, inserting their beaks into the soil to excavate every seed. A scarecrow set up for only 2 weeks will thwart them. Use scrap lumber or lath to outline the body and arms. An old bucket makes a head. Old clothes, a hat and gloves add reality. Dangle foil pie plates from the arms for added flashes of scariness. As soon as the radicle of each seed is firmly anchored, move Mr. Scarecrow to the second planting block; then the third. After all plantings have germinated and put up leaves, take him down, for to leave him in place would cause the birds to become accustomed to his presence.

The Time-Honored Scarecrow

Watering and watching for insects will be tasks not to be taken lightly until tasseling begins. As soon as tassels appear at the tops of each stalk, make sure each plant receives a copious supply of water without waterlogging the soil. Silks will then form and pollen from the tassels will drop to the silk. Each silk leads to a single kernel of corn in the ear. To assure pollination of plants on ends of rows, break off a pollen-laden tassel in the middle of the row and shake it over the silks of the end plants. If you are growing 3 or 4 plants of blue corn or any other novelty type, gently pull a clear plastic dry cleaners bag over the top of each plant as the tassels form. The pollen will fall to pollinate the silks without contaminating other blocks of plants.

Harvest as soon as the end of each ear is blunt. Squeeze it to find the bluntness; this means it is well-filled. You don't need to peel down the husk, but if you must, a thumbnail inserted into a kernel will squirt milk, not clear liquid, when the corn is at prime.

As soon as all ears have been harvested, dig each plant, grinding the stalks for the compost pile. Spade the soil to leave it rough and humpy over the winter so that winter's cold will penetrate deeply to kill overwintering insects and their eggs and to pry apart clay particles. The soil will be mellow and soft in spring, ready for smoothing with a rake. Rotate your corn crop every year without fail.

Cultivars

STANDARD

'Jubilee' - The #1 sweet corn in the world. Keep it well away from the super-sweet varieties, for if they cross-pollinate, both will be spoiled. Late.

SUPERSWEET[1]

'Northern Xtra-Sweet' - Good cold tolerance. Early

'Milk 'n Honey II'- Kernels are yellow and white. Main season.

'Skyline' - Early, uniform, high-yielding.

'Silver Queen' - The 'Queen' lives on. It has been the leading white corn cultivar for many years.

---

[1] *Geneticists have used genetic manipulation incorporated for sweetness of corn by using Supersweet (Su+) + Normal Sweet (N) = Sugar Enhanced (EH).*

■ POPCORN

Plant seed in peat pot strips and transplant without disturbing the roots. Plant in small blocks with rows 30 inches apart. Fertilize when 6 inches tall and again at midseason with 14-14-14. Water regularly, but deeply and infrequently. Harvesting at the right time is critical for popping. Let ears dry on the stalks, then pick when stalk and husks are completely brown and kernels are hard. Hang ears in loosely woven sacks to cure. Ears are ready for husking when kernels push off the cob easily. Place kernels in a large bowl outside and use a hair-dryer or the wind to blow away chaff and bits of corn silk.

Cultivars

'Pretty Pops'- Multi-colored kernels

'White Cloud'

'South American Hybrid' - Good for high altitude.

Troubles

See Chapter 4, Insects, Chapter 5, Diseases

INSECTS	DISEASES
aphid	corn smut
corn earworm	
corn-seed maggot	
cutworm	
earwig	
flea beetle	
grasshopper	
rootworm	
spider mite	
wireworm	

■ CUCUMBER

The lime-rich soils of the Mountain West grow superior cucumbers. Both vining and bush types are top producers. Sow seed indoors in cell-type containers; harden off and plant out, disturbing as little as possible, when soil temperature is at least 70°F. Plant 18 inches apart or in hills of 3 plants, 6 inches apart. Can be trained on a slanting trellis to save space. Trying to tie the vines upright usually leads to kinking the vines, which will cause curled fruits.

Cucumbers are heavy feeders and demand water the moment the soil becomes dry. They prefer a warm growing season. If you live in an area of cool summers, give them a spun-bonded fabric row cover supported by a hoop of wire. This will increase the temperature by about 7°F.

If you want to make pickles, choose a pickling cultivar, for slicing types do not make good pickles. Most cucumbers are *monoecious,* with separate male and female flowers. Many newer cultivars are predominantly *gynoecious,* producing only female flowers with an occasional male flower appearing when the plant is under stress from high temperature or lack of water. These also tend to produce an early crop and then decrease production quickly, which is useful if you are pickling the fruits.

The chemical *cucurbitacin* contributes to a bitter flavor in cucumbers and is said to contribute to indigestion. Cultivars such as 'Jazzer' and 'Marketmore 86' lack this chemical, and are touted as "burpless." Strangely, lack of this chemical affords a natural protection for cucumber beetles, but encourages attack by rabbits.

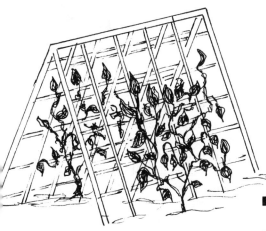

A-frame for growing cucumbers.

Cultivars

'Conquest' - Long harvest period.

'Northern Pickling' - 48 days, high yield of early pickle-size fruits.

'H-19 Little Leaf' - High quality fruit on a compact, multi-branching, vigorous plant.

'Jazzer' - burpless.

'Marketmore 86' - burpless.

'333 Suyo Long'- An excellent "burpless" fruit from China.

'147G Fanfare' - A small bush bearing big fruit.

Troubles

See Chapter 4 Insects, Chapter 5 Diseases

INSECTS	DISEASES
earwig	angular leaf spot
striped or spotted	anthracnose
cucumber beetle	bacterial wilt
	downy and
	powdery mildew

DANDELION GREENS

■ DANDELION GREENS

Late in the 19th century the hard-rock miners of the Mountain West were hard pressed to find sufficient greenery for their diets to ward off scurvy and anemia. The immigrants from Northern Italy or Wales were especially knowledgeable about the nutritive values of dandelion greens. We now know they contain Vitamin C and iron. With little level ground and no time or inclination to cultivate this weed, the miners' wives encouraged dandelions to grow beneath the board sidewalks of their mountain towns. These primitive sidewalks were a necessity in every mountain town to

protect milady's skirts during "mud season."
Since the boards were only here-and-there,
the dandelions growing beneath received
sufficient sun to produce a tender, blanched
plant.

The following cultural directions are a
long-standing family tradition and have
been handed down from the author's cousin,
Mrs. James A.(Lois) Clark, of Palisade,
Colorado. From the peach orchard rows, she
gathers entire plants, being careful to dig out
the taproot. Dandelions will usually be up
and growing strong the last of March or in
early April on the Western Slope of Colorado, but altitude and latitude will affect the
maturity date in your area. Pull off flowers
as they will impart an exceedingly bitter
flavor to the greens, but buds are choice
morsels. She fills garbage bags of the greens
to take to the yard where wash tubs are set
up and a strong stream of water from the
hose is used to push soil from every crevice
in the leaves and root. With each successive
washing, the greens are transferred to
another tub, where the water will gradually
become more clear. The greens are then left
overnight in the cold water to settle out
more silt and to crisp up. The following
morning she drains and transfers the greens
to plastic bags for refrigerator storage.

To prepare: Cut enough for a meal of the
greens, root, and buds into bite-size pieces.
Dressing for this salad is a mixture of diced
onion, salt and pepper, a good quality of
olive oil and vinegar. Mix with hands to
coat every piece, and serve at once.

■ EGGPLANT

A rich sandy loam should be spaded
deeply for eggplant. Start seeds indoors in a
sunny window where temperature is neither
below 70°F. at night, nor above 90°F. in
daytime. If flea beetles have been a
problem, grow the plants to gallon size
indoors before planting out. The one-
generation insects will be long gone. To
warm the soil, tuck black plastic over the
raised bed where transplants are to be set.
Transplant hardened-off plants through slits
in the plastic in mid-June when weather is
settled. Set stakes at the same time for
future need.

Harvest eggplant fruits before they get
seedy. The skin should be taut and shiny;
the flesh should bounce back when you
press. Rotate to where other nightshade
family plants have not been grown (tomato,
pepper, potato).

Cultivars

'Asian Bride' - Finger-slim, multicolored
and mild.

'Listade' - Italian.

'Violette di Firenze' - Italian.

'Imperial Black Beauty' - An old standard favorite.

■ GARLIC - see Chapter 3 Herbs.

■ HOPS - see Chapter 10, Vines.

■ KALE

Kale has taken the place of parsley as a restaurant plate garnish. This is unfortunate for our dining companions, for the parsley is a breath sweetner. However, the kale is cheaper. Its blue-green color and frilly texture add prettiness to a plate. For those willing to try it, it is is now becoming a steamed vegetable on our plates as well. It is especially suited to the northern-most reaches of the Mountain West, for it can withstand cold. Sow seeds in July, 1 per inch, thinning to 1 per 8 inches. A dozen plants are enough for a family. Cover the row with burlap until seedlings emerge, for July sun is cruel and they must be kept moist. Begin harvesting after the first frost and continue until snow depth makes it too difficult.

Cultivars

'Dwarf Blue Curled Vates' - A spreading plant with many leaves that are tender despite large size.

'Green Curled Scotch' - An early variety with a more yellowish leaf.

Troubles

See Cabbage

■ KOHLRABI

A cruicifer vegetable completely unlike its relatives, the bulbous kohlrabi is best grown in the cool days of spring or autumn; pull and cook when young and tender. Also good raw as a snack tray item. Sow seed 2 inches apart in open ground in late April or late July, thinning to 6 inches apart. Fertilize lightly as growth reaches maturity.

Cultivars

'Early White Vienna' - Bulbs mature quickly.

'Triumph' - Tolerant to disease 'Yellows."

'Grand Duke' - Award winning hybrid.

Troubles

see Cabbage

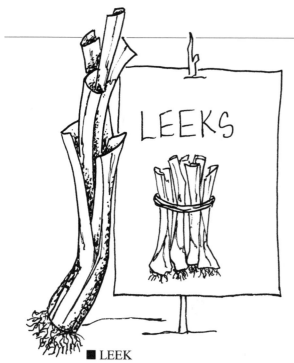

Cultivars
'Tital' - Extra early.
'Splendid' - Still 95 days to maturity.
'Arcona' - Very disease tolerant.
Troubles
See Onion

■ LEEK

A challenging member of the *Allium*
family, the leek is essential in the gourmet
household as a braised or steamed vegetable with a vinaigrette sauce or used in
soups, especially the famed Vichyssoise. It
takes time and patience to coax the
reluctant seeds into growth indoors in
warmth in January. They don't look
promising at first — thin wispy stems
topple easily. Prop them up with anything
handy — matchsticks come to mind —
until they finally take on some substance.
Plant hardened-off seedlings in May in
trenches dug 6 inches deep and enriched
with compost. A chicken wire-plus-
floating-row-cover covering over the
trench will protect them from battering
rainstorms, romping dogs, and hungry
birds. Gradually fill in the trench so that
each plant is covered up to the growing
point where the leaves divide to blanch the
bottom of the stalk. Dig the plants carefully
as needed throughout fall and winter.

■ LETTUCE

The lettuces we grow today differ from
those in fashion even ten years ago. With
health-consciousness in force, we are told
that the old standard 'Iceberg' does not
carry its weight. It is still the basis for many
homegrown tossed salads. Soil temperature
is critical for all lettuces. Cooler than 41°F.
or warmer than 70°F. will cause the
planting to fail. To find a soil cool enough
in midsummer, sow a crop in midsummer
in the shade of pole beans or tomatoes. You
can also fool the seeds by placing them in
moist vermiculite in a zip-lock bag in the
refrigerator at night. Remove the bag to a
place on the kitchen counter in daytime.
Alternating temperatures will germinate the
seed in a few days. As soon as you see the
radicle form, plant the seeds in the garden.
Open the seed row with a Warren hoe; then
dribble a line into the row of ammonium

sulfate at a rate of 1 cup per 10 feet of row. Cover with 2 inches of soil before sowing seed. Lettuce seed prefers light to germinate, therefore, cover lightly, and keep moist for good germination. Harvest head lettuce by cutting at the soil line as soon as wrapper leaves have formed a tight head and before any sign of elongation (bolting) has occurred. Harvest outer leaves of leaf lettuce by snapping them off, and new ones will form in the center; or harvest the entire plant.

Cultivars

BUTTERHEAD
'Buttercrunch' - A favorite
'Bibb' - Reliable
'Red Boston' - A colorful addition of thick, crisp leaves.

CRISPHEAD
'Ithaca' - An early head lettuce
'Great Lakes' - Slow to bolt; favorite in Mountain West.
'Frosty M' - For high altitude; light-frost tolerant.

LEAF
'Red Sails'- Winner of All-America.
'180B Brunia' - Redddish leaf tips; large, deeply cut leaves.
'Black Seeded Simpson' - An old favorite.

ROMAINE OR COS
'171B Guzmaine M.I. - Earliest
'171 Parris Island M.I. 318 - Tall, erect bunches

Troubles

See Chapter 4 Insects, Chapter 5 Diseases

INSECTS	DISEASES
aphid	aster yellows
armyworm	downy mildew
salt-marsh caterpillars	slime rot
earwig	tipburn
flea beetle	
leafhopper	
leafminer	
pill or sow bug	
slug	
spider mite	
webworm	
wireworm	

■ OKRA

Warm soil the latter part of May to the middle of June is best for planting okra seed which has been soaked overnight. Thin plants to 1 foot apart. Hill up each plant when it reaches 6 inches in height. Plants must grow steadily but without too much vegetative growth. Harvest pods when 2-3 inches long to keep production steady.

Cultivars

'Annie Oakley II' - Early.
'Perkins Mammoth Long Pod' - Slightly later, longer.

■ ONION

Onions are among the easiest of vegetables to grow. However, if you don't supply a balanced fertilizer program and a continuous well-regulated water supply, they disappoint your expectations. Onion "sets" are small onions grown closely in areas of long growing season and sold in garden centers. Transplants are sold in large garden centers. You can grow your own indoors in flats using "sets" or seeds to the transplant stage. The choice is up to you.There are advantages and disadvantages to all three. "Sets" are somewhat lesser in quality than seed-grown plants. Also, they are seldom available in all the remarkable varieties that have been developed. The same holds true for transplants unless you grow your own. Seeds take a little longer and are less of a sure thing.

Plant seeds, sets, or transplants in late April or early May, thinning to 1 1/2 inches for small green onions and 3 to 4 inches apart for large mature bulbs. Bulbing will begin after summer solstice. It is imperative that plantings be kept weed-free. One inch of water per week is an average amount for a well-prepared soil, easing up on both water and fertilizer as bulbing becomes apparent. It is normal for the "shoulders" of onions to emerge from the soil as the plants grow. As growth is complete, tops will topple on their own. It is now known that laying them over is not a good cultural practice. The necks will gradually narrow; thus increasing their keeping quality.

Cultivars

'Snow Baby' - A round white mini onion; a "pearl" onion may be allowed to grow to 1 to 2 inches to cook with early peas.

'Ailsa Craig Exhibition' - A British introduction for short growing season areas. Makes big onions of moderate pungency.

'Walla Walla Sweet' - The famed sweet mild onion of the Mountain West from Walla Walla, WA. Not a good keeper, but a must in every garden.

'Prince' - The best big onion for long storage. Tight tunic.

'White Spear' - A good quality scallion.

'Giant Red Hamburger' - Semi-flat with white flesh, red skin.

'Yellow Sweet Spanish' - The traditional Western cultivar. The brown tunic signals its good keeping quality.

■ SHALLOTS

This gourmet *Allium* adds mild flavor to sauces and salads. The foliage is used in Chinese dumplings. Share a pound of sets with a friend. Each one you plant will give you a dozen more at digging time. Good keeper.

Troubles

See Chapter 4 Insects, Chapter 5 Diseases

INSECTS	DISEASES
cutworm	onion smut
onion maggot	downy mildew
onion thrips	neck rot
wireworm	pink root
	purple blotch

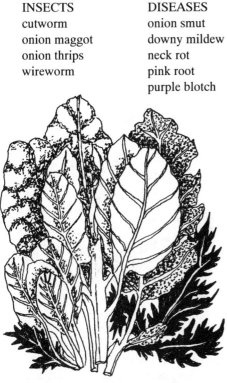

■ ORIENTAL VEGETABLES[1]

Chinese, Japanese, and Maylasian vegetables have intrigued North Americans since the international flavors entered our cuisine.

ROOTS

Burdock 'Takinogawa Long' - Requires a long growing season. Start seed indoors in peat strips.

Daikon (radish) 'All Season' - A long tapered white.

'Summer Cross' - A mild mid-summer white radish.

'Japanese Ball' - A large white fall radish.

LEGUMES

'Winged Bean' - A twining perennial that needs winter protection.

'Adzuki Bean' - A red bean used in pastry and for sprouts.

'Asparagus Yardlong Bean' - Needs very strong poles. Good stir-fried or steamed. Only for areas with hot summers.

'Mung Bean' - For sprouts.

Snow Peas - Edible pods grow in clusters on 25 inch bush. Harvest before peas make a visible swelling on the pod. 'Oregon Sugar Pod II' - 68 days. 'Snowbird' - earliest at 58 days.

GREENS

'Hon Tsai Tai - Tender purple flower stems and buds.

'Kyona/Mizuna' - A mustard green for salads

'Shingiku' (edible chrysanthemum) - Aromatic.

'Tatsoi' - The traditional black leaves for salads.

PAK CHOI

'Mei Qing Choi' - White stem, baby size.

'Joi Choi' - Tall, broad, heavy, dark-green leaves.

'Prize Choy' - Classic pac choi.

'Chinese Pac Choi' - Tender, compact.

BITTER MELON

Culture is the same as for other melons.

ICHEBAN

Chinese eggplant is more suited for stir-fry than conventional eggplant.

Troubles

See Lettuce

[1] *Available from Tsang and Ma, 1306 Old Country Road, Belmont, CA 94002 and, increasingly, from conventional seed stores and catalogs.*

■ PARSNIP

Give parsnips your heaviest soil, deeply prepared. Sow seed as early as possible in spring, covering the seed rows with burlap to prevent soil from drying. Seed is slow to germinate. Keep plants growing fast by side-dressing in July with 14-14-14. Not drought tolerant. Flavor is improved by freezing. Begin harvest in late fall and continue through the following March.

Cultivars

'All American' - Broad-shouldered, long.

'Hollow Crown Improved' - Short-topped, refined.

'Harris Model' - Long, slim roots.

Troubles

see CARROT and CELERY

■ PEAS

The flavor of canned, frozen, even "fresh" peas from the supermarket cannot compare to that of homegrown peas. Like sweet corn, peas begin to lose their sweetness the minute they are harvested. Raised beds suit them well, but they will need support in the form of chicken wire trellis or the traditional English pea sticks. The pea sticks actually allow for closer planting and are adequate for the weight of vines, except for the standard Sugar Snap Pea. The latter requires a stout 8-foot chain link fence. Save your brushy prunings from shrubs to use as pea sticks, thrusting them into the soil at the outer edges of the row so that the twiggy tops intermingle.

Planting is traditional on St. Patrick's Day, but you may wish to plant much earlier - November before soil freeze-up or January during a thaw period when soil is soft enough to cultivate. See earlier directions at *winter planting*. Use a *Rhizobia* inoculant to insure good germination. For spring planting, plant 2 seeds at the base of each peastick, with 1 drip irrigation tape positioned down the center. No thinning is necessary. The vines will grow over the brushy pea sticks, shading and cooling the soil so that water requirements are lessened.

Try growing 3 species - 1 for shelling, 1 sugar snap, and 1 Chinese edible pod variety for steaming or stir-fry. Sugar snaps are best eaten raw with a dip or sliced in salads. Plant a fall crop at the end of July. Pre-sprout the seed in a cool place indoors. Plan to protect this row with an arch of floating row cover which will increase the temperature inside by about 7 degrees, thus allowing the crop to mature after the first frost. Harvesting is a matter of your strength and inclination. Most prefer to pull all of the vines of a single cultivar, dragging them to a shady place for picking pods off the vines. Others can withstand the tedium and stooping to pick almost daily.

English pea sticks are a traditional necessity in growing peas.

Cultivars
'Green Arrow' - Voted the best and most prolific shell pea, with 2 to 3 pods at each growth node, each pod containing 8 to 10 peas. If pulling is your method of harvest, wait until pods are showing a little yellowing. The starch taste of raw peas will disappear with cooking.

'Wando' - A good cultivar for shelling that ripens all at once.

'Sugar Ann' - Voted the best sugar snap pea.

'Sugar Snap' - The standard 8 foot cultivar. Still one of the best.

'Yakumo' - Voted the best Oriental snow pea, also known as edible pod pea. See above for more cultivars.

Troubles
See Chapter 4, Insects, Chapter 5, Diseases
See "Oriental Vegetables" for more cultivars.

INSECTS	DISEASES
acorn-seed maggot	ascochyta blight
aphids	bacterial blight
grasshoppers	fusarium wilt
leafhoppers	powdery mildew
pea weevil	
spider mites	
thrips	
wireworms	

■ PEANUTS

melons, you can grow peanuts. They require a long, hot growing season, and are worth the extra work to be able to observe the extraordinary pollination and growth process. Plant 2 seeds 1 inch deep in "hills" 20 inches apart at the same time as you are planting corn and beans, using black or clear plastic to warm the soil around the planting hill. Do not apply an organic mulch. Take care not to break the thin brown, papery seed tunic or coat. If both seeds germinate, eliminate the weakest. The young plants will soon be covered with bright yellow male (staminate) and female (pistilate) flowers. The plant stems begin to elongate to lower the pollinated flowers to the soil where they soon go underground to set and develop their seed pods. Don't try to bury the flowers. They know how to do this on their own. It is important to hill-up around the foliage and to keep the soil weed free and soft. The first killing frost will blacken the plants, signaling it's time to dig the roots. Do this when soil is dry so that you can shake them off well. Stack the plants, tops and all, in a sheltered dry place to cure. Then pull off pods and dry them 2 to 3 weeks. A good place is on a screen near the hot water heater. Store peanuts in containers with tight lids. For best flavor roast them for 20 minutes in a 350°F. oven.

Cultivars

'Early Spanish'- Smooth buttery flavor.

'NC 17' - Bred for Virginia's sandy soils.

'Tennessee Red' - For northern and high altitude regions.

Troubles

See Peas

■ PEPPER

Peppers are an easy crop in the Mountain West if you can meet their requirement for heat. A challenge to germinate, the seed flats started indoors about March 1 are the most successful. Keep them at 80°F. or 90°F. in daytime and 70°F. at night until the shoots struggle to life. Take care not to overwater. A sunny window will bring them along. Keep the soil of the seed flat covered with a light colored material, aluminum foil or vermiculite, to avoid cooking the stems. Transplant hardened-off plants 18-inches apart in the row, using black plastic to cover the soil above the drip lines in areas where cool nights prevail. Keep them weed-free, but avoid deep cultivation, for peppers are shallow-rooted. Fertilize through the drip lines 3 times - the first 3 weeks after transplanting, and with successive applications 3 weeks apart, using 10-10-10. Harvest when the cultivar has filled out to its mature size or wait for it to turn red. Sweet red peppers are superior in flavor, and worth the wait. Remember that production of new fruits ceases when you fail to pick at mature size. Decreased production is the price you pay for the sweet red ones, but breeding is rapidly changing that penalty. With peppers, crop rotation is imperative.

Cultivars

SWEET

'California Wonder'- The old standard is still good.

'Ace' - dependable, prolific.

'Albino Bullnose' - A white blocky variety that turns orange.

'Chocolate' - Dark brown skin with green interior.

'Conquistador Spanish Paprika'[1] - Rich red paprika flavor, but no heat. Allow to dry to brittle stage; then pulverize in food processor.

'Earlired' - A good mild red for high altitude.

'Permagreen' - Almost black.

'Yellow Chinese Pimento' - Needs extra warmth

HOT[2]

'Aconcagua' - Mild or hot according to amount of heat at ripening time. From Argentina.

'Cayenne'- For the American, this one is hot enough.

'Hungarian Hot Wax' - Dependably productive.

'Pasilla' - A Mexican selection.

Troubles

See Chapter 4 Insects, Chapter 5 Diseases

INSECTS	DISEASES
Aphid	bacterial leaf spot
corn earworm	cercospora leaf spot
cutworm	damping off
flea beetle	mosaic
grasshopper	
leafhopper	
spider mite	
tomato hornworm	

■ POTATO

Very few potatoes are grown from seed today, though a flash of popularity came a few years ago. Although potatoes are the most popular vegetable in America, home gardeners often fail to harvest a good crop. Potatoes prefer a slightly acid soil not high

[1] Available from Shepherd's Garden Seeds, 30 Irene St., Torrington, Connecticut 06790, catalog free.
[2] A unit of pungency is called a Scoville. This rating of pepper hotness can range from less than 100 for a sweet bell pepper, to a mildly pungent 1000 in a New Mexico style chili. Ranging on toward a tangy 4000-6000 in Jalapeno, and onward to a blistering 200,000 - 350,000 in Habanero. A hotter growing season will usually result in greater pungency, but watering is also a factor. The pungency levels increase approximately ten to eleven fold when fruits are dried.

in organic matter. Highly alkaline soil leads to scab disease. Seed pieces are cut from purchased **certified** seed potatoes so that at lest one "eye" (sunken bud) is included. Small potatoes can be planted whole, especially Irish Cobbler. Pieces are allowed to suberize (callus) by placing them in single layers indoors for 3 days on the windowsill. Shake the seed pieces in a paper bag of sulfur dust to ward off scab disease. In May open furrows 4-6 inches deep; place a ribbon of superphosphate (0-45-0) in the furrow and cover with a little soil. Plant seed pieces 9 inches apart. Cover with a little soil; then place another ribbon of a high nitrogen fertilizer because many roots form *above* the seed piece; complete backfill and water well.

As weeding and cultivation begin, move your hoe toward the stems of each sprouting plant, thus hilling soil up around the stem. Apply a side-dressing of 10-10-10 about 1 month after plants have sprouted. Water to keep soil moist until flowering; then you will see that growth has ceased and can cut back on water and hill up to the foliage. Hilling-up helps stems to stand upright and protects tubers from heat and sunburn. In lower altitude climates, mulch the hill with dried grass or aluminum foil to keep soil cool. Digging can begin anytime at this point, or you may wish to leave them in the ground until mid-September. Dig with a garden fork or a traditional potato hook to prevent stabbing. Allow the potatos to dry in a warm, shaded place for a few hours before storing in darkness at as close to 40˚F. as possible.

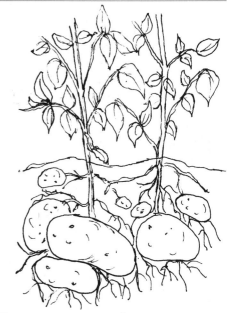

Potatoes are underground stems.

Cultivars

'Alaska Red'[1] - For high altitude. Can withstand summer frost.

'Irish Cobbler'- A standard for the home garden.

'Norgold Russet'- A good commercial cultivar

'Red Norland'-A red-skinned cultivar.

'Red Pontiac' - Susceptible to scab in some areas.

'Round Blue Andean' - Creamy yellow flesh with purple ring, prolific.

'Viking Purple' - Purple skin with stripes. Good keeper.

'Yukon Gold' - Good yellow-fleshed keeper. Served at The White House often.

Troubles

See Chapter 4 Insects, Chapter 5 diseases

INSECTS	DISEASES
aphid	bacterial Ring Rot

[1] *Available from Ronniger's Seed Potatoes, Star Route, Moyie Springs, ID 83845. Catalog $2.00.*

flea beetle	common scab
leafhopper	early and late blight
psyllid	fusarium and
	bactial wilts
wireworms	green-skinned
	tubers
	rhizoctonia
	viruses

■ PUMPKIN

Pumpkins are always important in the garden of a family with children. The Halloween pumpkin is more fun if you grew it yourself! See *Cantaloupe* for culture through the growing season, but sidedress with different compounds. Use a high nitrogen 10-5-5 three weeks after transplant. Use 5-10-5 when the fruits are about football size At harvest time the stem end will be very hard, unlike other cucurbits, such as squash or cantaloupe. The fruits are ready for picking when a pressed thumbnail does not leave an indentation. Pumpkins can withstand a light frost that will blacken the leaves but not the stems. Leave the fruits until the afternoon of a predicted heavy frost. Store at just above freezing temperature.

Cultivars

'Jack-be-Little' - A tiny fruit for table decoration.

'Baby Bear' - The right size for little hands at Halloween.

'New England Pie' - Dry, starchy, stringless; for pie.

'Connecticutt Field' - For a major Halloween pumpkin.

'Atlantic Giant' - For a BIG Halloween pumpkin.

Troubles

See Cantaloupe

■ RADICCHIO

Red-leafed chicory, popularly known as radicchio (ra-deek-ee-o) is a salad vegetable from Northern Italy. Its leaves can be rose red to bronzy maroon. It has a nutty, slightly bitter flavor. Sow seeds in late May, thinning to 18 inches apart. Keep seedlings growing vigorously with a sidedress of 10-10-10. As cool weather intensifies, taste-test the leaves. Harvest just as the ground freezes, cut the winter-softened plants back and some will re-grow in spring.

Cultivars

'Rossa de Verona' - Imported from Italy.

'Rossa di Treviso' - A taller cultivar with romaine-shaped leaves.

Troubles

See Lettuce

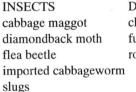

INSECTS	DISEASES
cabbage maggot	clubroot
diamondback moth	fusarium
flea beetle	root scurf
imported cabbageworm	
slugs	

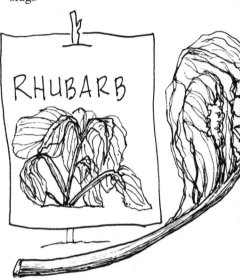

■ RADISH

Radishes can often be ready to pull and eat in only 26 days from sowing. It isn't easy to grow a mild one in the Mountain West; they tend toward fiery hot instead. Sow seed *thinly* as early as soil is thawed. Crowding will make large tops and useless roots. Take care that they don't get too dry, for they are not drought tolerant. The secret to a mild, non-pithy radish is providing a soil with extra sphagnum peatmoss and fertilizing once a week with a weak soluble fertilizer solution, using Peter's, RaPidGro, or Miracle-Gro at the rate of 1 tablespoon per gallon of water. Successive crops can be sown in May, June, August, and September. Rotation imperative. See CARROTS for interplanting.

Cultivars (see Oriental Vegetables for Daikon)

'Marabells' - The earliest.

'Red Pak' - Resistent to disease.

'Easter Egg' - Stays crisp even when large.

Troubles

See Chapter 4, Insects, Chapter 5, Diseases

■ RHUBARB

Purchase your rhubarb plants from a nursery or a neighbor because growing from seed is not reliable. Spring is the best time to plant or divide rhubarb. Rather than a specific date, use the emerging stems that look like shiny red boils as an indicator of the correct time. Give the soil an extra amount of weathered manure or compost, spaded in deeply. Plant at same depth as previous growth. For established plants, loosen soil around plants in spring and sidedress with a handful of a complete fertilizer, and again in late summer. Water well, especially in spring. Individual rhubarb stalks cannot be fully harvested until the third year of planting. Pull stalks from plant, do not cut. Never eat leaves, which are poisonous. Keep seed stalks pulled. Seed stalks are a sign of lack of nutrients.

Cultivars

'Valentine' - Relatively new, good color.

'Canada Red' - Very hardy

Troubles

See Chapter 4, Insects, Chapter 5, Diseases

INSECTS	DISEASES
aphids	downy mildew
curculio	mosaic (yellows)
	curly-top virus

RUTABAGA

■ RUTABAGA

This vegetable of yesteryear has a bad image problem. Its looks decree that the rutabaga is food fit only for starving armies. The flavor is a little like turnip, but more delicate and sweet. When soil temperature has reached 60°F, sow seeds 3 inches apart and barely cover. Keep moist until germination; then thin to 9 inches apart. Rutabagas get BIG! Keep moist throughout the growing season, sidedressing with 5-10-5 in July and August. Poorly nourished roots are fibrous. It is normal for the shoulders of the

roots to be above ground. Either harvest before a hard frost or mulch heavily for harvesting throughout the winter.

Cultivars

'York' - Sweet pale yellow flesh; resistant to disease.

'Pike' - A purple top that can be left in the garden late; larger top.

Troubles

See Chapter 4, Insects, Chapter 5, Diseases

INSECTS	DISEASES
flea beetles	bitterness - hot weather
	corky growth - too much nitrogen, hot weather

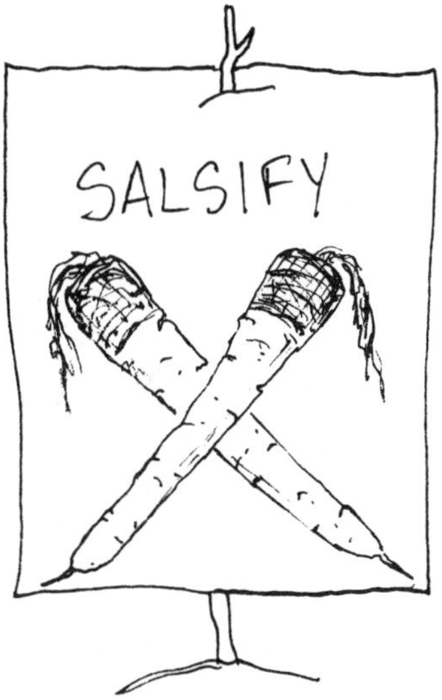

SALSIFY

■ SALSIFY/SCORZONERA

Root vegetables that have a flavor all their own are *Scorzonera*, black skinned and white fleshed, *Salsify*, white skinned and white fleshed. Leaves are grass-like to distinguish it from *Scorzonera*. The flavor of *Salsify* is that of an oyster and it is often called "mock oyster."

Culture for both is the same as for

parsnips. Digging should be delayed until the ground begins to freeze.
Cultivars
'Lange Jan' - A European strain of *Scorzonera*.

'Mammoth Sandwich Island' - The standard cultivar of *Salsify*.
Troubles
See Parsnips

SPINACH

■ SPINACH
With the introduction of the spinach quiche, America embraced this good-for-you green; then moved forward to accept spinach salads, but never took the leap to *cooked* spinach. Sow seeds broadly across the raised bed at the rate of 1 ounce per 100 feet of row. The plants seldom need thinning, but you may wish to pull a few to leave 3 inches between plants. Mulch with straw or dried grass clippings to prevent rain splashing soil into the leaves. Begin harvesting as soon as a plant has 4 leaves, or you can wait until a fairly mature rosette has formed, cut the whole thing 1-inch above the soil, and allow it to grow again. Harvest

all when you see signs of bolting, the elongation of the center rosette. Sidedress twice, at 4 inches, and again at 8 inches.
Cultivars
'Melody' - A smooth leaf Savoy that won the All America.

'Bloomsdale Long Standing' - An old cultivar; thick, crinkly, dark-green leaves.

'Avon Hybrid' - Slightly crinkled leaves; superb flavor.
Troubles
See Chapter 4 Insects, Chapter 5 Diseases

INSECTS	DISEASES
aphid	curly-top virus
cabbage Looper	damping off
leafminer	downy Mildew
	mosaic (yellows)

SQUASH

■ SQUASH
Even the smallest garden has room for a squash or two. Both the summer squash and winter keepers have the same cultural directions. Plant both types in basins, not hills, 4 feet apart each way. Sow seed as soon as danger from frost has passed, 6 seeds per basin, 2 inches apart and cover

with 1 inch of soil. Thin to the best 3 plants when they are 3-inches high. Cultivation should be shallow and soil moisture continuous, but not copious to insure steady growth. After thinning, sidedress with 1-ounce of balanced fertilizer per basin, applied in a ring 6 inches away from the plants and covered with an inch of soil. Water well. Do not pick up the vines to attempt to move them. Moving kinks the vines and the fruit will be deformed. Harvest the summer squash as soon as fruit reaches 4-6 inches. Harvest the winter squash when your thumbnail does not leave a dent. They are not frost tolerant, so harvest on the afternoon of a predicted heavy frost.

Cultivars
SUMMER
'Black Beauty' -A zucchini; green-black skin.

'Italian Black Zucchini' - The most famous.

'Coczelle' - An Italian strain; long slender fruits.

'Peter Pan' - A patty-pan yellow squash.

'Yellow Crookneck' - Easy to spot when harvesting.
WINTER
'Arikara[1] '- An antique grown by Northern Plains Indians; tolerant of borers; Early maturing; stringy but sweet.

'Buttercup' - More flesh than any other; mild.

'Delicata' - Tastes more like sweet potato.

'Hubbard' - The old traditional cultivar still very tasty.

'Spaghetti' - Harvest when skin is deep yellow.

'Turk's Turban' - Good baker.

Troubles
See Chapter 4, Insects, Chapter 5 ,Diseases

INSECTS	DISEASES
aphid	blossom end rot
cucumber beetle	mosaic
cutworm	powdery mildew
flea beetle	root rot
spider mite	wilt
leafhopper	
leaf miner	
squash bug	
squash vine borer	
whitefly	
thrips	
grasshoppers	

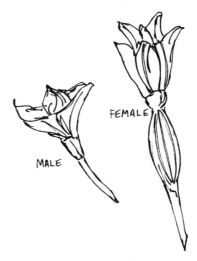

Male and female squash blooms. Both are edible dipped in a light batter and cooked as a pancake.

[1]*Available from Seed Blum, Idaho City Stage, Boise ID 83706. Catalog $2.00.*

■ SWEET POTATO[1]

Commercial production of sweet potatoes is thriving in the Mountain West where dry air precludes disease and vine borers are minimal. They are grown from rooted sprouts called "slips," which can be home sprouted or purchased from nurseries. If you can't plant your slips outdoors when they arrive, plant them in a flat of moist sawdust or vermiculite and keep them in a sunny window. Plants do best when set out in a very warm soil, to which has been added extra sphagnum peat, about 2 weeks after the last spring frost date. Heavy soils produce thin, fibrous roots. Warm the soil in the raised bed with clear or black plastic. Cut X's in the plastic to plant the slips 4 inches deep, 8 inches apart; then cover each with a bottomless plastic milk jug. Mulch when hot weather arrives. Sidedress each plant with 1/2 ounce of Miracle-Gro dissolved in 1 gallon of water 2 weeks after transplanting. In northern areas, install hoops over the rows and drape spunbonded row covers over them to keep the night temperatures high and the soil warm. Black plastic over the root run will ward off chill fall rains. Dig tubers when they reach desired size or immediately if soil temperature approaches 50°F. because keeping quality is impaired with chilling. Cure tubers for a week at 85°F.; then bring them to 85-90% humidity by placing in a plastic bag next to the furnace or hot water heater, or any area where continuous warmth is guaranteed. Do not refrigerate. Robust plants can produce 50 pounds of tubers per 25 foot row.

Cultivars

'Georgia Jet' - The best for the Mountain West.

Troubles

See Chapter 4, Insects, Chapter 5, Diseases

INSECTS	DISEASES
flea beetle	None
whitefly	
vine borer	

---

[1] *If you are confused about the difference between sweet potot and yam, both terms are used for the same plant. The true yam belongs to a tropical plant family and is seldom available in this country. The word "yam" is a marketing term used to distinguish southern-grown sweet potatoes from those grown in the north.*

tossed out sunflower seeds and hulls.

Cultivars

'Italian White'- A dramatic addition of creamy white petals, black disc flowers surrounded by a golden aura. Effective planted in the shrub border in full sun. Stems are somewhat lax, but easily draped over taller shrubs.

'Sunbeam' - A 5 foot plant with yellow ray flowers and green discs. A good cut flower.

'Sunspot' - A knee-high plant with 10-inch discs for good seed production. Makes a pretty edging for the vegetable garden.

'Velvet Queen' - Velvet red ray flowers with a black disc sprinkled with gold. 5 feet high.

■ SUNFLOWER

A vegetable garden is beautiful, that no one can deny. To add flowers at the row ends as indicated earlier in this chapter increases pollination of the vegetables by insects that are attracted to the pollen and nectar of the flowers. Sunflowers in a vegetable garden add other dimensions: an edible crop; height, if they are of the tall-growing cultivars; brightly colored flowers; and a third unseen quality, *allelopathy*. You will often see a farmer plant sunflowers on a particularly weedy piece of ground. The sunflowers transmit an allelopathic quality to the soil which will prevent the germination of many weed seeds. You as a home gardener can take advantage of this short-lived quality as well, if your garden is in the path of wind-blown weed seeds from a neighbor. Also, you may have seen a demonstration of the toxic substance emitted by sunflowers if you stock your birdfeeder exclusively with sunflower seeds. Very little plant growth will occur in the soil under the feeder where birds have

■ TOMATOES

Tomatoes will grow in almost any soil if it is warm and well-drained. Warm the soil for 2 weeks before planting with clear or black plastic. About the end of May or up to June 10, plant home-grown or purchased transplants that are about 6 inches high. Planting gallon-size plants is tempting but will not bring in an earlier harvest because they are woody and overmature. To protect from wind and to keep the soil warm, place a auto tire wrapped in 10-mil black plastic over the new transplant. If not wrapped, there is danger of the heavy metals used in tire manufacture being transferred to the soil. If you prefer to stake tomatoes, place the cage at planting time, but slip a plastic cage protector over it to hold in heat.

Planting is different from that of any other plant. The stem has the ability to form roots; therefore, we strip the lower leaves from the stem all the way to the top whorl of leaves. Dig a narrow shallow trench; mix a handful of complete fertilizer with soil in the bottom, and cover with 1 inch of soil. Lay the plant on its side in the trench, covering with 2 or 3 inches of soil. Water well. Within an hour or two the whorl of leaves will be turned upward. then cover the soil where the stem and root lie with clear plastic.

How to plant a tomato

Sidedress or apply fertilizer through the drip system monthly until blossoms form. Water as needed, but tomatoes are drought tolerant. Pinching or cutting out so-called suckers or side shoots has been proved an erroneous practice. The sucker shoots will bear as well as the main branches. Plants allowed to sprawl will also bear more heavily than caged plants. If you used the auto tire over the transplant, stack another on top — wrapped with heavy plastic as before — when weather is really warm and plant has reached the height of the second tire. The dark rubber will now serve a different purpose of shading the root. The vines will spill out over the second tire and down to the soil. Fruits will ripen quickly, above the danger of slugs and wireworms.

Auto tires wrapped in heavy black plastic make good tomato cages.

Cultivars[1]
Legend

V verticillium wilt resistant
F fusarium wilt resistant
FF race 1 and race 2 *fusarium* wilt resistant
N nematode resistant
T tobacco mosaic resistant
A *alternaria alternata* (crown wilt) resistant
L leafspot (*Septoria*) resistant
St *stemphylium* resistant

[1] *Experienced gardeners will defend their choice of tomato cultivars to the death. The author is mindful of scathing criticism against any attempt to guide a gardener toward a new culitvar. The cultivars listed are only a few of old and new cultivars considered by many to be the best.*

determinate - Those that produce only moderate vine growth after first fruit set.

indeterminate - Varieties continue to grow and produce additional fruit after fruit set and allow for a longer harvest season.

'Early Girl' - Earliest slicer; prolific.

'Quick Pick' VFFNTA - Best of the early varieties.

'Better Boy' VFN - Good yield of large fruits. A long-time favorite.

'Celebrity" VFFNT - An award winner of determinate plants producing a bounty of 8 ounce globe-shaped fruits that resist cracking.

'Lemon Boy' VFN - These are lemon colored not lemon flavored. Good tomato flavor on large fruits.

'Sweet Million Hybrid' FNTL - The highest performer of the cherry tomatoes.

'Roma' VF - The best of the paste tomatoes.

Troubles

See Chapter 4, Insects, Chapter 5, Diseases

INSECTS	DISEASES & CULTURAL PROBLEMS
aphid	blossom-end rot
blister beetle	cracking
cutworm	early & late
flea beetle	blight
grasshopper	fusarium wilt
leafhopper	leaf spot
tomato hornworm	psyllid yellows
tomato fruitworm	sunscald
whitefly	viruses
psyllid	weed-Killer
slugs	injury
thrips	
spider mites	
symphillds	
earwigs	
wireworm	

■ TURNIP

Turnips are more successful as a fall crop than those planted in spring. Turnips follow peas very well. After the summer solstice, plant seeds at the rate of 1/2 ounce per 100 feet of row. Cover with 1/2 inch of soil, and water well. When plants begin to crown[1] , thin to 3 inches apart. No fertilization is necessary. Begin harvesting at 2 inches in diameter.

Cultivars

'Purple Top White Globe' - The old standard is still good.

'Tokyo Cross' - A little radish-sized turnip good on the snack tray with a dip.

'White Lady Hybrid' - Vigorous, quick maturing.

Troubles

See Chaper 4,Insects, Chapter 5, Diseases

INSECTS	DISEASES
aphid	black leg
cabbage root maggot	black rot
flea beetle	

[1] See Glossary

45

■ WATERCRESS

The flavor of watercress is tradtional to the English tea sandwich and equally welcome in the North American dip or as a soup flavoring. Rather than grow from a questionable seed source, buy a bagful at the supermarket and root the cuttings in moist vermiculite or in water. Plant the rooted cuttings in the mud at streamside of a fresh cold-water stream. Anchor the cuttings with gravel. Watercress will also grow in a sandy, well-drained bed if it is doused with water every other day. A good containter crop, use a plastic bucket with drainage holes punched in the bottom. Hot weather can make the leaves taste peppery.

Troubles

See Lettuce

■ WATERMELON

Cultural practices are the same as for Cantaloupe. Watermelon can be grown indoors and set around the outside rim of a punctured, manure-filled coffee can. If black plastic is laid over the area where vines scramble, there is less danger of powdery mildew. Fruits are ripe when a sharp rap produces a hollow sound and when the stem end begins to shrivel.

Cultivars

'Sugar Baby' - A good 6 pound variety for a small family.

'Golden Crown' - A yellow skinned, red-fleshed award winnner.

'Sweet Heart Hybrid' - 9 pounders fit your fridge.

Troubles

See Chapter 4, Insects, Chapter 5, Diseases

INSECTS	DISEASES
aphid	blossom-end rot
cucumber beetles	powdery mildew
spider mites	fusarium wilt
leaf miners	
leafhoppers	

■ WHEAT

When you live in the country, there is a lure of learning to grow the unusual or sometimes the bizarre. The true dry land winter wheat, 'Turkey Red.' is a good choice for all of the Mountain West. Southern areas can grow spring wheat. A 10 foot by 10 foot plot will yield enough grain for 5 or 6 loaves of moist, rich-flavored bread. Seed is available at health food stores and in small quantities by mail order catalog. About Sept. 1 broadcast 1/4 pound of seed per 100 square-feet, and rake in, covering lightly. Keep moist by sprinkling. If the winter is extremely dry and open, water as needed. Spring rains are usually enough to mature the crop. Harvest when the grain is fully mature - falling out of the heads when you rub them, anytime from May to July 15. Bundle the stems into sheaves and dry in the sun away from the house because the sheaves are very flammable. When heads are no longer leathery, but fully hardened, thresh by shaking, jumping up and down on it with soft-soled shoes, or flailing on a tarp. Use a fan or hair-dryer to blow away the chaff. Take your bounty to a health food store that has a grinder to mill your flour. Wholewheat flour must be refrigerated.

Sources
W. Atlee Burpee Seed Co., Warminster PA 18974. Catalog free.

Gurney's, 110 Capital St., Yankton SD 57078. Catalog free.

Park Seed Co., Cokesbury Rd., Greenwood SC 29647-0001. Catalog free.

Thompson & Morgan, P.O. Box 1308, Jackson NY 08527-0308. Catalog free.

Fruits

Newcomers to the Mountain West are unaware that this is an ideal area for an edible landscape. Despite the vagaries of weather, fruit trees make good shade trees as well as beautiful boundary decoration trellised on fences. Fruiting shrubs become ornamental when grown in the foundation or border planting. Fruit trees or shrubs require little more care than those that are purely ornamental. The bonus of blossoms, fruit, shade and the brilliant color of fall foliage will make up for being cognizant of insect and disease control, the need of some species for pollination, and somewhat more than casual pruning. Apples, pears, plums, sour cherries, and black and hybrid walnuts as well as other nuts can be grown in all but the highest elevation (above 8,000 feet) area of the Mountain West states. Peaches, nectarines, apricots, sweet cherries, and a

larger assortment of nuts can be grown in the lower altitudes and the southern regions of the Mountain West. The bush fruits such as currants, gooseberries, quinces, and bush cherries enhance the border or foundation plantings, while raspberries and grapes, trained on perimeter boundary wire fences, serve as hedges. Strawberries, the backyard glamour fruit, should not be attempted unless the bed can be moved or the soil in the planting bed changed every 3 to 4 years.

On the negative side, the overall climate of the Montain West is not conducive to tree fruits. Cold, dry dessicating winds in winter, late spring frosts, and shallow, sometimes highly alkaline soils combine to make growing fruit tree a challenge. Nevertheless, with selected cultivars that are bred for the area, a sheltered planting site in full sun, and with reasonable care,

■ *Fruit trees or shrubs require little more care than those that are purely ornamental.*

we enjoy fruit with more palatable taste than that of any other area in the United States. The deep fluctuation between day and night temperature in late summer draws out the sugar/carbohydate ratio within the fruit. In California fruit production is far higher, but taste tests of Mountain West fruits rate higher.

Choosing the Right Tree Fruits for the Home Landscape

Your family's taste in fruit will guide your selection of species. Tart apples will never satisfy the person who likes sweet, dessert-type apples. The amateur wine-maker may want a grape of dusky flavor, while the salad-maker wants seedless grapes! Grapes, however, are severely pruned each year, so even the small landscape has room for more than 1 cultivar, even the fondly remembered grape arbor at Grandma's house. The problem of multiple fruit trees is easily solved as well, by trellising trees along the perimeter of the property. If you have room for only 1 apple tree, choose 1 grafted to 3 to 5 different cultivars. If this statement makes you suspicious of snakeoil salesmen tactics, be not afraid. Five-in-one apple trees are actually a good buy. It is possible in tree propagation to bud a different apple cultivar to each of the major limbs of a 3 year old tree. An added benefit is that the cultivars pollenate another so that crops are heavier. Each of the limbs will soon reach bearing age to give you 5 kinds of apples for years to come. Trellising these trees will give you better control over each of the grafted limbs. If allowed to grow freely, more than half of the more vigorous cultivars will overgrow the weaker. Make certain you mark each limb with a label to prevent accidental pruning of the grafted limbs.

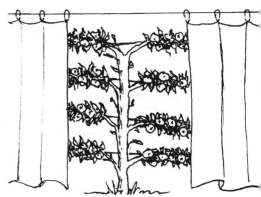

Trellised trees and a frost curtain being drawn over it at bloom time

Pears are a little more difficult to locate in the landscape. Two trees are best for good pollination by bees and not all cultivars will pollinate others. If you don't have space for a home orchard, plant a pear to frame both the front and back doorway. They are in good proportion for this task, and will give 4-season beauty. Pears are also good candidates for trellising.

Plums are universally loved for their abundant display of bloom in spring. With most being self-pollinators, they bear far more fruit than one family can consume. Grow a dwarf cultivar of the type your family likes best, and dry the surplus fruits for winter bird food. Plums are beautiful trelissed, as well.

Apricots and nectarines are possible to grow only in the southern reaches covered by this volume, unless you trellis them on a fence with accompanying frost curtains to be drawn over them at night during bloom time. The standard size (20 feet x 20 feet) of both trees are the best of climbing trees for children. Give them a location in full sun near the children's play area where they can become shade as well as look-out posts for invading armies. If climbers wear soft shoes, the trees will withstand the traffic of several generations.

Cherry trees, both sour and sweet cultivars, are not difficult to place in the home landscape. Use the dwarf cultivars as tall background shrubs for the perennial border or mixed with the tree-and-shrub border on the perimeter boundary of the home. Bush cherries make a satisfactory hedge, but the fruit is mainly taken by birds, for it is mostly stone and very little flesh.

Nut trees pose the only difficult placement. Make sure you wish to deal with falling nuts before you plant a nut tree. With growing the hybrids of English, Persian or Carpathian walnuts possible only in the southern areas of the Mountain West, the squirrels are formidable foes. With black walnuts, the squirrels are welcome to carry off the excess nuts, for there are not many people who develop a taste for them, and recipes for their use are not abundant either. Squirrels seldom stash the nuts a-la-tree cavities as in fairy tales. They bury them in the lawn. In addition, they are given far more credit than they deserve for remembering where they buried them; therefore, the nuts germinate in the spring and you are faced with a feat of strength to remove the seedlings. Either black or English hybrid walnuts make magnificent shade trees, however. They are one of the few trees that put down deep roots. If you have a country property, give them a deep-soil site above the flood plain of a creek bottom. Generations to come will thank you.

For other species of nuts, the jury is still out. Many of those you will see listed have had only minimal testing in the Mountain West. Others are doubtful for permanence in commerce. Only you, the gardener, can make the tests that will determine the efficacy of nut growing in the Mountain West. Share your information and knowledge gained with the Cooperative Extension agent in your county, as well as with garden club members.

Planting a fruit tree to shade your patio has its hazards. The dropping of immature fruit in June ("the June drop") is messy, but far more messy is the dropping of fruit throughout the season and into winter. While placing a plastic tarp under a tree makes disposal of the dropped fruit an easy task, the tarp is not the thing of beauty you may want decorating your patio. Then again, the pick-up may become the task of youngsters in the family and a good way to acquaint them with observing nature.

For country dwellers with room to plant a home orchard the guide on p. 52 will give you the picture of how many more dwarf fruit trees you can plant than the standard size. In addition, the dwarf trees will begin to bear in the 3rd year, while the standard-size trees will not bear until the 5th to 7th year, and 20 years may pass before full bearing capacity is reached. On the down side for dwarf trees, there is some evidence that dwarf trees are more susceptible to temperature extremes than standard size trees.

The upper areas of gently rolling terrain are the ideal site for a small fruit orchard because natural air drainage down the arroyos on frosty spring nights will protect the blooms. Freedom from competitive roots of shade trees or evergreens is also a necessity. The water source for a small orchard must be at a gravity point above the orchard or you must install a small pump to pump water uphill to begin the irrigation.

Weeding of tree fruits is as important as fertilization. Until a perennial grass is tightly knit under the trees and in the

■ *Squirrels seldom stash the nuts a-la-tree cavities as in fairy tales.*

51

irrigation furrows, cultivation with a small tiller or handing weeding will have to suffice. Weeds are notorious gobblers of soil nutrients and water.

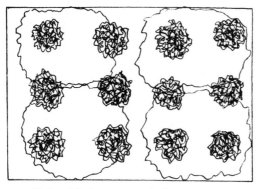

12 dwarf fruit trees grow in the same space as 4 standard trees.

13 Strikes Against You

To give you the odds that you face in growing tree fruit, please study the chart **pp. 53** that lists the environmental pitfalls and hazards. The chart does not include insects, which are considered a controllable hazard. Keep in mind that this chart is the worst-case scenario. There will be years of good harvests without undue effort.

Watering Methods

Drip irrigation is the preferred method of water application for the home orchard or for tree and shrub fruits in the border or foundation planting. Place 6 emitters per tree within the small root zone of young trees. Enlarge the ring of emitters as trees grow to the dripline of each tree. Sprinkler irrigation is adequate but wasteful. If you choose sprinkler irrigation, take precaution to make the arc of water very low. Protect each trunk with a metal shield. The force of water repeatedly striking the trunk will cause serious damage. Micro-sprinklers do not present this problem. With any method of irrigation, test the depth of water

penetration after each irrigation to make certain water has reached deeply.

Direction for protecting tree and small fruits is found in Vol. I, Chapter 7, p.67. Chapter 9 "Pruning" p.95-102 will give you direction in pruning tree and small fruits, as well as trellising directions. Please read these chapters carefully before choosing the fruit cultivars.

Furrow Irrigation

For the home orchard where drip irrigation is not feasible, furrow irrigation is the best method of watering. A head ditch is installed at the highest point of gravity, with furrows leading from it at a 90° angle. The furrows are 2 to 2 1/2 feet apart and run with the force of gravity to a deeper ditch that is installed parallel with the head ditch at about the midway point of the orchard. This is known as the "waist" ditch. This ditch is necessary only in the larger orchard where the furrows may be too long for water to run through to a different kind of ditch by the same name, but with a different spelling - the waste ditch (see below), at the bottom of the orchard. By installing a midway ditch (the "waist" ditch), water is collected in sufficient amount to have enough force (also known as "head") to complete the run through to the waste ditch. In all orchards under furrow irrigation, the water is run slowly through a few furrows at a time until good penetration is seen as "black across the row." At the bottom of the orchard, the lowest point of gravity, the waste ditch is installed to collect water to be channeled elsewhere to water another crop, or to a neighbor who needs water. Gated (flexible or rigid) pipe is also a method of furrow irrigation that may be chosen. It eliminates the need of a head or waist ditch. See Vol. I, Learning To Apply Water, p.74.

Hazard	Apples	Apricots	Cherries Sour	Cherries Sweet	Cherry Plums	Crab-Apples	Peaches	Pears	Plums Prune (European)	Plums Japanese Hybrid	Plums Native American
Spring frosts	X	XXX	XX	XX		X	XX	XX	X	XX	X
Winter freeze	X	XX	X	X		X	XX	X	X	XX	
Insufficient chilling		X	XX	XXX			XX			X	
Brown rot		XX	X	X			XX		XXX	X	X
Rain cracking		X	X	XXX			X			X	
Bird damage		XX	XX	XXX			X	X	X	X	X
Tree borers		XX	X	XX			XX		XX	XX	
Hail	XX	XX	XX	XX	XX	XX	XX	XX	XX	XX	XX
Excessive high temperatures			X	X					X		
Insuffiecient moisture	X		X	XX			X		X	X	
Poor soil drainage		XXX	XX	XX			XX		X	XXX	X
Bacterial disease	X	XX	X	XX		X	X	XXX	X	XX	X
Viral diseases		X	X	XXX			XXX			XX	XX

X = slightly susceptible
XX = moderately susceptible
XXX = highly susceptible

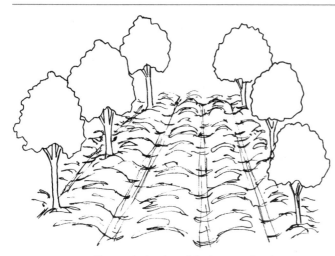

Furrow irrigation of the home orchard.

The Orchard Floor

If furrow irrigation is chosen as the method of applying water, weeds will be a problem unless a grass species is planted to choke them out. Creeping Red Fescue has been the traditional grass for the orchard floor. It does not compete with roots, requires about the same amount of water as the fruit trees, and can withstand the shade of fruit trees. Growing at about 4 inches high, it does not require mowing. A new variety of perennial ryegrass 'Elka' has been found to establish itself faster than the common species. 'Elka' is a European cultivar, bred for sports turf, but we find it has an additional use as a good ground cover for orchards. Sources for it can be found in Washington state or below.[1]

In late fall, scatter ryegrass seed over the established furrow, and rake in lightly to bury the seed without disturbing the contour of the furrow. Winter snow and rain will bring on germination in early spring.

Apples (*Malus sylvestris.*) and Other Fruit Lore

We have choices to make when selecting apple trees for the home landscape. Because the apple is the most popular of fruits, concentrated research has given us a bewildering array of colors, tastes, growth characteristics, and sizes from which to choose.

Size and Other Characteristics

Spur fruit trees are universally accepted nowadays as being the most fruitful. A spur is a shortened limb with reduced internodes and several fruiting buds. It usually lasts about 3 years before snapping off. New spurs form from latent buds nearby. Many of the antique apples much sought after by some growers do not have this characteristic, so these trees do not bear heavily.

An apple limb has many spurs.

The apple is easily manipulated by grafting its root or trunk in pieces. For example, a root of extraordinarily fast growth or of resistance to cold, insects, or disease may be chosen to graft to a stock of a choice tasting variety. But what if the

---

[1] *'Elka' is sold in a mixture with Creeping Red Fescue under the name of "Companion Mix", available from Arkansas Valley Seed Co., 4625 Colorado Boulevard, Denver CO 80216. Tel.: (303) 320-7500.*

proposed scion is incompatible to the chosen root? To muddy the heritage further, another stock that is compatible to both scion and root can be grafted to the first stock. This stock can possess its own desirable characteristics, such as a better shape or enhancement of the keeping quality or the harvesting date of the fruit. Any number of characteristics can be chosen for grafting.

Grafted root and two stocks.

The East Malling Research Station in England is similar to the Cooperative Extension Research Stations in the United States. It was here that the first dwarfing rootstocks were used to make small, easily harvested trees. A standard apple tree with minimal pruning will attain a height of 30-40 feet. The smallest of the dwarfs will be 7 to 9 feet. This dwarf, EM9, (for the village East Malling) will have shallow, brittle roots, but it is still excellent for trellising where the trunk is supported by the wire and brittle roots will not break from the swaying of a trunk in a windstorm or the weight of a heavy crop. The cultivars continue with numbers from 1 to 27 in the naming system. Not all are available. Next to appear in commerce were the Malling Merton strains, MM, numbers 1 to 115. Nurseries are sometimes reluctant to divulge the names of rootstocks of the trees they offer for sale.

We, as consumers, can hope that the Truth in Advertising statutes will prevail to prevent fraud.

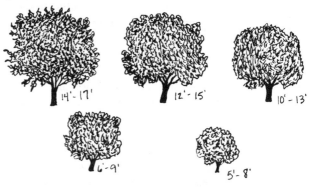

Mature Height of Dwarf Apple Tree Cultivars[1]

Many apples are not self-pollinating. For the best fruit yield, plant 2 different cultivars according to the chart below.

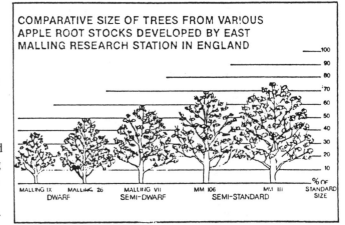

---

[1] *Dr. Harrison Hughes, Colorado State University, Department of Horticulture.*

Some varieties produce pollen that is sterile; others bloom earlier than the blooms of a potential pollinizer variety. Some produce pollen that is incompatible; hence there is no fruit despite prodigious crops of blooms. But, take heart, a nearby flowering crabapple tree will often serve as a pollinizer for a whole neighborhood of backyard apple trees. If all else fails, however, beg a bouquet of blooms from a tree of a cultivar that will pollinize your tree or from a crabapple tree. Cut small branches of blooms, placing the stems in a bucket of warm water immediately. Prop the bucket in the lowest crotch of your tree. The bees won't know the difference and will move from the blooms of the cut branches to the blooms on your tree.

Buying Fruit Trees

Many nurseries sell 3 year or older stock as potted trees. These are the poorest of choices, for they suffer transplant shock and will not come into bearing as soon as a 1 year or 2 year bare-root or just-potted sapling. With the younger trees, you can begin training immediately. With an older tree, corrective pruning is often necessary to overcome the lack of pruning in the nursery.

Growing Fruits from Seed

If you have unlimited time, a large parcel of land with good soil and water, intense interest, and a gambler's heart, planting fruit seeds can become a compelling hobby. Chance seedlings are the stuff upon which family fortunes are built, and no matter how remote the possibility of the surfacing of a

rare characteristic, the breeder, like the seeker of gold, always has hope. Keep your sights set high. Don't steadfastly maintain your seed-grown backyard peach is ambrosia just because you grew it, when actually it tastes like "ditch water and fuzz."[1]

What Is A Benchgraft?

The term *benchgraft* comes from the practice of laying a row of apple rootstocks and scions on a potting bench for quick grafting. A good propagator can do hundreds of these in a day. When you purchase a benchgraft, you select the root that best suits your need and the cultivar you want. The two are grafted, wrapped, sealed, labeled, and callused (healed at the union) before being sent to you or your local nursery. Sometimes an interstock graft is necessary if the stock and scion you chose are incompatible. You are urged to plant these saplings in a protected area where they will receive extra care before being planted in their permanent location.

Planting a Fruit Tree

Planting instruction for a woody plant is included in Vol.I. The planting of a fruit tree is slightly different. **Spring planting is favored over fall planting.**

1. Dig a wide hole deep enough to set the tree, **if it is a standard, not a dwarf**, so that the graft union will be 2 inches **below** the finished level grade. Set aside the topsoil in a pile on a plastic tarp. Set aside the subsoil in a different pile.
2. Use 1/3 of the subsoil in compost-making at a later date. Mix sphagnum peatmoss with the remaining 2/3.

[1] *A Mountain Westernism arising from the natives' observartion of tourists who eat Palisade, CO peaches as they return to Denver driving up De Beque Canyon. The seeds they toss out the window germinate and grow along the banks of irrigation ditches and the Colorado river. The fuzzy fruit these trees produce is watery and tasteless.*

3. Using the topsoil, build a hill inside the hole.
4. Prune the root tips of your tree <u>lightly</u> to remove all broken or ragged tips, and to make fresh cuts on unbroken roots. This procedure will expose firm vigorous cell structures that will quickly form a network of fine root hairs.
5. Spread the tree roots over the hill evenly, holding the tree in place with one hand or with the tines of a spading fork.
6. Use some of the mixed subsoil to cover the roots lightly.
7. Fill the hole 1/2 full. **If your tree is a dwarf, not a standard cultivar,** the graft union must be 2 inches **above** the finished grade to permit the dwarfing root system to influence the tree through-out its life.
8. Keep your feet out of the hole! Roots are too often broken by tamping with your feet. Fill the hole with water, allowing it to seep away. This will eliminate air pockets and settle the soil.
9. Finish filling the hole, leaving a saucer-like depression to hold water around the tree. Mulch with pole peelings or dried grass.
10. Water again; then allow the soil to become almost dry before watering again. Root hairs will push through slightly moist soil more quickly than through sopping wet soil. This time period may be from 5 days to 2 weeks. Test the moistness of the soil with fingers plunged deeply. Water through-out the summer to keep the soil moist, but not soggy, at all times.
11. Prune those limbs or twigs that are crossing and rubbing together. The tree needs all the leaves it can muster to promote a good root system during the first growing season.

12. About November 1, paint the trunks of fruit trees with white latex paint or wrap each one with commercial tree wrap, beginning at the bottom. This precaution prevents sunscald, one of the greatest causes of tree demise in the Mountain West.

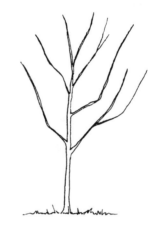

The newly planted fruit tree.
See Vol. I Chapter 9 Pruning for training and pruning fruit trees.

Training

Though the spreading and bending of limbs of fruit trees **after growth begins in spring** is demonstrated in Chapter 9 of Volume I, the reason for this action is not given. The more horizontal a branch grows, the more likely it is to form fruiting spurs for earlier production. Also, wide-angled crotches are stronger than narrow crotches and more able to bear a heavy fruit load or snow load. The horizontal branches restrict movement of carbohydrates from the ends of limbs to the roots. Instead of accumulating in the roots, the carbohydrates accumulate in the limb, slowing down growth in the limb as well. With the slowing of vegetative growth, fruiting buds are more likely to initiate at the end of June.

Fertilization

Fruit tree fertilization has changed recently. Nursery trees are pushed with fertilizer to salable size. If you are planting dwarf trees or whips to be trellised, apply 1 cup per tree of a complete fertilizer, such as 10-10-10, each spring after the trees have leafed out. The nitrogen will push them into making a large leaf crop, which, in turn, will increase growth and fruiting in the third year. Water well after the fertilizer application; the trees will be making 15 to 30 inches of terminal growth per year. If trees are near a lawn, there is no need for fertilization. The annual application of complete fertilizers to the lawn is sufficient. Make certain, however, that there is no herbicide present in the lawn fertilizer, for it will kill trees, shrubs, and flowers with roots under the turf surface. For the remaining nutrients needed by the trees, rely on spading in homemade compost plus the fallen leaves of each tree in autumn. The slow release of major and micro-nutrients will keep the trees in good production. If there is failure of trees to grow, apply a combination of 1 bushel of compost and the standard application fertilizer recommendation on the package. Apply around the root run of the tree, spading in lightly.

Spraying for Insects

Insect control on fruits or vegetables is not a part of this volume or of Vol.1. Chemicals and their regulation by the Environmental Protection Agency change too swiftly to warrant the inclusion. However, stages of growth of buds is pictured below. Use this as a guide for spray dates. Your horticulture agent at the Cooperative Extension Service will guide you in controlling insects.

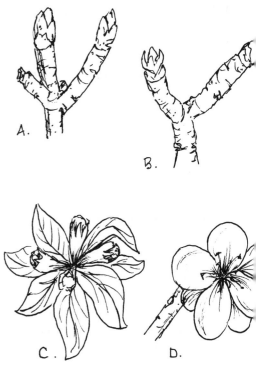

Stages in bud growth of apples. (A) Dormant stage. (B) Delayed dormant or "green tip". The bud has broken slightly. (C) Pre-bloom; buds show some color but petals have not begun to unfold. (D) Full bloom (E) Post-bloom petal-fall or calyx stage.

The June Drop

You will notice the first drop of fruit when spent blooms fall. These have not been pollinated and can't hang on. Almost all tree fruits, especially apples, experience a dropping of immature fruit in June or early July. Commerical growers may prevent this with a cover spray not available to backyard growers. The drop is caused by lack of pollinizers (another cultivar), lack of pollinators (bees and other insects), lack of nutrients or water, attack by disease and insects, and/or low-temperature injury.

There will be many years when a gardener will whistle a sigh of relief when a cold snap during bloom seemingly leaves his crop unscathed; then in June he is dismayed when all or almost all of the developing fruits drop. This happens because the stem was frost-damaged. When the weight of the developing fruit is too much for the damaged stem, the fruit drops, even though it was undamaged.

Fruit Thinning

We have a chemical method of thinning fruit, and we also thin by hand. Within 10 days after petals have fallen from fruit blooms, spray the tree lightly with carbaryl (sold as Sevin) if you want to eliminate a few fruits, or spray to a point of dripping if you want to eliminate all of the fruit. Carbaryl is an insecticide that combats chewing insects. It is very toxic to bees, but since the bloom period is over, the bees are no longer interested in your trees. The chemical affects the peduncle (stem) and nutrients can no longer pass to the fruit and it drops. There is also a product called "Florelle" which will eliminate unwanted fruits.

Thinning by hand is a tedious job. We thin to increase the size of the fruit and to decrease incidence of alternate bearing. While thinning any fruit, it is well to keep a carrot in front of the nose, such as visualizing peeling 4 apples for a pie instead of 14. Break the clusters of fruit, leaving only 1 fruit. The distance between fruits should be 4 to 5 inches, edge to edge, not center to center. It takes 32-40 leaves to mature every fruit. Experience will teach you when the balance between leaf surface and number of fruits has been reached. Place a plastic tarp beneath the tree before you begin thinning to make quick work of the cleanup. Pears are self-thinning, dropping fruits about 6 weeks past bloom.

Alternate Bearing

Some apple cultivars, pears, plums, and sometimes cherries will bear heavily one year and almost none the next. The reason lies in the nutrient absorption mechanism of some cultivars and in the manner of bud initiation. The buds that eventually develop into fruits are initiated a full season ahead of the time of fruiting. Thus, the blossoms that produce the crop this year were initiated in June last year. If a heavy crop was carried by the tree last year, the flower buds for this year's crop were competing for the nutrients with last year's fruit. Thinning aids in preventing alternate year bearing. The earlier after bloom the apples are thinned, the less stress on the tree and the less likely it is to bear alternately. The apple cultivars most likely to go into alternate year bearing are Wealthy, Baldwin, and Golden Delicious. The annual bearers that seldom bear alternately are McIntosh, Cortland, and Delicious.

Fall Blooming

Apples, lilacs, and many other woody plants are prone to put out a scattering of bloom in fall during dry years. The drought has been substituted for their dormancy period and they sense "winter is over." It is not a phenomenon to be welcomed. It is a signal of poor maintenance.

Harvesting

Apples and pears are harvested by lifting up and twisting to the side rather than pulling down. Think of how you unbutton a button. The action is the same and is less likely to snap off the spur. The stem on the apple is preserved as well. The intact stem increases the keeping quality.

Apples are the only fruit that keep their ripeness to themselves for a time. Plums, peaches, apricots, nectarines, and cherries proclaim their ripeness with a slight softening and bright coloring. Pears (except for Asian pears) are picked green. Only apples require a little sleuthing to find the best time to pick. The best test is the taste test. When the cultivar has reached its typical coloring, pick one and take a bite. If it tastes starchy, it's not ready. If the seeds are still green, it's not ready. If you aren't sure, do the iodine test. Pour a little iodine (that medicine chest treatment for skinned knees) in a saucer. Cut an apple in half and place it, cut side down, in the iodine for 2 or 3 minutes. Iodine stains starch. If the apple fails to take up the iodine, the starch has been converted to sugar and it is ripe. Blotchiness means it is half-ripe. You may have a sufficient number of trees to justify the purchasing of a pressure gauge to press against the skin of an apple to determine ripeness.

Testing apple ripeness with a saucer of iodine.

"Bloom" — What Is It?

Many tree fruits develop a white powder over the skin as they ripen. It is known as "bloom" and the term has nothing to do with a blossom. It is thought to be the fruits' adaptation to sunlight. The white bloom protects the fruit from sunscald by reflecting the unwanted rays. A few apples, nectarines, grapes, and almost all plums produce bloom.

Storage

Store apples as close to 40°F as possible. Cool down all fruits quickly as possible after harvesting. Peaches, plums, apricots, and nectarines should be wrapped individually in tissue paper squares, though this technique prolongs their shelf-life only a little. It's all downhill the moment they are picked. Also, there is no further ripening after harvesting. They must be allowed to ripen on the trees. Pears, except for Asian pears, are harvested green when both the calyx end and the stem end are well-rounded, and the seeds are brown. They can be stored in the hydrator of your refrigerator until a few days before use. Then bring them to room temperature in a pretty basket, and in a few days they will be colored up, soft and juicy, and ready to eat.

A method of home storage of apples was devised many years ago and it is still a good method. Partially bury an old refrigerator flush to the door. The shelves become separators for different varieties of apples. When extreme temperatures threaten in late November, mulch the door with straw mats you make yourself from a bale of straw or those made of excelsior and wrapped in nylon netting purchased from an air-conditioner store. Most refrigerators no longer have latches. If they do, these must be knocked off with a sledge hammer to avoid the possibility of a curious child crawling into the fridge while playing and being trapped.

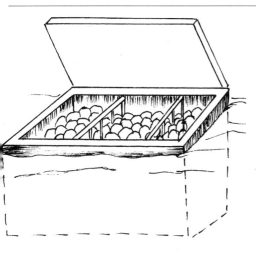

Old refrigerator buried flush to the door is used as storage for apples.

Commercial orchards store apples by controlled atmosphere storage, CA for short. You can approximate CA storage with a half-buried barrel or by digging and constructing a storage cellar in your utility area. Spray the earthern floor of your cellar with water frequently to bring up the humidity. The greenhouse sunpit discussed in Vol.I, p. 243 is also a good storage unit for apples, potatoes, carrots, turnips, and other root vegetables.

Tree Fruits

■ **APPLE** (*Malus sylvestris*)
Cultivars
'Braeburn' - New Zealand 1952. Orange-red blush over yellow-green background. Some tartness; very crisp. Superb keeper needing 160 ripening days.
'Cortland' - New York 1915. A cross between Ben Davis and McIntosh. Large dark red with heavy bloom. White flesh is crisp, tender, and subacid; slow to discolor, making it ideal for salads and pies. Ripens after McIntosh and before Red Delicious.

'Cox Orange Pippin' - England 1830. Medium size, dull orange-red, thin tough skin. Yellow flesh is firm, tender and very juicy. A parent to Gala.

'Criterion' - Washington 1973. A cross between Red Delicious, Yellow Delicious and Winter Banana. Large with smooth clear yellow skin, blushed with reddish pink. Flesh is firm, crisp, very juicy, slightly subacid. Good fresh, for cooking, freezing, drying or canning. Excellent keeper. Heavy producer and late bloomer, therefore, ripens late.

'Dolgo Crab' - A good pollinizer for all others. Vigorous, tall (25 feet) ornamental tree with dense, willowy branches. New foliage reddish. Large crimson fruits, excellent for jelly and spiced apples. Resistant to cedar apple rust, mildew, fireblight, and scab.

'Discovery' - England c. 1900. Striped and splashed red; very flavorful; not a good keeper, but extremely hardy. This may be the apple that can be grown well at Ouray, Vail, Aspen, on the Wasatch, or in the deeply cold valleys of the Bitterroots and Glacier National Park.

'Fameuse' - recorded arrival from France into Canada in 1739. The is the snow apple in the orchards of George Washington and Thomas Jefferson. It does better in the cool soils of the Mountain West, however. Deep crimson fruit; very white, tender, sweet, juicy flesh. Very long lived.

'Fuji' - Japan 1962. Yellow-green flesh, sweet, aromatic, subacid. Needs 170 days to ripen properly. Hardy only in the southern reaches ascribed in this volume. Good keeper.

'Gala' - New; firm flesh; vigorous tree; harvest this tree more than once, picking only ripe fruits each picking; fair keeper.

'Golden Delicious' - Old reliable for backyard culture as well as in orchards. Sweet, firm flesh; moderate keeper.

'Granny Smith' - New Zealand. A very crisp, hard, juicy white flesh; bright green tough skin. Long keeper. Requires long growing season. Ripens late October.

'Grimes Golden' - West Virginia 1804. Very large bright golden yellow fruit; crisp, fine grained yellow flesh. Aromatic and spicy flavor. Superior dessert quality. Keeps until January. A good pollinizer.

'Haralson' - Minnesota 1923. Medium fruit bright red striped to solid yellow. Crisp, juicy, tart. Very hardy to Zone 2. Slightly susceptible to fireblight.

'Jonagold' - New York 1953. A cross between Jonathan and Golden Delicious. Large, round yellow with light red stripes. Very firm, sweet flesh. Heavy producer. Keeps well. Good for drying and fresh eating. Not a good pollinizer.

'Jonamac' - New York 1972. A cross between Jonathan and McIntosh. Medium size, red, firm fruit with tart McIntosh flavor. Hangs well on tree, ripening before McIntosh. Hardy to Zone 3.

'Jonathan' - New York 1826. Medium size lightly striped, round bottomed; white flesh is juicy, tart, tender, aromatic. Not a good keeper. Susceptible to fireblight. Hardy through Zone 4.

'Lodi' - New York 1911. A better choice than 'Yellow Transparent' as a summer apple. Good sauce and as canned slices. Very hardy, annual crop. A fair keeper.

'McIntosh' - Ontario 1870. A cross between 'Fameuse' and 'Detroit Red'. Medium large, deep red fruit with crisp, perfumed, very juicy white flesh. Thin skin, tart, spicy flavor. Hardy to Zone 2. Not a good keeper.

'Prairie Spy' - Minnesota 1940. Large, crisp, juicy cream-colored flesh. Good for pie and sauce. Very long keeping and hardy through Zone 3. This is the apple for the hardship situation on the Great Plains.

'Rome Beauty' - Ohio 1848. It was once a large, pale yellow with mixed bright red flushes. Newer cultivars are all red. Flesh is yellow, coarse, tender, medium juicy and subacid. Early to bear; very productive. Blooms late. Good for baked apples.

'Wealthy' - Minnesota 1880. Medium to large with yellow red color. Crisp, tender, very juicy subacid flesh. Smaller, open spreading tree of superior hardiness. Fruit ripens over long period. Scab, fireblight and rust resistant. Hardy to Zone 2.

'Winter Banana' - Indiana 1876. Large yellow fruit with suture mark on one side. Flesh is crisp, moderately juicy, mildly subacid, not thought of as flavorful. Annual bearing. This is the best pollinizer, often grown as a colonnade to save space in a small orchard. NOTE: "Red Delicious" is a much-manipulated variety sold in supermarkets that has lost taste appeal.

A Winter Banana apple growing as a colonnade for its ability to pollinize in small orchard.

Tree Fruits In Containers

Mountain dwellers, as well as those who live in apartments with balconies, can grow the new colonnade trees in 15-inch containers on wheels. These trees will produce about 1/4 bushel each. Growing them in open flower beds or against a wall will make them a sculptural interest as well.

Cultivars (all have been introduced by Stark Bros, Louisiana, Mo 63353).

'CrimsonSpire'™ - Clean white flesh; tangy taste. Ready to harvest in mid-September.

'EmeraldSpire'™ - Green with golden blush; Mid-September.

'Maypole' - A flowering crab with the colonnade growth habit. Acts as a pollinizer for the others.

'ScarletSpire'™ - Red over green; late September ripening.

'UltraSpire'™ - Very compact growth. Red fruits with yellow-green blush. Tart, tangy; mid-September.

Troubles

See Chapter 4, Insects; Chapter 5 Disease

Insects	Diseases
aphids	apple scab
apple flea beetle	cedar apple rust
apple maggot	fireblgiht
cankerworm	powdery
codling moth	mildew
curculios	
leafrollers	
red spider mites	
scale, oyster shell	
shot hole borer	

■ **APRICOT**
(*Prunus armeniaca*)

Apricots will be found growing in surprising places in the Mountain West. Northern Montana, Idaho, and southern Canada are ideal because the weather stays good and cold throughout the winter without temperature fluctuation. Spring, when it finally arrives, is there to stay. Apricots insist upon blooming April 1 in more southerly regions. Frost is almost always the reason for crop failure. Crown borer is the second reason. Being of the genus *Prunus,* apricots are susceptible. This insect damage is often unnoticed until it's too late. See Chapter 4, Insects.

Pruning is limited to selecting scaffold branches and opening the crown. Apricot trees do not heal wounds well, and tree paint will not help. Prune correctly only in late winter. Insect and disease problems are best controlled with clean culture or a drip-irrigation system topped with fabric weed barrier and pole peeling mulch.

'Goldrich' - Most popular cultivar among commercial growers from statistics of numbers purchased.

'Harcot' - Exceptional cold hardiness; winning flavor.

'Manchurian Bush' - In northern sections this is an ornamental shrub that may have a few fruits. Pink blooms about April l, which are promptly frozen. Blooms again sporadically in later spring which may produce fruits. Requires corrective pruning to give it a pleasing shape.

'Moongold' - Bred in Minnesota for hardiness, late blooming, freestone, and juicy aromatic apricot flavor. Needs a pollinizer.

'Smith' - An old cultivar with very large fruit seldom seen in commerce. If you find a tree, beg budwood and graft your own tree. This is a superior plant.

'Sungold' - Bred for withstanding harsh climates. Good flavor and texture. Needs a pollinizer.

'Tilton' - An old cultivar with very large

fruit seldom seen in commerce. Look for it in backyards of older homes and beg budwood to make your own tree.

'Wilson' - A good all-purpose apricot; heavy bearer with sweet, distinctive flavor.

Troubles

See Chapter 4, Insects; Chapter 5, Diseases

Insects	Diseases
aphids	black knot
crown borer	brown rot
curculios	gummosis
leafhopper	plum pocket
mites	

■ CHERRY, SWEET
(*Prunus avium*)

'Bing' - The traditional long-stemmed dark, rich flavored sweet cherry. Requires a pollinizer such as 'Van.'

'Lapins' - New from Canada; split resistant; late blooming and, therefore, frost tolerant. Ripens late July.

'Royal Ann' - The old French light yellow/pink cultivar for pickling and fresh eating. Pollinizer can be 'Montmorency' or 'Stella'.

'Stella' - British Columbia 1968. Large, short-stemmed, sweet, juicy fruits with large stone. Vigorous, self-fertile.

'Van' - A dark, sweet, short-stemmed pollinizer that is a good substitute for 'Bing.'

■ CHERRY, TART (*Prunus Cerasus*)

'Montmorency' - France 1700. Spur type; medium size, bright red fruits with firm yellow flesh and clear juice. Self fruitful. Rich, tangy, tart flavor. Good for pies, jam, jelly, pancake syrup, and wine. Requires very good drainage and aeration. Will succumb quickly to overwatering. Ripens late June to mid-July.

'Northstar' - A cross of Siberian Cherry and English Morello, 1950's. Large fruit with thin, light red skin, red flesh, red juice, and small free stone. Upright habit. Self-fruitful. Hardy to -40°F.

Troubles

See Chapter 4 Insects; Chapter 5 Diseases
See Apricots

■ NECTARINE (*Prunus persica cv nucipersica*)

The "fuzzless peach,"as the nectarine is known by many, is not a cross of peach and plum. It is its origin that is fuzzy, for geneticists are unsure of its beginnings. The existence of the nectarine goes back centuries. It is a mutation of a peach that has evolved to become very stable. As first recorded, the nectarine had white flesh, but now it has yellow-orange flesh and is larger and more firm. Nectarines and peaches can be budded to each other, for both have the same cold tolerance of -15°F. before the tree dies. It is self-fertile, and is availble in both dwarf and standard size.

'Hardired' - Red skin, freestone with yellow flesh.

'Garden State' - Sweet yellow-fleshed freestone. Ripens at same time as 'Hale Haven' peach.

'Redchief' - White-fleshed freestone. Resistant to brown rot. Good size and color.

Troubles

See Apricots

Nuts

Nut trees and shrubs are seen more commonly in the East, but there is no reason why we in the Mountain West cannot enjoy nuts grown on our own property. They require a well-drained slightly acid soil. Acidify the soil within the **expected** root run of the mature tree with compost or sphagnum peatmoss. Each fall dig in finished compost plus the fallen leaves of the tree to keep the soil acid.

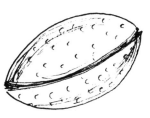

■ **ALMOND** (*Persica amygdalus*) For the areas of the Mountain West in Zone 5, almonds are a possibility, though you must be prepared to protect them during the bloom time. The exquisite pink flowers appear a month earlier than peaches, which will be the end of March through April 10. See Volume I, Chapter 7 "Plant Protection". The trees are cultivated in the same manner as the peach, with the nuts ripening from peachlike, fuzzy fruits in late August and early September. Keep a plastic tarp under the trees for easy harvesting, for the nuts fall when ripe. If birds such as Crossbills are around in summer, they may get the nuts unless you protect the tree with netting.

'Hall's' - A small spreading tree suitable for anchoring the perennial border or to grow along with other shrubs and small trees in a border or windbreak. Pink flowers are the first breath of spring. Plant 2 for good pollination.

Troubles
See Chapter 4 Insects; Chapter 5, Diseases
See Apricots

CHESTNUT

■ AMERICAN CHEST-NUT
(*Castanea dentata*)
The blight that destroyed the American Chestnut seems likely to be spent in the next several years. Cultivars have been found in the wild that are blight

free. These have been used to breed new trees that should become magnificent 40-60 feet shade trees as well as producers of quality nuts. Plant at least 2 trees for good pollination.

■ CHINESE CHESTNUT
(*C. mollissima*)
A smaller tree worthy of a cityscape, but best in a small grove in the country. Plant budded or grafted trees, more than one to assure pollination, or you will get a crop of "blind" nuts (empty shells). Nuts are very perishable and must be gathered from the ground within 2 days after falling or the nuts will be hard and inedible. Refrigerate harvested nuts immediately.
Troubles
See Chapter 4 Insects, Chapter 5 Diseases
    Insects
        chestnut maggot

FILBERT
■ FILBERT (*Corylus avellana*) A small tree to 18 feet with taproot habit. Thick spreading foliage good in the windbreak or tall hedge.

■ FILAZEL
(C. cornuta x C. avellana)
The hardiness of a hazel nut is combined with the flavor and size of a filbert. Maturing in September on a 15 foot tree within 4 years after planting.

'Gellatly Filazel' - Nuts ripen early.

'Big Red Filazel' - Large early-ripening nuts. Of suckering habit and a good candidate for the windbreak.

Troubles
lack of nuts • lack of pollinizer
See Chapter 4 Insects; Chapter 5 Diseases

Insects	**Disease**
bud mite	filbert blight

HAZELNUT

■ AMERICAN HAZEL
(C. americana)
Blight resistant; good productivity; may reach 30 feet in the Mountain West. Zone 4.

■ TURKISH TREE HAZEL
(C. colurna)
Non-suckering cross with European filbert and British Columbia 'Laroka'. Nuts crack out very clean. Pyramidal tree to 50 feet. Drought-resistant; corky bark. Zone 4.
Troubles - See Filbert

PECAN *(Carya illinoinensis)*
There are successful pecan trees in sheltered areas of Western Colorado, of Eastern and of Southern Utah, of New Mexico, and of Nevada. They are wide-spreading shade trees of 30-40-feet.

■ SHELLBARK PECAN
Prefers a deep rich moist soil with shelter of evergreens north and west of the planting and about 25 feet away.
Troubles - See Filbert

■ WALNUT
(Juglans sp.)

There is a saying, "He who has nothing to give to his children should plant a walnut grove." The wood of either Black or English walnut is extremely valuable for furniture, but we are cautioned to allow an expert in its preservation to cut and season the harvested trunk. Walnut trees are very deep rooted and slow growing, and prefer a deep rich bottomland above the floodplain with a constant source of water. They are easy to cleft graft if you come upon a superior cultivar. The trees require early training and a knowledgeable pruner to form strong limbs. The shells of the black walnuts are deeply ridged and thick-walled. The stains from the husks are long-lasting; therefore, use your car to run over the husked nuts to avoid the stains and to separate the husks from the nuts.

■ BUARTNUT
(Juglans cinerea x J. ailantifolia cordiformis)
A cross between Butternut and Heartnut. It retains the sweet heart-shaped kernel that cracks out whole. Leafs out late. Withstands -46°F. in Alaska.

■ BLACK WALNUT
(J. nigra)

Towering handsome trees with bright

yellow fall foliage. Two needed for pollination. The squirrels will plant it many times over.

■ ENGLISH CARPATHIAN WALNUT (*J. regia*)

Fast-growing trees up to 30-feet with thin-shelled nuts. Two needed for cross pollination. Bears in about five years.
Troubles
See Chapter 4 Insects

Environmental problems
• blind nuts from lack of pollination;
• kernels black from high temperatures in August;
• moldy nuts from rain or leaving husks on too long;
• nut shortage from frost.
Insects
Chestnut weevil
Tent caterpillars
Walnut husk maggot
Webworms

WHAT IS JUGLONE?

The mystery of untimely death of plants growing near walnut trees was solved early in this century when a chemical dubbed *juglone* ($C_{10}H_6O_3$) was found in its leaves, roots and wood. Members of the *Solanaceae* and *Rosaceae* families are particularly susceptible. Many other shrubs and trees seem unaffected, as is turfgrass. The only solution is to test the area with one or a few plants of the desired species before committing to planting it *en masse*.

■ PEACH (*Prunus persica*)

Peaches are traditional in the lower altitudes and river valleys with a long growing season in the Mountain West. River valleys are noted for their swift air currents that whisk threatening frost away. As stated earlier, the sharp temperature fluctuation between day and night temperatures and low humidity during the ripening period are thought to be the reason why Mountain West peaches have a flavor far superior to those of California, Georgia, or Michigan.

Peaches prefer a sandy loam, but will succeed in any soil that is well-drained. They cannot withstand wet feet or high alkalinity, and they are unusual in that they do not require winter watering. As members of the genus *Prunus*, they are susceptible to the crown borer. It is imperative to thin the fruits to 6 to 8 inches apart, as every tree sets far more fruits than the tree can hold or ripen. Don't pick peaches when green! Wait until the fruit has changed to a yellow with 25% blush. A bushel of green peaches picked today would yield almost 2 bushels in 5 days; almost 3 bushels if you wait another 5 days.

'Bellaire' - Good flavor; blushed freestone. Taste-tested in Western Colorado. Good for canning. Popular at farmer's market.

'Champion' - A white fleshed freestone peach preferred by many.

'Cresthaven - The most popular for orchardists.

'Elberta' - The old standard that some regard as still the best flavor peach ever developed. Yellow with almost no blush;

freestone; late ripening. "It ain't purty, but it's the best" is the motto of Elberta lovers.

'Glohaven' - A blush of red on yellow background. Good flavor, good keeper; freestone.

'Halehaven' - Very large fruits, reliable, self-pollinating; good disease resistance. Ripens in early September.

'Polly' - Small tree for higher altitudes; somewhat freestone; nearly white flesh. Not long-lived.

'Redhaven' - The most popular at the momemt; freestone; beautiful glowing red color.

'Reliance' - Said to withstand very hard winters, though trees will be killed at -15°F. Red-skinned freestone splashed with yellow.

Troubles

See Chapter 4 Insects Chapter 5 Diseases
See Apricots

■ PEARS, ASIAN
(Pyrus pyrifolia)

The fruits of an Asian pear have the crisp texture of an apple and the flavor of a pear, only sweeter. The fruits ripen on the tree and often appear in the second or third year. The fruits set heavily and must be agressively thinned to increase fruit size. The trees are small, somewhat upright in habit, and turn a glorious orange yellow in fall. They are susceptible to fireblight, a bacterial disease. All are hardy to at least -20°F. See Vol. I "Plant Protection" Chapter 7 pp. 59-60 for methods of protecting a tree in a more harsh climate.

'Hosui' - Large russeted fruits of superior flavor. Somewhat susceptible to fireblight.

'Korean Giant' - Also known as 'Don Bae' or 'Muk Gul'. Crisp juicy flesh; russeted very large fruit. Keeps until March. Bears early, but does not ripen until after the snow flies, usually November.

'Shinko' - Most fireblight resistant; very juicy, sweet.

'Singo' - Yellow-tan fruit with very white, tender juicy flesh that keeps until spring. Very vigorous upright tree. Acts as a pollinizer for 'Korean Giant.' Needs a warm wall behind it. Ripens mid-October.

■ PEARS, EUROPEAN
(Pyrus communis)

These pears are picked green when the calyx and stem ends are well-rounded and when the seeds are brown. They can be stored 6 weeks to 3 months, depending upon variety, just above 40°F. When you want pears on the menu, bring a few into room temperature and they will ripen within a day or two. If allowed to ripen on the tree, European pears develop tooth-breaking stone cells.

If you live in an area where the temperature can drop below -20°F, graft a colder climate variety, such as 'Flemish Beauty' on standard roots and plant with the graft union below ground level to assure survival, and healthy growth.

'Bartlett' - The most famous and flavorful of all pears. Needs a pollinizer. Red foliage in fall; upright in habit.

'Harrow Delight' - Two weeks earlier than Bartlett, but similar in taste and juicy quality.

'Magness' - USDA introduction 1960.

Medium, greenish- yellow fruit with light russetting. Tough skin against insect attack. Long storage life; no grit cells. Requires pollinizer such as 'Maxine,' 'Harrow Delight' or one of the Asian cultivars.

'Maxine' - Ohio 1923 aka 'Starking Delicious'. Medium large, golden fruit, firm, crisp white flesh, free of stone cells. Resistant to fireblight. Needs 'Magness' as a pollinizer.

'Seckel' - The little, extra-sweet, juicy pear used for baked desserts, pickling, spicing and canning whole. Slow growing, semi-dwarf, self-fertile.

'Ure' - An introduction from the Morden Research Station in Manitoba, Canada. Fruit is greenish-yellow, a blush of red. Very sweet, juicy, and aromatic. Tree is very hardy and may be the pear for the high country. Zone 3.
Troubles
See Chapter 4, Insects; Chapter 5, Diseases
See Apples

■ PLUM
(Prunus sp.)
Plum culture is similar to apricot, but a crop is certain more often than it is for apricot. Cross pollination is sometimes difficult if there are no other trees in the neighborhood or in the home orchard. The different types of plums tend not to pollinate each other, *i.e.,* Japanese plums will not pollinate American or European plums. Give the trees plenty of space away from a frost pocket, for they bloom in early spring.

'Blue Damson' - European. Said to go back to biblical days; the name comes from Damascus. It is said this is the only fruit known to come true from seed. Rounded, well-branched tree. Blue fruits with greenish flesh.

'Green Gage' - American. Introduced in early 1800's. Small smooth green fruits on extremely hardy tree of low-branching habit. Gardeners have a history of devotion to this old cultivar. Ripens in early September.

'Kaga' - American. Developed by Dr. N. E. Hansen of Hansen's bush cherry fame at the North Dakota Experiment Station. Fruit is small, crimson, and plentiful. Tree is a dependable pollinizer. Ripens in late August.

'Santa Rosa' - Japanese. The favorite from California possible in Zone 4 only as a trellised specimen with frost curtains drawn over when frost threatens blooms. Best pollinizer is 'Hybrid Oka.'

'Stanley' - A European introduction with large, oval, dark blue fruit. Rich flavor. Excellent for canning, preserves, drying or eating fresh. Bears early, blooms late and is a heavy producer.

'Waneta' - A Japanese hybrid from South Dakota. Very fertile, bears annually. Hardy to an astounding -50°F. Buy a tree grafted on American Plum stock to get this hardiness rating.

NATIVE PLUMS

■ AMERICAN
(Prunus americana)
This is the native of thickets along country roads and arroyos. Though multi-stemmed, it can be trained to a single trunk for a picturesque twisted small tree hanging over a lily pool. White blooms before leaves in early spring; very long lived. Fruits are small, flavorful; loved by birds.

■ WILD GOOSE PLUM
(Prunus munsoniana)

The plum thicket of Kentucky, Missouri, Arkansas, and Texas, not the Mountain West, but still one of the most popular plums for wildlife plantings, jams, and jelly.

■ CHERRY PLUMS
(Prunus cerasifera)

Both 'Opata' and 'Sapa' are recommended by the USDA High Plains Grassland Research Station, Cheyenne, Wyoming, for the high altitude areas of the Central Great Plains and all altitudes over 6,000 feet. Pollinizes all other plums that are blooming at the same time.

'Hybrid Oka' - a clingstone with almost black skin and purple-red flesh. Ripens in late August. Needs a pollinizer.

Troubles

See Chapter 4, Insects; Chapter 5, Diseases

See Apricots

■ QUINCE
(Cydonia oblonga)

Quince shrubs are good in the foundation planting or in the tree and shrub border, bearing large fruits at the base in about the sixth year. A bowl of quince in your home in late summer will produce a fruity fragrance that is superior to any aerosol room freshener. Wait until the fruits are yellow, however, to pick them. Though inedible out of hand, they make a jelly of unusual flavor; contact the home economist at Cooperative Extension Service for directions.

Troubles

See Chapter 4

Insects

aphids	red spider mites
wormy fruits	

SMALL FRUITS

The widely varied small fruits have a place in every home landscape. Grape arbors, strawberry towers, raspberry patches, and the shrubs that provide edible fruits are growing in the gardens of gourmet restaurants as well as in the private gardens of gourmet cooks. There is no substitute ingredient for freshness.

If you are from the northern tier of Mountain West states, you lump all small fruits into a category called "brambles." The following list is alphabetical. The brambles are of the genus *Rubus*.

■ BLUE-BERRY
(Vaccinium sp.)

This section will be very short. Domestic blueberries are being grown in the Mountain West, but the author has never found a gardener who has maintained them and faithfully defended their flavor for more than a few years. Blueberries require an acid soil with a pH of 4.6, which can be manufactured on the home grounds with a lavish effort. Sulfuric acid is the chemical that will acidify the soil quickly, but it is also the most dangerous to use. Soil scientists tell us that soil sulfur or aluminum sulfate works very gradually to bring down the pH, but only if there is a large amount of organic matter present. Oak leaf compost is one of the best acidifiers, but not every gardener has access to a quantity of oak leaves. Even when soil acidity is artificially produced, it is difficult to maintain, for the water in the Mountain West is often strongly alkaline. Flavor in the blueberry apparently depends greatly on its happiness with where it is growing. When blueberry experimenters finally make the honest analysis of the blueberries they have laboriously produced, it is almost always "thumbs down." The day will come when hybridizers will succeed in producing a flavorful blueberry that we can grow, but until then..... Native *Vacciniums* are a possibility, but you'll have to put up with suckering and a somewhat unsightly growth habit. The flavor of the native berries will not equal the domestic cultivars.

BRAMBLE FRUITS: *RUBUS SP.* BOYSENBERRY, BLACKBERRY, DEWBERRY, LOGANBERRY, RASPBERRY BLACK, RASPBERRY RED

■ BLACKBERRY
(Rubus macropetalus)

The days of blackberry canes long enough and strong enough to strangle a moose are over. Newer cultivars are sometimes thornless, are gentler, and definitely have sweeter berries. Though trailing blackberries are sometimes called "dewberries," the selections from the wild are now named cultivars. There are erect, thornless, and trailing cultivars selected or bred for the Mountain West that can grow in your backyard without invading other plantings. A watchful eye as to their habit is still somewhat necessary, however. The best site is one sheltered from the west and north by evergreens, and

where snow will lie deep throughout the winter. They will sucker widely; keep a sharp shovel handy. Blackberries are biennial. Canes grow 1 season, fruit the second season; then die and are replaced by another set of canes. Plant in spring or late August. For those in Zone 5 the choice is broad, but there are still 2 cultivars for the colder regions. Sugar content is up from those grown even 10 years ago. Wait until the berries are dead ripe before picking, however. They should be a little soft, and dull, not shiny. Zone 5.

'Chester' - Hardy to about -10°F, thornless; low acid; very sweet compared to the first thornless cultivars offered. Ripens mid-July.

'Black Satin' - Thornless, non-suckering; berries ready when dull black in mid-July.

'Darrow' - Thornless; ready for picking in early August. Zone 4.

'Illini Hardy' - Bred at U. of Illinois for -25° F. Ready for picking in early August.

■ BOYSENBERRY, DEWBERRY, LOGANBERRY

The boysenberry is a cross between loganberry, raspberry, and blackberry. Berries are long — sometimes more than 2 inches — and a prized gourmet item. Canes are long and thorny and must be covered in winter. A thornless cultivar is offered, but does not produce as heavily as the armed.

The loganberry is a hybrid originated by a Judge Logan. It is a cross between a western black dewberry and a red raspberry.

The dewberry (*Rubus ursinus*) is native of California, but will prosper in the Mountain West with protection.

■ RASPBERRY, BLACK
R. occidentalis
(also called Blackcap)

Plant black raspberries as far away as possible from red raspberries or other cultivated brambles. They are susceptible to *verticillium wilt*, which is also found on other brambles, tomatoes, peppers, potatoes, and eggplant. Therefore, avoid planting where these plants have been grown in the recent past. Full sun is the best site, with at least 12 hours of sunlight daily.

Soil preparation for black raspberries is all important if you are to get non-crumbly berries of worthwhile size. Spade in compost and sphagnum peatmoss until you have a mellow soil that will hold water without waterlogging, for these plants also demand more water than red raspberries. Plant in very early spring spacing plant 3 feet apart in the row with 8 feet between rows. After planting as soon as frost is out of the ground, cut all canes back to the ground to eliminate possibility of disease-carrying canes. Protect new growth from spring snows and frosts with spunbonded row cover or cardboard boxes. Summer topping to 1 foot is necessary about mid-July for spring planted plants and topping to 2 feet for the years thereafter. This process keeps the canes from growing long and spindly, arching over to touch the soil. As they touch the soil, they form a *ratoon,* a rooted plantlet, and nutrients surge to the plantlet instead of toward blooms and berries. This activity also produces the ferocious, tangled thicket of fairy stories. Pick berries when they are glossy and totally black. Harvest usually begins at the end of the strawberry season in June

'Black Hawk' - The choice for canning; disease resistant, midseason.

'Cumberland' - Old favorite of rich flavor; glossy when ripe; mid-July.

'Haut' - Ripens 3 to 5 days later than other cultivars and has a longer picking season.

'John Robertson' - Developed in South Dakota. Self-pollinating.

■ RASPBERRY, RED
(Rubus idaeus, var. strigosus)

Red raspberries in Mountain West gardens are the envy of all our neighbors. We wallow in them. We eat them out of hand, we make jam and pie and serve them on ice cream. We even strain out the seeds and make jelly or gourmet vinegar. This plethora doesn't drive down the supermarket price, however. If your children are wishing for money-making projects, raspberries are the very thing.

■ RED RASPBERRY CULTURE

Red raspberries are the only bramble fruit that can withstand some shade. Six hours of sunlight will suffice, provided the source of shade is NOT nearby trees that possess roots that are competing with the raspberries. Soil of moderate fertility is needed, with additional organic matter spaded into the rows each spring. One inch of water per week is the one big drawback for red raspberries. They will never tell you they need water by wilting. They sulk and balk in producing instead.

Methods of culture vary. The row culture shown offers ease of cultivation. A drip irrigation system and a covering of old carpeting between rows eliminates weeding, saves water, and discourages suckering of the plants. Thin the canes to 6 inches apart each spring after they are well up. Choose only the strongest canes to remain. After planting, the canes will bear on the tips in fall of the first year. In November after leaves have fallen, prune the canes back by half. In the second year these canes will bear on side shoots, then die. New canes will have formed to begin the cyle again. This system gives you 2 crops per year beginning in July, ending in September or whenever temperatures are too low for berries to ripen. Go through your rows to remove the dead canes frequently. They are dark brown with shreddy bark.

Fertilize with an all-purpose fruit/vegetable fertilizer, such as 8-10-8 or 10-10-10 is recommended in early spring as leaves are unfolding.

Row culture posts are located at the ends of each row, with wires strung at 5 feet and 2 feet above the soil surface. Cross bars attached to the end posts will serve as a place to anchor the wires. Make a hook at the end of each wire to fit into a hole on the crossbar. Unhooking the wires makes harvesting and pruning easier.

Protection of canes will be necessary in some areas. The county extension office can supply information for your area. Bending canes over while wood is still green is not an easy task. Ways to hold them down include: u-shaped aluminum tent stakes, lath nailed to wood stakes, and clods of soil; carried from another area, not soil gathered from between the plants, which is then piled over the canes. Remove the soil gradually as spring comes on.

Mowing of canes in fall is still another method of culture preferred by some. Cut the canes to within 6 or 7 inches of the soil surface; then mow the remaining stubs down with the lawn mower. This is a system that is the easiest of all methods, but it limits harvest to 1 crop.

Troubles

See Chapter 4 Insects, Chapter 5 Diseases

Insects	Disease
aphids	anthracnose
raspberry cane borer	orange-rust
	spur blight
spider mites	viruses
stink bugs	
raspberry fruit worm	
raspberry sawfly	
rose chafer	

Row culture of red raspberries made easy.

CULTIVARS OF RED RASPBERRIES

'Boyne' - The preferred cultivar for the high country.

'Fall Gold'- A very sweet yellow berry preferred by some.

'Heritage' - Red berry; vines exceptionally hardy.

'Indian Summer' - A self-supporting vine with thimble-shaped red berries.

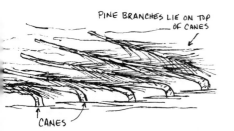

PINE BRANCHES LIE ON TOP OF CANES

CANES

Winter protection of raspberry canes.

'Pathfinder' - Exceptional cultivar developed by USDA High Plains Grassland Research Station, Cheyenne, Wyoming and rescued from oblivion in November, 1975, by Dr. Samuel C. Litzenberger, retired plant pathologist and volunteer Master Gardener for Boulder County Cooperative Extension. The vigor and productiveness of this cultivar has been preserved through home garden culture in Colorado. It is unknown whether any commercial sources for 'Pathfinder' are available. Make friends with a Colorado Master Gardener!

Cane Borer is virtually eliminated by using a power blower in November to blow every vestige of leaves from the rows. The cane borer overwinters in leaf debris.

■ CURRANT
(Ribes sp.)

Currants can occupy the most difficult space in your landscape — the base of the downspout. They prefer a soil constantly moist, but the wet/dry place near the downspout will suit them well if it isn't too long between storms. They can also withstand some shade. Both currants and gooseberries carry the disease White Pine Blister Rust, and should not be grown within 900 feet of a white pine or a white pine seedling nursery. See pruning procedures for currants and gooseberries in Vol. I, p. 99.

Though promoters of xeriscape will urge you to grow the native species, the dry, tasteless berries from Squaw currants are not recommended. To sally forth to pick Golden Currants *(Ribes aureum)*, and other natives in the wild is also not recommended. Leave the wild fruits for the birds and creatures of forest and plain: Their life depends upon them. Yours does not. If you intend to incorporate a currant bush planting into a xeriscape, use a drip system beneath a mulched weed barrier and provide adequate water.

'Coronet' - A black cultivar from Ottawa, resistant to blister rust. Excellent for wine, syrup, and cordials.

'Crusader' - A black from Ontario also resistant to white pine blister rust. The finest cultivar for jam. The syrup is used extensively as a health tonic in England and Europe to provide Vitamin C in the diet.

'Jonkeer van Tets'- Imported from Holland, this red cultivar is the top producer of all time (so far). Self-fruitful.

'Cherry Red' - Larger fruits; mildew resistant. An excellent thorny shrub to direct traffic along walks in parks or as a barrier along your property edge.

'Red Lake' - The leading domestic red currant. Disease free, large crop; good flavor.

'White Imperial' - White translucent fruit with slight pinkish blush when ripe. Sweetest and richest flavor of all currants. Ripens in late July.

Troubles

See Chapter 4 ,Insects; Chapter 5, Diseases

Insects	Disease
aphids	blister rust
cane borer	leaf spot
currant borer	powdery mildew
currant fruit fly	
currant sawfly	
currant spanworm	
flea beetle	

■ ELDERBERRY
(Sambucus canadensis)

Though this is a native plant of Canada, the cultivated varieties produce a larger, juicier berry. For pies, jam, jelly, and especially wine, this berry-like drupe is growing in many farmyards throughout the Mountain West. Preferring a rich, moist soil, it will sucker freely at the base to become a thick, tousled shrub 5 feet across and 5 feet high. Two cultivars are recommended for cross pollination.

'Adams' - The largest berries of all the cultivars.

'Johns' - Fruits ripens 2 weeks earlier than 'Adams'.

'Nova' - Very productive; ripens later than 'Adams'.

Troubles

See Chapter 4, Insects; Chaper 5, Diseases

Insects

aphids

mites

spindle worm, aka elder borer, see cane borer of raspberry for control.

■ FIG (*Ficus carica*)

The growing of figs has become a status symbol among gardeners in the Mountain West. In tropical climes a fig is a tree fruit, but in the Mountain West, it is a shrubby bush; therefore, will be placed among the small fruits. Actually, except for the physical strength required to move a fig in a half-barrel on wheels, it is not as complex nor difficult a horticultural feat to grow a fig as it seems. Gardeners living below 4,000 feet, in New Mexico, the Western Slope of Colorado, Eastern/ Southern Utah, and Nevada can grow figs in the ground outdoors, for they can withstand 0 to -10°F. But protection should

be in place before temperatures reach -10°F. Give them full sun against a south-facing wall where plenty of moisture is available. The fig is not a fruit in the truest sense. It is a fleshy receptacle with a cluster of minute flowers inside. A tiny hole at the apex of the fig allows a gall wasp to enter to pollinate the flowers, which precipitates the formation of the true fruits, which are the seeds you encounter when you eat a fig newton. Another fascinating fact about figs is that they are thought to be the second cultivated crop known to the human rare — the grape being the first.

'Brown Turkey' - The soft, brown, juicy fruits appear in mid-summer. They can be dried or stored in the refrigerator for several weeks.

'Celeste' - Pale pink flesh that is sweeter than 'Brown Turkey,' but is also a more tender plant. For heavy winter protection, give it a circlet of snow fence and a packing of leaves and straw in and around the branches; heavy mulching of root zone with evergreen boughs; then cover the entire structure with strong plastic. All of this should be in place before the temperature reaches 10°F.

Troubles

See Chapter 4, Insects, Chapter 5, Diseases

Insects	Disease
aphids	scale
spider mites	

■ GOOSEBERRY
(*Ribes hirtellum*)

The culture of gooseberries is similar to that of the currant, though gooseberries can withstand harsher conditions. They prefer a cool, rich, moist soil, but will make do with whatever you've got. They make an excellent barrier hedge around basement windows or the property perimeter, or as a protective screen around your prized rhododendrons. Not even a cat can get through their formidable thorns. Give them a drip irrigation system[1], topped by a fabric weed barrier and a mulch of pole peelings. This will prevent the natural layering of branches that touch the soil and take root, for a single gooseberry can become an impenetrable thicket in no time. Severe pruning is necessary to keep them in bounds. See Vol. I, Chapter 9 Pruning, p. 100.

'Champion' - Large green berry, late fruiting; mildew resistant.

'Downing' - An American cultivar adapted to all conditions of the U.S.; very productive; aphid resistant.

'Welcome' - Large fruit, red purple; sweet; branches have softer thorns than other cultivars.

■ GRAPES
(*Vitis labrusca*)

The fruit that requires the least work and worry is the grape. The soil requirement is of broad range. Added organic matter each year will improve quality and quantity of fruit, however. A drip irrigation system on a time clock will increase the ease of culture. Pruning is the only item that requires some skill, and it is better to prune as best you can rather than not at all.

Vines are sold as 1-year or 2-year olds. Select a site in full sun and away from the root competition and shade of nearby trees.

In the high country or in the northern latitudes select a south-facing site on a wall or on a sloping site above a lake or river. Water is slow to warm and slow to cool. The cold air above a body of water will prevent spring frosts from reaching the blooms. The warm air above a body of water in autumn allows higher sugars to mount in the fruits.

Planting

The planting hole is deeper than for a tree or shrub, being about 2 feet deep and as wide. Mix compost, weathered manure and/or sphagnum peatmoss with the backfill. Set the vines 8 feet apart if possible. If you'd prefer to prune harder and grow more cultivars, plant the vines as close as on 5-foot centers. When the plants are set and watered well, prune the top back to 2 buds, one on either side of the stem.

Setting the posts and stringing the wire is completed at the same time as the planting. Set metal posts 8 feet long 2 to 3 feet into the ground. String the first strand of number 9 wire 5-1/2 feet from soil level and the second strand 2 feet below the first. They may seem high, but when the trunk enlarges, you will see that this will give good exposure of the greatest leaf surface and fruit clusters to the sun. The first season is a critical one for water, for roots are expanding rapidly and must not want for water. In the second and subsequent years, keep watering to the same amount as for turfgrass until fall; then harden off by reducing watering. Fruit sugars will rise with lessening of the water and winter hardiness will be increased. Use a screwdriver thrust into the soil to tell you when

---

[1] *Drip irrigation systems are remarkably trouble-free, but it doesn't hurt to stop and listen intently when the system is running. If you hear an inordinate rush of water, remove the mulch, peel back the fabric, and you may find that a system has developed a leak or that an emitter has dislodged.*

it's dry, then water long and deeply.

See Vol. I, Pruning, p. 101 for grape pruning direction.

Fertilization

Grapes respond quickly to nitrogen and potassium, but not at all to phosphorous. Mountain West soils are rich in natural potassium; therefore, only 1/3 pound of ammonium sulfate per vine is needed each spring. Scatter it widely, not at the base of the trunk, and spade in shallowly; water very well, for this is a "hot" fertilizer.

Harvesting

Grapes are slow to ripen in all but the lower altitudes of the range of this volume. Pick off leaves that are shading the clusters to expose them to the sun. Tie small brown paper bags around each cluster. Not only will this increase the heat and hasten ripening, but it will also protect the clusters of berries from birds, hornets, wasps, and marauding children.

Spraying the maturing clusters with gibberellic acid[1] will increase the size of berries, thus, the size of bunches. It is expensive — about 50 dollars for 20 ounces. Share the cost with a neighbor — perhaps several.

Table Grapes

'Canadice' - A beautiful red seedless that hangs on the vine well, increasing in sugar.

'Concord Seedless' - The same characteristic flavor as the seeded variety. Good for juice, pie, jelly, marmalade.

'Glenora' - A blue seedless earlier than Concord.

'Himrod' - A quality green seedless grape, not as tasty as 'Thompson's Seedless' which is iffy in the Mountain West.

'Interlaken Seedless' - Early white; sweet, small.

'Niagra' - A white seedless cultivar also used for a dessert wine.

'Reliance' - A sure performer in a red seedless grape; ripens in late August.

Wine Grapes *(Vitis vinifera)*

The attraction to Colorado and other areas of the Mountain West for the growing of wine grapes rests in the absence of the Phylloxera, a plant louse that attacks grape roots, weakening and eventually killing the vine. The wine industry is growing fast, using locally grown wine grapes as well as other pome and drupe fruits grown in the area. The winter-kill rate of the vines in these areas is high, however. As hardier cultivars are introduced, the industry will grow even faster. Home gardeners, in the meantime, are encouraged to grow the European cultivars of their choice for home winemaking. Taking a chance on the winter-kill seems absurd, however, when methods of protection are available for the few vines grown in the home vineyard that may not be economically feasible with a commercial operation.

---

[1] *Gibberellic acid is available in 20 ounce quantitites from Mellinger's, Inc., 2310 W. South Range Rd., North Lima, Ohio 44452-9731. Catalog free.*

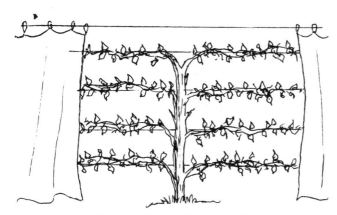

Grape vines trained on wires with extra wire above for drawing curtain over.

Wine Grape Cultivars of Proven Hardiness[1]

Barbera	Pinot Noir
Limburger	Rkatsitelli
Merlot	Sauvignon Blanc
Muscadet	Reisling
Muscat Blanc	

Troubles

See Chapter 4, Insects, Chapter 5, Diseases

Insects	Disease
flea beetle	anthracnose
grape berry moth	black rot
grape phylloxera	downy and
grape rootworm	powdery
mealy bug	mildew

■ HUCKLEBERRY

(Solanum nigrum)

An annual bush fruit often seen in catalogs, huckleberries are touted as a tasty substitute for blueberries, to which they are not related. Catalog writers are known for their dementia regarding

Kingdom Planta, and are, therefore, excused. The blackish fruits are insipid out of hand, but if enough lemon juice and sugar are added to the puree of berries along with a liberal pinch of nutmeg, a passable pie is created. Grow them from seeds planted indoors in January or February, or as purchased plants in May. The berries ripen in mid-August.

Troubles

aphids

■ JOSTABERRY

(say yohstaberry)
(Ribes nigrum x R.hirtellum)

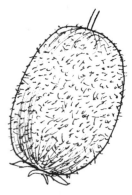

This cross between a black currant and gooseberry is a novelty that appeals to those with the space to accomodate its 5 foot height and width. It is self-pollinating and thornless; producing a generous harvest of plump, blue-black, berries of tangy flavor. Not great to eat out- of-hand, but good in pies and jam. Zones 3-5.

Troubles

see Currant

■ KIWI

(Actinidia arguta, and A. kolomikta)

The interest in growing this grape-size, smooth green fruit with the sweet/tart green

[1] *From test at the Colorado State University Orchard Mesa Research Center, Grand Junction, Colorado, completed and published in Progress Report 1983.*

flesh is easy to understand. The vines have beautiful pink, green, and white foliage. The thumb-nail sized fruits have the same flavor as the brown fuzzy cultivars (*Actinidia deliciosa*) from warmer climes and found in supermarkets. Purported to withstand -20°F, the hardy cultivars do not achieve full hardiness until they are 2 years old; therefore, laying down the vines and bundling them into straw-packed packets is necessary. Both male and female vines can climb the same trellis, adding a vertical element to the vegetable garden or patio container. Both cultivars can withstand some shade, with *A. kolomikta* preferring more. Prune as little as possible to keep the plants in bounds until their sixth year; then annual whacking back of too rampant growth is all that is necessary.

'Ananasnaja' - From Russia; stores well.

'Geneva' - Developed by New York State Experiment Station.

'Issai' - A plant that does not need another plant to bear, though production will be higher if a second cultivar is planted.

'Meador' - Developed by Prof. Elwyn Meador. Early ripening.

Troubles

Insects

beetles

Cats are attracted to them and chew on trunks; protect with hardware cloth cylinder.

■ STRAW-BERRIES

(*Frageria Ananassa*)

The taste of homegrown strawberries leaves no doubt that home-grown are best.

The commercial berry must be bred for shelf-life and to withstand shipping. The cultivars for backyard growing are sweeter, juicier, and quicker to spoil. Success, if it is to be continued year after year, requires some plain and fancy procedures that may put off a gardener with little time or space.

Insects and disease are the main deterrents. Chemicals to deal with them are harsh or require a license to purchase. They also may be obsolete before this volume is published. The alternative is to move the bed or change the soil every 3 years. With this in mind, the following method of growing strawberries is set forth for its ease of culture with the least amount of back-breaking labor. And besides, it's pretty.

Select a site in full sun near a hose bib. The three-tier raised bed of 1x8 redwood boards makes a very attractive centerpiece for the vegetable garden. If you install old carpeting as a pathway around the pyramid, kneeling to pick the berries is far easier than stooping. Slugs, the nemesis of all strawberry beds, seldom find their way into the pyramid because the board sides are too dry for their mode of travel. The berries are raised to meet the sun, thus making them easy to see as well. Winter protection of the tiered bed is possible with the new styrofoam insulated, velcro-fastened blankets, or you can fashion your own with plastic sheets and a goodly volume of straw. Don't forget to add a few mothballs or a warfarin container to discourage mice. Protection from birds is also simple for the pyramid bed. Use nylon bird netting draped over the bed, and held above the berries with bamboo stakes, available at garden supply and oriental import stores. Hold it in place around the edges with clip-type clothespins clipped onto the boards.

Mix the soil on the site by volume with 1/3 sphagnum peatmoss or homemade compost. As you construct the pictured three-tier bed, fill each layer with the mixed soil, tamping down slightly. Allow the soil to settle naturally, however, for best results. Install the drip irrigation system, ideally with a computerized clock timer to eliminate possibility of your forgetfulness.

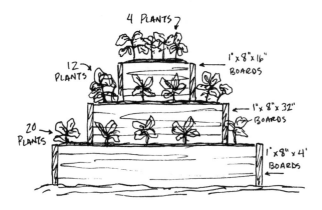

The Three-Tiered Strawberry Bed

The next step is to install a fabric weed barrier over the drip system. Tuck it into the sides of the structure or light will trigger weed growth.

Purchase strawberry plants in spring. They are offered for sale usually in bundles of 25, bare-root, bound up with rubber bands. Their appearance resembles nothing but flimsy, lifeless twigs, but once trimmed up and planted, they spring to life without delay. Cut x's in the weed barrier 1 foot apart. Trim the roots of the plants with scissors to expose fresh root initiation cells. With your trowel, make a small depression in the soil with your trowel and build a hill inside the depression. Hold the plant with one hand while fanning out roots over the hill with the other. The crown node is at the juncture of the leaf stems. See the illustra-

tion to position it before backfilling. Replace the points of the weed barrier around the plant. Water plants in with a starter solution made with 2 tablespoons of superphosphate 0-45-0 to 1 gallon of water before installing a bark chip or pole peeling mulch on top of the weed barrier. During the growing season, your strawberry tier will need 1 inch of water per week. The pictured 3 tier bed accomodates 36 plants, which will yield enough berries for a family of 3.

The Growing Season of the Everbearing Strawberry

As the plants grow the first season, they will form flower buds as well as runners. Pinch off all blooms and runners until about July 4; then allow 1 runner to form at the side of each plant. Pin it down to the soil surface so that it will root about 6 inches away from the mother plant. At this time fertilize with 10-10-10 or a complete fertilizer of your choice. The mother plants will bloom and bear, but not heavily, in the fall of the first year. Fertilize in early spring the following year as leaves are greening with 10-10-10 and again on August 1. In June the mother plants will bear heavily, and again in fall, after which they are destroyed. Meantime, the runners have become mothers, and are treated in the same way as last year's mothers. If your plants show no signs of disease by the third year. remove them and set aside while you change the soil in the tiers. In this manner you will never have the shock of losing an entire bed. The discarded soil can be used in composting or can be solarized. After spreading it in a thin layer, cover with a clear plastic, securing at the edges. Two months of sunlight will kill pathogens.

STRAWBERRY CULTIVARS

Everbearers

'Fort Laramie' - A cold-hardy everbearer developed by USDA in Cheyenne, Wyoming. Fruits are very sweet, but firm in areas of cool nights; softer where nights are warm. Plants are very vigorous. Keep foliage dry as it is susceptible to mildew.

'Ogallala' - A winter-hardy everbearer developed by USDA in Cheyenne, Wyoming. Berries are soft, medium in size, dark red, sweet, good flavored. Early ripening.

'Quinault' - An everbearer with sweet, firm fruits. Habit is sprawling. Ideal for the patio hanging basket. Very productive.

June-bearers

One-crop strawberries are grown mainly by commercial growers because they produce fruit over a period of time in June from buds formed the previous August. Cultivars that do well in the Mountain West are 'Dunlap', 'Fairfax', 'Catskill', 'Kent', 'Guardian', 'Honeoye', and 'Arrowhead'.

Day-Neutral Strawberries

Strawberries that keep on making flower buds all summer without caring about how many hours of daylight they get appeared on the scene in the early 1970's when a wild strawberry plant from the Wasatch range in Utah was crossed with cultivated berries. Maryland breeders have used one of the progeny to produce the two leading cultivars, 'Tristar' and 'Tribute.' The production of day-neutrals is, understandably, limited to the care they receive, for they require constant light fertilization to keep up the pace. Day-neutrals produce very few runners, and those that do appear should be pinched out. The overall size of each plant is taller and broader than other cultivars. After planting, once again remove all flower buds to force the plant into making an extensive root system. Beginning in July, allow the blooms to form, and from then on you will receive a bounty of berries. Drought and heat are their nemeses. A fabric weed barrier and adequate water needs will overcome both. The top of the plant can withstand tremendous heat if the roots are cool and well-watered. Day neutral strawberries last about 3 years, after which they should be replaced.

During the peak of the fruiting season pick strawberries every other day. Harvest only those berries that are fully colored. No need for you to pick the white-shouldered berries like those in the supermarket. Pick the berries with the caps and stems attached. To do this, snap or cut the stem with your fingernails. Keep harvested fruit out of the sun and refrigerate as soon as possible. Avoid picking berries when the plants are wet. Berries damaged by birds or slugs, or rotten, overripe berries must be picked as well. Leaving them invites disease.

Troubles

See Chapter 4 Insects, Chapter 5, Diseases

Insects	Diseases
aphid	black root rot
crown borer	botrytis or
earwig	leaf spots
leafhopper	red stele
millipede	viruses
slug	
spider mite	
spittlebug	
strawberry leaf roller	
strawberry root weevil	
tarnished plant bug	
white grub	
wireworm	

A Thought On Growing Fruit

You may never become an orchardist, a berry farmer, or a triple-threat competition to the growers of exotic fruits in the Middle East, but what you can grow to perfection is fruit with a higher quality of taste than is grown in any other area in the world. The Mountain West grows it best!

Sources

Bear Creek Farms
 P.O. Box 411
Northport WA 99157
Catalog free

Mellinger's
 2310 W. South Range Rd.
North Lima OH 44452-9731
Catalog free

New York State Fruit Testing Cooperative Association
 P.O. Box 462
 Geneva NY 14456
Membership $5.

Southmeadow Fruit Gardens
Lakeside, MI 49116
Catalog $8

Stark Brothers
Lousiana MO 63353
Catalog free

Herbs

If the chemical makeup of herbs had not been analyzed and synthesized, herbs would be growing in every climate in North America, and we, as gardeners, would be growing our own herbs. As it stands today, herbs are not an important part of every garden, and few market gardeners bother growing them. However, that does not mean that they are not important in the preparation of foods and remedies. A small section of every super-market produce department is devoted to packaged fresh herbs, and the dried herbs are displayed with the spices. Specialty shops and the manufacturers of the so-called "natural" products are big consumers of fresh and dried herbs. Despite these sources, culinary herbs are not as important as they once were in this country, while herbal medicine seems on the brink of a resurgence. The *uses* of herbs will be listed but not addressed here, since it is neither a herbal nor a cookbook. Growing the basic culinary herbs plus lavender (and catnip if you are a cat fancier) is the topic of concern here. You are directed to the end of the chapter for sources of information on the medicinal uses of herbs.

If you devote just one row in your vegetable garden to growing herbs, you will soon be looking for places where you can tuck in more herbs, such as in the perennial border, back behind the firewood storage, or in a patio or windowsill pot.

If you are inclined to gathering herbs in the wild with the mistaken belief that wild herbs will be more potent, be advised that they are few and far between in the Mountain West. The health and vigor of a plant and, therefore, its potency, depend on soil quality and environmental conditions. You as a gardener can meet the needs of herbs as to soil type, moisture or lack of it, sun or shade and protection from all the elements that endanger plants. Your cultivated herbs will overtake and display as much potency as the wild offerings. Mountain West soils need all the cover that Nature, meager as she is at times, can muster. Let wild herbs remain where they are.

Locating the Herb Garden

The admonition is always the same — grow herbs in full sun as close to the kitchen door as possible. Nothing is more disagreeable than to stumble through the dark to gather a pinch of an herb that will rescue a so-so dish you are preparing. Therefore, give the herb garden a bright overhead spotlight as well.

Growing Herbs in Concrete Blocks

The design of a concrete block is an invitation to plant something in the 2 spaces separated by a center wall. There isn't a gardener who has ever looked at one of these without feeling an urge to stuff those 2 spaces with something green and growing. There are many herbs that will fit nicely in these. In addition to enjoying the additional heat that is soaked up by the concrete walls, many species will stay within bounds and, best of all, look good while doing it. A walkway on all sides of a vegetable garden is a standard feature. Place the blocks on their sides along the walkway; fill with the soil mixture that the species will enjoy; plant with care, for the sharp concrete quickly severs roots and stems if the plants are handled carelessly. A drip irrigation line can be placed along the top of the line of blocks. Foliage will quickly disguise it. Bees, attracted to the herb blooms, will linger to pollinate vegetable crops. Easily harvested and a

temptation for nibbling, concrete blocks will satisfy the growing conditions for many herb species.

Soil Myths

Tall-tale tellers give beginning gardeners false information that herbs grow best in poor soil. That may be true in black-dirt Iowa or rich loam Indiana, but only Mountain Westerners can know the depths of "crud-ity" into which poor soil can fall. Soil preparation for herbs is the same as for the vegetable garden. After the initial soil preparation as stated in Vol. I., Chapter 4, Soils, each year spade in 1 pound of organic matter per square foot and 1 pound of triple super phosphate per 100 square feet. For the perennial herbs, side dressing[1] in spring will bring more foliage or flowers. If the leaves of the herb are to be used, your nitrogen-rich lawn fertilizer will be best. If flowers and seeds are used, a fertilizer with a high phosphorous number is best. The phosphorous percentage is the second number on the front of the fertilizer bag. Add organic matter in midsummer and spade in fallen leaves after the leaf fall is complete in the autumn. If plants need winter protection, use evergreen boughs, laced down with strong ropes or twine if yours is a windy area.

The Herb Garden Knot

The herb garden knot dates back to the Renaissance, especially Elizabethan England, when it became a status symbol to grow herbs in an elaborately fashioned pattern resembling an intricate knot. The setting for the knot garden was a brick paving that allowed dry footing for the gatherer of herbs as well as a way to keep them in bounds within the pattern, since most herbs are somewhat invasive. Martha Washington's herb garden follows a simple

[1] See Glossary

pattern and one that is easy to copy.

Plants to choose for the knot are those with small habit and foliage. Choose those with dark red, yellow-green, very dark green, gray or silver foliage. Trimming the knot requires some time and effort. At the point where 2 species of plants meet, try to prune one ribbon to flow over the other in the pattern for the best picture. Viewing it from above will give you the perspective needed.

The center of the knot is traditionally a sundial, but this location is also excellent for placement of a single hive of bees, decorative bee skep or gazing ball.

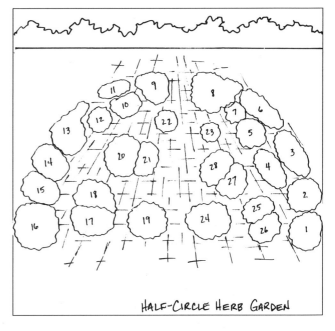

HALF-CIRCLE HERB GARDEN

HERB GARDEN KNOT

The Half-Circle Herb Garden

A half circle added to the patio will give you the opportunity to grow a greater variety of herbs than can be grown in the knot garden, as well as the benefit of beauty, scent, ease of culture and a conversation piece. Keep the taller growing

Plant List

1. Borage
2. Tub of Assorted Mints
3. Dill
4. Lettuce Leaf Basil
5. Garlic
6. Lemon Balm
7. Winter Savory
8. Parsley 'Curlina'
9. Lavender 'Hidcote'
10. Chervil
11. Fennel
12. Summer Savory
13. Cilantro/Coriander
14. Catnip
15. Caraway
16. Lemon Thyme & Burnet
17. Sweet Cicely
18. Basil, Opal
19. Sorrel
20. Tarragon
21. Thyme
22. Garlic Chives
23. Rosemary
24. Oregano, Greek
25. Marjoram, Sweet
26. Parsley 'Darki'
27. Anise

species toward the back. Don't hesitate to take the lopping shears to them when rampant growth threatens; new growth will be more attractive and useful.

■ *Angelica archangelica*
ANGELICA

We begin with an herb that does not belong in the herb garden because it looks better in a shade garden. Though you may find a plant or two for sale at a very posh herb nursery, you will probably resort to growing it from a pinch of fresh seed begged from a neighbor or swiped from a botanic garden. The plant is as splendid as its name, with wheels of compound foliage and umbels of yellow-green flowers. Give it a prominent place where its attractive basal foliage and 4 foot flower stems can be viewed from bottom to top. It prefers a partly shaded site, rich soil, and a constant source of moisture. It may not live after flowering, but allowing it to scatter seed will assure you of a constant supply of seedlings to transplant. Don't confuse this plant with our native species, *Angelica ampla*.

A. archangelica is used to flavor brandy, chartreuse, vermouth, and tea. Leaves stewed with fruits will flavor jams and jellies nicely. Since it is extremely hardy and grows wild above the Arctic Circle, the Finns, Laplanders, and Norwegians use it as an early spring vegetable, steamed and lightly buttered.

■ *Pimpinella anisum*
ANISE

Only 2 feet high, the dainty anise is an annual grown for its seed. It needs a long growing season (120 days). Most gardeners will start it indoors in March and set out the plants only 4 inches apart in early June when the soil is thor-

oughly warm. When seeds form from the blooms, cut the plants to the ground; thrust them head-first into brown paper bags; close the bags and hang them from the rafters in the attic or any warm, dry place where the seeds will fall into the sack for easy collection.

Anise is used in tea and in baking. The flavor of licorice is in the seeds, which are often used to improve other flavors.

■ *Ocimum basilicum*
BASIL, SWEET

A tender annual plant, basil is the harbinger of frost, for none is more susceptible to Old Jack. It is easily started indoors from seed where its requirement for a warm germination temperature of at least 60°F. can be met. Transplant when night temperatures are above 60°F. If the plants become chilled early in the season, they will never amount to much. The usual height is 18 inches. Plants can be tucked here and there in the vegetable or herb garden, but give it a row of its own to see it flourish at its best. Harvest leaves before blooms form for the best flavor. Prevent flowering by snipping off the buds until such time as you want seed to form.

Cultivars

'Cinnamon' - Short, stocky plants with purplish leaves and deep rose blooms. Strong cinnamon scent. Used in chutney.

'Fine Green' - Ornamental dwarf plant for planters and patio pots. Keep pinched for compact growth.

'Green Ruffles' - A green version of 'Purple Ruffles'(which see). Both cultivars slow to start. Plant indoors early in March.

'Lemon' - Long, thin leaves with lemon scent. Good as a poultry and fish seasoning. Resents transplanting. Plant seeds after weather is reliably warm.

'Lettuce Leaf' - Large serrated leaves with familiar basil scent and flavor. Floppy plants may need staking.

'Licorice' - Anise flavor is added to tomato dishes for those who like the licorice flavor. Easy.

'Mammoth' - Reputed to be the best of the lettuce-leaf basils. Large enough to use for wrapping pieces of chicken or fish before grilling. Does not get bitter after long cooking.

'Opal' - Purple leaves. Better than 'Purple Ruffles' for making vinegar. Hard to find. Available at Cook's Garden, P.O. Box 535, Londonderry VT 05148. Catalog free.

'Purple Ruffles' - Deeply cut ruffled purple leaf is highly ornamental. Attractive planted with lavender flowers in the perennial border.

'Spicy Globe' - A small perfect green globe 6 inches high. Very light basil taste. More ornamental than useful.

'Sweet Genovese' - The best pesto basil. Shiny long leaf. Widely grown under glass in Italy.

■ *Borago officinalis*
BORAGE
    Although the most attractive of all herbs, borage has the fewest uses in the kitchen. The 36 inch perennial plant with a width of 2 feet will be covered with hundreds of aquamarine blue flowers in midsummer. Even the bristly leaves are endearing. In the kitchen the leaves and flowers are steeped in tea. However, the herbalist has many uses for it in herbal medicine. Never let seed fall, for it can become an invasive plant.

■ *Sanguisorba minor*
BURNET, SALAD
    The low rosettes of blue green foliage are pretty enough for the rock garden or flower border edging. The flowers are pink globes, held high about the foliage. In Germany burnet is known as *pimpinella* where finely minced leaves are mixed with quark, a dairy product similar to yogurt, and served over boiled potatoes and hard-boiled eggs. The flavor imparted is somewhat like cucumber.

■ *Carum carvi*
CARAWAY
    This biennial of the carrot family is easily grown from seed. Growing to 24 inches high, it needs full sun and moderate watering. Since it is grown for its seed, you must harvest the umbels just as the first seeds form, placing them in brown paper bags as described above for Anise. The seed will finish ripening inside the bag.

■ *Nepeta cataria*
CATNIP
    A hardy perennial, catnip is easy to grow, but difficult to get started because your cat and the

neighbors' cats will eat or trample the seedlings. The gray aromatic leaves and pale lavender flowers make an attractive addition to the dry sandy soil of the outdoor cat box. Your cat does not require catnip for health, but for blissful temperament and for staying young, your cat will thank you for growing it.

■ *Anthriscus cerefolium*
CHERVIL

A delicate-flavored annual, chervil thrives in cool weather and requires some shade and good drainage. The basal leaves are only 6 inches high, but the flower stalks reach 18 inches. Sow seeds where it is to grow, for transplanted plants bolt[1] quickly. Let a few seeds fall from the seed heads at harvest time for a continuous supply of plants. Chervil is used in gourmet sauces.

■ *Allium schoenoprasum*
CHIVES

Chives are perennial, growing from 8 to 12 inches high, preferring a rich, well-composted soil, and tolerating some shade in summer. The leaves are chopped and used in green and potato salads, and in omelets and other egg dishes. The mild onion flavor is welcome in many other dishes. The purple flowers are attractive in bouquets in well-veltilated rooms where the onion scent is wafted away.

■ *Coriandrum sativum*
CILANTRO/ CORIANDER

A staple in Mexican and chinese recipes (where is is also called Chinese Parsley), cilantro/ coriander is an annual grown for both its seed and its strong-smelling foliage. Seed is slow to germinate and is planted direct because seedlings resent transplanting. The plants will reach 36 inches high and bloom in late summer. Harvest the seeds as above for Anise. Coriander seeds are used in baking and to flavor gin and liqueurs.

■ *Anethum graveolens*
DILL

The seeds of dill gave dill pickles their name, but nowadays the leaves as well are used in flavoring fish, poultry, salad dressings, butter and cream cheese,and vegetable sauces, and in dumplings and biscuits. It thrives in light sandy soil; is quick to germinate, but does not transplant well. The plants will grow 36 inches high and are not able to withstand wind. Harvest the leaves as needed; harvest seed heads, preserving as above for Anise.

Cultivars

'Bouquet' - Compact, dwarf habit.

'Dukat' - Also known as Tetra Dill, this cultivar produces abundant foliage and will regrow new leaves to replace those

[1] *See Glossary*

harvested. Plant seeds in hills with 4 or 5 seeds per hill to give stability.

'Dwarf Fernleaf' - A ferny little plant 8 inches high that is useful as a bedding plant or for its crop of abundant foliage.

■ *Foeniculum vulgare dulce* FENNEL, COMMON SWEET

In the Mountain West, fennel will need winter protection of evergreen boughs. This perennial will grow 5 feet high with thread-fine leaves and yellow umbel flowers. The minced leaves are used in salads, in butter sauces for vegetables, and in a stuffing for poached fish. The seeds are often added to other herbs and steeped in tea. Do not confuse fennel with Florence Fennel (*finocchio*), which is an Italian vegetable, as tricky as celery to grow.

Cultivar
'Smokey' - A red-leaved cultivar much sought after for its ornamental qualities. Flavorful seeds are added to fish chowder or salad.

■ *Allium sativum* GARLIC

Garlic is such a staple in the American diet that it is hard to think of as an herb. The bulbs are baked whole; the cloves (segments of the bulb) are minced or bruised for adding to every kind of dish. Garlic is best planted in the fall or in very early spring in the high country in well-drained soil that will not puddle. Separate cloves from the bulb and plant, pointed tip upward, 3 inches deep and 4 inches apart. Keep the plants weeded well during the following season, and cultivated on the dry side. The bulbs will be ready for digging when the foliage yellows. Store garlic bulbs at 60°F. in mesh bags, a ventilated garlic pot, or braided and hung in an airy place.

Cultivars
'Red German' - Especially suited to cold climates, the bulbs are large with only 8 to 10 cloves each.

'Sicilian' - A soft neck makes this cultivar non-bolting. It produces more cloves per bulb. White skinned with a papery tail at the top of the tunic

'Spanish Roja' - The tunic has a slight purplish tinge; clove color varies with the soil from teak-brown to very dark brown. 7 to 13 cloves per bulb. often produces topset bulbils. Good for eating fresh.

■ *Allium tuberosum* GARLIC CHIVES

Like chives, garlic chives is a hardy perennial, but with white flowers reaching 30 inches in height. The green leaves are not tubular and hollow like chives, but short and triangular. The leaves are used raw in the same dishes in which ordinary chives are used, but the garlic flavor is also present. The flowers are welcome additions to summer bouquets.

■ *Lavandula officinalis*
LAVENDER

The premier scent for milady in days gone by and ever popular today in bouquets, potpourri, scenting the linen and clothes closet, lavender deserves a more prominent place in the landscape than the herb garden. The lavender-blue blooms and ever-gray foliage are a nostalgic sight at the foot of a 'Simplicity' rose hedge. A plant or two combined with the deep maroon foliage and white spires of Penstemon 'Huskar Red' is another attractive thought. This is one herb that will be more aromatic if grown in gravelly soil on the dry side. The dimensions of the plants will vary with severity of the climate. Protect in winter in the high country. Cut blooms for drying as first blooms on stems open.

Cultivars

'Hidcote' - Named for an English garden in the Cotswolds of the United Kingdom, this cultivar has deep violet blooms.

'Loddon Pink' - A somewhat satisfactory pink bloomer; good for constrast.

'Munstead' - Named for the home of Gertrude Jekyll, famed landscape designer. Blooms are lavender blue.

■ *Melissa officinalis*
LEMON BALM

A hardy perennial, lemon balm will grow 48 inches high. The lemon-scented foliage is similar to nettle, but without the prickles. It seeds around and seedlings are easy to transplant. Use it minced in salads or steeped in vinegar or tea.

■ *Origanum majorana*
MARJORAM, SWEET

This herb is semi-hardy in the Mountain West. Sweet marjoram plants are set 12 inches apart and grow to 8 inches in height. Protect heavily in winter. The Germans use this herb in sausage and in potato soup. Italians use it in sweet spinach fritters and in a stuffing for chicken. Tea made from majoram, lemon balm, and mint is pleasant.

■ *Mentha spp.*
MINTS

Mint plants are exceedingly invasive if they find the growing conditions they prefer. Moist, rich soil will see them take off with vicious runners throughout your garden. If you care to contain them, a big box or half-barrel with drainage holes, parked beside the hose bib on deck or patio shows off their beautiful foliage and blooms, yet makes it handy for you to water them and (most important) snip off the blooms before seed is formed. Use leaves, dried or fresh in tea, or salad, or to flavor desserts.

■ *M. rotundifolia variegata*
APPLE MINT

A mint bed would not be complete without these woolly round leaves flecked and bordered with creamy white. Smelling of apples and spice, it will grow best in a lightly shaded, moist corner of the 'mint box'.

■ *M. x. p. chocolate*
CHOCOLATE MINT

Tastes and smells like chocolate. Not as rampant as other mints, with attractive bronze-green foliage. Height is 12 to 15 inches. Pale lavender flower stalks appear in late summer.

■ *M. requienii*
CORSICAN MINT

A creeper for between paving stones. The scent when stepped on is unmistakable. Honeybees crawl over it from morning till night. It flavors Creme de Menthe.

■ *M. cordifolia*
ENGLISH MINT

An early mint with crinkly, heart-shaped leaves of excellent flavor.

■ *M. pulegium*
ENGLISH PENNY-ROYAL

Another creeper for groundcover duty between paving stones or in a rock wall. The flower stalks rise 4 inches with whorls of lavender blooms. Used as an insect repellent, it can also be used steeped in tea.

■ *Pycnanthemum tenufolium*
MOUNTAIN MINT

Paradoxically though not a true mint at all, the crushed leaves of the mountain mint emit the mintiest of odors. The compact plants are only 4 to 6 inches with delicate, mid-green foliage.

■ *Mentha piperita crispula*
PEPPERMINT

The curly leaves are very dark with purple tones; stems are also purple. It is very strong when fresh, but when dry the flavor is the true peppermint.

■ *M. suaveolens*
PINEAPPLE MINT

The beautiful light green and white foliage is an excellent foil for the darker foliage of Peppermint. The flavor and scent, of course, are that of pineapple.

■ *M. spicata*
SPEARMINT

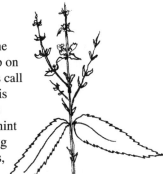

The name tells us that the leaves are spiked and sharp on the edges. The Southerners call this the 'julep' mint, for it is used to flavor their famous pick-me-up. It is also the mint for general uses in flavoring lamb, jelly, boiled potatoes, carrots, or peas.

■ *Origanum vulgare*
OREGANO

Also called Wild Marjoram, this hardy perennial is grown very dry if the leaves are to be strongly scented. In truth, an old cultivar handed down in the Mountain West and known as 'Knock You Dead Greek

Oregano' will have tall floppy growth and bland-tasting leaves in a rainy summer or if given an inordinate amount of moisture. Used in Italian and Greek dishes.

■ *Petroselinum crispum*
PARSLEY

A biennial started from seed, parsley must have the seed coat scarfied before it will germinate. Rubbing the seed between two sheets of coarse sandpaper will do the job quickly. Started in a flat indoors, the seedlings should be thinned quickly, for they make a little tap root that disturbs their neighboring plant when pulled. The curly cultivars make attractive additions to the mixed planter on the patio. Traditionally, parlsey decorates the dinner plate so that the diner may eat it last to sweeten the breath. Dried flakes or fresh leaves are used in soups, salads, and casseroles. Watch a plant closely for the swallow-tail butterfly pausing to lay a few eggs. The fearsome, colorful parsleyworm that hatches from the eggs will spin a chrysalis at the end of summer, and you will have this beautiful butterfly again next year, but very little parsley to cast around seed.

Cultivars

'Abravour' - Long stems with large, finely curled dark green leaves. Good cold weather tolerance.

'Catalogno' A flat-leaved cultivar from Italy that has a stronger flavor than the curled varieties.

'Champion Moss Curled' - The best as a bedding plant to set off the colors of flowers.

'Curlina' - The earliest strain. Globe shaped plants have strong stems and leaves that stay dark green in hot weather.

'Darki' - Leaves are black-green, with very tight curled foliage.

'Garland' - Very uniform triple-curled leaves.

'Krausa' - Also called 'Dutch Moss Curled', this imported cultivar is rated very high.

'Sherwood' - Early, bright green for early summer and early fall.

'Unicurl' - Finely curled, dark green leaves curl in instead of out. Therefore, the foliage shakes clean of dust and dirt. It is also tolerant of rust, which can be a problem disease in fall.

■ *Rosemarinus officinalis*
ROSEMARY

Rosemary is a prostrate houseplant in the Mountain West. We can keep hanging baskets of it growing outdoors in summer, but it must be overwintered in the sunroom or greenhouse. It likes a sandy soil in full sun. The gray needle-like foliage is aromatic of pine and camphor and is used in flavoring meats, poultry, and sauces, and is a common ingredient in perfume and medicines.

Cultivar

'Miss Jessup' - An upright growing cultivar with tight foliage and strongly scented silver foliage. It is a good candidate for the contrasting foliage needed in the knotted herb garden. For protection methods, see Vol. I, Chapter 7, Plant Protection.

■ *Salvia officinalis*
SAGE

The sages like a light sandy soil and plenty of sun. The fragrant leaves vary in taste, but the scent is always the same. The culinary sage does not flower, and is an annual. Use it to flavor meats, stuffing, poultry, and sauces.

■ *Satureia hortensis*
SAVORY, SUMMER

An annual that prefers light, rich soil in full sun. It does not transplant well. Sow direct and thin to 8 inches apart. The leaves are used fresh in soups and salads, but if you dry them, they lose their flavor quickly.

■ *Satureia montana*
SAVORY, WINTER

A very hardy perennial that grows into a neat bush about 8 inches high. It is also a good candidate for the knot herb garden design, for its height and habit can substitute for the boxwood edging of herb knots treasured in Williamsburg, Virginia, the Old South, and Great Britain. Used in soups, stews, and casseroles.

■ *Allium ascalonicum*
SHALLOTS

See Chapter 1, Vegetables.

■ *Myrrhis odorata*
SWEET CICELY

A hardy and beautiful perennial with foliage about 2 feet high, this herb likes a rich, moist soil and partial shade. The flowers are 4 foot umbels of white similar to Queen Anne's Lace. It makes a nice background plant in the border, and its emerging fronds in spring are especially complemented if daffodils are planted among them. Pieces of the root must be transplanted very early in spring, for it starts growth well before the last frost. It is used to cut down the acidity of fruit, to flavor liqueurs, and as a tea.

■ *Rumex scutatus*
SORREL

Sorrel is a perennial that is grown for the large leaves with lemony/ peppery flavor used to wrap fish, and chicken, and to mince in salads. Seeds do not germinate quickly or well. Seed direct and thin plants to 12 inches apart. Sorrel is the first plant to green up in spring. Keep stalks trimmed back to encourage continued leaf growth.

■ *Artemisia dracunculus*
TARRAGON

The true French Tarragon cannot be grown from seed, and seed lists containing it will be Russian Tarragon, which is of inferior quality. French Tarragon, a hardy perennial, grows to a

height of about 2 feet with glossy deep green leaves. The flavor is warm, aromatic and slighly biting. Russian Tarragon has very little of any kind of flavor. French Tarragon needs a sunny position where water will not stand in winter, for it is root rot that will kill it in winter, not a cold temperature. Tarragon is used in vinegar and as a flavoring for many dishes.

■ *Thymus vulgaris*
THYME, ENGLISH GARDEN

A hardy perennial that becomes woody after three or four years, English thyme must be started anew from cuttings from the old plant or from a newly purchased plant or from seed. The taxonomy of Thymus is unclear. According to herb experts, there are two cultivars of culinary Thyme, English (also called Winter) and French. English Thyme grows about 10 inches high. It is difficult to germinate seed. French Thyme (botanic name unknown) grows about 18 inches high and germinates easily from seed. Both are used in the kitchen for flavoring. Industrially, it is used in embalming fluid, perfumes, deodorants, and insecticides.

■ *T. x citriodorus*
LEMON THYME

This small creeper can be sheared to stand upright, but it is a natural to spread moderately in the rock garden or dripping daintily over the edge of a patio pot.
Cultivar
'Aureus' has yellow-green leaves that contrast with darker leaved cultivars. Lemon Thyme is used with baked fish, in salad dressings, and in sauces.

Suggested Seed and Plant Sources

The Cook's Garden,
P.O. Box 535
Londonderry VT 05148

The Sandy Mush Herb Nursery
Rt 2, Surrett Cove Rd.
Leicester NC 28748-9622

Stokes
Box 548
Buffalo NY 14240

Park Seed
Cokesbury Rd.
Greenwood SC 29647-0001

Thompson & Morgan
P.O. Box 1308
Jackson NJ 08527-0308

Insects

I n comparing the number of insect species in the Mountain West with the number in other regions, we are winners. Cold winter temperatures, low humidity, brilliant sunlight, and low precipitation in summer have their advantages. The number and diversity of insects may seem incredible to you, the gardener, if destruction is the name of their game on a particular day as you survey your domain, but, by and large, we can't lay claim to infamy as the bug capital.

In the *Kingdom Animalia,* the joint-footed animals known as *arthropods* are, unquestionably, the dominant life form. No other animal comes remotely close in diversity and number of species. Over 80 percent of all animals are *arthropods* (close to 2 million species), and 80 percent of *arthropods* are insects. Some other noteworthy *arthropods* are mites, milli-pedes, and pillbugs. If it appears critical

that we set about at once destroying this overwhelming number of enemies, let us remember that many of this frightening number are going about their life cycle by pollinating flowers, recycling nutrients in the soil, parasitizing or gobbling up the injurious species, and, in general, quietly serving a role in the balance of nature.

Insects are identified by characteristics that are unlike those of the remaining *arthropods.* In identification we look at the 3 body regions — head, thorax, and abdomen — 3 pairs of legs and often a winged stage that distinguishes the nymph (juvenile) from the winged adult. These features also separate them from the *Arachnids* —the spiders with 4 pairs of legs, head and abdomen only, and without a winged stage.

You must become a bug-watcher before you can fully understand the term *metamor-phosis.* Its literal meaning is "change in

■ *. . . we can't lay claim to infamy as the bug capital.*

■ And when your resolve and stomach falter, use gloves.

form." You may have come upon a cluster of insect eggs on the back of a leaf, you may have caught the breathtaking unfolding of a butterfly as it emerged from the chrysalis, when you earlier saw the caterpillar feeding on a leaf; yet it's often difficult for a gardener to understand the progression from egg or live birth to adult.

Complete metamorphosis occurs in the insects that emerge from an egg to enter the immature stage as *larvae.* This is the stage that usually causes the most injury to plants and animals, for the larvae feed heavily, often 4 or 5 times their weight daily, in order to grow to maturity. As they grow, they shed their skins (actually *exoskeletons*) periodically, each time growing a new and larger outer covering. After reaching full development, the time of year and the temperature determine what happens next. Under some conditions the adult will enter a state of suspended animation called *diapause* for 6 or more months when getting ready for winter. In other instances the larvae shed their last larval skin and begin to form the hard or semi-hard shell that will cover them as *pupa.* It is during this stage that seemingly magical changes occur. Insects in the pupal stage do not feed and seem to be unmoving, though close watching will be rewarded with notice of a twitch now and then. A few or many months may pass when, according to species, the adult stage emerges as a moth, butterfly, beetle, ant, or lacewing.

Among the insects that undergo *simple* or *gradual metamorphosis*, are aphids, earwings, grasshoppers, and the "true" bugs. Upon hatching from the egg, these individuals are miniature look-alikes of the adult form, with a few variations, such as spots or stripes, hairiness or smoothness. They molt their skins as they outgrow them. It is often these shed skins that betray their presence

on a surface. Each time they molt, typically 6 or 7 times, they emerge with a new skin and proceed with feeding in the same manner as before. They are often found together in few or enormous populations, and they resemble each other in stages of development. The metamorphosis complete, they are sexually mature, sometimes winged, and ready to found a new generation.

Integrated Pest Management

Integrated Pest Management, often referred to as IPM, is an effective pest management program that uses cultural and mechanical means in a timely fashion FIRST before using, if necessary, selective chemical control that will be least harmful to the environment.

No attempt here will be made to address control of harmful insects through either chemical or biological control. The objective here is to aid you in identifying the insect. The Cooperative Extension Office in your county will give you the most up-to-date research findings about the timely application of a chemical or biological control. Sometimes the extension agent's advice may be "Pick it off with your fingers," which may not be what you want to hear. Big guns are not needed when a slingshot does a better job. Lose your squeamishness. Move forward in becoming a better gardener. And when your resolve and your stomach falter, use gloves.

The Orders of insects follow the recognized features of wings, mouthparts, and the metamorphosis process they undergo as they develop. Thankfully, the Mountain West is not the home of all of the Orders of insects on this planet. **The following Orders are common garden visitors.**

96

■ *Orthoptera*
Grasshoppers, Crickets, Katydids

It's hard to find something to love about a grasshopper; yet they are fascinating to watch up close as they chomp on your favorite plants. The wiseacre look on their face plus their seeming watching of *you* makes you a little more tolerant of their damage. A good child's project is to collect all 5 of the species of grasshoppers that damage cropland in the Mountain West[1] . There are 5 more of minor importance.

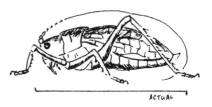

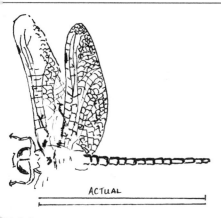

■ *Odonata*
Dragonflies, damselflies

All of us as children chased dragonflies. If you progressed beyond the chasing, you watched these beautiful insects in rattling flight as they dipped low over a lily pool, the females shedding eggs as they flew or gliding down to deposit them at water's edge. The nymphs hatch in the water to live on other insects in the pond, using their extensible clawed lower lip (*labium*) to capture them. The metamorphosis is gradual as they progress to adulthood and full fledged flight. Also, you may have been privileged to see the tandem mating flight of male and female, which must take some practice to accomplish. The damselflies include the beautiful "**blue darner**" darting over your pool as they feed on mosquitos and other harmful insects. All stages of dragonflies and damselflies are beneficial.

Grasshoppers lay their eggs just under the soil surface in fall. They resemble a cluster of grains of wheat stuck together. In spring when the eggs hatch, the minute hoppers are fast walkers, chewing new foliage everywhere with strong jaws and rasping mouthparts. As they progress through gradual metamorphosis, 2 pairs of wings form, and it's off to the races to see which one can devour more of your garden.

---

[1] *Migratory grasshopper, Red-legged grasshopper, Differential grasshopper, two-striped grasshopper, Packard grasshopper. From Cooperative Extension Bulletin 502A, Colorado State University, Fort Collins CO.*

Crickets and Katydids aren't much of a threat to your garden. Learn to distinguish their cheery songs in the evening as you weed.

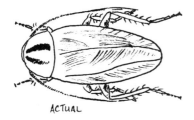

■ Blattnia
Cockroaches
Cockroaches are not a threat to your garden, but they are a real threat to your well-being in your home because they are carriers of fungi, bacteria, and perhaps viruses that are harmful to the human being. Learn to fear the cockroach. Little changed since prehistoric times, the cockroach is a survivor *par excellence.*

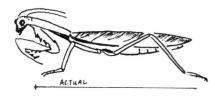

■ Mantodea
Mantids are fierce predators of other insects, though they may not destroy as many harmful insects as a single cell of fungus. Their common stance is that of prayer, thus the name **Praying Mantis**. The hooked forearms clasp and hold their prey as they devour it alive with a powerful mandible. A mantis can dispatch a tomato hornworm in about 20 minutes. If you wish to pick up a mantis to carry it to a prospective prey, grasp it lightly behind the head or it will swing the hooked arms around to attack you.

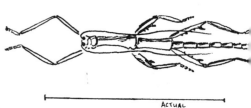

Walkingsticks are the harmful mantid. Their name describes them perfectly: If you see a stick walking, you have seen a walkingstick. Their mandible is strong and they are not particular about the plant parts they attack. Though wingless, it's everything in sight and within walking distance. They are plentiful in the southern range of this volume.

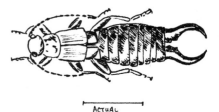

■ Dermaptera
Earwigs illicit strong emotions in those who behold them. The pincer-like posterior is actually a clasping device used in mating, but folk tales persist that the earwig pinches people while they are sleeping, takes up residence in their ears, and other nonsense. In normal numbers the earwig is a beneficial insect, cleaning up debris, and digesting fragments of dead plant and animal matter. It makes a nest for its young, usually next to the warm concrete foundation of your home. It is a nurturer of sorts, being one of only a few insect species to be present during the hatch of its young, to bring food, and to defend the young. In large numbers the earwig becomes a

harmful insect. It attacks flowers, especially zinnias, hiding among the petals in daytime and feeding at night.

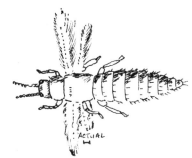

ACTUAL

■ *Thysanoptera*

Thrips are seldom noticed insects due to their small size until their damage becomes apparent. When you see foliage silvered and dry in long streaks, you learn to look for thrips. They are slender and whitish, with a segmented abdomen and sucking mouthparts. Wings, when present, resemble feathers. They most commonly attack gladiolus and onion foliage. Their gradual metamorphosis is complex, with the stage just prior to adulthood often encased in a cocoon.

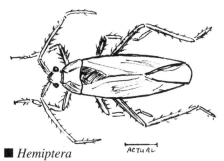

ACTUAL

■ *Hemiptera*

To a gardener, almost any insect is a bug, but to an entomologist "bug" refers to the Order *Hemiptera,* or "true bug." These are among the gardener's most feared order of insects because their sucking mouthparts contain damaging saliva that causes areas of stems and leaves to wilt and die. In addition, the damaged areas of plant tissue are susceptible to diseases. True bugs hold their wings flat across the abdomen, a characteristic distinguishing them from *Homoptera* that hold their wings rooflike over the body. From the smallest **leaffoot bug** to the largest **squash (stink) bug,** their colors and the shield forms must be studied carefully by every gardener. Learn to recognize the **tarnished plant bug, boxelder bug, lace bug, four-lined plant bug, harlequin bug,** and **Lygus bug.** The small species are fast flyers. You have only a fraction of a second to identify the culprit.

A few species of *Hemiptera* are beneficial:

Minute Pirate Bug — lies in wait among flower petals to attack other insects as they gather or feed from flower pollen. It might be classed as semi-beneficial, for it attacks honey bees without mercy.

Water Strider — The sight of a water strider merrily skating on the surface of your pond can brighten anyone's day. They feed on other insects in the water.

Ambush Bugs — They wear a golden and brown camouflage, lying in wait for other insects among flowers of their same colors.

Assassin Bugs — These brownish to black insects occur on foliage, although a few will enter houses. They prey on other insects, and they can also inflict a painful bite if you disturb them.

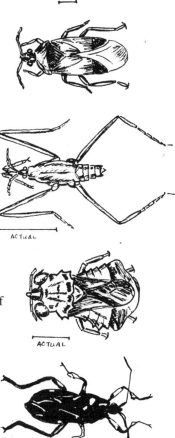

ACTUAL

ACTUAL

ACTUAL

ACTUAL

■ *Homoptera*

Cicadas, leafhoppers, psyllids, whiteflies, aphids, and scales are among the most diverse order of insects.

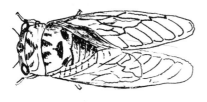

ACTUAL

Though there are many **cicadas** feeding on native plants, we seldom see (or hear) cicadas in our gardens. If you hear a loud noise in late summer like that of a wind-up toy, you have heard the cicada. Midwesterners pay them no mind, but the sound stops a Mountain Westerner in his tracks. The sound, of course, is a mating call. The damage is a chewing of twigs and new growth. If the area below your trees is littered with twigs, bark shreds, and debris, get out the binoculars to look up into the tree for cicadas. They favor Aspen trees and other members of the *Salicaceae* family.

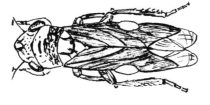

ACTUAL

Leafhoppers are a diverse group, some resembling small grasshoppers, others like frogs. The **buffalo treehopper** has a humped back like a buffalo, while still another resembles a thorn. All are jumpers; all are sucking insects found in every type of vegetation

ACTUAL

Psyllids are one of the most harmful insects, especially to tomatoes and potatoes where they produce the plant disease "psyllid yellows." The psyllid is a gall-maker, causing its host plant to form a nubbin of extraneous tissue over the area of insect entry. An example is the **Hackberry nipple gall**. The insects are active jumping insects with wings held roof-like over the body when they are at rest. Nymphs are oval and flat and look very little like the adults; many producing a large amount of a waxy filament, making them look like blobs of cotton. The presence of psyllid adults is always detected by migrating warblers who feed upon them in spring. When you see a Hackberry tree filled with a variety of warblers, you know the psyllid is present in large numbers.

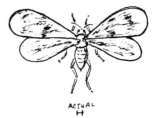

ACTUAL
H

Whiteflies are minute, glistening white, and fast-moving. When infested foliage is disturbed, they fly out in clouds. Difficult to control, our hard winters will sometimes diminish a population, but the chance is strong that you will purchase a whitefly again in spring when you purchase transplants from a greenhouse, where they are a persistent pest.

100

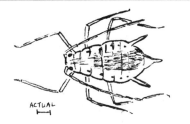

ACTUAL

Aphids are the most complex insect family. They come in many colors, but can also be almost colorless. They can be winged or wingless, born live or hatched from an egg. The adults can also chose the sex of their offspring! Their common identifying characteristic is a pair of cornicles near the posterior end of the abdomen. These cornicles resemble thin thorns. Aphids discharge from the anus a thin liquid called *honeydew* at regular intervals. Ants keep colonies of aphids like we keep cows, and they feed the honeydew to their young.

Scale insects resemble their name when their quiescent stage is clustered in colonies on branches of trees, shrubs, or greenhouse plants. Their sucking activity will eventually kill a plant. Identification of scale insects is so complex that only the females display the identifying characteristics as seen when the specimen is mounted on a microscope slide. Dormant and summer oil are often effective controls, but chemical controls are virtually useless unless you happen to hit the small window of time when the insect is in its crawling/flying stage.

■ *Neuroptera*
Dobsonflies, fishflies, and alderflies aren't big in the gardener's life unless he also happens to be a fisherman. The larvae of the dobsonfly is the hellgrammite which is prized as a lure by fishermen. However, **green lacew-ings** and their larval form, as well as **antlions** are beneficial insects we must all learn to identify. They feed on aphids. Lacewings fly in clumsy clouds. If you bike on summer evenings, you are likely to run into a mass of them, resulting in nose/eyes/hair distress. They lay their eggs at the ends of tiny stalks, usually on foliage. The larvae have long sickle-shaped mandibles; they pupate in small pea-shaped cocoons.

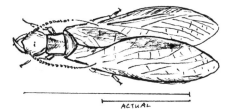

ACTUAL

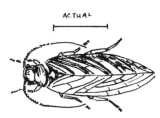

ACTUAL

Antlions resemble damselflies, and have knobbed antennae. Larvae, sometimes called "doodle-bugs," have long, sicklelike jaws and live at the bottom of a conical pit in dry sandy or dusty places. They feed on ants and other insects that stumble into the pit.

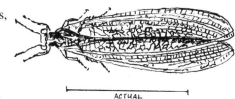

ACTUAL

■ *Coleoptera*
Beetles are easily identified by the horny, leathery front wings (*elytra*) that meet in a straight line down the middle of the back. The front wings cover the membranous wings that are folded underneath. The membranous wings are used in flight. The leathery wings act as protective hovering tools. The mouthparts vary in size and design, with astounding efficiency in chewing ability. With complete metamorphosis, the larvae are variable in form, hardness, and appendages. Some are grub-like, others greatly flattened or segmented. Beetles occur in a hundred or more habitats, including aquatic. The most common in the Mountain West are presented here alphabetically.

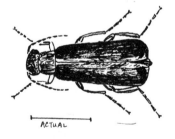

Blister beetles are the dreaded enemy of the horse owner and the gardener. The long, narrow body may vary in color, gray, bronze, or black. The adults often search out and lay their eggs in the soil next to a pod of grasshopper eggs, thus giving a food source to their young when they hatch. That's about the extent of their beneficial activity, however. Larvae can also latch onto bees and be carried back to the hive, where they attack bee eggs. The body fluids of the adults contain *cantharadin*, a substance capable of blistering skin and killing a horse. The adult beetles are fond of tomatoes, potatoes, beets, clover, and alfalfa hay.

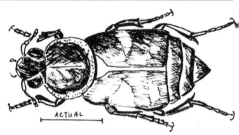

Carrion beetles are beneficial. They are the clean-up crew of highway and byway. Also called Dung Beetles, you will find them under dung piles in a pasture. Like all scavengers, they are smooth-bodied with no crevices in which harmful bacteria might lodge.

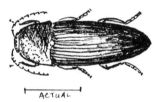

Click beetles have been known to collect a cheering section. If the beetle is on its back, the elongate-narrow body gives it the ability to bend the head and prothorax backward; then it straightens the body with an audible click and the beetle is propelled into the air. If it doesn't land right side up, it continues the performance until it does. Perhaps the cheers help. The adult beetles feed on flowers and foliage. The larvae are the infamous **wireworms** that chew on roots and newly planted seeds.

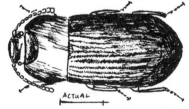

Darkling beetles are similar to ground beetles, though not as shiny. Their beneficial activity is the same, that of eating decaying vegetation. The most common species emits a foul-smelling black fluid when disturbed. They are abundant throughout the Mountain West.

Elm-bark beetle is responsible for the spread of Dutch Elm Disease, which is a fungus they carry on their bodies as they move from an infected tree to one that is not infected.

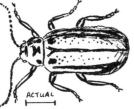

ACTUAL

Elm-leaf beetle feeds exclusively on the foliage of elm species. With 2 generations per year, they are difficult to control.

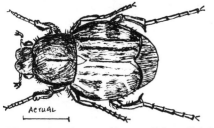

ACTUAL

Flower beetles are almost all beneficial. Usually black, with red, blue, green, orange, or yellow markings, they feed on pollen or nectar, but are also predators of aphids, scales, and other soft-bodied harmful insects. Flower beetles tumble when disturbed.

Ground beetles are beneficial. They are shiny black, voracious hunters of other insects. They are most often

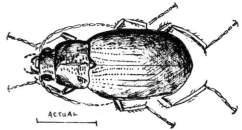

ACTUAL

nocturnal and will fly clumsily toward light. They more often scurry or walk rapidly rather than fly. They feed on some of our worst pests — gypsy moth larvae, cutworms, and cankerworms, and will climb trees and shrubs in search of prey.

Ladybird beetles need no introduction to any gardener. The familiar orange-red, shiny elytra with a variety of black spots is

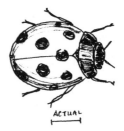

ACTUAL

recognized the world over as a beneficial insect. Sit down quietly with your eyes at the same level as a Ladybird some summer afternoon. Sometimes you will see them eating aphids like popcorn, and yet another time you will see them walk right over the aphid without seeming to notice. Their spots vary according to species —2, 3 or 9. A harmful relative, the **Mexican Bean Beetle**, is a lighter orange, with 15 or 16 spots. It lays golden clusters of eggs on the underside of

ACTUAL

bean foliage. These hatch into a harmful orange and black larvae that pupate to the adult stage.

COLORADO
POTATO
BEETLE

FLEA
BEETLE

CUCUMBER
BEETLE

Leaf beetles include the **Colorado Potato Beetle, 2 species of asparagus beetles, cucumber beetle, and flea beetle.**

Long-horned beetles have long antennae, as their name implies. **Raspberry cane borer** is a long horned beetle with larva that is a pest of the raspberry patch.

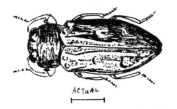

ACTUAL

Metallic Wood-Boring Beetles are the dreaded enemy of orchardists, berry growers, and home-owners. The adults are shiny blue-black or bronzy like metal. The adults feed on foliage and bark or flowers. The **bronze birch borer** is in this family. You will find colonies of them basking in the sun on trunks and branches of trees that are sometimes already unhealthy or dying They are rapid runners, taking off in flight at the sight of you. After basking in the sun and feeding for a few weeks, they mate and lay eggs in bark crevices, and then die. The hatching larvae are the *flat-headed borers* with armour-plated heads and jaws of incredible strength, able to chew into hard and soft wood trees a day or two after hatching. Their galleries are familiar sights to the lumberman.

ACTUAL

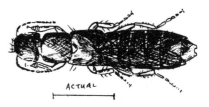

ACTUAL

Rove beetles are easily recognized because the front wings don't cover the abdomen. The segmented abdomen is readily visible from a distance. Though some will eat carrion, they are generally considered a harmful insect, eating flowers and other vegetation. They are fast runners, bending the tip of the abdomen upward, which suggests to the collector that they sting. They bite; they do not sting.

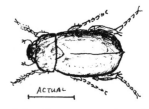

ACTUAL

Scarab beetles are sometimes beneficial as scavengers, but most are plant feeders. They include the **rose chafer, June beetle,** and **Japanese beetle.** Larvae are plump, white, and lie C-shaped under the soil surface.

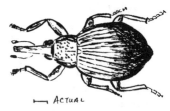

ACTUAL

Snout beetles also called **curculios** have an elongated head with drilling mouthparts that drill into the calyx of rose buds, the fruits of plums and peaches, nuts, seeds, and stems.

Twig borers are beetles that attack the new growth twigs of peaches, apricots, nectarines, and plums.

■ *LEPIDOPTERA*

Butterflies and Moths belong in the Order of insects that is most beautiful or least frightful of all the Orders. The butterflies are usually thought of as daylight flyers, while moths often fly at night so that no one sees their beauty.

The 4 membranous wings are largely or entirely covered with scales carrying the colors and markings of each species. A sucking proboscis forms a long coiled tube that the insect carries coiled up under what might be a chin, if it had one. Feeding for the adults consists of sipping nectar of flowers. A few have no mouthparts and do not feed. Some, such as the **Monarch butterfly** migrate for long distances. The metamorphosis is complete (egg to larvae to chrysalis to adult); the antennae is knobbed in butterflies and feathered in moths. The larvae are typically called **caterpillars.** The majority have 3 pairs of thoracic legs and 5 pairs of abdominal prolegs. Many caterpillars are brightly colored with hairs or spines; often very ferocious looking, but harmless to handle. A few exude unpleasant odors or have irritating, rash-producing hairs that alarm mothers of children who play with them unwittingly. The larval forms of both butterflies and moths are harmful, eating many times their weight in foliage, flowers, vegetables, and fruits. Only you can decide

whether the harm outweighs the beauty of the adults.

Butterfly larvae pupate in a silken tube called a chrysalid (*chrysalis* is plural); some are brightly colored or have a shape remindful of the butterfly shape. Moths pupate in smooth cocoons, usually dark brown or black, and often attached with a strong strand to a twig.

Swallowtail butterflies are easily recognized by the elongation on the hind wing. Their background color is usually black,

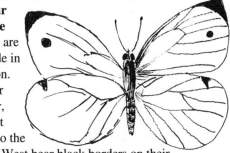

with turquoise, gold, red, blue, or orange marks. The larvae are varied, some green with black, orange, and gold stripes. Others are smooth green with false eye-spots to frighten their predators. If disturbed, foul-smelling horns extend from their heads.

Sulphur and White butterflies are world-wide in distribution. Named for their color, those most common to the Mountain West bear black borders on their wings and have single black spots on both sets of wings. The sulphurs are yellow to orange; the whites are a cloudy white easily recognized as they fly their zig-zag erratic flight over the *Brassica* crops in your vegetable garden.

Milkweed butterflies include the beloved **Monarchs** that travel great distances each season, returning with tattered wings to the area of their origin. Feeding on the bitter sap of milkweeds gives the butterfly body the same flavor. Thus it is thought they elude their predators who quickly learn they are not a tasty meal.

Brush-footed butterflies are mainly the **Fritillaries,** named for the tiny forelegs, hairy and useless for walking. Most are medium in size. Their caterpillars feed at night on violets and other garden flowers.

Buckeye butterflies are brightly colored with a large eyespot on the upper side of both hind and fore wings. These spots trick birds into mistaking them for an enemy owl.

Thistle butterflies are represented mainly by the **Painted Lady** that blows in on a fair wind

regularly from the Southwest. It cheers farmers and gardeners alike, for its larvae relish the foliage of the despised Canada thistle.

Admiral butterflies are quickly recognized by their black and white wings with greenish edging. The Admirals are found only on the eastern edge of the Mountain West region.

Hairstreak butterflies have almost invisible hairlike tails on the hind wings. They are usually blue, coppery, gray or dull brown on the under side. The Colorado Hairstreak is more purple and the underside has a banded pattern, typical of all hairstreaks. It is found around the scrub oaks (*Quercus gambeli*) in Western and Southern Colorado.

Elfin butterflies are small to medium-size, brown and drab. The larvae of the **Western Banded Elfin** feeds on pine.

The **Blues** are small and usually blue above. Most common in the Mountain West is the **Western Tailed Blue** which is always a welcome sight above timberline.

Sphinx moths are common in the Mountain West. Also called **Hummingbird moths** and **Hawk moths**, they resemble the birds as they hover over flowers on early summer evenings. The larvae of these moths have a large hook at the end. The most infamous is the **tomato horned worm.**

Giant Silk moths are represented in the Mountain West by the **Cecropia moth.** Its knobby larvae sports colored horns that quickly spurt forth when it is disturbed. The cocoon is often noticed attached lengthwise on a tree twig. It resembles a fuzzy, cigar-shaped piece of cloth.

Isabella

moth is well known for its caterpillar, the **Woolly bear,** which is supposed to foretell the severity of the coming winter by the amount of black wool on each end of the body. There are 2 broods — spring and summer. The adult moth has spotted white forewings and light orange hind wings.

Fall Webworm is the green worm with white tufted hairs well-known for the ugly web nests it scatters

throughout deciduous trees in late summer. The adult moth has white wings spotted with light brown, and almost pure white hind wings. Eggs are laid in masses on the undersides of leaves, with pupa overwintering in cocoons.

NOCTUID moths are serious pests in the Mountain West as well and the North American continent. They include the well-known **Armyworm, Cutworm,** and **Corn Earworm.**

Cutworm moths are dusky, scaly, light to dark brown, about 1-inch long. Some are present in fall, others only in

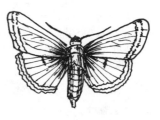

spring. Most are migratory. The larvae of all species feed at night and lie C-shaped just beneath the soil surface in daytime. Some, like the **Pale Western Cutworm,** are climbers.

Loopers are, as their name implies, larvae that move by means of moving their 3 pairs of front

legs forward; then humping their back as the back legs catch up. The adult moths are undistinguished, under 2 inches in length, and almost always night flyers.

Corn Earworm adult moths are pale yellow with only a few spots. The larvae are both

the **tomato fruitworm** and the **corn earworm.**

Leaf Tier moths are brown with wavy dark lines on the wings. The wingspan measures 3/4 inch. The larval

caterpillars are pale green, turning yellow when grown. They tie leaves together with strands of silk, feeding inside that protection. Aspen, celery, clover, hydrangea, and oak are attacked.

Gypsy moth was accidentally introduced from Europe. It overwinters as

egg masses that resemble a piece of cloth. It is often attached to the underside of a vehicle, the garage door, or a tree trunk. The larvae feed on the foliage of deciduous trees, oak being a favorite. Great time and effort is given each year to prevent this insect from entering the Mountain West because it might change its diet to include evergreen trees. We could control it on the deciduous trees in cities and towns, but it would be very expensive to control in evergreen forests.

Western Tussock moth is a pest of evergreen trees, especially Blue or Green Spruce (*Picea pungens),* the native tree indigenous to the north slopes and stream banks of the Mountain West. Unfortunately, this tree is also a favorite of city and suburban home landscapes, where it is often in poor vigor from lack of water and care, thus becoming a prime target for the insect. It begins its foray into the tree at the top; therefore a good pair of binoculars and frequent inspection is the best prevention of damage.

LASIOCAMPIDS are moths of medium size with stout hairy bodies. They are attracted to light at night.

Eastern Tent caterpillars are the most notable of the Lasiocampids. Despite their name, their territory covers the entire

Mountain West. The bristly blue bodies of the larvae are easily distinguished from the **fall webworm.**

Carpenter moth larvae, the **carpenter worm,** are wood borers in shade trees and evergreens. Among them are **lilac/ash borer, locust borer,** and borers of other deciduous trees.

CLEARWING MOTHS resemble wasps, but are moths with see-through wings. They fly in daytime and feed at flowers. The larvae are borers in bark, trunks and roots of trees.

Peach Tree Borer adult clearwing moths lay eggs at the soil line of plants of the genus *Prunus.* The hatching larvae drill into the trunks to travel upward. The tree responds with great boils of resin in its attempt to wash out the offending insect. Trees affected are: peach, apricot, nectarine, plum, cherry, and almond.

Of the **CASEBEARER MOTHS,** the larvae of **Leafminers** are universal throughout the Mountain West and the rest of the United States. The small, smooth, green worms that feed in between the upper and lower surfaces of leaves, most notably those of the *Salicaceae* family. The adult moth is very small and dark gray. The damage is observed as a light-colored, circuitous path through a leaf.

The **OLETHREUTID MOTHS** are noted economic pests. The **Oriental Fruit** moth is a pest only of the East and Southwest as yet, with the remainder of the Mountain West working hard to keep it at bay. The small brown moth lays eggs that hatch into larvae that drill directly into the twigs of peaches in early spring. A later generation enters the fruit.

The **Codling** . **Moth** is present where apples grow. After wintering as larvae in cocoons, moths emerge to lay eggs in early spring at about the

time the petals are falling from blooms. The hatching larvae infest pears, apples, crabapples, and walnuts. Several generations are possible throughout the summer.

The **European Pine Shoot Moth** is a serious pest of Scots, Austrian, and Mugho Pines. The adult lays eggs in late spring near the emerging candles of new growth. The

larva feeds on needles, then drills into the candle to destroy it.

The **Pitch Mass Borer** adult moth lays eggs on the trunks and twigs of pines. The hatching larva tunnels into the bark, causing the

tree to put forth masses of pitch in its attempt to "pitch" it out. The partly grown larva overwinters in twigs and needles and feeds in spring and early summer.

Among the **PRODOXIDAE MOTHS**, only the **Yucca** moth will be of interest to a gardener. The female moth carries pollen to the stigma of yucca blooms, fertilizing the eggs which form seeds. The larvae feed in the seeds, but damage is slight. The larvae then pupate in spring.

■ *DIPTERA*
Flies, Mosquitos, Midges, Gnats

Though it is a household pest, a serious carrier of human and animal disease, and a tormenter of horses, cattle and other animals, the Order *DIPTERA* does not contain many species that attck our gardens. Their chief identifying characteristic is of having only 1 pair of wings. The mouth-parts are piercing, sucking, or lapping.

Mosquitos are not harmful to plants, but are placed here because they are dangerous to gardeners. Though the Mountain West does not harbor the malaria mosquito, *Anopheles,* encephalitis is a mosquito-borne disease that can be permanently disabling with its side effects. The male mosquito has a feathery antennae and does not bite. The female has only a few short hairs on the antennae and does bite. The species most often found in this area is *Culex.* Bites from mosquitos are annoying and can become infected. If mosquitos are multiplying in your garden, you can be counted as the culprit in leaving standing water in flower pots, watering cans, and other vessels or tools. Water gardens that do not contain fish are also an excellent breeding place for mosquitos. With these dire consequences in mind, let all gardeners be more diligent in disposing of standing water and in keeping water gardens well stocked with fish.

Fungus gnats are slender, mosquito-like insects that appear suddenly in our homes, having developed from larvae in the soil of our indoor plants. Non-pasteurized potting soil is responsible for the infestation. Fungus gnats are slow fliers, and, in general, a nuisance, but they do not eat foliage. Their food is decaying organic matter in the soil.

Window flies, as their names implies, are often found in window sills or basement window wells. They are smaller than a House fly, usually gray or black. Larvae usually occur in decaying wood or on fungi. They are predaceous and feed on a variety of insects.

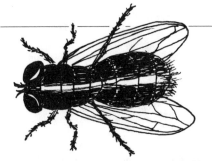

Cluster flies are the large, buzzy flies with a metallic sheen that suddenly appear when you open the windows for the first time in spring. They are short-lived and a nuisance only for a few days.

Syrphid flies are also called **Hover flies** because of their habit of hovering in mid-air for a few minutes. Adults vary in size, color, and appearance; many are brightly colored with yellow, brown, and black markings. Syrphids do not bite or sting. The larvae are colorless globs that are often seen feeding in the center of a large population of aphids.

Fruit flies are troublesome little black flies that erupt in clouds from a box of overripe fruit. They will also invade the home if fruits or vegetable are left out uncovered.

Leaf miner flies are minute flies that are seldom noticed. They lay eggs on foliage, such as columbine, birch, spinach, and beets; the

eggs then hatch to drill in between the upper and lower leaf surfaces to make circuitous white markings on the leaves.

Tachinid flies resemble a House Fly, but may be larger and more hairy. The larvae are parasites of other insects, and many are of value in keeping noxious species of flies under control.

■ HYMENOPTERA
Sawflies, Ichneumons, Chalcids, Ants, Gall Wasps, Wasps, Bees

Sawflies are small, black, four-winged insects with a segmented abdomen. Their presence is seldom noticed, but their larvae,

a shiny, slug-like blob, is a common skeletonizer of fruit tree leaves such as pear, cherry and plum. Another common name is **pear slug.**

Ichneu-mons are slender,

wasplike insects that are beneficial unless you try to handle one, which will result in a painful sting. Their normal activity is to fly low over areas where harmful larvae, such as **sod webworms** and **armyworms,** are present. Eggs are laid on the harmful larvae, which hatch to feed on and destroy the host.

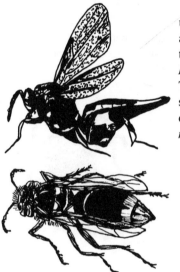

Chalcids are uniformly black and smaller than the *Ichneumon.* Their activity is similar to that of the *Ichneumon.*

Wasps are hard to love, but we, as gardeners, should not be unduly afraid of them. Be watchful that you are not harboring a wasp nest in your trees, under the eaves of your home, or in a tool shed or carport, and you will go a long way in avoiding unpleasant contact with them. The insects themselves are beneficial because they seek out and gather soft-bodied harmful insets to feed to their young.

Gall wasps are seldom noticed as they fly around an oak or willow tree. They sting the foliage, which, in turn, reacts to form an abnormal growth, a gall. It is difficult to determine whether these galls harm the tree.

Velvet ants are not ants, but members of the family *Mutillidae*. They resemble hairy ants with red and black markings. They are important parasites of the larvae of ground-nesting bees and wasps.

Ants are given a bad name by unwitting gardeners. Ants have long been studied for their intelligent behavior. Their activity is beneficial to the soil. Their relentless search for food aids in controlling harmful insects. The species deemed harmful, such as **Carpenter** ants are doing what they do best — demolishing old, rotten wood and rendering it back to the soil. The little annoying ants known as **sweet** and **sour ants** are attracted to our own poor house-keeping habits. It is not thought **Fire ants** will invade the Mountain West, but the adaptability of any insect is unknown in its enormity.

Leaf-cutting bees are the frustration of rosarians with a show bloom ready for cutting. These insects cut a circular piece from a leaf to fold carefully into a cell in which to rear their young. Because of their beneficial pollinating activity, rose show judges are directed to look the other way when foliage with circles cut away accompanys a bloom.

Bumble bees are heard before they are seen. The deep buzzing sound announces their arrival at a flower. Larger than any other bee, they are often feared and destroyed, but their pollinating activity is needed for fruits and flowers. Learn to recognize them.

Honey bees are the gardener's best friend, but there are still those who fear them. Unfortunately, honey bees can sense fear, probably because of perspiration. "Buzz pollination" is a bee activity that can cause fear in those who hear it. A bee works its wings rapidly to shake pollen loose so that it can gather it. The sound is loud and mistaken for anger. Gain confidence by close observation of bees. Learn to work among them by wearing light-weight clothing and cotton gloves to absorb perspiration. You will soon have them crawling over your bare hands in a friendly manner. Teach your children to observe

them closely. They will find no more fascinating friend.

The Other Creepy Crawlers—Diplopods, Gastropods, Isopods, and the Eriophyid Mites

■ *DIPLOPODS*

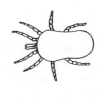

The **milli-pedes** are noticed only when they have been bad. For the most part they go about their business burrowing in the soil and eating bits of organic matter they come upon. As their name implies, they have multiple legs. Their shiny brown, many-segmented bodies shed the moisture where they prefer to live, and they move quickly. The gardener's main complaint about them is their burrowing into ripe strawberries. Eliminate the wet conditions they prefer, and you've won half the battle. Pick ALL of the strawberries that are ripe; don't leave those that are overripe and rotten, and you've won all of the battle. In fall you may get a few millipedes in the house. Under dry conditions they soon succumb.

■ *ERIOPHYID MITES*

These cousins of the ordinary spider mites you are familiar with will never be obvious with their presence. They are 5 times smaller than a spider mite. In other words, they are no see'ems, which is a term usually reserved for the biting gnats of the Colorado Plateau. Dr. Whitney Cranshaw, Coopera-tive Extension Entomologist for Colorado

State University, calls them "little walking carrots." They have only 4 legs, all up front, and they drag the rear end.

The presence of an eriophyid is made known when you see the damage. They are gall-makers, the most interesting gall being the Flower Gall, a fanciful and elaborate affair that somewhat resembles a cluster of flowers. You will see these on Green Ash and Chokecherry. A russeting of pears, a rusty blister on leaves of apple, crabapple, and pear signals their presence. White, dry sections on raspberry fruit are also a symptom, but this can be drought stress as well.

They are controlled by many natural enemies, including predator mites, predator thrips and minute pirate bugs. They overwinter around the buds on fruit trees and Green Ash, therefore, they can be controlled by a spray of dormant oil in early spring.

■ GASTRO-PODS

Slugs are of great concern to the gardener who has them. These pale blobs of slime feed at night, laying a silvered trail of mucous to ease the passing of their bodies, and sometimes consuming an entire planting of young lettuces or a favorite and rare flower you've been waiting to behold. To control them you must give up the nightly watering you favor as a water-saver; give up the mulch of moist compost or wet grass clippings. Instead, lay down a mulch of dry, sharp pole peelings that will pierce their bodies as they travel. Water only once a week, and avoid crowding your plantings.

Eliminate bits of debris that lodge here and there, such as in cracks in the patio. Sunny, dry conditions are not to their liking. Toads and snakes will eat them and Daddy Long-Legs spiders (*Pholcidae*) will gang up on a slug to nibble it to death.

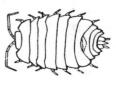

ACTUAL

■ ISOPODS

The Sowbugs and Pillbugs are interesting creatures, and your children will bring you these prized possessions cradled in dirty little hands. The pillbug, when disturbed will roll up into a globe-shaped curl that protects and conceals it, while the Sowbug cannot maneuver in this manner.. Both are long-lived, but slow-growing. Eggs and newly hatched young remain inside the mother several months, much like a marsupial animal keeps its young. After they outgrow the pouch, they undergo several molts until they emerge as adults at about 1 year. They are soil-builders of sorts, but when the population is too high, their control is to eliminate the conditions they favor.

Now that you've become a bugwatcher, keep notes on the controls you have tried, what works and what doesn't. Use your Cooperative Extension office for up-to-date information, and seek the wise counsel of a qualified entomologist to learn more about the insect life of your area.

Suggested Reading

"Pests of the West," Dr. Whitney Cranshaw, Faculty of Entomology and Cooperative Extension, Colorado State University, Fulcrum Publishing, Golden CO 1992.

"Butterflies and Moths," Robert T. Mitchell and Herbert S. Zim, Golden Press, New York NY.

"The Gardener's Bug Book," fourth edition, Dr. Cynthia Westcott, Doubleday, New York NY.

"A Field Guide to the Insects of America North of Mexico", by Donald J. Borror, Faculty of Entomology, Ohio State University and Richard E. White, Systematic Entomology Laboratory, United States National Museum, Houghton Mifflin, Boston MA 1970.

"Rodale's Color Handbook of Garden Insects," by Anna Carr, Rodale Press, Emmaus PA.

Diseases of Plants

COOPERATIVE
EXTENSION OFFICE

I n the Mountain West we can thank the low humidity, cold winters, lack of soil organic matter, and brilliant sunshine for fewer plant diseases that must be controlled. For the most part we can live with the few diseases that are present, or we can use cultural methods to overcome disease. We cannot control, except by elimination, the disease(s) of decline or old-age, but, as we advance in knowledge even these can be forestalled to allow a plant to live longer.

What We Can Do To Prevent Disease

The most heartbreaking happening for a gardener is the death of a plant from disease. Prevention of disease is not always possible, but before you buy a plant or plant a mail-order plant, give it the 5-point checkup.

1. Check the growing point. If it is broken, wilted, shriveled, or off-color, the chance of recovery is slim. It is possible to prune off the affected area, but if the problem is disease, it has probably already spread throughout the vascular system.

2. Check the leaves, both upper and undersides. If there are stippled spots or larger irregular spots or if any of the leaves are entirely affected and have lost color, the problem is probably irreversible. Raised spots on leaves are often a symptom of edema, caused by irregular watering practices. This is not a serious problem and can be overcome by removing the affected leaves and changing your watering practice to keeping a plant evenly moist, not alternate drowning and drought.

3. Check the stems or trunk, if this is a tree or shrub. Mistreatment during transit can cause areas of peeled bark that will never heal properly. Tree wrap can hide

■ *. . . before you buy a plant or plant a mail-order plant, give it the 5-point checkup.*

117

trauma as well as canker represented by sunken, pitted areas. Sunscald will also be seen as sunken areas, with old scars blackened and partly healed.

4. Check the crown by knocking the plant out of the pot to examine the root system. If this is a bare-root plant, check the roots for signs of drying. The *crown* is located at the point where the root joins the stem. Look for a swollen, soft, knobby, spotted area on the crown. This is *crown gall*, whereas a graft at that point would be smooth and hard.

5. Check the roots for *root knot,* which is described by its name — swellings along the course of the root. *Root Rot* is a blackened, soft, rotten root that can be caused by disease, overwatering, or crowding in the pot. Circling of the roots within the pot is also a sign of poor culture. This condition can be overcome with scoring the root mass lightly and vertically so that each root is gently nicked with a sharp knife. Adventitious buds will then be activated and the roots will venture outward into new soil.

Cultural Practices Can Invite Disease

The most common diseases are activated by poor cultural practices.
1. Plant not adapted to this area.
2. Overwatering.
3. Underwatering.
4. Roots cut while weeding.
5. Too much shade or sun for the preference of the plant.
6. Planting in fall resulting in failure of plant to establish before winter.
7. Leaving disease-infested plant debris in area of growing plants.
8. Poor soil preparation weakens plant, thus making it susceptible to disease.
9. Overcrowding, leading to poor air circulation.

10. Temperature stress, either too high or too low, leading to weakness and susceptibility to disease.

Are You the Garden's Worst Pest? Do you...

1. Walk around among the plants when they are wet? Fungal spores are easily spread from plant to plant when transferred to your clothing and on to the next plant.
2. Leave jagged pruning wounds? From the smallest annual to the largest tree, a jagged wound means easy entry for disease organisms.
3. Leave tools lying about that are clogged with dried soil and disease organisms? Cleaning your tools of soil not only keeps them sharp but destroys clinging disease organisms.
4. Carelessly bash a tree trunk with the lawn mower? Arborists claim that many tree diseases begin with a wound caused by a lawn mower. They even give it a name — lawnmoweritis.
5. Use the same soil year after year for starting seedlings? Soil quickly becomes infected with *Fusarium sp.* Use a soilless seed-starting media.

Physiological and Environmental Disorders

Chlorosis is a yellowish discoloration of the leaves with the veins and midrib a normal green. It is caused by alkalinity in the soil wherein the iron that is present in all Mountain West soils is not available to the plant. Changing the pH will make iron available and gradually restore normal leaf color. You may add sphagnum peatmoss or hire a professional to make a careful and controlled addition of sulfuric acid.

Sunscald is caused by a extreme temperature fluctuation between night and day.

The bark or stem tissue develops a corky spot, then a dry sunken area. Decline and death can follow.

Herbicide damage is widespread throughout any area where the human population is more oriented toward the use of chemicals as opposed to muscle power in removing weeds. Without knowledge of where a root system lies, there is a definite chance that desirable plants will take up the chemical herbicide through the roots and be damaged, if not killed outright. Symptoms of herbicide damage often mimic those of diseases. The upcupping of foliage is one of the most sure symptoms of herbicide damage that is not included in the symptoms of diseases. Parallel venation on leaves that are normally net-veined; chlorosis; wavy or curled leaf margins; and curled, twisted, disproportionate growth are additional symptoms. Needle cast and clubbing of tip growth are exhibited in evergreens affected by herbicides.

If yours is a country property, you will probably have occasion to use a phenoxy or hormonal-type herbicide. Be aware that these materials can travel in the soil and into the vascular system of a plant as far distant as a city block. Litigation is often begun when neighbors infringe upon rights by using a soil sterilant herbicide.

Causal Organisms

The fungal organisms affecting plants greatly outnumber the bacteria and viruses. Fungi reproduce by *spores* that resemble fine dust. They are released by the thousands and are blown about by wind or carried in water droplets. Upon alighting on plants they begin inoculation by growing an extension along the leaf surface. The fungus then grows down into the leaf, thus infecting it. As it matures, the fungus ripens, the spores are once again released and the cycle is repeated.

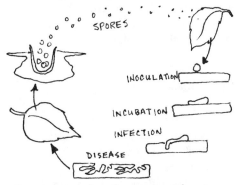

Fungus spores, how they are spread.

Bacteria are microscopic one-celled organisms that reproduce by division, thus increasing rapidly under favorable conditions. The bacteria that cause plant diseases dissolve plant tissues with enzymes or plug the stream of sap, causing the plant to wilt. Bacteria are motile, and can move also through splashing water or infected seed. While insects transmit some bacterial diseases, high-moisture conditions are necessary for a bacterial infection to succeed; therefore, it follows that the Moutain West is not host to many bacterial diseases. An additional type of bacteria, known as a *mycoplasma,* infect cells of the phloem (sap stream) and produce aberrations of plant growth such as grotesque, bushy, or distorted new growth.

Viruses are the no-see-ems of the three causal organisms. Being microscopic, they are detected only when the following symptoms occur: streaking of foliage, yellowing of leaves, leaf curling or crinkling and ring spots on leaves or blooms. Many viruses are transferred when plants are overcrowded or by certain insects, notably aphids and leafhoppers.

Viruses are the no-see-ems of the three causal organisms.

119

Descriptions of Diseases

Only those diseases that are a possibility in the Mountain West are listed. The rare occurrence of a disease not listed is not considered a threat to the spread of the disease.

Fungus Diseases
FLOWERS

Blight *(Alternaria sp.)* causes a circular leaf spot with a brown center and dark brown border. All parts of the plant, even the root, are eventually involved. The leaves are blighted and the leaf stems rotted at the base. Blossoms and seed heads are often destroyed. Seedlings are at times very susceptible. The very small sclerotia which carry the fungus through the winter are imbedded in diseased petioles.

Crown Rot *(Sclerotinia sp.)* causes a crown and stem rot which is followed by drying, wilting and eventual death. Large, flat, black sclerotia, or small, round ones, the size of mustard seeds, are often visible in the decayed stems.

Damping-Off *(Pythium sp., Pellicularia sp.)* attacks the stems of seedlings, causing them to topple without warning.

Gray Mold *(Botrytis sp.)* coats branches and flower stalks with a gray exudate which causes a wilting of the flowers and the development of light brown areas on stems at the base of flowers. The fungus enters the plant through the flower parts and grows into the stem, forming cankered areas. It spreads by water droplets on leaves.

Leaf Spots *(Ascochyta sp., Phyllosticta sp., Cercospora sp. Cercosporella sp. Didymaria sp., Discosphaerina sp., Leptothyrium sp., Ovularia sp., Phyllachora sp., Ramularia sp, Septoria sp.)* are many and varied. Flowers, stems, and leaves become discolored in spots,

dwarfed and distorted.

Mildew *(Erysiphe sp., Phyllactinia sp., and Podosphaera sp.).* Powdery mildew is a dry whitish scum on upper leaf surface, while Downy mildew is a fluffy, downy growth on leaf and stem surfaces.

Root Rot *(Pellicularia sp.)* causes a sudden wilting and death. It is carried in debris left lying beneath plants. Overwatering increases susceptibility.

Rust *(Tranzschelia sp)* is characterized by rust-colored pustules on undersides of leaves. It can overwinter on fallen leaves.

Smut *(Urocystis sp.)* Dark brown powdery pustules appear on swollen regions of the leaves and petioles. When ripe they break the skin and scatter their spores, which are united in balls. The smut overwinters in the root and crown. In some countries, the smut balls are a delicacy to be served at the table.

Bacterial Diseases

Bacterial Leaf Spots *(Xanthomonas sp., Pseudomonas sp.)* are seen as similar to those caused by fungus.

Crown Gall *(Agrobacterium tumefaciens)* causes a warty, tough growth at the point where the stems meets the root.

Viral Diseases

Aster Yellows is apparently caused by a mycoplasma-like organism carried by leafhoppers and is most often seen on asters and carrots. Symptoms are a yellowing of stems and foliage, and an aberration of the flower to make it appear light-colored and completely uncharacteristic of the species. Rogue immediately.

Fungal Diseases
TREES AND SHRUBS

Gnomonia and its asexual stage *Gloeosporium* are lumped together as the causal fungi for a disease called **Anthra-cnose.** Depending upon the species affected, the symptoms can be bud, twig, and shoot blight; leaf spots; and stem cankers. Ash, elm, maple, sycamore, walnut, and white oak are commonly infected. Look for lesions on the midvein of oak, leaf distortion and curling in ash, twig girdling, and branch cankers as the last phase before death.

Black Knot of Cherry and Plum is caused by the fungus *Apiosporina morbosa.* It is of concern for commercial fruit growers of the Mountain West, favoring Stanley and Blue Damson plums, though all cultivars are candidates. The disease is characterized by production of elongated swelling or knots on the limbs of susceptible cherry and plum. These corky outgrowths predominate on small twigs and branches and on the trunk. Knots, which are longer than they are wide, may reach 1 foot or more. Fruiting capacity of the trees is markedly reduced. Prune out the knots in August if possible, as this is the time they are fully extended. Cuts should be made 2 to 3 inches behind the swelling. Remove knots on the trunk or main branches by cutting away the diseased tissue down to the wood and at least 1/2 inch outward beyond the margin.

Black knot on chokecherry.

Brown Rot of Stone Fruits is of little importance where rainfall is low. Nevertheless, in irrigated areas the relative humidity can increase disease incidence. Brown rot is usually first seen as the fruit approaches maturity. Small, circular, light-brown areas of decay appear on the surface of the fruit, expand rapidly, and within a few hours may encompass the entire fruit. The fruits either drop to the ground or remain attached and become mummified. In warm, wet, humid weather, tufts of ash-gray mold develop over the surface. The mummified fruits become carriers of to the disease the next growing season. Control starts with removal of all fruit, mummies, and blighted twigs from trees in the fall. Cultivate around trees before first bloom. Prune to promote good air circulation. Do not plant near wild trees which may be a source of inoculum.

Cedar-Apple Rust *(Gymnosporangium sp.)* is rampant during a wet spring throughout the Mountain West. It causes great consternation when observed by gardeners, but it is not a dangerous or debilitating disease in this area. Two hosts are required — juniper (cedar) and apple. It begins during a wet spring when telial horns extrude from lesions, galls, swelling or brooms on Junipers. These are gelatinous masses, sometimes as great as 5 inches in diameter, yellow to orange in color, and with finger-like projections not unlike similar objects in monster movies. The teliospores can actually be seen to grow with the naked eye. The drippy mass dries and ascospores blow to attach themselves to other junipers or to species of apple or crabapple. The latter display spotted leaves, but are seldom damaged. Control is the elimination of one or the other host or a 2-mile separation between the cedars and the apples. This disease is widespread in Texas and the Midwest, but not in the Mountain West.

■ Do not plant near wild trees which may be a source of inoculum.

121

Cytospora Canker of Cottonwood, Willow, and Aspen is of major concern throughout the Mountain West. It is a disease of stress. Cankers on trunks and limbs are elongated, slightly sunken, discolored areas of the bark. Bark often splits along the canker margin because of callus formation by the host. It quickly girdles and kills twigs, then trunks. Fruiting bodies develop in dead bark, with the fruiting bodies forming first as small pustules; then during moist weather, yellow to reddish-brown spore masses or tendrils exude from the pycnidia causing consternation among gardeners because this disease can be seen to grow before the naked eye. As dripping begins from the tendrils, hardening occurs and the tendril falls away. Death usually occurs within 5 years. There is no cure or treatment. Maintain healthy trees and you will never see this disease. The most susceptible are weeping willow, 'Lombardy' and 'Bolleana' poplar, and 'Siouxland' cottonwood. Those usually resistant include the hybrid poplars 'Noreaster,' 'Mighty Mo,' 'Ohio Red,' and the species black and peachleaf willow (*Salix nigra* and *S. amygdaloides*). 'Norway' poplar is relatively resistant. Aspen grown at low (below 7,000 feet) altitude will always be susceptible to numerous maladies and *Cytospora Canker* is usually the last hurrah.

Dutch Elm Disease, also known as Phloem Necrosis, is caused by the fungus *Ceratocystis ulmi*. It has destroyed 90% of the American elms in the Mountain West, but there are enough left to warrant the narration of the problem. In susceptible species such as American elm, the first symptoms are yellowing of foliage, followed by wilting and browning. Usually a single branch is affected first in early summer, then symptoms spread to adjacent branches. It may take several years for a tree to die. When bark on affected branches is peeled back, brown streaks in the wood indicate vascular infection. Other wilt-producing fungi can cause the same symptoms; therefore, positive diagnosis requires a laboratory test in which chips of wood (not bark) from streaked branches are tested with specifically devised tests. Control is removal by professionals and disposal of the wood according to the local or state law. Most municipalities have land-fills specifically constructed for Dutch Elm diseased wood.

Leaf Spot of Cottonwood and Aspen (caused by a fungus *Marssonina sp.*). Many cottonwoods and also aspen that are grown at the Plains altitude exhibit black spots on leaves beginning as soon as leaves unfurl. Individual spots on severely infected leaves coalesce to form angular, necrotic blotches. The leaf spots vary in size, and are circular or lens-shaped. A yellow to golden margin often borders each spot. Elongate black lesions develop on veins, leaf petioles, and terminal section of new shoot growth. Early senescence results and a gradual decline of the affected tree begins. The disease cycle begins with fallen leaves of the previous season. Keep each fallen leaf picked up and you may win the battle with this disease.

Leaf Spots of Cottonwood, *Caragana*, and Maple (caused by a fungus *Septoria sp.*). Symptoms vary according to the time of infection, the hosts, and the texture and age of leaves. Brown circular spots may have a yellow margin. Small flecks, commonly with angular margins, may coalesce to form spots. White or silvery spots, or irregularly shaped large spots that are light tan in the center and dark brown on the margin may form as the leaves increase in size. Sanitation is the key to control.

The fungi *Phyllosticta sp.* are common causes of leaf spots on Maple and *Caragana* throughout the Mountain West. Trees and shrubs affected are Silver Maple (*Acer saccharinum*), Sugar Maple (*A. saccharum*), and Rocky Mountain Maple (*A. glabrum*). Spots begin as dark brown and irregularly circular, developing a light tan color and dropping out of the leaf as the disease progresses. Margins of the spots can be reddish purple with black dots (pycnidia).

The fungus *Rhytisma acerinum* is responsible for **Tar Spot** of Maple. The spots appear ridged and tar-like, resulting in the name "wrinkled scab." All maples are affected, but this disease is only spreading slowly from east to west.

Powdery Mildew of Lilac

(*Microsphaera alni*) affects not only lilac, but also alder, birch, maple, honeylocust, walnut, sycamore, oak, elm, and linden. During mid-summer, leaves develop small white or gray dusty-looking patches. These patches enlarge throughout the summer, and by early fall the entire leaf surface may be covered with a white powdery substance. Later in the fall, small pinpoint-sized brown to black structures develop throughout the powdery area. These dark spots are the sexual fruiting bodies of the fungus. The pathogen overwinters in fallen leaves as partially developed ascospores. These spores mature during wet spring weather and are then exuded from the black fruiting bodies and are blown or splashed onto non-infected foliage. After germination, haustoria of the fungus penetrate the leaf tissue and are restricted to a single layer of cells, the palisade layer. Mycelium growing on the leaf surface produces asexual spores, which are powdery white. These asexual spores are dispersed by wind and rain to other leaves, beginning the cycle anew. The fungus grows best during warm, damp summer weather. At the onset of cool weather, growth slows or ceases and the sexual fruiting bodies are produced that overwinter on dead leaves.

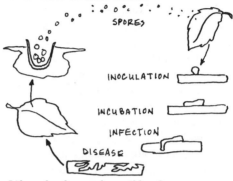

Life cycle of a powdery mildew fungus.

■ *. . . sexual fruiting bodies are produced that overwinter on dead leaves.*

Shoot Blight of Spruce caused by the fungus *Sirococcus sp.* is present throughout North America, mainly on spruce, but it can also be present on pine. Symptoms are tip dieback and cankers on current year's growth. Foliage becomes chlorotic, dies, turns reddish-brown, and is shed, leaving bare shoots throughout. Infected elongating shoots may curl and become hook-shaped. Cool, shady conditions favor infection. Tips should be clipped back behind point of infection.

Thyronectria Canker of Honeylocust is caused by the fungus *Thyronectria austro-americana*. It is a disease of stress. The symptoms include dieback of branches, reduced yellow foliage, premature fall coloration and premature leaf drop. Cankers appear on branches and trunks, which turn wine-red. Yellow pycnidia blacken with age to become black dots within the canker. Trees most often affected are those under drought stress or with a lawnmower wound at the soil line. Death is not immediate, but usually occurs within 5 years.

***Tubercularia Canker* of Siberian Elm and Russian Olive** caused by the fungus *Tubercularia ulmea* is widely distributed fungus disease throughout the Mountain West. The symptoms are elongated cankers on trunks, branches, and twigs. Flagging (wilting of mid-season foliage) occurs with dead leaves firmly attached, thus indicating girdling of a main branch by the canker. The surface of the bark is red-brown and becomes brown to black as it dies and dries out. Gum deposits may be found on Russian Olive branches. Fungal fruiting bodies emerge on the bark surface.

As the Russian Olive (*Elaeagnus angustifolia*) becomes more of a nuisance weed tree in the Mountain West, we can assume we might be less concerned with the canker. However, we can predict that the disease will attack more species in the near future. Watch for and remove diseased specimens of both Siberian Elm and Russian Olive. Manage remaining trees with winter watering and weed and insect control. Disinfect pruning tools with household bleach if pruning is necessary.

Wetwood (Slime Flux) of Elm, Cotton-wood, and Mulberry. These species are more often affected than other trees, but wetwood can strike any tree species. Symptoms are found in the trunk, branches, and roots. A dark colored, moist exudate forms, usually in spring, that fluxes down the trunk or branch. Air-borne bacteria, yeasts, and other fungi contaminate the sap, resulting in a frothy, slimy, foul-smelling liquid. Upon drying it leaves a light gray to white crust. Abundant gas is produced in wetwood-affected tissues by the fermenting action of bacteria on carbohydrates in the sap. Wetwood is associated with tight soils with poor drainage. Driving a drain into the site is no longer recommended. Washing the affected area daily with detergent in a car-washing tool is known to keep the infection to a minimum.

Witches'-Broom of Hackberry is more unsightly than harmful. The proliferation of twiggy growth into one mass at first resembles a bird's nest; then it becomes apparent it is an aberrant growth resembling a broom made of twigs. The only control is pruning. The cause is not understood, but thought to be related to eriophyid mites.

BACTERIAL DISEASES

Fire Blight, caused by the bacteria *Erwinia amylovora,* is the first plant disease shown to be caused by a bacterium. It is found only in North America and was first observed in 1780 in the Hudson River Valley. It is a major threat to susceptible apple, crabapple, *Cotoneaster,* European mountain ash, flowering almond, pear, and *Pyracantha*. The disease begins at bloom time when bees and other insects visit to collect the pollen. They carry infected pollen from the bloom of a diseased tree to the bloom of a healthy tree. If temperature and humidity conditions are right, the disease spreads immediately through the bloom, shoot, and into the twig, which turns dark red-brown. The foliage flags but does not abciss, hanging on to tell the gardener something is amiss. If the affected twig is not cut with sterile shears, the disease proceeds down the branch and into the trunk. When fiery cankers appear on the trunk, control is seldom achieved. Spraying with a bacteriacide every 3 days, beginning when 50% of the blooms are open, will often achieve success. Usually 3 sprays are necessary before petals fall.

Western X-Disease of Chokecherry

The disease pathogen for X-Disease was thought to be a virus, but is now thought to be a spiroplasma, a spiral- shaped bacterium without a cell wall. It affects sweet and sour cherries, peaches, and especially chokecherry, which are all of the genus *Prunus*. American plum, (*Prunus americana*) might be expected to be susceptible also, but is showing remarkable resistence, even when planted among susceptible species. Symptoms include leaves turning greenish-yellow in late June, becoming reddish in July and August, then turning deep red. Shoots are stunted and rosettes result from shortened internodes. Infected fruits are somewhat pointed and yellow-red. Both diseased and healthy fruit may be found on the same tree.

TURF

Lawn and other turf grasses vary in their susceptibility to diseases. Diseases are more likely to occur when lawns are improperly established without soil preparation and are poorly maintained. Inadequate soil aeration or drainage, overwatering, and improper fertilization or mowing may lead to disease problems. Some lawn diseases can be controlled by using fungicides, but unless this is a high profile turf, such as a golf green, chemicals are no longer recommended for control of diseases in turf.

Environmental Factors

Injury from causes other than pathogens is often mistaken for disease symptoms. Such injuries include burning with chemical fertilizers, dog urine damage, insect damage, burning of the grass by placing rugs, mats, cans, or similar objects on the lawn in hot weather, burning by chemical weed killers, and DROUGHT!

Chlorosis in Turf is a physiological condition, chiefly a problem in highly alkaline soils which "tie up" the iron in the soil, the element necessary for green

cholrophyll formation. Grass foliage turns pale green, yellow or ivory-colored except for the green veins. If chlorosis is severe the grass may die. A simple method to alleviate the condition is to dissolve 2 tablespoons of iron sulfate in 1 quart of hot water. Dilute this with 2 1/2 gallons of cold water and apply to 1,000 square feet of turf.

Damping-Off occurs on newly seeded turf during warm weather on heavy, moist or water-logged soils and where seeding rates have been excessive. Infected seeds rot in the soil; grass stands are thin and weak in irregular patches. Seedlings are stunted, water-soaked, turn yellow or brown, wilt and collapse. Avoid over-watering. Seed in late summer or early fall at the rate recommended on the package.

Diseases of Turf
FUNGAL DISEASES

Brown Patch (*Rhizoctonia solan*) attacks all cool-season turf grasses, including bentgrasses, fescues, Kentucky bluegrass and ryegrass. It results in round patterns of dead grass from 1 inch to 3 feet in diameter. Leaves are first water-soaked and dark, but soon dry, wither, and turn light brown. In light attacks, turf recovers in 2 or 3 weeks. Brown Patch occurs in hot humid weather when night temperatures are above 60°F. and leaf surfaces are covered with free moisture for long periods. It occurs less frequently when available nitrogen is adequate or low and when phosphorous and potassium levels are high.

Dollar-Spot (*Sclerotinia homeocarpa*) is a fungus disease that is most severe on Bent grass, Kentucky bluegrass, and ryegrass. The fungus causes bleached or straw-colored spots on the turf about the size of a silver dollar. If the fungus is growing actively, a fine white, cobwebby mycelium can be seen when dew is still on the grass.

■ . . . *chemicals are no longer recommended for control of diseases in turf.*

Sometimes only the uppermost grass blades are affected, giving each blade a narrowed area of tan color between areas of normal width of green color. The disease is most prevalent in spring and fall during periods of cool nights and warm, humid days, and also on lawns low in nitrogen. Often a light application of a high nitrogen fertilizer will clear the problem.

Fairyring (*Marasmius oreades* and other mushroom type fungi) is not a disease but a condition in which the causal fungus grows vigorously underground in an ever-widening circle. Occasionally, during spring and fall, fruiting bodies appear above ground in a circle or arc corresponding to growth below the surface. Although mushrooms may be unsightly in turf, the chief objection comes from damaged grass within the circle. The area outside the circle usually is bright green with very healthy grass. Beneath the dead grass in the center is a tough layer of mycelia. The grass dies as a result of drought because water cannot penetrate the mycelia. There is no chemical treatment. Piercing the mycelia with a garden fork and force-watering with a hand-held hose is often effective, but the only cure is to remove the soil and dead turf in the area. Often as you dig down to remove the soil, you will come upon buried debris from the house construction — lath, dry wall, broken boards, etc. This is feeding the fungi, and the condition will clear when it is removed and new soil and sod installed.

Frog-Eye aka Summer Patch (*Phialophora graminicola*) has a character-istic pattern of light green patches 1 to 2 inches in diameter. As the disease progresses, the color of the grass changes to a dull reddish brown, then to a light straw color. Within a few days, the discolored grass area may enlarge to a total width of 2 feet or more. In the final stages, distinct streaks, crescents, and uniformly blighted circular patches of grass will be scattered throughout the lawn. Centers of green apparently healthy plants, occur within the circles of dead grass; hence the name "Frog-Eye." The disease usually appears first in late June or early July when weather turns hot. It is seen first in areas of direct sun, such as a south-facing slope or near a sidewalk. The disease is most severe during periods of high humidity and when excess nitrogen has been applied.

Melting Out (*Helminthosporium sp.*) causes reddish-brown to purple-black spots on yellowed leaves of Kentucky bluegrass and sometimes spreads to the ground line. At first individual grass plants die in a random pattern and the turf appears thin and shabby. Infected grass dies out rapidly in irregular spots. Finally, large areas of dead grass result from the infection. The disease is often most severe during cool, moist weaher in the spring. Avoid over-stimulation with nitrogen.

Necrotic Ring-Spot (*Leptosphaeria korrae*) is a cool season disease character-ized by a fading of the turf with individual plants dying in an irregular pattern until the entire turf has a moth-eaten appearance. The frog-eye symptom (see above) can also be present. The remaining plants are resistant to the fungus and can be counted upon to spread by stolons to fill in the area eventually. Rake out dead grass with a thatching rake and mix enough sharp sand with moist sphagnum peatmoss to give the entire lawn a topdressing of 1/4 inch. If yours is a highly alkaline soil (pH of 8.5 or above) mix in a shovelful of soil sulfur with the topdressing.

Powdery Mildew on turfgrass looks the same as it does on your lilacs or roses — a grayish-white mold coating foliage, especially in shade or where air circulation is poor or soil is not well drained. Keep the lawn vigorous with proper fertilization and maintain adequate moisture in the soil. Avoid excess nitrogen. Mow frequently at the recommended height.

Snow Mold *(Fusarium nivale)* causes pink snow mold; *Typhula itoana* causes gray snow mold. Snow mold is a problem for high country golf courses, but treatment is not often justified in the home landscape situation. You will never know that you should have treated for it last fall until the snow melts and you find patches of dead turf in the spring. For a golf course or home putting green, treatment consists of applying a chemical recommended by your Cooperative Extension Service just before the first snow in autumn. Since we often have periods of snow and no-snow in early winter, your educated guess or that of an old timer will guide you. Raking through grass as soon as snow melts will usually cure snow mold in the home landscape. Lifting the blades to warmth and sunlight will kill the offending fungi.

Stripe-Smut *(Ustilago Striiformis)* causes great consternation when you discover it. Grass blades are curled and have black stripes running parallel up and down the length of the blade. If you touch it, a black soot-like explosion of spores fills the air. The problem occurs most often in a cool spring and in areas next to the sidewalk or drive. This disease is not widespread and does not pose any great danger to turf. It usually clears if you sweep it off with a broom.

VEGETABLES
(NOTE: Diseases are listed on vegetables alphabetically, not grouped by casual organisms.)

Diseases in the vegetable garden are greatly decreased with cultural practices. If you use sprinkler irrigation, you create the exact conditions needed for disease — high humidity, water droplets on leaves, and high velocity water splashing disease organisms between plants. However, drip irrigation or furrow irrigation keeps the water where the roots are and keeps the leaves and air dry.

Asparagus
RUST *(Puccinia asparagi)* appears as red or brown elongated spots on asparagus spears, shoots, or needles. This organism is exclusive to asparagus. Heavy dew favors development of the disease.

FUSARIUM WILT AND CROWN ROT *(F. oxysporum* and *F. moniliforme)* causes weak, spindly spears. As the season progresses, shoots from a severely infected crown may exhibit brilliant yellow coloration. Stem lesions near the soil line are frequent symptoms.

Beans
ANGULAR LEAF SPOT is caused by *Isariopsis griseola.* Leaf spots appear on the oldest leaves; the spots are dark brown to gray with a distinct margin, and angular in shape. Severly spotted leaves senesce prematurely and drop off. The fungus can survive for 2 years in residue from diseased plants and in soil.

ANTHRACNOSE is caused by *Colletotrichum lindemuthianum.* Black, sunken lesions appear on pods, cotyledons, and stems. Spots are 1/2 inch in diameter, raised, and covered by a salmon-colored ooze during moist conditions. The fungus is spread by wind or rain, animals, and implements.

■ *The fungus can survive for 2 years in residue from diseased plants and soil.*

BACTERIAL BLIGHTS are caused by 3 bacteria. *Pseudomonas phaseolicola* causes HALO BLIGHT, numerous small dead spots of leaves, each with a yellow halo. Halo blight is favored by cool wet weather. Common Blight and Fuscous Blight are caused by the bacterium *Xanthomonas phaseoli* that is characterized by large dead areas on leaves. Spots begin as small water-soaked or light green areas which later dry out and turn brown. Brown-Spot Blight is caused by the bacterium *Pseudomonas syringae.* Symptoms are more common on lima beans. Look for small reddish-brown irregular leaf spots with distinct margins and a darkening of some veins on the lower surface. The spots enlarge and drop out.

CERCOSPORA LEAF SPOTS are caused by the fungi *Cercospora canescens,* and *C. cruenta.* The spots on stems, leaves, and pods are brown to rust-colored, irregular, and form a checkerboard pattern. The undersides of leaves are dark and fuzzy.

MOSAIC is a virus disease known as BV-1, BV-2, and PSV. Mottled, puckered, stunted plants result. Veins die and drop out; pods are distorted. All 3 viruses are spread from sweet white clover and gladioli, and from diseased to healthy plants by aphids, by leaves rubbing, and by the gardener handling healthy plants after handling diseased plants.

POWDERY MILDEW is caused by the fungus *Erysiphe polygoni.* It begins with faint discolored leaf spots from which a grayish white talcum-like growth spread to all above-ground parts. Young leaves dwarf and curl, and then turn yellow and drop.

ROOT ROT is caused by 4 different fungal organisms: *Fusarium solani, Rhizoctonia solani, Pythium sp.,* and *Thielaviopsis basicola.* Characteristics include black rot of the taproot, sunken reddish-brown stem cankers near the soil line, reddish taproot, and wet rot of the root.

Beets

CERCOSPORA LEAF SPOT is caused by *Cercospora beticole.* Spots on leaves are brown to gray with distinct reddish-purple borders. The fungus overwinters in residue from diseased plants or on seed, and is spread by splashing water, insects, and tools.

ROOT ROT COMPLEX is caused primarily by *Pythium ultimum.* Symptoms include a postemergence damping-off, root rot, stem rot, and external and/or internal dry rot of fleshy roots. It is prevalent where beets have been grown in the same soil year after year.

Carrots

ASTER YELLOWS is caused by a mycoplasma, and is characterized by production of yellowish, dwarfed leaves, usually arranged in a tight rosette. Older leaves may develop reddish margins. The root at the crown bulges up into a cone and hair-like roots develop on the carrot taproot. The mycoplasma overwinters in many perennial weeds and is spread by leafhoppers.

ROOT ROT infected carrots may have forked roots and irregular round galls and spindle-shaped enlargements on the tap and side roots. These symptoms are caused by the same kind of root knot nematodes (microscopic worm) that causes root galling on tomatoes, cucurbits, lettuce, and other vegetable crops.

Celery

PINK ROT is caused by *Sclerotinia sclerotiorum.* Plants appear to suddenly wilt and collapse. The center is watery, pinkish, and moist. The disease develops during years of high rainfall and cool temperatures.

YELLOWS is a fungus disease caused by *Fusarium oxysporum*. The plants tend to be brittle and taste bitter. Continuous celery growing in the same location permits the disease to be soil-borne.

Corn

COMMON RUST is caused by *Puccinia sorphi* that begins as oval to elongated cinnamon brown pustules scattered over both leaf surfaces. The pustules rupture and expose dusty red spores and later black spores. The wind spreads the red spores to infect other leaves immediately. The black spores overwinter to hit next year's crop. The disease is favored by cool temperatures and very high humidity.

LEAF SPOTS develop from *Helminthosporium maydis, Phyllosticta maydis, Colletrotrichum graminicola,* and *Pseudomonas alboprecipitans.* More than one can be present on the same plant! All are characterized by lesions that are white to straw-colored and several inches long. Stalk, shank, and husk then rot.

SMUT is caused by the fungus *Ustilago maydis.* Large fleshy irregular galls appear on leaves, stems, ears, and tassels. Immature galls are white and spongy; mature galls turn brown, are explosive, and contain dark powdery spores. The smut fungus overwinters in soil. Smut development is favored by dry conditions and temperatures between 79°F and 94°F. Hail, cultivation, and insects can also spread the disease.

Crucifers
CABBAGE, CAULIFLOWER, BROC-COLI, BRUSSEL SPROUTS, and TUR-NIP.

BLACK LEG is caused by the fungus *Phoma lingam.* Symptoms begin as dark sunken cankers at the base of the stem and as light brown circular leaf spots. Stem cankers enlarge and girdle stems, and plants wilt. A diagnostic feature of Black Leg is the presence of distinct black pycnidia (speck-size reproductive structures) within stem cankers and leaf spots. The fungus overwinters on residue from diseased plants.

FUSARIUM YELLOWS is caused by the fungus *Fusarium oxysporum.* It affects all crucifers. Affected plants have a sickly, dwarfed, yellow appearance. Leaf edges frequently become purple and bases become brown. Lower leaves drop one by one. The fungus can remain in the soil many years. Disease development is promoted by high soil temperatures.

Cucurbits
CUCUMBER, MUSKMELON, CANTA-LOUPE, WATERMELON, SQUASH, and PUMPKIN

ANGULAR LEAF SPOT is caused by the bacterium *Pseudomonas lachrymans* and affects cucumber, squash, and pumpkin. It begins with angular-shaped leaf spots that appear gray or tan and finally drop out, leaving ragged holes. Fruit infections appear as small sunken water-soaked spots, and fruit rot follows. Bacteria overwinter in crop residue and are spread by splashing water.

ANTHRACNOSE is caused by *Colletotrichum lagenarium,* and affects cucumbers, cantaloupe, and watermelon. Leaf spots begin as yellowish or water-soaked areas that enlarge rapidly, turn brown, and shatter to form a ragged hole within the spot. Young fruit may be killed, but large fruits develop depressed dark-bordered cankers with creamy pink-colored ooze in the center. The fungus overwinters in residue from diseased plants and is spread by splashing water.

■ *Hail, cultivation, and insects can also spread the disease.*

■ *Touch a clean knife blade to the cut and slowly withdraw it.*

BACTERIAL WILT is caused by *Erwinia tracheiphila*. Wilting and drying of individual leaves is seen first, followed by wilt and death of entire plant. A diagnostic test is to cut a wilted stem near the crown and squeeze sap from the cut stem, watching for a white exudate from the vascular bundles. Touch a clean knife blade to the cut and slowly withdraw it. If you see a white ooze that strings out in a fine thread between the newly cut stem and the knife, it is bacterial wilt.

CHOANEPHORA WET-ROT is caused by the fungus *Choanephora cucurbitarum*, and is a summer squash fruit rot that affects wilted blooms and spreads to attached fruit. Infected fruit rot rapidly and fungus mold appears on the rotted area. It somewhat resembles Blossom End Rot of tomatoes. It is promoted by sprinkler irrigation.

DOWNY MILDEW is caused by *Pseudoperonospora cubensis*. Symptoms are irregularly shaped yellowish to brown spots on upper sides of leaves, followed by a downy purple fuzz on the undersides. Spots drop out of leaves as they die. Moist conditions such as the garden under sprinkler irrigation favor the disease.

FUSARIUM WILT is caused by *Fusarium oxysporum f. sp. melonis* and is characterized by stunting, yellowing, wilting and death of vines. A streak appears at the soil line on one side of the vine first, looking water soaked, then turning yellow-tan, and finally turning dark brown. This fungus lives in the soil many years and can be prevented with a heavy mulch to keep the soil cool in areas of extreme summer heat.

GUMMY STEM BLIGHT is caused by *Didymelia bryoniae* and affects winter squash, pumpkins, gourds, cantaloupe, cucumbers, and watermelons. It begins with pale brown or gray spots on leaves, petioles, and stems. Stem spots appear first at the nodes, and a gummy exudate appears. Leaves turn yellow and die. Sometimes entire plants die, but most often 1 or 2 stems will go ahead and produce fruit. The fungus overwinters in diseased plant parts.

POWDERY MILDEW is caused by *Erysiphe cichoracearum* and affects cucumber, muskmelon, pumpkin, and squash. The white powdery growth on leaves is introduced by wind at high temperatures, and is predominently a problem in warm winter regions. Keeping soil dry under the vines with weed barrier cloth or old carpeting will aid in preventing this disease.

Eggplant

ALTERNARIA BLIGHT is caused by *Alternaria solani* and occurs on tomato as well. Leaf spots are dark and leathery and when they become numerous, leaves die and drop. Fruits can also have sunken leathery spots.

Lettuce

ASTER YELLOWS is caused by a mycoplasma characterized by a yellowing and curling of the youngest leaves. Heart leaves remain dwarfed and curled, and heads remain soft. The mycoplasma overwinters in many perennial weeds and is spread by leafhoppers.

BOTRYTIS GRAY MOLD is caused by *Botrytis cinerea* and appears on plants in all stages of development. Seedlings look like they have damping-off. Older plants rot at the stem or lower leaves where they touch the soil. Dense fuzzy gray mold appears on exposed surfaces and plants fail to develop.

Onions

BLAST is caused by *Botrytis spp.* and appears first as numerous white specks on leaves. As spots expand, leaves die from the tips and turn brown. Plant tops may be killed and topple over within a week. This disease often occurs where thrips and mildew have taken their toll.

PURPLE BLOTCH is caused by *Alternaria porri* and may develop where white specks associated with Botrytis blight are present. It begins as water-soaked spots which rapidly turn brown. The spots expand and turn purple with a darker margin surrounded by a yellow zone. They may be as large as 2 inches in diameter. The fungus overwinters in plant residue.

Parsnips

CANKER AND LEAF SPOT is caused by the same fungus, *Itersonillia perplexans*. Leaf spots appear as small silvery areas which enlarge and become brown with a dark border. Cankers are prevalent near the shoulder of the root. The fungus overwinters in "field-stored" parsnips and is promoted by cool wet conditions in fall.

Peas

PEA STREAK is caused by a combination of the bean yellow mosaic, BV-2, and pea stunt viruses. It comes on as purplish brown flattened pods, purplish brown streaks on stems, death of veins, yellowing on some leaves, and eventual wilting and death of terminal growth.

POWDERY MILDEW is caused by *Erisiphye polygoni* and is characterized by a talcum-like mold on leaves, stems, and pods. Germination is promoted by sprinkler irrigation. Spores are borne on the wind or introduced in seed.

ROOT ROT organisms are present in all soils. They are activated to attack peas in a wet spring where soils do not drain well. Use raised bed culture; keep plants growing

vigorously, and you will never see this problem.

Peppers

BACTERIAL SPOT is caused by *Xanthomonas vesicatoria* which affects leaves and fruit of peppers and tomatoes. Leaf spots appear first on lower surfaces of leaves as small irregular water-soaked areas; then they enlarge up to 1/4 inch in diameter and become purplish gray with black centers and yellow halos. Spots on upper surfaces of leaves are depressed; those on lower surfaces are raised. Fruits sunscald and fail to develop. Bacteria is spread by sprinkler irrigation and in plant residue.

CERCOSPORA LEAF SPOT is caused by *Cercospora capsici* that causes large circular or oblong spots on leaves and stems. Light-gray centers with dark brown margins occur, and severely affected leaves turn yellow and drop. The fungus is carried on seed and survives at least one season in plant residue.

SUNSCALD often appears to be a disease. Affected areas are light-colored, soft, and slightly wrinkled. These areas later dry and become sunken, whitish, and papery. Fungi of various diseases often enter these areas to kill the plant. Wind, as well as sun, can cause sunscald.

Potatoes - see Tomatoes

Radishes

BLACK ROOT is caused by *Aphanomyces raphani*. Skin of the root turns purple to black in an area that finally girdles the root. The root becomes constricted and may crack. The black discolored area extends inward in radial streaks and generally remains firm. Disease development is favored by a warm spring.

■ *Bacteria is spread by sprinkler irrigation and in plant residue.*

Spinach

BLIGHT is caused by the cucumber mosaic virus, CMV, and begin on young inner leaves and later appears on outer leaves. Leaves are mottled, curled, and wrinkled; later they yellow and finally die. Plants are severely stunted. The virus overwinters in perennial weeds, builds up in many vegetable crops, especially cucurbits, and is spread from infected plants by aphids. This disease is worse during a warm spring.

Sweet Potatoes

SCURF is caused by the fungus *Monilochaetes infuscans* and appears on fleshy roots as small brown superficial spots. The spots expand and coalesce, but remain superficial. In storage, affected tubers dry out and shrivel more rapidly than do healthy tubers. Scurf fungus overwinters in affected roots, in residues, and in soil. The disease occurs in heavy, wet soils which contains abundant organic matter.

STREPTOMYCES SOIL ROT, also referred to as pox and pit, is caused by the fungus *Streptomyces ipomoea.* Symptoms begin as small dark dry surface spots on tubers. The dried tissue later falls out, leaving a pit or pock mark. Root growth around these spots is checked as other parts continue to grow, and the root becomes distorted. The fungus is prevalent in soil when sweet potatoes are repeatedly cropped. Disease occurrence is promoted by a high alkaline pH.

Tomatoes

Tomato diseases are grouped into symptom categories to help with diagnosis. Categories include blights, fruit spots and rots, leaf spots and blights, herbicide damage, viruses, and wilts.

Blights

EARLY BLIGHT is caused by the fungus *Alternaria solani* and is present throughout the Mountain West. It doesn't always strike early in the growing season, and is generally observed on older plants. Dark brown spots with dark concentric rings develop first on oldest leaves. Spotted leaves may die prematurely, resulting in substantial early defoliation, fruit sunscald, and poor fruit color. The disease overwinters in residue; it is also seed borne and can be introduced on transplants.

LATE BLIGHT is caused by *Phytophthora infestans* and affects both tomatoes and potatoes. Irregular greasy-appearing grayish areas develop on leaves. These expand rapidly during moist conditions and a white downy mold appears at the margin of the affected area on the lower leaf surface. Suspicious leaves without this down can be placed in a plastic bag with a wet paper towel for 1 day to promote appearance of this diagnostic sign. This disease may be introduced on transplants or wind-borne from other areas, and is promoted by cool, wet conditions.

Fruit Spots and Rots

ANTHRACNOSE is a common rot on ripe fruit caused by *Colletotrichum coccodes.* It first appears as small slightly sunken circular spots which increase in size. Fruit may rot entirely as a result of secondary infection. Anthracnose overwinters in soil, in plant residue, and in seed. The fungus can become established on early blight leaf spots. Green fruit can become infected, although spots will not appear until fruits ripen. The disease is prevalent on fruit that is overripe and in contact with soil.

BLOSSOM-END ROT in the East is the result of a lack of calcium in the soil.

Mountain West soils are derived from calcium-bearing parent material, but we as gardeners have this penchant for giving a plant too much water, followed by allowing it to become too dry. Shrink/swell of cells is probably responsible for Mountain West blossom-end rot. Root pruning during cultivation can also be partly responsible.

CATFACE is an abiotic disease caused by factors that seriously disturb initial fruit development during blossoming. Symptoms are extreme malformation and scarring of the fruit. Cool weather during fruit set and injury from 2,4-D herbicide can be traced as the cause.

SUNSCALD is characterized by white leathery spots on fruits. It often follows a leaf blight when leaves drop, exposing fruits to unaccustomed sun.

Herbicide Damage

2,4-D HERBICIDE DAMAGE can be clinched when you see light-colored parallel veins on leaves. Terminal shoots have leaves with distinct points and lobes. Possible sources include drift, fertilizer or pesticide contamination with an herbicide during storage, soil contamination, clothing and gloves contaminated from previous herbicide use.

Leaf Spots and Blights

TOBACCO MOSAIC is caused by a virus that affects tomatoes, eggplants, peppers, and potatoes. Symptoms on tomato foliage include light- and dark-green mottling with curling and slight malformation of leaflets. Sometimes green fruit are mottled. Affected plants may be stunted. The virus is very persistent and infections, and can be spread by merely brushing against plants. The virus is not spread by aphids, but it is spread by humans who smoke cigarettes. The virus

can be present in every cigarette and discarded butt, as well as on the hands and clothing of the smoker.

Wilts

The wilt organisms: *Verticillium sp.* affects tomatoes, potatoes, eggplants, peppers, strawberries, and raspberries. Oldest leaves turn yellow first, then dry up, often without wilting and drop prematurely. Shoot tips wilt slightly during the day and may curl upward. Internal woody stem tissue is dark. This soil-borne fungus can last many years in the soil. *Fusarium oxysporum f. sp. lycopersicae* affects only tomatoes and, unlike Verticillium, is characterized by leaf yellowing that progresses upward from the base of the plant. IT MAY OCCUR ON ONLY ONE SIDE OF THE PLANT. Woody stem tissue is dark throughout the plant. This fungus also can last many years in the soil, but is restricted by a cool soil at higher altitudes. Many tomato varieties bred to resist this fungus become susceptible to the recently detected race 2 — *Pseudomonas solanacearum* is a bacterial wilt that affects tomatoes, potatoes, eggplant, and peppers. The plant wilts suddenly without leaf yellowing. Stem centers (pith) become water-soaked, later turn brown, and sometimes become hollow. Pith discoloration helps distinguish bacterial wilt from Verticillium and Fusarium wilts. Woody stem tissue turns brown and roots may start to form on the stem. The bacterium overwinters in cold-frame and greenhouse soils. Walnut wilt is present when tomatoes are grown within the root zone of walnut trees, which exude juglone, a highly toxic chemical that may last in the soil many years after the trees have been removed.

Spotted Wilt is caused by a virus that is spread by thrips. Foliage becomes light-

■ *. . . we as gardeners have this penchnat for giving a plant too much water, followed by allowing it to become too dry.*

green mottled, accompanied by numerous small grayish brown thin dead spots. Spots on fruit are about 1/2 inch wide, have concentric rings, and are numerous.

When You Suspect Disease...

Your first move is to collect a typical sample of the problem plant. This may entail removing an entire plant. Wrap it carefully in several sheets of newspaper and take it to your local Cooperative Extension Office. There is a Cooperative Extension Office for every county in the United States and its territories. Several counties may share an office, but this is only in remote areas of low population. The Extension horticulturist will examine the specimen, ask you questions regarding the culture of the plant, and make the diagnosis. If he or she is unable to make the diagnosis, there is a back-up army of specialists at the state unviersity level who have the laboratory facilities to diagnose the problem and make recommendations. If they, in turn, are unable to make the diagnosis, there is another back-up army of specialists at the United States Department of Agriculture in Beltsville MD.

CHAPTER 6

Unwelcome Visitors

Newcomers to the Mountain West have idyllic notions of living in the foot-hills or mountains above the town or city where they work. The oft-repeated and tortuous ascent and descent via 4-wheel drive during a howling blizzard soon gives them pause. However it's the unfriendly or too friendly critters that most often cinch their decision to move to town. Tolerance levels for mischievous, annoying, or vicious wildlife will vary with the individual, and this section is designed to give information only. What one wants to attract, another wants to shoo away, and still another wants to whack. Loss of habitat and increasing human population will only exacerbate the problem.

Ants — Beneficial insects like ants can

sometimes make a nest where they are intrusive, such as in a crack of the house foundation or under the floor of a mountain cabin. If they are in a flat place, such as between the patio stones, a kettleful of boiling water will dispatch enough so that the remainder will leave. If they are in a vertical space, such as a crack in the foundation, push crystals of boric acid into the space repeatedly until you no longer see ants. Then repair the foundation. If they are the large carpenter ants, the boric acid crystals or Diazinon spray may control them. However, ants are busy reducing rotting wood to compost, which is their part in the web of life that covers this planet, so it is best to remove the source of their food instead. Flying ants are a demonstration of overcrowding in the colony. The queen of the crowded colony lays eggs that will become a winged queen and winged adults.

■ *. . . ants are busy reducing rotting wood to compost, which is their part in the web of life. . .*

135

These promptly begin migrating as intended. They may stop off on your roof or patio for a spell, but don't panic. They will move on shortly. Consult your Cooperative Extension office if ant problems persist.

Bats — If we gardeners could attract more bats, our gardens and mosquito-bothered patio picnics would be far better off. However, if bats choose to hang (literally) out in your attic, you're in trouble. The weight of the guano has been known to collapse the ceiling. They sleep by day, roam by night. Wait until full dark in the evening when they have flown away to nail closed their exit from your attic. This may require some searching for a tiny hole. Their flexible bones make it possible for them squeeze through small openings.

Bees are welcome visitors, but their spring-time swarms are sometimes troublesome. The new queen often chooses a low-hanging tree limb to alight upon, and the others follow. There is nothing to be alarmed about. Simply call the local bee association, a beekeeper of your acquaintance, or your Cooperative Extension office. They will have a list of beekeepers and will call one who is looking for a new hive. They will come with all their equipment and take the swarm away. It's fascinating to watch them at work.

Bears — It is common for bears, which are omnivorous, to eat everything in sight before denning up in winter. Your berry patch, fruit orchard, and garbage cans may be raided even in the cities of the Mountain West. Take care NOT to feed your pets outdoors. Keep garbage cans washed and sweet smelling and INDOORS! If a bear becomes troublesome, call your state division of wildlife.

If you encounter a bear in your yard or while hiking, don't run. Remain calm and SILENT. If the bear comes toward you, make yourself appear big by waving your arms. Begin screaming as loudly as you can at this time also. Your sudden vocalization may make them more frightened than you are.

Birds — The troublesome birds—blackbirds, crows, grackles, house sparrows, jays, rock doves, (pigeons), and woodpeckers are sometimes loathsome, but mostly just a nuisance.

Get rid of their food and roosting source, and you're halfway there. Habit is a very

136

strong influence on all birds. Break the habit, whatever it is. Food sources such as pet food dishes, feeding bunkers for cattle, sheep, hogs, chickens, and other domestic animals must be under cover so that they cannot be penetrated. Sweep and dispose of uneaten food in corrals. Never put out bread crumbs or garbage for songbirds to eat. You will attract trash birds, instead.

Roosting can be interrupted with a strong stream of water from the hose. Starlings and many other birds prefer communal roosting. They will fly at the first squirt of water, but come back 20 minutes later. Squirt them again each time they return until they disperse to seek roosting elsewhere. Usually, this task can be turned over to a teenager who will thrill at the opportunity of staying up all night fending off the "enemy" of the family.

The pump-action air gun is legal in many cities and towns. It can be used legally on starlings, crows, magpies, and rock doves in many areas. Check with your Cooperative Extension office to learn the legal status of your problem bird. If it is legal to shoot, it is often necessary to shoot only one bird. Hang it by the feet high in a flyway in a very visible place. Its kin will soon recognize it and go elsewhere. Birds have very little blood. The body dries without emitting an odor.

Birds will often gather in a tree before flying over a swimming pool. As they lift off, they defecate, making their presence even more disagreeable. Erect the necessary supports for a piece of nylon bird netting all the way across and in the way of their flight pattern. Their acute vision will pick up the new barrier and they will go elsewhere. When their habit is broken, you can take down the net.

Birds of prey, such as owls, hawks, falcons, and eagles are almost never a nuisance, but here following are a few instances that may require a behavior change on your part or theirs.

Owls mate in winter. Their calling to attract a mate can be annoying when you are trying to sleep. Be aware that these calls are of short term. Invest in some earplugs, and as soon as mating occurs, they will return to their normal silent lifestyle.

The **Great Horned Owl** is a vicious predator of anything it can kill. Housecats are favorites. Bring your cats indoors at dusk to protect them.  Hawks, falcons, and eagles will prey on domestic chickens. Cover their pen with wire netting to protect them.

The **Sharp-shinned** and **Cooper's Hawk** will take one bird about every 3 days from those coming to your feeder. This is a natural course of events in the wild and nothing should be done to harm the predator.

Woodpeckers, being cavity-nesters, mate in late winter. It is normal for a male to display what a fine

137

fellow he is by pecking loudly on anything handy within sight of the lady of his choice. This din can make sleeping nearly impossible. Give him a new drumming sight. Nail a tin can lid in a prominent place about 10-12 feet above ground to a tree far from your hearing. He will be delighted with his new noise-maker. Woodpeckers will also search out food by pecking holes in the siding of homes where insects have laid eggs or spun cocoons between and in or around the boards. Wash down your house with a strong stream of water frequently. Re-stain cedar shakes and siding.

Bird-scaring devices are available at your nursery. Flash-tape is easy to apply. Attach one end of a long piece to a fence post, twig, or limb. The reflective tape flutters and reflects light in flashes to scare birds away.

"Avitril" is a registered bird repellent that requires a license to purchase. Call an exterminator who has a license if you have a widescale problem in a rural setting with a large population of trash birds — **starlings, house sparrows**, **crows, grackles, rock doves, and magpies**.

Movable bird netting on a frame is the answer for a row of peas, a block of corn, or the raspberry or strawberry patch. Use a grid of PVC pipe, glued at the joints, to attach bird netting. Secure it around the pipe by hemming it with a length of stiff wire.

Moveable bird netting protects a row ready to harvest.

Deer — The burgeoning population of **mule deer** and **white-tail deer** in the Mountain West is alarming. Their preference for "the good stuff" is understandable. Your watered and fertilized roses, zinnias and vegetables are much more nutritious than the dry, harsh grass of the foothills. Their damage to your evergreens, especially junipers, in winter is also natural. Ruminent animals must have "browse" to aid digestion. A fence 8 feet high is required to keep out a **mule deer**[1] until you throw in the towel and go for electricity. The wire does not have to be strong — chicken wire will do unless a buck gets his antlers tangled in it.[1] A **white-tail deer** is smaller than the **mule deer** and cannot jump as high, however, and the fence needs to be only 6 feet high. Gardeners have been known to plant a wide band of prickly pear cactus outside their fences because the deer won't risk a thorn in his hoof, and he is not a proficient broad-jumper. Deer can jump high but not broad. Another ploy in a similar vein is the outrigger fence, especially if you live at the base of a small hill. A normal 4 foot fence is erected with a broad 8 foot outrigger on the outside of the fence. The deer won't risk entanglement with the outrigger boards and move on to your neighbors.

[1] *Lou Feierbend of Sunshine Canyon in Boulder, CO, has had success with this method.*

138

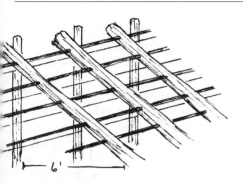

Outrigger fence.

Electric fencing is not as expensive or as troublesome to erect as one might think. The fibrglass poles are less than 1 dollar each and available at your local hardware, as are the wire and insulators that attach to the poles with a screw. The wire is hooked directly into your house current. The amount it will use will not be noticed on your electric bill. Your hardware dealer can show you the entire unit. For deer, place the wire at the 3 foot height early in the season before you plant the vegetable garden. Rub the wire with a rag dipped in peanut butter. The deer will smell the much-loved peanut butter and touch the nose to the electrified wire. A jolt to any other part of his anatomy is not severe enough to teach a lesson. Learned behavior is very swift after the nose is in jeopardy and that animal does not return. This method works equally well for **elk**.[1]

In late winter both **deer** and **elk** shed their antlers. Instead of letting them use your evergreen trees as a rubbing-off place, give them a sturdier and more attractive (to them) structure. Use a 10-foot post of 4x4 lumber. At irregular intervals nail several cross pieces of 2x4. In summer when the digging is easy, erect the contraption and set it in concrete in a prominent location.

Unfortunately, this thing cannot be hidden or the animals won't see it. The animals will use it for rubbing off their antlers, thus saving your trees.

Dogs and cats wandering onto your property can be repelled with the new lingering and bitter tasting compounds containing denatonium saccharide. These are non-hazardous and ecologically-sound repellents. They are available at stores such as nurseries and hardware stores.

Lions are eating poodles like popcorn up and down the Mountain West. Domestic **dogs and cats** are easier to catch than wild prey. However, wildlife officials tell us that cougars, also known as mountain lions, are attracted to large deer populations. They might be successful in killing one a week. It is normal for them to feed on their kill a little each day, covering it with pine duff and branches to hide it between feedings.

If you encounter a lion on your property or on a hiking trail, do not run. Back away slowly speaking in soft tones. If the animal comes toward you, make yourself as large as possible. Wave your arms and scream and hiss as loud as you can. As with bears (see above), your sudden vocalization will alarm them and they may slink away.

[1] *From lecture by Roger Swain, Aug. 1992.*

139

Pack rats are strange little rodents with a penchant for stealing bright-colored or shiny objects to bring to their nest. They abound at the montane altitudes all over the Mountain West, and, although they aren't considered harmful, if they carry off your diamond ring, you're going to consider it the *crime capitale*. Be aware of their presence *everywhere;* place your valuables in boxes or drawers that close tightly. Leave them little balls of foil if your valuable object is hard to move or hide. They are perfectly happy with simple things.

Moles are non-existant in the Mountain West. Many newcomers swear they have moles when they view puffed-up soil in circuitous routes through their gardens. The tunnels are those of **pocket gophers** or **ground squirrels**. These rodents do not hibernate, but feed on roots all winter. The ground is snow-covered; therefore, their tunneling pushes soil upward against the packed snow. When the snow melts, the perfectly formed tunnels are left as random, raised, circuitous routes. In addition to feeding on roots encountered while digging, they also feed on vegetation pulled into the tunnel from below, and on ground vegetation near the tunnel, though many never appear outside the tunnel in

their entire lives. They are ruinous to alfalfa fields and native grass lands. They also wear down their continuously-growing teeth on buried utility cables. Give them their very own piece of utility cable, placing it near a burrow, and they may leave the real thing alone. On the beneficial side, they increase soil fertility by adding organic matter, increasing soil aeration, and water filtration, reducing soil compaction, and increasing the rate of soil formation by bringing up subsoil and subjecting it to weatherization.

For control, place gopher traps near the main or lateral tunnels, preferably one with the freshest mound of soil. Remove the soil plug with a garden trowel. Secure the trap with a wire and marker stake. Visit the trap twice daily. If an animal is not caught within 48 hours, move the trap to a new location. Trapping is usually most successful in spring and fall when gophers are active.

Porcupines are slow-witted, slow-moving, and appear docile. They can, however, do a great deal of damage to your evergreens by girdling the tops. They can also dig and destroy your bulb plantings. For porcupine, gopher, and mouse protection of your bulb plantings, use a shallow layer of gravel on top of and all around each bulb so that the animals cannot smell the bulbs. If you are unsuccessful in controlling porcupines, call the Division of

Wildlife of your state government and they will advise you.

Prairie dogs are the most successful of all rodents in the Mountain West. Their "towns" are seen throughout the plains, foothills, and lower montane zones. If you should be so unfortunate as to have a colony on your property, the most realistic and efficient method of removal is to call a professional exterminator. In areas where the discharge of firearms is not forbidden, shooting them one by one will gradually decrease the population, but be aware they have sentinel dogs on duty at all times who bark a warning of your presence. Getting close enough to shoot is almost impossible. Above all, do not try relocating them by running water down the holes and catching them when they emerge. Relocating any animal into strange territory almost always condemns them to a slow death.

The not-so-smart rabbit digging, outline of wire under soil.

Rabbits are fairly easy to repel once you understand that they aren't smart enough to concentrate their digging efforts beyond the wire you erect. To explain: Make a tight chicken wire fence 4 feet high, bending 6 inches of the wire outward at the soil line. Cover this portion with a little soil. The rabbit will try to dig under the fence at the base of the upright portion. Encountering wire, he doesn't know to move backward 6 inches and try again. If you also have racoons, see below before making the wire taut.

If **rabbits** gnaw on the bark of your fruit trees or evergreens in winter, give each tree a cylinder of hardware cloth from a point 2 inches beneath the soil at the base of the bole to as high as snow can be expected to lie and the rabbit be expected to stand, for rabbits will stand on their hind feet to reach delectable morsels above. Spraying the limbs with Thiram will deter them somewhat. This is a fungicide, but the Taste Terrible deters rabbits.

Racoons are fairly easy to repel once you understand that they aren't as smart as they look. There's something about the little bespectacled face with the wiseacre expression that confounds the human species. They can climb any fence except one that flips them on their back. Therefore, make a wire fence that is attached tightly to the posts at the bottom and for 3 feet upward; then allow it to flop without attachment. Mr. Racoon climbs till he reaches the floppy part and tips backward. He will do it again and again, complaining loudly, until he tires and goes elsewhere.

Racoons can't climb a floppy fence.

If you elect to construct the electric fence explained under *deer,* attach 2 more wires at the bottom. One will be 4 inches from the soil line, and another 4 inches above the first. These two low electric wires will repel **rabbits, racoons, skunks, pocket gophers, squirrels, and thirteen-lined ground squirrels,** and **sometimes chipmunks.**

Scarecrows - See Chapter 1, Vegetables.

Skunks are fairly easy to repel. If you are a good housekeeper in keeping the outdoor areas clean of food debris, and if you do not have grubs in the turfgrass, you will be free of all except a wandering skunk that passes through. If, however, a skunk makes its nest to have its young under your porch or deck, be ready with a plan. Place as close as you can get to the culprit a small battery-operated radio, set to a rock-and-roll station with the volume turned on full. They will quickly leave to make their nest elsewhere and taking their young with them. Don't worry, you will only have to put up with the noise for an hour or two.

Snakes are seldom a problem in the Mountain West. The **prairie rattler** is almost always put off by construction noise and, if he lived on your property before construction started, he's no longer a resident by the time you move in. The other little snakes are beneficial, especially the thick dark bull snake. The author's family had a bull snake that resided in the root cellar, stretching himself across the door lintel. You can bet we youngsters, sent to the cellar to fetch a quart of peaches, said a quick "howdy" and did not tarry. If you have a lot of rock work in your landscape, snakes, being cold-blooded animals, are attracted to warm stones. Stretched out on a garden walk, they are reluctant to move. If you have too many of these insect and rodent-eating beneficial animals, dust rotenone on their favorite sunning spots. Rotenone is a fish-killer and a reptile irritator. It irritates their skin and they seek a home elsewhere. Your nursery has rotenone in the organic insecticide department. They may also carry "Snake-Away", which is reported to be a good snake repellent.

Spiders are another beneficial animal. They eat only live insects. Some spin intricate webs of beauty when spangled with dew on a sunny morning. Others spin clumsy funnels and messy tangles. In early fall the widow family moves in. These are the **Black Widows,** feared by many. They are seeking a warm, dark place that has access to the small insects that are its food. A crack in the foundation or just behind the front or back entry is a favorite place. Since this spider is poisonous, it is best to deal with it with the vacuum cleaner.

The **wolf spider** is a large fuzzy black fearsome thing that is mildly beneficial and should be allowed to go its way. It wants nothing to do with your home, so don't fear it will enter. It is about 12 years old before it's big enough for you to notice. Keeping wolf spiders in a covered, ventilated aquarium with a saucer of water and small live worms to eat is educational for your children. If you encounter one with a huge white egg sac on its back, it's even more entertaining to watch the spiderlings from

day to day. However, when they have eaten the egg sac, it is time for them to climb to a high place to be wafted away by the wind. Catch as many as you can in a baby food jar, one by one, and release them. The mother may live on for a time, too, but it's best to release her at the same time so your children aren't traumatized by her death.

The squirrel that is bothersome in city and town is the **Fox Squirrel**, which is not native to this area. They are voracious strippers of bark and leaves, thus killing trees, and destroyers of the nestlings of our songbirds. The overpopulation of the Fox Squirrel has led homeowners and gardeners to devise many methods of destruction. To prevent squirrels from gobbling food from your bird feeders, locate first a window that will be convenient to open so that you can fill the feeders. Then hang the feeders opposite the window placing the screw eye for the feeder on the facia under the eaves of your home. You won't have to go outside on a cold day to fill the feeder, and squirrels are completely shut off from reaching it. If your windows won't open so that filling a feeder is convenient, use instead a pole with an all-metal feeder that closes down if too much weight is placed on it. For suet feeding, use the wire cages that are available in nurseries or wild bird food stores. Hang the cages with long, thin, strong wires.

Trapping is the most successful method of destroying squirrels. Bait the trap with peanut butter, leaving the trap unset for several days to gain their confidence. Then set it to catch the offender. Do not take

them to a nearby park or out into the country to release them. Shifting the responsibility for damage control is not a favor. Kill them in the most humane way by placing the animal, trap and all, inside a plastic garbage bag. Pleat the bag opening around the exhaust of your car, holding it securely while a second person starts the motor. Start the motor at idle speed. The bag will fill with exhaust fumes containing carbon monoxide almost immediately. Shut the motor off at that time or the bag will blow up, and before the exhaust pipe becomes hot. It will be only a minute or two before the animal is dead.

Termites are not rampant in the Mountain West, but there are enough to make you worry when you purchase a home. In most communities

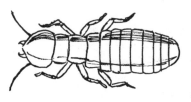

the building codes adopted in the late fifties insisted that termite flashing be installed on the footers of concrete to prevent subterranean termites from attacking wood members attached with rebar to the concrete . If your home was built before that time, it is wise to have it inspected by a licensed exterminator before you buy. If you suspect termites, it is also the best policy to allow a licensed exterminator deal with the problem. It can be costly. Get bids from two or more licensed exterminators before you choose.

Toads are the most welcome guest in any garden. They can dispose of more harmful insects than most of the predaceous insects and all other animals. Your pet cat, however, will bother the toad to death by patting it gently to keep it moving until it dies of exhaustion. Give the toad a hideaway of an overturned clay flower pot with a little entry dug into the soil beside it. There are also "toad houses" available at your nursery. In winter, leave a corner deep with leaves and debris so that toads can find a refuge that will remain unfrozen for the winter hibernating period. Your lily pool will be the repository of eggs the following spring. After the tadpole stage, the toad will crawl onto the bank and remain a dweller in moist, dank places by day, and a marauder at night, eating insects and slugs.

Turtles are not a harmful intruder on your home grounds. However, if a snapping turtle, with its powerful jaws and vicious temper, should happen to choose your property to make its home, it is unsafe to allow one to linger. The Mountain West, being too dry overall, is on the boundary of the limits of their habitat, and it is unlikely you will see any. Bait a cat or dog trap with ground meat and set it near the place of the last sighting of this reptile. If several days pass without success, call a professional exterminator.

Voles are tiny rodents that can be very troublesome in towns and cities during a snowy winter, or if you own a mountain cabin. They do not hibernate, preferring to make runs under the snowcover, where they dine without interruption all winter on the turfgrass you have worked hard to maintain. When the snow melts, the 4 inch wide runs, devoid of vegetation, become visible, and your entire lawn looks like the circuitous route of the roller coaster at the amusement park. There is very little one can do during the winter. When snow lies deep and long, you can, however, count on vole damage. Fortunately, with fertilizer and water, turfgrass recovers quickly. In summer if the vole paths continue to the degree that your turf is being totally destroyed, you can bring down the population to a tolerable level by placing unbaited mouse traps across their trails. They have poor eyesight and move at a dead run. Clean the traps daily until damage is under control.

Voles and the common **house mouse** can also cause damage to spreading evergreens, such as Pfitzers and Tammys, by girdling the trunks with their incisor teeth. Remove mulch and any grass that may be growing beneath the shrubs. Crush chickenwire so that it fits loosely around the base of the spreading and upright evergreens. Make a repellent that has an unpleasant taste that discourages feeding on the bark. A new coat must be applied each fall.

Mix 1 gallon of denatured alcohol with 7 lbs. of pulverized rosin Let stand in a warm place for about 24 hours. This mixture is flammable, so do not expose to open flame. Shake occasionally. When the rosin is dissolved, spray or brush repellent on the dry bark of trees and other plants to be protected. All surfaces should be covered to at least 2 feet above the normal snow line.[1]

Moth balls scattered under the shrubs at approaching winter will help. A tray of warfarin for each 6 spreading evergreens will also aid with control.

Wasps, hornets, and yellow jackets are a threat to young children and adults alike. Fortunately, we have aerosols sold as "Wasp and

[1] Harold Davidson, Extension Horticulture Agent, Michigan State University.

Hornet Killer" that are effective if used correctly. These insects cannot see at night. Wait until full dark; then attach a piece of red cellophane over the lens of a flashlight. Insects cannot see red light. Locate the nest's entry point, which is usually near the bottom. Spray directly into the opening, using the red lens flashlight to aid your aim. Use the amount directed on the can. If the nest is in the ground, use moist soil to seal in the aerosol contents after spraying. If the nest is in a wall, call a professional exterminator. The point where the insects are exiting is usually not anywhere near their actual nest, and an exterminator has the necessary long hose attachment for safe control.

To avoid being stung by wandering wasps, hornets, or yellow-jackets, avoid using hairspray, perfume, or scented lotions, including sunscreen. Wear light-colored clothing — long sleeves, long pants. Avoid walking barefoot outdoors. Search the shrubs and trees often for signs of nests of these insects. If you are or even think you are allergic to the stings, keep an anti-venom kit on hand at all times. Other members of the family should be informed of the allergy and be prepared to drive you to the emergency room of the nearest hospital.

As gardeners we use our close tie with nature to sharpen our senses to detect the unwelcome visitors. With progress as a gardener, we make less and less fuss over the intruder.

CHAPTER 7

Weeds

Weeds are often defined as plants out of place. The tenor of this definition is that if they were located elsewhere, someone would love them. This isn't true, is it? At least for most of them, no one loves them.

The war on weeds takes a begrudged and inordinate amount of time. Each individual engaged in any kind of agriculture or horticulture finds it necessary to make a battle plan, new each year. Have you ever considered how much more time you would have to enjoy your garden if you didn't have to weed? While it's true that weeding helps in abating the frustrations and irritations of a day at the office, the cost to you of water, soil nutrients, and *space* are greater than anyone can measure. Crops are literally choked out by undesirable plants. Livestock are affected by irritating (**Leafy Spurge**) and poisonous (**Larkspur**) plants that cause weight loss, other afflictions, and often death.

The costs of weed control in croplands, as well as in lost productivity, are reflected back to you and all consumers through higher commodity prices.

Weeds also threaten human health. According to the National Institute of Health, weed allergy is the principal allergy in the United States. Ten million dollars are spent annually treating hay fever alone.

Perhaps the greatest threat that weeds pose is to the lifestyle we hold dear in the Mountain West. Our greatest natural resource is our scenic beauty. There isn't a Mountain Westerner, even those living in cities, who doesn't look daily to a mountain and breathe a sigh of thankfulness. Outdoor recreation activities are greatly affected by weed infestations. Wildlife are known to abandon weed infested range and to move to surrounding cropland and residential areas causing extensive damage. Loss of ecological diversity, native plant communities, soil, and the habitat of all animals —

■ *Have you ever considered how much more time you would have to enjoy your garden if you didn't have to weed?*

from the tiny meadow mouse to the climax beast, such as the antelope, moose, elk, bison, bear, and cougar — continue the decline of our lifestyle, our opportunities to make a living, and the matchless composition of our world.

Americans tend to accept blame for the introduction of many harmful insects into this country, but with weeds, we can lay the blame on the ships of other countries carrying our immigrant forefathers to these shores. The holds of ships held grains and other foods coming to this country. Ballast and packing materials can be credited with vast numbers of weed seeds as well. The seeds germinated quickly in the wide open fertile lands and, with no enemies, proliferated to the point of receiving *pest* designation. We've been engaged in a fight for our lands and lives ever since.

Weed Control, Mechanical and Chemical

Before examining the worst weeds individually, let us look at ways to combat them. It's easy to think first of a chemical that will kill weeds and prevent further growth. However, soil sterilants are not the answer to weeds and have no place in the home gardener's chemical cupboard. Their use in the home landscape will migrate in the soil to roots of desirable plants, resulting in the death of trees and shrubs and all other vegetation to the point that the soil will never again support plant life. These chemicals are not worth the damage they do. There are several chemical mixtures on the market that are available to home gardeners that border on the soil sterilant. Read the label carefully before you buy. Look for restrictions as to the root run of desirable plants. We have NO WAY TO MEASURE where a root run might be. Chemicals travel quickly through the soil to damage desirable plants' roots.

The two chemicals homeowners can use to control weeds are glyphosate and 2,4-D. Glyphosate (sold as Roundup, Kleenup, Killzall, etc.) kills grassy and broadleaf plants except for **Bermudagrass, Zoysia grass** and **purslane**, but does not kill woody plants if used correctly. Be careful not to spray the green bark of a young tree or the sucker shoots around a tree. Glyphosate breaks down in the soil to harmless elements, but it can be stored in the roots of a woody plant. If you spray the same area within the root run of a tree or shrub year after year, eventually the plant will show droopy, up-cupped foliage with burned tips, and the plant will finally die.

In Chapter 14," Growing Wildflowers," you will find ways of controlling weeds that have lain dormant as seeds for long periods of time, sometimes over a century. For weeds that have germinated in spring, the most effective method of control is with a Dutch hoe, also called a scuffle hoe. Its back and forth rocker action is easy to manage, and it cuts off seedling weeds at the soil level. It isn't necessary to rake up the cut weeds; they are young and have not formed seeds. Let them dry to form a mulch.

For weeds that are older, your own muscle action is the most effective. Soak the soil well the day before, set a goal for yourself, such as a bucket a day, and plan to spend a half hour each day pulling each weed.

For the giant weeds that are older still, the main effort must be in cutting them off at the soil line before they can bloom and set seed. This isn't too difficult if you carry a pair of sharp pruning shears and drag a large square of plastic to hold the debris. If the offender is a perennial, it will put forth new foliage that will then be very susceptible to either glyphosate or 2,4-D, but if you prefer not to use chemicals, be aware that this plant will eventually put up new foliage, flower, and set seed. If you persist in cutting it off again and again, each time it is forced to grow new foliage the nutrient reserves in the root will be depleted until it dies. The leaves are the factory, remember, and being deprived of the factory eventually takes its toll. This method is especially good for **bindweed** during the growing season. A method using a chemical on **bindweed** follows (p. 155).

On a piece of weedy ground, use the tried-and-true method of watering up the weeds. After you find that no more are emerging, spray the entire area with glyphosate. Wait 3 weeks, then spray any that are still living. After that, you can plant individual plants, but if you are seeding a turfgrass lawn, take care to cultivate only very shallowly so that deeply buried weed seeds will not migrate to the surface to germinate.

In treating individual weeds that are growing among desirable plants, open both ends of a cardboard box, place it over the weeds and spray with glyphosate or 2,4-D down into the box to coat the foliage of the weeds; wait a few minutes for the drift to settle; then remove the box and move to the next one.

For weedy grasses growing in among the desirable turfgrass, mix a bowl of glyphosate; don a pair of rubber gloves, then a pair of cotton gloves over the rubber ones. Carry the bowl of glyphosate to the weedy area. Dip your hands into the solution and wring your hands together slightly so that the solution does not drip. Stroke each offending blade of weedy grass. Make certain that you do not irrigate the area for 6 hours. The weedy grasses will be dead in about 3 weeks. Re-treat, if necessary, for those you missed.

■ *Achillea millefolium*
YARROW, MILFOIL is a fern-leaved perennial introduced from Europe. It spreads by seeds and runners. Stems are 1 to 2 feet, erect and hairy, branching near the top. Leaves alternate, covered with fine hairs which give a grayish-green cast. Flowers are cymose, white or pinkish, with a very rank odor. Difficult to control with chemicals.

■ *Agrostis paulustris cvs.*
BENTGRASS is a very desirable species for the golf green, but it has no place in the home landscape. For **bentgrass** that has invaded a bluegrass, buffalograss, rye, or fescue lawn, spray the infested area with 2,4-D according to the directions for dandelions on the container. For unknown reasons, 2,4-D kills this grass used on golf greens.

REDROOT PIGWEED

■ *Amaranthus retroflexus*

REDROOT PIGWEED is a non-native plant introduced from Europe or tropical America and is an annual reproducing by seed. The stem is light green, stout, tough, rough-hairy, with many branches and is 1 to 6 feet tall, with a long, somewhat fleshy, red taproot. The leaves are alternate with the lower ones ovate, about 3 to 6 inches long, pointed at the tip, dull green, rough-hairy, with prominent ribs and veins. The upper leaves are smaller, narrower and more lance-shaped. Flowers are small, green, and densely crowded in a large bristly, simple or branched, terminal or axillary cluster. Redroot Pigweed grows in cultivated fields, pastures, roadsides, and waste places up to 8,500 feet throughout the Mountain West.

COMMON RAGWEED

■ *Ambrosia elatior*

COMMON RAGWEED is a member of the Aster family, Ragweed tribe. It is a native annual which reproduces by seed. The stem is 1 to 3-1/2 feet tall, erect, finely haired and much branched. The leaves are thin, 2 to 4 inches long, once or twice dissected, dark green above and paler underneath. Both male and female flowers are found on this plant. Solitary clusters of flowers can be found in the axils of the upper leaves and they are cup-shaped forming numerous drooping heads. The pollen of Common Ragweed is said to cause many people to suffer from hay fever. It is common in cultivated fields, meadows, roadsides, and waste places from 4,000 to 6,000 feet.

SILVER-LEAF POVERTY WEED

■ *Ambrosia tomentosa*

SKELETONLEAF BURSAGE or SILVER-LEAF POVERTY WEED is a member of the Aster family, Ragweed tribe. It is a native creeping perennial which reproduces by seeds and horizontal roots. The stem is 4 to 18 inches high, branched and somewhat bushy. The leaves are alternate, 2 to 5 inches long, white beneath with minute hairs, smooth green above, and dissected into narrow, irregularly margined lobes or segments. The flowers are very small and heads are formed in a pale green, elongated cluster that is 1 to 3 inches long. The seed capsules are straw-colored when ripe and have sharp, short spines on the surfaces. It grows in arid environments, prairies, pastures, waste places, and roadsides, and is a weed in cultivated, irrigated fields. It is most common from 5,000 to 8,000 feet, but may be found wherever land is cultivated.

WHITETOP

CHEAT GRASS

■ *Bromus tectorum*
DOWNY BROME aka CHEAT GRASS, a non-standard common name, a member of the Grass family, Fescue tribe, is an annual or winter annual introduced from Europe. It usually germinates in the fall, lies over winter and produces seed early in the spring. It has smooth, slender erect stems. The plant grows 6 inches to 2 feet high from a much-branched base. The sheaths and leaves are covered with fine, soft hair. The leaves are 1/8 to 1/4 inch wide and flat. The head is much-branched and somewhat drooping. Seeds are long and flat with an awn about as long as the seed. It matures seed in early spring before most other grass species or crops. It is a strong invader and creates a serious fire hazard when mature. Mature plants turn purple or brown. It grows in fields, waste placs and roadsides and is widely distributed from 4,000 to 9,000 throughout the Mountain West. The name **Cheat Grass** comes from its lack of nutrients for livestock because they show no weight gain when grazing this plant.

■ *Cardaria draba*
WHITETOP is a member of the Mustard family and was introduced from Europe probably in alfalfa seed. It is a creeping perennial which reproduces by seed and creeping roots. The extensive root system spreads horizontally and vertically, with frequent shoots arising from the root stock. It grows erect from 10 to 18 inches high and has a gray-white color. The alternate leaves clasp the stem and are oval or oblong with toothed or almost smooth margins. The leaves are often covered with very fine white hairs. Each leaf is 1/2 to 2 inches long with blunt ends. The flowers are white, 1/8 inch across, and are numerous in compact flat-topped clusters which give the plant its name. The seed pods are heart-shaped and each contains 2 oval, finely pitted red-brown seeds, each about 1/12 inch long. **Whitetop** is one of the earliest perennial weeds to emerge in the spring, with flowers and seeds produced in late April and early May. It has become a major problem in pastures and cultivated areas from 3,500 to 8,500 feet.

151

MUSK THISTLE

■ *Carduus nutans*
MUSK THISTLE is a member of the
Aster family, Thistle tribe. It is an introduced biennial, winter annual, or rarely
annual which reproduces by seed. The first
year's growth is a large compact rosette
from a large, fleshy, corky taproot. The
second year stem is erect, spiny, 2-6 feet
tall and branched at the top. The leaves are
alternate, deeply cut or lobed with 5 points
per lobe, very spiny, 3-6 inches long and
clasp down the stem. The wavy leaves are
dark green with a light green midrib and
mostly white margin. The large and showy
flowers are terminal, flat, nodding, 1-1/2 to
2-1/2 inches broad; purple, rarely white;
and surrounded by numerous lance-shaped
spine-tipped bracts. Blooms appear in late
May and early June and the seed in June or
July. Seeds are straw-coloraed and oblong.
Musk thistle is commonly found on
roadsides and waste places. It prefers moist,
bottomland soil, but can be found on drier
uplands also. It is an increasing problem at
all altitudes of the Mountain West up to
10,000 feet.

SANDBUR

■ *Cenchrus longispinus*
SANDBUR is a member of the Grass
family, Panicgrass tribe. It is a non-native
grass introduced from Europe and reproduces by seed. Stems are 8 inches to 3 feet
long, ascending or prostrate, and often form
mats. Early in the season the stems are erect
and later they are reclining and much
branched. The leaf sheaths are somewhat
flattened, very loose and smooth with hairy
margins. Leaf blades are flat, smooth,
green, and round on their margins. The
plant has 10 to 30 burs with each bur about
1/4 inch in diameter and thickly set with
stiff, barbed spines. Sandbur grows in
cultivated fields, roadsides and waste
places, but favors sandy soil. It is widespread from 3,500 to 6,500 feet.

DIFFUSE KNAPWEED

■ *Centaurea diffusa*
DIFFUSE KNAPWEED is a member
of the Aster family, Thistle tribe. Diffuse

knapweed was introduced from Europe and is a biennial or short lived perennial forb[1] which reproduces only by seed. The plant usually produces a single main, much-branched stem that is 1 1/2 to 3 feet tall. In young plants a basal rosette of leaves is present with each leaf divided into narrow segments. Young leaves have a thin nap. Stem leaves in the mature plant become much reduced, alternating 1 per node. Flowers are mostly white, sometimes purple, and are located on each branch tip. The bracts surrounding each flower bear 4 to 5 pairs of lateral spines and 1 terminal spine. Diffuse knapweed can be found in riparian areas, roadsides, waste areas, and in home gardens. It is poisonous to horses. It is a tough competitor on dry sites and rapidly invades and dominates disturbed areas. It is widespread and becoming a threat to the entire economy of the Mountain West.

In other Mountain West states, desirable native plants are being reduced as this plant spreads. It branches high on a 1-to 3-foot tall stem. Basal leaves are elliptic and up to 6 inches long. Stem leaves are needle-like. Flowering heads are solitary at end of branches, bracts are stiff and with dark spots tipped with a comb of fringe. The ray flowers are pink to purple or, rarely, white. Seeds are 1/8 inch long, tipped with a tuft of bristles. Herbicides are most effective when applied to the basal rosette in early spring.

RUSSIAN KNAPWEED

■ *Centaurea repens*
   RUSSIAN KNAPWEED is a member of the Aster family, Thistle tribe, and is a creeping perennial introduced from Europe. It reproduces by seeds and rhizomes. The vigorous roots are black. Rhizomes which are both vertical and horizontal in the soil, may or may not be black. The ridged stems are erect, rather stiff, branched, and 1 to 3 feet tall. Young stems are covered with soft gray hairs or nap. The upper leaves are small and narrow with broken edges. Leaves attached midway up the stem have slightly toothed margins, while basal leaves are deeply notched. The flowers are thistle-like, solitary, terminal, 1/3 to 1/2 inch in diameter and lavender to white. The plant flowers from June to August and seeds are

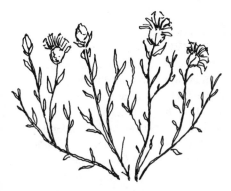

SPOTTED KNAPWEED

■ *Centaurea maculosa*
   SPOTTED KNAPWEED is a biennial or usually short-lived perennial with a stout taproot, introduced from Eurasia in alfalfa and clover seed. It is the number one weed problem on rangeland in Western Montana.

[1] *See Glossary*

produced in late summer to early fall. Russian knapweed is one of the most serious noxious weeds of the Mountain West. It is extremely poisonous to horses. It is very difficult to control or eradicate once it becomes established. It is distributed throughout the Mountain West from 4,500 to 7,500 feet.

CANADA THISTLE

■ *Cirsium arvense*

CANADA THISTLE is a member of the Aster family, Thistle tribe and it was introduced from Europe. It is a creeping perennial which reproduces by seeds and fleshy, horizontal roots. The erect stem is hollow, smooth and slightly hairy, 1 to 5 feet tall, simple, and branched at the top. The leaves are set close on the stem, slightly clasping, and dark green. Leaf shape varies widely, from oblong to lance-shaped. Sharp spines are numerous on the outer edges of the leaves and on the branches and main stem of the plant. The flowers are small and compact; about 3/4 inch or less in diameter, and light pink to rose purple in color. The seeds are oblong, flattened, dark brown and approximately 1/8 inch long. Canada thistle emerges in April or May. It is one of the most wide-spread and economically damaging of the noxious weeds of the Mountain West. Infestations are found in cultivated field,

riparian areas, rangeland, forest, lawns, and gardens. It is distributed from 4,000 to 9,5000 feet.

Canada thistle is a difficult plant to kill, but long years of research have found that the best time for a good kill is to apply glyphosate just as the plants' blooms are showing the typical lavender color. If the plant is among desirable plants, use the bottomless box method described earlier in the chapter.

BINDWEED

■ *Convolvulus arvensis*

BINDWEED is a member of the Morning-glory family. This creeping perennial was introduced from Europe. It reproduces by seeds and horizontal roots, which have been found at a depth of 20 feet. The stems are smooth, slender, slightly angled, 1 to 4 feet long, and spread thickly over the ground or twine around erect plants or other objects. The leaves are alternate, 1 to 2 inches long with great variation in shape. They are more or less arrow-shaped with spreading, pointed, or blunt lobes at the base. The flowers are bell or trumpet-shaped, white or pink, and about 3/4 to 1 inch wide. Bindweed is a problem throughout the Mountain West, and is one of the most competitive perennial weeds. Because a 2-or 3-year food supply is stored in the extensive underground root system, it is hard to kill by cultivation. Seeds can stay viable in the soil for up to 40 years. It is widespread throughout the Mountain West from 4,000 to 8,000 feet.

Bindweed can be killed totally if it is sprayed with glyphosate or 2,4-D in early winter after all other plants have been cut down by freezing weather. Strangely, it remains green, though a pale green, late in the season which means that it can still absorb the chemical. Spray the plants to the point of run-off on a warm, sunny November day. More plants may come up from seed the following spring, but you will eventually win the **bindweed** battle. If you live in an area where winter snow will cover the ground before November, use your own judgment as to the moment to spray after your first hard frost.

CRABGRASS

■ *Digitaria sanguinalis*
CRABGRASS is a member of the Grass family, Paniceae tribe. It is a tender annual spread by seed and stems which root at joints. It may be erect or prostrate. Leaves and stems sometimes hairy, wiry. Seed stalk produces 3 to many "fingers" maturing in late summer, often with a purple shading. Seed may remain dormant in soil for many years. Crabgrass is a problem only in domestic turfgrass, not in pastures or grasslands of the prairie. It is said to be

Lucifer's gift to lawns, diabolically adapted to survive in cultivated turf where it becomes a demon, running over the surface like a green tidal wave, robbing permanent grasses of water, nutrients, light, and space.

Crabgrass is the weed of cartoons and stand-up comics, but it is a nuisance, real and terrible, to the gardener who wants to see weedfree turf in his yard. Crabgrass most often invades a lawn that is cut too short, for it is an annual that needs light to germinate and the scalped lawn suits it very well. It germinates about April 15, and can, therefore, be controlled with a pre-emergent weed control chemical. A pre-emergent kills the seed before it can germinate. Pendimethylin is the pre-emergent ingredient of a dry mix fertilizer that can be spread over the area. This chemical will control **crabgrass** as well as **prostrate spurge.** The latter is a mat-like growth of very small leaves that eventually forms a rosette 6 inches or more wide.

FLIXWEED

■ *Descurainia sophia*
FLIXWEED is a member of the Mustard family, and is very similar to and often confused with Tansy Mustard, *Descurainia pinnata*. It is an introduced annual or winter annual which reproduces by seeds. The stem is erect, branched and 4 to 30 inches high. The leaves are alternate,

2 to 4 inches long, and dissected to give a lacy appearance. The stem and leaves are covered with fine hairs. The flowers are small, and pale yellow, and occur in small clusters at the tips of elongated racemes. The seed pods are 1/4 to 3/4 inches long and on a stalk. Tansy Mustard seed pods are shorter and fatter. Flixweed is widely distributed throughout the Mountain West up to 8,000 feet.

LEAFY SPURGE

■ *Euphorbia esula*
   LEAFY SPURGE is a member of the Spurge family and was introduced from Europe. It is a creeping perennial which reproduces by seed and extensive creeping roots. The roots can extend as deep as 30 feet and are extremely wide spreading. The shoots grow erect, 1 to 3 feet high, and are pale green and unbranched except for flower clusters. Leaves are alternate, narrowly linear with smooth margins, about 1/4 inch wide and 1 to 4 inches long. The small yellow-green flowers are enclosed by a pair of heart-shaped, yellowish-green bracts, which have the appearance of flowers. The pods are 3 seeded. The plant, including the root, has a milky latex that will seriously harm those with sensitive skin. This highly alkaline latex will take the hair from the legs and bodies of cattle. Leafy Spurge rivals the knapweeds in being the most serious noxious weed threat in the

Mountain West. It is adapted to a wide variety of habitats, wet and dry, and is very competitive with other plant species. It may exclude all other vegetation once it becomes established. Although it is unpalatable to cattle, sheep eat spurge without ill effects and do well on it and are, therefore, a useful cultural control tool.

PROSTRATE SPURGE

■ *Euphorbia maculata*
   PROSTRATE SPURGE is a member of the Euphorbiaceae family. It is an annual containing milky sap that exudes when you break a stem. Small leaves are simple, alternate or opposite, growing in clinging mats on the soil surface. Flowers are pink at leaf axils. It can smother turf, but is easily pulled. It is difficult to control with chemicals. See above for pendimethylin.

FOXTAIL BARLEY

■ *Hordeum jubatum*

FOXTAIL BARLEY is a member of the Grass family, Barley tribe. It is a native perennial grass which grows in thick tufts or bunches. The stems are smooth, up to 2 feet tall, erect, and sometimes reclining on the ground at their base. The leaf sheaths are smooth, loose, and 2-to 5-inches shorter than the internodes with erect, rough, narrow, flat, gray-green blades. Its heads or spikes are 2 to 4 inches long, nodding, with spreading, slender barbed awns each 1 to 1 1/2 inches long. The seeds are yellow, hairy at the tip, and about 1/8 inch long. Foxtail Barley is injurious to livestock, piercing gums and tongue, and causing ulcerations and swellings. It grows on any soil, wet or dry, and is a threat to lawns and gardens from 3,400 to 10,000 feet. The Japanese, however, grow and sell it in the cut flower trade.

KOCHIA

■ *Kochia scoparia*

KOCHIA is a member of the Goosefoot family and was introduced from Europe. It is an annual, reproducing by seed. The stems are erect, round, slender, pale green, much branched, and 1 to 6 feet high. Leaves are narrow, bright green, hairy, numerous, and attached directly to the stem. The upper leaves are narrow. The flowers are inconspicuous, in the axils of upper leaves. Seeds are about 1/16 inch long, wedge-shaped, dull brown and slightly ribbed. Kochia can be found in cultivated areas, roadsides, waste place, and home landscapes. In autumn, the plant may become red and later brown; it breaks away from the root, tumbling over the ground, and scattering large amounts of seed. It is found throughout the Mountain West up to 10,000 feet.

PRICKLY LETTUCE

■ *Lactuca serriola*

PRICKLY LETTUCE is an annual or winter annual, reproducing by seed. This introduced weed is a member of the Aster family and grows 2 to 6 feet tall. The stem is erect, round, smooth or sparingly prickly at the base. Its leaves are bluish green, and deeply lobed, with wavy, prickly toothed margins and white midribs. The leaves are also alternate, oblong, clasp the stem and are often twisted to a vertical position. The flowers are numerous and yellow. Prickly lettuce can be found in cultivated fields, roadside areas, waste places, and home landscapes from 4,5000 to 6,000 feet.

PERENNIAL PEPPER-GRASS aka TALL WHITETOP

■ *Lepidium latifolium*

PEPPER-GRASS is a member of the Mustard family. It was introduced from southern Europe and western Asia, and is a deep-rooted perennial plant with an extensive, vigorous creeping root system. It reproduces by seed and rootstalks. Perennial Pepper-Grass is similar to whitetop; however, it is taller, standing 3 to 5 feet and has a heavy, sometimes woody crown. The lower leaves are oblong with toothed margins and the upper leaves do not clasp the stem as in whitetop. Flowers are white. Perennial Pepper-Grass can be found along streambanks, in waste places, and in home landscapes. It has a limited range in north-central and south-central Colorado from 5,500 to 8,000 feet along the South Platte drainage and in the San Luis Valley. Thousands of acres have been taken over by this plant.

YELLOW TOADFLAX aka BUTTER AND EGGS

■ *Linaria vulgaris*

TOADFLAX resembles the snapdragon and is a member of the Figwort family. It was introduced from Europe as an ornamental and has now become a serious weed in mountain meadows. It is a perennial reproducing from seed as well as from underground rootstalks. The stems are from 8 inches to 2 feet tall and leafy. Leaves are pale green, alternate, narrow and pointed at both ends. The flowers are bright yellow with deep orange centers. These flowers are about an inch long and blossom in dense clusters along the stem as it lengthens and grows. The fruit is round, about 1/4 inch in diameter, brown and contains many seeds. Yellow Toadflax emerges in April and May and is adapted to both moist and dry habitats. It displaces desirable grasses and reduces ecological diversity, increases erosion, and is difficult to control throughout the Mountain West from 4,000 to 10,000 feet.

LOOSESTRIFE

■ *Lythrum salicaria*

LOOSESTRIFE is a North American and Old World native perennial herb with 4-angled stems 3 to 4 feet high; opposite and entire leaves. The flowers are pink, sometimes white or purple in a terminal leafy inflorescence. It is often planted in

perennial borders where moisture is not
lacking. It will be up to you to determine if
this plant is a weed in your area. On the
deserts of New Mexico, Utah, Nevada,
Western Colorado, or Utah, you will
probably never see it. In the over-watered
pastures of the 5-acre farmer near a city, it
may be abundant and should be eliminated.
It is easily pulled in moist ground. It's
pronged roots make it difficult to pull in dry
ground. Clip and collect the blooms and
wait for a rainy spell to eliminate it.

BLACK MEDIC

■ *Medicago lupulina*
   BLACK MEDIC is a member of the
Leguminosae family, subfamily *Faboideae*.
It is an annual or perennial with clover-like
foliage, long reclining stems, small yellow
flowers in axillary racemes. The fruit is
indehiscent, coiled in a spiral, and blackish
at maturity. The long taproot makes it easy
to pull if you soak the soil first.

MALLOW

■ *Malva neglecta*
   MALLOW is a member of the Mallow
family introduced from Europe, but is a
native of Asia. It is annual or biennial,
reproducing by seeds. Stems are round,
smooth, prostrate, 6 inches to 2 1/2 feet
long and spread over the ground in all
directions. The deep taproot forms quickly
after germination. Leaves are round or
kidney-shaped, slightly lobed with scalloped and toothed edges. Flowers are
clustered in leaf axils, pale blue to white,
sometimes pink. The fruit is about 15
kidney-shaped carpels arranged in a circle.
It ranges throughout the Mountain West
from 4,500 to 7.000 feet.

OXALIS

■ *Oxalis stricta*
   OXALIS or **WOODSORREL** or **SOUR
GRASS** is an annual of the Woodsorrel
family. With clover-like leaves, yellow
flowers, and a slender taproot, it is found
from 4,500 to 8,500 feet in moist places. It
is an attractive clover-like plant, 4 inches
high, that can be either deep red/purple or
light green. Both varieties have a yellow
bloom. The seed is expelled forcefully

which is why it spreads far and wide throughout areas that are cool, moist and sometimes shaded. It is easily pulled, but you may wish to use a 2-4-D solution that also contains dicamba and is labelled for **spurge, oxalis, and chickweed.** Read directions carefully and apply the chemical to the offending plants only.

PASTURE GRASSES are invasive in every home landscape. Much of the developed land in the Mountain West was once in pasture; therefore, the seeds have lain dormant a century or more, ready to germinate the moment you begin irrigating your new turfgrass seeding. We identify the majority as *Echinochloa crus-galli* **BARN-YARD GRASS;** *Eleusine indica* **GOOSEGRASS;** *Setaria viridis* **GREEN FOXTAIL;** *Muhlenbergia schreberi* **NIMBLEWILL.** They can be dug individually as they appear. Be ready to fill the hole with a piece of sod cut to fit the size of the hole so that new pasture grasses won't have the opportunity to germinate. You can also kill the clumps of pasture grass with an overdose of a high nitrogen fertilizer to burn out the offenders. Water well, then pour 1/2 cup of a fertilizer such as ammonium sulfate into the center of the clump. Water again gently to dissolve it. The clump will be seriously damaged or dead within two weeks.

ANNUAL BLUEGRASS is the short, light green annual grass that is usually a winter annual spreading to form large patches in the lawn. Fluffy seed heads appear in June, and the plants die out during hot weather; then seed germinates in the cool weather of fall. It is easily pulled, but the real answer to control is in a thick, impenetrable turf that is mowed at 2 1/2 inches or more to shade out the germinating seedlings.

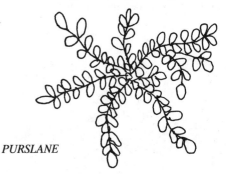

PURSLANE

■ *Portulaca oleracea*
Purslane, also called Pussley, is a member of the Purslane family. It is an annual succulent with diffuse stems and flat, shiny, thick fleshy leaves. Flowers are yellow. It is found throughout the Mountain West from 4,500 to 7,000 feet. It is somewhat allelopathic, killing its own species within a certain radius. Wait to pull it until just before it blooms. Never hoe it and leave the debris, for it quickly roots. Chemicals are useless against it.

RUSSIAN THISTLE

ANNUAL BLUEGRASS

■ *Salsola iberica*

RUSSIAN THISTLE is a member of the Goosefoot family. It was introduced from Russia and is an annual that reproduces by seed. It is a round, bushy, much-branched plant growing 1 to 3 1/2 feet high. The branches are slender, succulent when young and woody when mature. The leaves are alternate with the first being dark green, soft, slender, and 1 to 2 1/2 inches long, with 2 sharp-pointed bracts at the base. The flowers are small, inconspicuous, green-white or pink and are usually solitary in the leaf axils. Seeds are 1/16 inch in diameter and conical. At maturity the plant breaks off at the base and because of its round shape becomes a tumbleweed, scattering seeds for long distances. Russian thistle grows on dry plains in the Mountain West up to 8,500 feet.

VOLUNTEER OR WILD RYE

■ *Secale sp.*

WILD RYE is mostly an annual that is believed to be derived from *S. Montanum*, a perennial native in the mountains of southwestern Asia. The first blade is tall, narrow, and vertical. Blades are covered with short hairs and have prominent veining above and a midrib below. Sheaths are covered with short hairs. The spikes are 4 to 6 inches long, slender, and long bearded. Volunteer Rye has become a major problem

in wheat fields and has spread to cities and towns.

COMMON CHICKWEED

■ *Stelaria media*

Common Chickweed is an annual or winter annual of the *Caryophyllaceae* family with creeping stems that turn up at tips and root at joints. Numerous small leaves cover the ground like a green mat. Leaves are opposite, not more than 1/2 inch in length, and pointed. Flowers are small and white. Its low creeping habit makes mowing difficult. It can be controlled in late fall or early spring with 2,4-D plus dicamba. Do not spray if the plants are within the expected root run of desirable plants.

DANDELION

■ *Taraxacum officinale*

DANDELION is a member of the Composite family, Agoseris tribe. The pinnatifid to toothed leaves lie flat in a rosette, giving rise to a bare stemmed, hollow scape with flowers of yellow ray heads that quickly form reddish or greenish

161

achenes attached to white down dispersed by the wind. **Dandelion** succumbs quickly to 2,4-D if the foliage is young and the air temperature is above 70°F.

■ *Tribulus terrestris*
PUNCTUREVINE, GOATHEAD is a member of Zygophyllaceae (Caltrop) family. It is the annual, prostrate, mat-forming vine that punctures your bicycle tires, sticks in the soles of your running shoes, and vexes your pets to distraction. The leaves are opposite and divided into 4 to 8 pairs of leaflets. Flowers are yellow, borne in the leaf axils. The fruits have 5 sections, which, at maturity, break into structures that resemble a tack. Each section has 2 to 4 seeds. This weed was introduced from southern Europe, and is now widely scattered over the U.S.

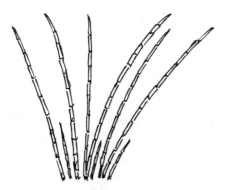

JOINTED GOATGRASS

■ *Triticum cylindricum*
JOINTED GOATGRASS is a member of the Grass family, Barley tribe. It is a non-native grass introduced from Turkey in the late 1800's. It is a winter annual, reproducing by seed and grows 15 to 30 inches tall in erect stems which branch at

the base to give the plant a tufted appearance. The leaf blades are 1/8 to 1/4 inch wide, usually smooth, with small auricles at the base. The root system is shallow and fibrous. The most distinguishing characteristic is the 2- to 4-inch jointed, cylindrical, balanced seed head. Seeds of Jointed Goatgrass are attached to their rachis segment, resembling a grain of wheat, and are shed in June and July.

Weeds are the enigma of horticulture. Weed specialists are few. The student finds them boring and the teacher at wit's end to find a way to make them interesting. The new gardener deals with them in a "let's get on with it" way. The advanced gardener slyly plots an overall battle plan that will get them out of his hair forever. He won't succeed, but the sharpening of his skills will keep the tyrant weed at bay.

Suggested Reading
"Weeds of the West" published by Western Society of Weed Science in cooperation with the Western United States Land Grant Universities Cooperative Extension Service; Whitson et al, revised 1992, University of Wyoming, Laramie WY.

Propagation

Plant propagation is the ancient art that formed the foundation of civilization. When hunters and gatherers began to lodge continuously in one place and to be mindful of the increase of plants from existing ones, propagation had its beginnings as a science. The first *Homo sapiens* to understand primary propagation began the long road toward the embodiment of *civilization*. They began by learning to plant and cultivate kinds of plants that fulfilled nutritional needs for themselves and their families. Survival depended upon plant improvement. Selection of a plant from the wild that displayed characteristics superior to its neighbors was probably the first farming activity. We see examples of these today in plants such as the lima bean, tomato, barley, and rice. The next step was selecting plants that arose as natural hybrids. They were carefully preserved and passed from father to son. Changes in chromosome numbers in these hybrids make them unique in cultivation because they have no single wild relative. Examples of these natural hybrids are: maize, wheat, tobacco, pear, and prune. The third plant improvement to be noticed and preserved were naturally occurring plant oddities and monstrosities, such as heading cabbage, broccoli, and Brussels sprouts.

None of these plants could have been preserved to be continued in cultivation through the generations, however, without the ingenuity and intelligence of the human species. Tentative attempts antedate recorded history. It is not by chance that the oldest cultivated crops known to mankind, the grape, olive, and fig, are also the easiest to propagate by hardwood cuttings. We know

■ It is not by chance that the oldest cultivated crops known to mankind, the grape, olive, and fig, are also the easiest to propagate by hardwood cuttings.

that not many eons passed before budding and grafting techniques were stumbled upon or craftily devised. We know that it was the nineteenth century before glass houses made possible the rooting of leafy cuttings. The twentieth century would see the discovery of root-inducing chemicals that revolutionized the nursery industry. Likewise, seed crops were revolutionized by the discovery of genetic principles that made possible the production of hybrid seed. The twenty-first century will see the common garden workshop use of tissue culture as a means of propagation.

Types of Propagation

There are three basic types of propagation: sexual, asexual, and apomixis.

Sexual

Seeds are the result of self-pollination and fertilization or by various sources of pollen carried by wind, and by bees and other insects. Therefore, the variability of seedlings with characteristics differing from the parent is sought after by the propagator who wishes to choose the seedling with superior or distinctive qualities. On the other hand, the variability of seedlings may lead to the gardener's disappointment. That's why saving seed is a chance you take with the vagaries of nature.

Asexual

Vegetative propagation eliminates the risk of variability because the cuttings, divisions, layers, etc. result in a plant exactly like the parent.

The greatest number of plants we enjoy today came to us by *natural selection*, not by breeding. A good example might be the Blue Spruce. In nature the greatest number of spruce in a forest are green. Yet you have seen one with blue foliage shine out on a hillside where it is growing among those that are green. Asexual plant propagation methods have allowed that one blue spruce to be multiplied by cuttings and sold thousands of times. We still call a spruce with very blue foliage a *shiner*.

Apomixis

In some species an asexual reproductive process takes place whereby no fertilization is needed. The embryo of the seed develops directly from an egg nucleus without fertilization. Apomixis is significant because it is a means of assuring uniformity in seed propagation. Many citrus species produce apomictic seedlings which are used as rootstocks. Apomixis is also significant because many virus diseases are not transmitted by seed. Growing apomictic seedlings provides a means of rejuvenating an old cultivar that has become infected with a virus disease.

Sexual Propagation

Seeds

Seeds are produced from plants in 2 classes: those from *angiosperms* which are vascular plants that bear seeds in a closed, protected ovary, such as a petunia or a maple tree; and those from *Gymnosperms* which are those that bear seeds that are open and unprotected by an ovary. The conifers are *gymnosperms*.

A seed is a fertilized ovule that contains all the genetic information to result in a plant with characteristics *similar* to the parent. The miracle that never fails to stir a gardener is that even the most microscopic seed contains the means to make a root that grows *down* and a shoot that grows up, and the whole process can take place in spite of or because of you and without your presence.

A seed has 3 basic parts: an embryo, an endosperm (a place to store food), and a covering for both. The embryo is an undeveloped plant that was created when male and female cells united during fertilization. It contains an *axis* with growing points at each end, 1 for the shoot and 1 for the root, and 1 or more seed leaves which are called *cotyledons*. The number of these depend upon the plant's hereditary direction. For example, monocotyledonous plants such as grasses or lilies have a single cotyledon. Dicotyledonous plants such as beans or pansies have 2. Gymnosperms, such as pines, may have as many as 15.

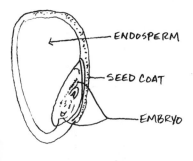

The corn seed. Embryo, endosperm, seed coat.

The endosperm contains a group of cells well filled with food, usually starches and sugars. In many dicotyledonous plants the endosperm is digested by the growing embryo before the seed is fully ripened. Only orchids do not produce seed with an endosperm; it is said that if one ever develops, orchids will blanket the earth.

The composition and structure of the seed coat varies with each species of plant.

Fruits

The fruit is the ripened ovary and any other structure that is closely associated with it. Many actual fruits are known as "seeds" and "vegetables" to the gardener and farmer. The kernel of corn, wheat, or oats, in addition to the so-called "seed" of the sunflower, carrot or parsnip is in reality a fruit containing 1 or 2 seeds. The edible portion of the latter 2 are roots. To many people a "fruit" implies a fleshy structure, which is true only part of the time.

To avoid confusion later, the types of seeds, together with the "fruits" that surround or contain them are listed below.

A few botanic/horticultural terms are necesary to understand the classification of seeds and fruits.

Carpel - One of the individual parts of a compound ovary.

Dehiscent - A fruit that opens naturally to release the enclosed seed or seeds. A violet seed capsule, for example, dehisces explosively. That's why violets proliferate uncontrollably.

Dry - Dry at maturity. For example, a bean pod is fleshy and edible when young, but becomes dry upon ripening.

Fleshy - Succulent and watery at maturity like an apple, cherry, peach, or tomato.

Indehiscent - A fruit that does not open to release the seed or seeds. Fleshy fruits are almost always indehiscent as are most dry 1-seeded fruits. The seed eventually may germinate and force its way through the walls of the fruit unless these have already decayed away. Examples are peach and plum. The 2 halves of each seed are held together by a gummy material containing *pectin*. During winter or seed stratification, the rain and melting snow break down the *pectin*, releasing the seed to germinate in spring.

Locule - 1 of the compartments of any ovary or fruit.

Classification of Seeds and Fruits Useful to a Gardener

Accessory - A fleshy fruit like a strawberry, made up of a succulent receptacle covered with several to many pistils, each forming a dry achene-like fruit.

Accessory Strawberry, achenes.

Achene - Dry indehiscent 1-seed fruit with the seed connected at only 1 point. The sunflower has achenes.

Aggregate - A fruit with the receptacle not fleshy. Examples are blackberry and raspberry.

Berry - a fleshy fruit formed from 1 compound ovary containing few to many seeds. Examples are currant, banana, grape.

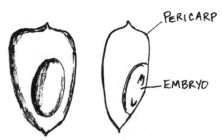

Caryopsis - Dry indehiscent 1-seeded fruit, the seed connected at all points. The corn kernel is a caryopsis.

Capsule - A dry dehiscent fruit made up of more than 1 carpel. It may be 1 celled with 1 line of dehiscence, but the placentae would be more than 1. This is a very common type of fruit, such as a poppy seed head.

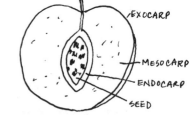

Drupe: A fleshy indehiscent fruit, 1 seeded, with a stony covering. Peaches, plums, and apricots are examples.

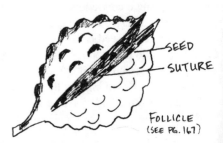

Follicle - A dry 1-celled, 1 carpel fruit splitting down 1 side only, as in the milkweed.

Nut - Dry indehiscent 1-seeded fruit with a hard coat. Too often a misused term.

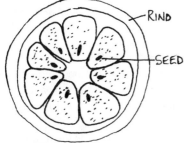

Hesperidium - A berry-like fruit with a thick leathery covering. An orange is a good example.

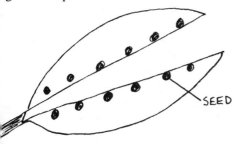

Legume - A dry 1-celled, one carpel fruit splitting down 2 sides. Often called a "pod."

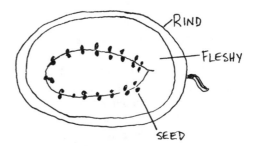

Pepo - Fleshy fruit formed from an inferior compound ovary with a hard tough outer wall. Watermelon and cucumber are examples.

Multiple - a fleshy fruit formed from several to many separate flowers. An example is the mulberry.

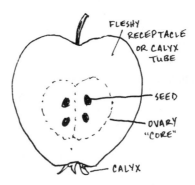

Pome - Fleshy fruit formed from an inferior compound ovary, the receptacle being the calyx tube of the flower, which becomes thick and fleshy. Apples and pears are pomes.

Spores

Reproduction by spores occurs in ferns. Two separate stages are involved. One is the asexual generation in which the plant has roots, stems and leaves called fronds. The other is the sexual generation in which the plant is a small inconspicuous oddity without roots, stems, or leaves and is called a *prothallium*. Spores are produced on the underside of the fronds in dusty clusters that appear brownish and often alarm the gardener who thinks the plant is diseased. Spores drop and dispurse and, under favorable conditions, undergo a pseudo-germination to produce the *prothallus*, which is a flat green plate of cells directly on the soil or media surface. This structure grows to about 1/4 inch in diameter before forming male and female parts on the underside. Sperm are discharged in the presence of water and are attracted to fuse with the egg. The developing embryo develops a foot through which it absorbs water and nutrients from the prothallus. A root is produced which grows downward. At the same time the primary leaf and stem develop into a rhizome from which fronds and more roots follow.

Seed Sources

The provenance of seed is important to you as a gardener only if you live in an area where -40° F is experienced often in the winter. It is reasonable to assume that seed collected in Texas will not have the same hardiness as that collected in Montana, yet many of the same plants grow in a range from Texas to Montana. Grasses, for example, are notable geographic wanderers. Those species grown in the warmer clime will not harden sufficiently in the fall to be grown in the colder climate. Even if the plant survives, the growth rate will be very slow. If you are buying seed of doubtful hardiness, ask the nursery to provide source information.

Germination of Seed

Seeds may be grouped into several classes in regard to the type and cause of germination and reasons for delayed germination.

Thermodormancy is the dormancy of seeds at temperatures over 75° F. It is usually associated with freshly harvested seeds, and can be overcome with after-ripening in dry storage. Lettuce, celery, endive, delphinium and other cool weather flowers are notably among this group. Dry chilling of freshly harvested seed at 41° to 50° F. for 24 hours will suffice. Seeds of some woody species are inhibited by high temperatures.

A hard seed coat prohibits or retards gaseous exchange of oxygen and carbon dioxide, and the absorption of water, and prevents the protrusion of the root and shoot. We can overcome the problems of penetrating the hard seed coat by using one or more methods of scarification, which follow:

1. Chemical: Immersion of the seed into sulfuric or other strong acids for periods ranging from 5 to 60 minutes. Though this method is often listed as if we all knew how to handle acid/water combinations, acid is extremely dangerous and this method is not recommended. Hydrogen peroxide, on the other hand, is typically found in every medicine cabinet. It can become a seed soak that is effective. Penstemon species will germinate after a soak of 1 hour in the latter.[1]

[1] *Information comes from Andrew Pierce, director of Horticulture and Program Development for Hudson Gardens (ten miles south of Denver) and former propagator and assistant director of Denver Botanic Gardens.*

2. Mechanical: Rubbing seed with an abrasive, such as sandpaper, emery boards, a file, or even mixing it with gravel in a concrete mixer.

3. Hot water soak for as long as it takes the water to cool.

The seed may contain an embryo that is undergoing a condition after maturity in which the seed will not germinate even though external conditions are favorable. The process of treating such seeds to promote germination is known as "after-ripening." There are many seeds having after-ripening requirements.

Stratification is the term used for the chemical changes that occur when seed embryos after-ripen in a cold, moist environment for periods ranging from 30 to 120 days. The temperature range is from 32° to 50°F. with the optimum for most seeds at 41°F. The quantity of moisture should be enough that the seed coat may absorb some water (*imbibition*), but not so much that the entrance of oxygen is prevented. The length of exposure will vary with each species and cultivar of plant. The media used for stratification can be sand, peatmoss, sawdust, vermiculite or perlite. Storage in a zip-closed bag placed in a household refrigerator is the usual method. You may wish to plant the seeds where they are to grow in the fall. They will stratify naturally over the winter and germinate in the spring.

The changes occuring inside a seed during stratification include increased water-absorbing power, increased enzyme activity, increased acidity, and gradual changes of the insoluble complex of stored materials into soluble, simpler substances.

The great majority of temperate zone deciduous trees and shrubs, fruit trees, nut species, and conifers respond well to stratification.[1]

Double-dormant seeds are those that require 2 years to germinate fully. They are characterized by having very hard seed coats as well as an internal dormancy of the embryo. A second cold period to simulate winter is necessary to after-ripen the section above the cotyledon leaves, known as the *epicotyl*, after the *radicle* (root) has already developed. **The double-dormant seed puts down a root the first growing season and a shoot appears the second growing season.** Examples of seeds with double-dormancy are: *Cotoneaster, Crataegus, Cornus, Sorbus, Symphoricarpus, Taxus, Tilia, Viburnum, Trillium,* and *Smilacina.*

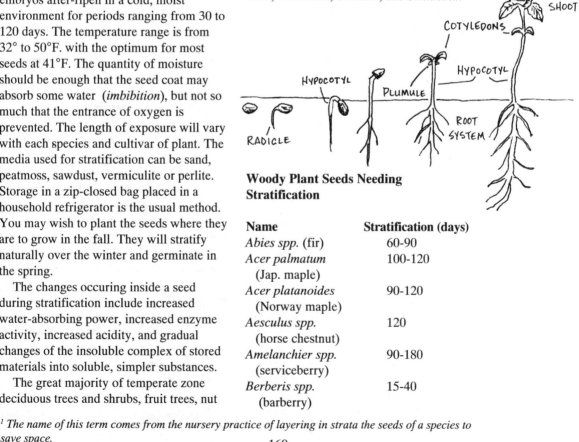

Woody Plant Seeds Needing Stratification

Name	Stratification (days)
Abies spp. (fir)	60-90
Acer palmatum (Jap. maple)	100-120
Acer platanoides (Norway maple)	90-120
Aesculus spp. (horse chestnut)	120
Amelanchier spp. (serviceberry)	90-180
Berberis spp. (barberry)	15-40

[1] *The name of this term comes from the nursery practice of layering in strata the seeds of a species to save space.*

Celastrus spp. (bittersweet)	90
Celtis spp. (hackberry)	60-90
Cladrastis lutea (yellow-wood)	90
Cornus kousa (Chinese dogwood)	120
Elaeagnus angustifolia (Russian olive)	90
Fraxinus spp. (ash)	30-90
Juglans nigra (black walnut)	60-120
Juniperus spp. (juniper)	90-120
Ligustrum spp. (privet)	60-90
Liriodendron tulipifera (tuliptree)	70
Lonicera (honeysuckle)	30-60
Malus spp. (apple)	30-90
Picea pungens (spruce)	30-90
Pinus spp. (pine)	30-90
Prunus spp. (plum, apricot, cherry, peach)	60-120
Pseudotsuga Menziesii (Douglas-fir)	30-60
Rosa spp. (rose)	120
Syringa vulgaris (lilac)	30-90

Seeds that require a high temperature followed by a low temperature are rare, but exist often enough to confound the gardener. In nature, ripe seeds fall to the ground where they are exposed to the warmth and moisture of late summer and fall, and are then subjected to chilling in winter. With this sequence, germination occurs the following spring. If this sequence of events does not occur, germination may be delayed until the second spring. In wild ginger, several lily species, herbaceous and tree peony, and a number of *Viburnum* only the radicle grows at high temperatures. Low temperatures must follow to after-ripen the epicotyl and cause

the shoot to grow. Two to 6 months at high temperatures are required for root growth before a chilling period of 1 to 4 months to induce shoots to appear.

Chemical Inhibitors

Seeds that exhibit *allelopathy* exude chemicals that prevent the germination of seeds nearby. Crested Wheat is a primary example of this trait. See Chapter 11 Ornamental Grasses.

During fruit and seed development many different chemicals accumulate in the fruit, seed coats, and the embryo. Especially in fleshy fruits, such as the orange, these chemicals prevent germination of the seed while it is within the fruit. The orange seeds are prevented from germinating, even though conditions are ideal, by the juice of the orange and its chemical inhibitors. Chemical inhibitors are especially impor-tant in desert ephemeral plants. The seeds fall and lodge in crevices and cracks in the desert "pavement," but only a strong downpour of rain will wash away the chemical inhibitors and allow the seed to germinate. A light shower will not. The perpetuation of the plant species is assured because the downpour has allowed enough water to accumulate to wash away the inhibiting chemicals, germinate the seed, and keep the plant in a moist environment as it grows, flowers, and sets seed once again. Thus, the cycle is complete.

Germination Requirements

1. A disease-free media that allows the seed to complete the process. Native soil, soilless media, sand, and vermicu-lite are examples.

2. Suitable temperature for the species. This can be from 41° to 86° F. Follow direction on seed packet or research the

requirement for each species in books and manuals.

3. An adequate supply of moisture. The seed imbibes water rapidly and in large quantities during germination.

4. An adequate supply of *oxygen*. The seeding medium should be well aerated. Seeds respire rapidly while germinating and need a large supply of oxygen.

5. Some seeds need light. Not bright sunlight, but subdued light from a thin covering of the seeding media. Lettuce and bluegrass are examples.

Seeding Method

Every nursery has a department displaying dozens of items that will help you successfully grow a plant from seed to maturity with success. Explore all of these and choose which suits you best. The following is only one proven method used by Cooperative Extension Master Gardeners since 1973. It is adapted for home use from a method known as the USDA Method which was devised by scientists at the USDA research laboratories in Beltsville, Maryland, for use by greenhouse growers.

Materials Needed:

  1/2 gal. milk carton
  ice pick
  knife with serrated edge
  waterproof tray, such as styrofoam meat tray, to fit milk carton
  bottle caps
  commercial potting soil
  vermiculite
  aluminum foil
  plastic bag
  soil thermometer
  misting bottle
  seeds of your choice

Step 1. Close open end of milk carton; cut top edge (white) away. Push flaps closed, no stapler needed.

Step 2. Slit edge of milk carton to form a lid.

Step 3. Pierce bottom side of carton with ice pick at for least 25 drainage holes.

Step 4. Fill with pasteurized (see below) soil mix, tamping lightly.

Step 5. Tamping will allow you to top with 1/2" of vermiculite.

Step 6. Water thoroughly.

Step 7. Sow seeds, choosing appropriate method of covering. Large seed is covered with additional vermiculite or perlite. Sow small seed on top of vermiculite without covering. The vermiculite or perlite will serve two functions: being sterile, it will prevent *damping off* disease, a fungal disease that often attacks seedlings. Both of these materials also will prevent *strangulation* of the stem. When the carton is placed in full sun, the dark soil mix attracts heat which can reach lethal levels on the tender stem of a seedling, causing a narrowing or cooking of the stem. The light-colored vermiculite or perlite reflects heat; thus the seedling stem is saved. Label carton and enter sowing data in notebook.

Step 8. Fold a sheet of aluminum foil over lid to act as reflector.

Step 9. Close lid unless the seed requires light for germination. Place styrofoam tray under carton, using 4 bottle caps as support to prevent carton from touching tray and to allow oxygen to enter drainage holes and excess water to escape.

Step 10. Enclose carton and tray in plastic bag, loosely folding over excess.

Step 11. Place carton where temperature on thermometer registers 75-80° F. If light is required for germination, place under a fluorescent light tube 16 hours per day. No additional watering will be necessary until after germination is complete. You may wish to invest in a rubber propagation mat, which has imbedded electric heating cables and an attached thermostat. These make for more precise temperature monitoring of seed cartons and are available at nurseries.

Step 12. Check carton daily. At the first sign of germination, remove carton from bag; adjust the lid so that it stands upright. Place carton and tray in a window with at least six hours of direct sunlight or one inch under florescent lights for sixteen hours daily. Germination will continue to progress. Enter germination data in notebook.

Step 13. Water only when soil and vermiculite feel dry when a finger is pressed into the mixture. Overwatering is a hazard to seedlings.

Step 14. The first pair of leaves is known as the *cotyledon* leaves or seed leaves and seldom resemble those that follow. When the second pair of leaves appears (known as *true* leaves), thin the seedlings to stand one inch apart. Transplant excess seedlings to more prepared milk cartons or the seedling container of your choice.

Step 15. Check the average date of the last frost in your area. One week before the expected transplanting date out-of-doors, begin *hardening-off* of the seedlings to get them accustomed to the great outdoors. Place them out-of-doors in sunlight, but out of wind for 15 minutes the first day; on the second day increase the time to 30 minutes; on succeeding days increase the time until the seedlings can stay out-of-doors overnight.

Step 16. Three days before the date of transplant, use a sharp knife to score through the soil in a block around and in between each plant. This will cut through tangled root hairs and force the seedlings to make new root hairs within their own soil block.

Step 17. Choose a cloudy day or early evening for the transplanting procedure. Set each soil block and plant at the same level it was growing previously. Water the seedlings gently with a starter solution of 1/4 tsp. of soluble fertilizer to 1 gallon of water. Mulch with one inch of dried grass clippings, straw, or any other light-colored material. Shade each seedling for a few days with a non-metal object, such as a berry basket, shingle, or flower pot that will prevent wind damage. Keep the seedlings moist but not soggy.

Step 18. Seeds that have been stratified can be started in the above method after the stratification period is completed.

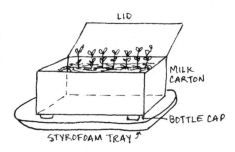

Asexual Propagation

Substances related to plant growth were discovered and replicated in 1934. *Auxins*, *cytokinens*, and *gibberellins* are hormones of the plant body that act similarly to hormones in the human body. Of these, auxins are the most important in relation to forming roots on cuttings. A naturally-occurring auxin, *indoleacetic acid*, has been synthesized and is most often used by the propagator, while synthetic auxins also used are: *naphthaleneacetic acid, indole-butyric acid,* and *2,4-dichlorophenoxyacetic acid.* Fortunately for the gardener, these jaw-breaker named compounds are sold in nurseries in powdered form, labelled "rooting pow-der."[1]

Making Cuttings

Your grandmother called them "slips." You will call them "cuttings" as you increase your stock of herbaceous and woody deciduous and evergreen plants. As you progress as a gardener, you will gain greater satisfaction with the use of the following procedures to propagate your most rare or unusual plants.

Materials Needed for Stem, Leaf, Heel, and Root Cuttings:

Clear plastic box with lid and drainage holes or a

Greenhouse flat or shallow fruit crate with clear plastic bonnet to affix over the top of the cuttings to increase relative humidity during the rooting process and

Equal parts mixture of perlite and vermiculite

Rooting hormone

Pencil

Sharp knife

Notebook and pen

Herbaceous Softwood Stem Cuttings

Step 1. Fill the container of your choice with an equal portions mixture of perlite and vermiculite.

Step 2. Herbaceous cuttings can be taken at any time of the plant's active growth. Cut 1/2 inch below a leaf node of the tip of a branch that is of typical diameter for the species, usually less than 1 feet to 2 inches in diameter. Taking a cutting from a stem that is very young will result in failure. The cause is thought to be related to juvenility.

Step 3. Strip leaves from lower end of stem that will be below media level.

Step 4. Dip cut end in saucer of powdered rooting hormone. Tap lightly to remove excess.

Step 5. Using a pencil, form holes in rows in the rooting media. Place each cutting in a hole, firming media around stem.

Step 6. Gently mist with warm water.

[1] *Both natural and synthetic hormones induce growth of root cuttings. Examples of trade names are: Rootone, Hormodine #1 and #2, Dip and Grow.*

Step 7.   Adjust cover or bonnet over cuttings and place in good light, but out of direct sun. Room temperature is adequate for rooting of most herbaceous cuttings.

Step 8.   Record date, species information in notebook.

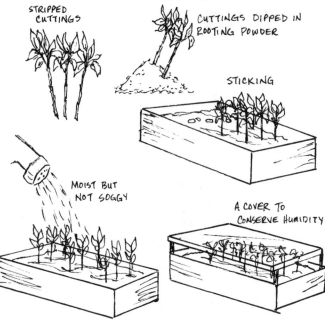

Cutting procedure.

Herbaceous Leaf Cuttings

Every beginning gardener has rooted a leaf of an African Violet successfully in a bit of water in a tumbler on the kitchen windowsill. It takes very little more doing for many other plant species to be rooted by leaf cuttings.

Meristem cells in a plant are those that are capable of dividing indefinitely and giving rise to the definitive cells of the species. Meristem cells may be located at many places throughout a plant. Even meristem cells located at the tip of a shoot make possible the growing of a new plant with roots, shoots, flowers, and seeds.

The meristematic tissue *sometimes* used in leaf cuttings is that of plants that display foliar embryos, which is a very early stage of leaf development. Examples of these are: *Bryophylum* species that have the ability to give rise to small plantlets in the notches of their leaf margin; *Tolmiea* (Piggy-back Plant) with miniature replicas of the parent riding on top of a leaf surface, or *Camptosorus* (walking fern) that forms root primordia at the tip of the leaf.

The meristematic tissue *most* often used in leaf cuttings is secondary meristem. Examples are *Begonia rex*, *Sedum*, *Saintpaulia*, *Sansevieria*, *Crassula*, and lilies that produce new plants from mature cells at the base of the leaf blade or from the petiole. In several species, such as the sweet potato (*Ipomeoa batata*), Peperomia, and Sedum, new roots and shoots form on callus tissue which develops over the cut surface through activity of secondary meritem tissue. Callus tissue on a plant resembles a callus on the human body — a thickening of cells.

Materials Needed:

Plastic box with lid and drainage holes. Fill it with a mixture of equal portions of moist perlite and vermiculite.

Clean, sharp knife or new razor blade
Rooting hormone powder
Plants of your choice

Step 1.   Select a leaf from African Violet or Streptocarpus that is young, but fully grown. Cut at the juncture with the root. Dip violet leaf in root hormone as above.

Step 2.   Lay the Streptocarpus leaf on a

flat surface and cut into several sections, each one or more inches long. Maintain polarity [1] by dipping the cut ends closest to the juncture with the root into rooting hormone. Tap to remove excess.

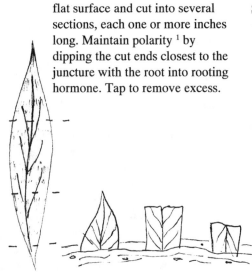

Strep cutting laid out to maintain polarity.

Step 3. Stick[1] cuttings into the rooting media in depressions made previously with a pencil or similar tool. Firm the media around the cutting.

Step 4. Close the lid and place the container in bright light, but not sunlight.

Step 5. Check media frequently for moisture. Keep it moist, but not soggy.

Step 6. After two or more weeks, tug gently on the cuttings to see if rooting has taken place. Some species may take several months to initiate roots.

Step 7. Pot up the rooted cuttings as soon as roots are strong. Waiting until roots become tangled does not do the plant a favor.

[1] See Glossary

Sticking Callused Cuttings

Step 1. Select a young, but fully grown leaf, from a *Sansevieria, Crassula, Sedum* or *Aloe*. Cut with clean, sharp knife or new razor blade at the juncture with the root or stem.

Step 2. Set the cut leaves aside in bright light in a place where you won't forget them, such as the kitchen counter. Check daily for a drying of the cut end and a pad of callus at the base of the leaf. This is an irregular mass of cells in various stages of hardening. The formation of callus and the formation of roots are independent of each other, but they often occur simultaneously.

Step 3. Proceed as with Step 3 above, taking care that the media is not too moist. Do not cover unless cuttings show signs of shriveling.

Why We Don't Root Cuttings In Water

Rooting cuttings in water initiates a root that will demand more water after it has been potted up in soil. It's an amateurish method that does not hold merit. *Coleus*, for example, will root with amazing speed in water, but the resultant plant will not be as healthy or vigorous as one rooted in a solid media.

Herbaceous Heel Cuttings

Some plant species can be propagated by leaf cuttings if a small portion of the stem is included. This is called a *heel*.

Step 1. Using a sharp clean knife or new razor blade, cut a leaf to include a small portion of the stem without cutting it through when the leaf is taken.

175

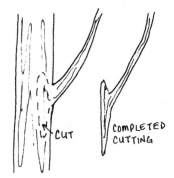

Completed heel cutting.

Step 2.   Proceed as above.

Herbaceous Root Cuttings

At times most gardeners have tried to save a plant that, from accident or weather-related event, has lost all its above-ground parts. Replanting the root or portion of root will sometimes result in the activation of a dormant bud along the root called an *adventitious* bud which will throw a shoot and the plant is thus saved. *Adventitious* buds are a back-up army of buds found along stems and sometimes roots that are capable to bursting forth when disaster has befallen the existing roots or shoots. They are seldom discernible to the naked eye, but can be excised when dissecting a stem or root. Evolution has given adventitious buds to the roots of a few plant species, but other plants have not evolved to this degree.

Experiment with root cuttings by exposing a portion of the root of a very young tree, such as a bird-planted seedling that appears in an unwanted place. Take the cutting from a root that is about the diameter of a pencil and 4 inches long. Dip the cut surfaces in rooting powder. Tap to dislodge excess. Lay the cutting on a bed of moist vermiculite as above and proceed as for Herbaceous Leaf

[1] *See Glossary*

Cuttings above. Portions of root from a *Dieffenbachia* are also good candidates for root cuttings. Often a year will pass before roots and shoots arise from the cutting.

If you wish to take root cuttings from an herbaceous perennial such as a *Phlox paniculata*, lift the plant in the fall to a tarp; wash the soil from the roots and cut off all the roots to two inches below the crown. Replant the crown, cutting back the stems and foliage to four inches. Cut the remaining large roots into two-inch lengths, dusting the cut surfaces with rooting hormone. Plant these by laying them on a bed of sand in a flat. Cover with one-half inch of sand. Keep moist in the cold frame over the winter. Transplant the rooted shoots the following spring.

Softwood Cuttings of Woody Plants

The list below is of woody trees and shrubs that can be propagated by softwood cuttings taken as the new growth hardens in late spring or early summer. Evergreens will seldom harden their new growth until August 1. If you fail with rooting a cutting, try again next season when the new growth snaps as you bend and break it.

Acer campestre	Hedge Maple
A. Ginnala	Amur Maple
A. griseum	Paperbark Maple
A. palmatum	Japanese Maple
A. rubrum	Red Maple
A. saccharum	Sugar Maple
Azalea spp.	Rhododendron spp.
Berberis spp.	Barberry
Buddleia spp.	Butterfly Bush
Caragana arborescens	Siberian Pea Shrub
Caryopteris x clandonensis	Bluebeard
Clematis spp.	Clematis
Cornus spp.	Dogwood
Cotoneaster spp.	Cotoneaster
Cytisus spp.	Broom
Deutzia spp.	Deutzia
Elaeagnus angustifolia	Russian Olive

by supplying constant moisture nding the stoma will allow it to make and roots more quickly. Still another l is to bathe the rows of cuttings in a st for one minute in five, or any nterval of time chosen by the ator. Perlite is usually chosen as the for sticking misted cuttings, for it more quickly than sand, vermiculite, other media. It is also less likely to infested with algae or bacterial ination. You can rig your own mist ation area out-of-doors or in a home ouse.

al Parts of a Mist System

lenoid valve to cut water on and off ally (a).

-hour timer so the mist is cut off at).

nterval timer to control the percent mist is on and off (c).

 nozzles vary from the deflection vhich has a flat surface, or the anvil roduces a fine mist spray when a zed stream of water is deflected The anvil nozzle performs best, but ce is yours. Use plastic pipe fitted rn-off valve.

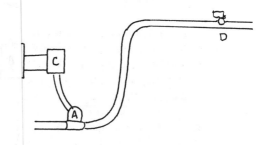

ient mist using a house plant can be injected directly into the Follow package directions. For low concentrations of nutrient, mist is applied at every misting period. For high concentrations, apply once or twice weekly during the evening. Leaf scorch, poor growth, dieback and the presence of mosses and liverworts over the surface of the medium are indications that the concentration of nutrient applied is too high.

Soil heating cables can be installed within the rooting medium for quick rooting in a greenhouse. Standard temperature at the base of the cuttings is 85°F., with 75° F. for the air.

Harden-off the cuttings by gradually decreasing the mist environment into the open and/or cooler greenhouse. Rapid deterioration will occur if the rooted plants are left under the mist too long. Premature leaf drop is a primary symptom.

Dorothy Wallace and Paula Boyle's Rose Cuttings

Gardeners with years of experience in rose growing are legion throughout the Mountain West. Dorothy Wallace (Mrs. Frank E.) of Longmont, CO and Paula Boyle (Mrs. Don) of Loveland, Colorado, are two experts who have devised a method of rooting rose cuttings successfully. Their methods follow.

Dorothy Wallace's Method For Propagating Hybrid Tea, Floribundas, Grandifloras and Shrub Roses

Prepare the soil where the cutting is to be planted with sphagnum peatmoss and compost. Roses dislike being transplanted, so it is best to root them in their permanent position. In September or early October cut a stem that has flowered and has six sets of leaflets. Cut off the spent bloom and remove the lower three leaflets, being careful not to damage nodes at the base of each leaf. See illustration.

Node at the base of a leaf.

Dust lower stem cuts with rooting compound before pushing into the prepared soil almost to the three leaves remaining at the top. Water well. Roots will form at the cuts below the soil. New growth will strike from the barely visible buds above the soil level.

Cover the cutting with a muddied two- or three quart jar. To "muddy" a jar, slosh a mixture of soil and water inside a jar until all the glass is coated. This will dim the light reaching the cutting and reduce shock. Invert the jar over the cutting, pressing the rim an inch or more into the soil. Mound soil around the jar to create a miniature greenhouse. Keep the jar in place and the soil around the cutting moist until spring. When temperature is above freezing in late April, you can peek to see if the cutting is growing. Replace the jar until danger of frost is past in May, or later in the high country. Once the jar is removed, protect the tender cutting by shading it with an inverted milk carton with top and one side removed so that it can be pushed into the soil to keep it upright in wind. Once the rose is hardened off and starts growing, this cardboard tent may be removed - probably in two to four weeks.

Paula Boyle's Method for Propagating Miniature Roses

In September make the cutting below a five-leaf leaflet on a stalk with a spent bloom. Cut off the spent bloom and the lower three leaves with manicure scissors. Wound the lower end of the stem slightly by scraping it with a credit card. This will activate adventitious buds to form roots. Dust the cuts as above with rooting hormone. "Stick" in a styrofoam drink cup that has drainage holes in the bottom and fill with vermiculite almost to the remaining leaves. Cover with a clear drink cup and place in a sunny window in a tuna can saucer for it to drain into. Keep moist. The cutting should be rooted by February and ready to pot up for indoor growing until it can be transplanted into its permanent growing position outdoors after the danger of last frost has passed.

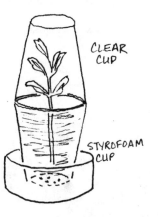

CLEAR CUP

STYROFOAM CUP

Paula's method of propagating mini roses.

Deciduous Hardwood Stem Cuttings

Increasing your trees and shrubs by cuttings is an economical and satisfying procedure. Usually, cuttings taken in autumn are the most sucessful. Wait until the tree's or shrub's leaves have dropped and the plant has gone dormant. Roots won't appear on your cuttings until next spring. Use the following procedure:

Step 1. Take cuttings from a mother plant that is healthy and vigorous. Look for one-year-old wood, which is lighter in color, but behind the wood made this year. The stem's thickness will vary with the species. Do not use pruning shears. A sharp knife will be less likely to squeeze closed the cells on the cut end. The most suitable cutting material will be determined by stem firmness. Those undesirably low in carbohydrates are soft and flexible, while those higher in carbos are firm and stiff, and break with a snap rather than bending.[1] Take damp paper towels or newspaper with you to the garden to wrap the cuttings as you take them.

Step 2. At your work table. Begin by discarding the top inch or two of each stem, since this does not contain enough stored plant nutrient to survive the winter. Then cut the stems into 6 to 9 inch pieces, each with 3 or 4 leaf nodes. Maintain polarity: Cuttings won't grow if planted upside down! Make the end closest to the

---

[1] *Take softwood cuttings of the genera* Prunus *and* Malus *in spring when new growth is about 2 inches long. Lilacs, also, will root only by making softwood cuttings during the short period in the spring when the shoots are several inches long and in active growth.*

soil a square cut, the top cut at a slant. Dip the square bottom ends into rooting hormone and tap off the excess.

Step 3. Bundle the cuttings with rubber bands, labelling each species. Make sure all the slanted top ends face the same way. Place the bundles with the bottom ends facing upward in boxes filled with slightly moist vermiculite, sawdust, or sand and store them in an unheated room that remains above freezing throughout the winter. This might be a crawl space in a basementless home, a garage, or root cellar. You can also store outdoors in a pit of well-drained soil below the frost line of your area. Stand the bundles upright with bottom end "up." This will increase the amount of callusing and root development, and also retard the growth of the tip end. If buds begin to grow before the roots are formed, they take up the nutrients that should go into a good root system. The top portion of the pit or box is warmest, which helps development of the callus and subsequent rooting. Cover with soil. Water lightly, but don't allow the soil to be soggy. Then cover the bundles with an insulating layer of leaves, roofing paper, or thick foam plastic. During the winter the cuttings (no matter where stored) will form callus tissue on the basal end.

Step 4. Retrieve the cuttings in March or April before leaves unfurl on outdoor shrubs and trees in spring.

Plant the cuttings in a prepared nursery area that is protected from wind, but in full sun. Dig a trench about three inches wide and as deep as your cuttings are tall. Place a two-inch layer of coarse sand or pea gravel in the bottom of the trench. Stick the cuttings about six inches apart, standing upright on the sand, and leaving only the top bud exposed above the top of the trench. Backfill with the excavated soil mixed with compost, sand or perlite to make a very light but moisture retentive mix. Firm the cuttings and water well.

Step 5. Give the nursery bed a cover of shade cloth, lattice, or ventilated fiberglass. Once the top buds break and new leaves form, remove the cover and feed monthly with a complete fertilizer. The rooted plantlets will be ready to be transplanted to their permanent position or potted up for your garden club's fund raiser by the following spring.

Rooted cuttings lined up in a trench ready to grow.

Evergreen Hardwood Cuttings

Follow Step 1. above, except that heel cuttings are taken by carving a small portion of stem to include with the stem; then make two or three longitudinal cuts along the stem down through the bark and into the wood. See illustration. Dip in rooting powder and tap off the excess. Reduce the tip to lessen the leaf surface. If possible, insure a better rate of success by using mist propagation. Then proceed to Steps 4. and 5. above. Broad-leaved evergreens will root more readily if the cuttings are taken after the spring flush of growth is complete and the wood is partially matured. Timing will vary from summer to fall. Narrow-leaved evergreen cuttings will be more successful if the cuttings are taken between from late fall and late winter.

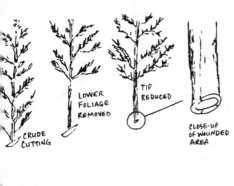

LOWER FOLIAGE REMOVED

TIP REDUCED

CRUDE CUTTING

CLOSE-UP OF WOUNDED AREA

Division

Division of herbaceous perennials is a spring and fall task for every gardener. The usual rule-of-thumb for timing is spring division for plants that bloom in midsummer to fall; and fall division for plants that bloom in spring. Only German bearded iris defy all reason. They prefer a mid-summer division right after they bloom. See Vol. I, pp. 53.

Indoor plants are divided when they outgrow their container.

Chrysanthemums are best transplanted annually in very early spring. Discard the woody center of the plant.

Perennials will often tell you when division is needed by failure to grow in the center of the clump, which becomes woody and tangled with roots. Dividing will stimulate a species toward more blooms, and you will soon set aside time each spring and fall to renew your perennial border.

A sharp spade, a plastic tarp, and two spading forks may be the only tools needed. Taking up the entire clump may not be an easy task, and you may need a long-handled shovel to lever the clump out of the soil and onto the tarp. Once there, you may wish to hose off the soil that is clinging to the roots so that you can better view the task ahead. Two forks prying opposite each other will do the least amount of damage to the roots, but use whatever works for you. A tangled mass of daylily roots may require an axe or chain saw to persuade them to part.

When re-setting a perennial, trim the roots to expose new, viable tissue. Give three divisions a triangular position, and you will see them fill in during the growing season and bloom with renewed vigor. An excess of plants can be potted as a gift or sold to support your gardening mania!

A few perennials resent transplanting by turning up their toes if disturbed, or at least languishing without bloom for several seasons. Rather than lifting the entire clump, trick the plant by slicing a triangular piece-of-pie with a sharp butcher knife. Fill in the excavation with a good soil mix and the plant may never miss the theft.

Perennials That Resent Transplanting

Aconitum napellus	Monkshood
Asclepias tuberosa	Butterfly Weed
Dictamnus albus	Gas Plant
Gypsophila paniculata	Baby's Breath
Helleborus niger	Christmas Rose
Limonium latifolium	Sea Lavender
Paeonia sp.	Peony
Polemonium caeruleum	Jacob's Ladder

See Vol. I, pp. 192 for a list of annuals that resent transplanting.

Daylily Stem Division

An interesting property of daylily bloom stalks is their ability to root. After your daylilies have bloomed, pinch off the spent blooms, grasp the stalk and pull. Quite often the stalk will separate from the crown with a snap, leaving you with a stalk with one strappy leaf. Cut off the stalk to the point of the strappy leaf and stick the remainder of the stalk as you would a cutting into good soil in sunlight where you want the division to grow. With moderate watering, roots will form at the base of the strappy leaf and the plant will put up several more leaves before the end of the season. The following season will see the division increase, with bloom the third year.

Division showing two forks prying apart.

Layering

With one or a few plants to be propagated, there are simpler methods that the gardener can employ with even less care and effort than with rooting cuttings. Layering gives an almost 100% success rate. If a shrub has handsome lower branches that are pliable enough to bend to the soil, you have a possible new plant that appears to be full grown in one growing season.

Tip Layering

Trailing blackberries, dewberries, and black and purple raspberries have arching stems that, by the end of summer, have touched the ground. At the point of contact, they form a ratoon, and roots will grow without your aid. However, help it make roots by making a hole three to four inches deep to bury the end of the shoot and cover it with soil. Darkness under the soil will encourage the process of etiolation in which a plant develops in the absence of light, which, together with moisture and soil contact, will cause it to develop roots. After three weeks, give each cane a tug to see if rooting has taken place. If it has, cut it away from the mother plant and transplant to its permanent location.

Tip layering can also be used with tip cuttings of annuals to be brought into the house before frost. Use the foam block method described in Chapter 12, Container Growing.

Simple Layering

To propagate a shrub by simple layering in early summer, bend down a branch to the ground; then cover the branch   with soil and place a heavy stone on top, leaving the tip exposed. The tip is then sharply bent to an upright position, which often cracks the stem. If it doesn't crack, wound it slightly on the underside where it will touch the soil. The sharp bending may be all that is necessary, but you may also use any of the pictured techniques to induce rooting. If rooting does not occur within a few weeks, you may apply indolebutyric acid rooting compound by mixing a pinch of the powder with a dab of lanolin and wiping the wounded area of the cutting. The stone serves three purposes: It holds the branch in close contact with the soil, it etiolates the layer by keeping it in darkness, it helps to conserve moisture under and around the layer.

The following spring the layer will be ready to cut away from the mother stock and planted in its permanent location or potted up for sale or give-away.

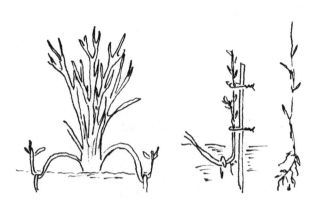

Simple Layer Propagation.

Compound or Serpentine Layering

This type of layering is useful when propagating vines, such as grape, *Wisteria, Clematis, Philodendron*, climbing rose, or honeysuckle. The etiolation of the portion of stem that is underground will allow roots to form. Cleanly cut the sections apart when rooting has been induced and pot up or plant in a permanent location.

Air Layering

Air layering is a highly overrated method of propagation. You might be better advised to buy a new plant. However, it is well to try all propagation methods if you are to progress as a gardener. If you come upon air layering in ancient books at the library, you will find it called *marcottage, gootee, circumposition, pot layerage,* or *Chinese layerage,* for air

BEFORE ROOTING   AFTER ROOTING

SHOOT BENT TO A SHARPE "V"

SHOOT CUT OR BROKEN ON LOWER SIDE

SHOOT CUT ON THE UPPER SIDE: TERMINAL END BROUGHT UPRIGHT BY TWISTING AT THE CUT

GIRDLING DONE BY REMOVING BARK FROM STEM

GIRDLING ACCOMPLISHED BY WRAPPING COPPER WIRE AROUND STEM

COPPER WIRE

Techniques used to stimulate rooting by simple layering.

layering is a very ancient method of propagation.

Step 1. Girdle or cut the bark of the stem at a point six to twelve inches or more from the tip end. Remove a narrow band from around the stem. Scrape the exposed surface with a credit card to insure removal of the phloem and cambium to retard healing.

Step 2. Apply a root-promoting powder such as indolebutyric acid by mixing it with lanolin as above directed and wiping the wounded area.

Step 3. Pack about two handfuls of slightly moistened sphagnum peatmoss around the wounded area, securing it with a sheet of polyethylene film plastic,which is gas permeable. Secure with electrical tape, beginning well above and below the points of contact with the remaining stem.

Step 4. Place the mother plant in bright light, not full sun. Daily misting will aid in keeping high humidity around the layer-in-progress.

Step 5. The plant can survive on its own and be cut away from the mother stock when rooting is visible through the plastic. Pot up in suitable media.

Mound Layering, also known as Stool Layering

This method of propagation is most often used in grower-nurseries in areas with long growing seasons, but it can also be used by a gardener as a means of fund raising. Large numbers of plants can be propagated from a single, mature (mother stock) shrub.

Step 1. Improve the soil around the mother-to-be with compost or weathered manure, for this plant will be highly stressed for the next several years.

Step 2. Before new growth starts in the spring, cut back the mother to an inch above the ground level. New shoots will break from this single stem. When new shoots are 3-5 inches high, mound loose soil or sawdust up to half their height.

Step 3. At the end of this growing season, roots will have formed at the base of each of the covered shoots.

Step 4. These rooted layers are cut below their new roots and potted up for sale or planted in the permanent location.

Step 5. The mother plant is now at the same stage as in Step 2. and ready for the process to be repeated the following spring.

Step 6. Maintain fertility of the soil around the mother plant with annual fertilization as each growing season begins.

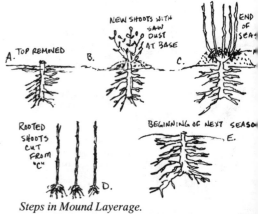

Steps in Mound Layerage.

Trench Layering

This method of layering is for the home nursery or home gardener who wants to start a number of plants for his own use or for sale. "Lining out " stock is purchased from a grower nursery. These are seed-grown trees and shrubs that are usually sold after one year of growth.

Step 1. Plant the plants at an angle of 30° about30 inches part in rows.

Step 2. The following spring before growth begins, dig a trench four to six inches deep in front of each plant in the row. Bend each plant to the ground until it is lying flat in the trench. Remove weak and crossing branches as well as weak wood. Head back each branch slightly.

Step 3. Pin down the entire plant securely with U-shaped pins.

Step 4. Firm soil in between branches and over the entire plant. Water well. Shoots will develop at buds over each of the branches

Step 5. At the end of the growing season, remove soil, cut rooted portions apart, and pot up or transplant to the permaent location.

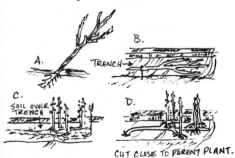

Natural Layering

Gardeners interested in propagation often overlook the plants that layer themselves naturally. Runners are specialized stems that develop from the axil of leaves at the crown of a plant. They then grow horizontally along the soil to root and form a new plant at a node. The best example is strawberry; others are *Ajuga* and *Vinca minor*.

A *stolon* is also a horizontally growing stem that produces adventitious roots when the stem contacts soil. The underground stem that produces the potato is a stolon.

An *offset* is a type of lateral branch that develops from the base of the main stem in some plants. It is generally thought of as a shortened, thickened stem of rosette appearance. The date palm and pineapple are both propagated from offsets.

A *sucker* is a shoot that arises from an adventitious bud on the root or from the vicinity of the crown.

Budding

Learning to bud and graft is the ultimate in the progress of a gardener to a horticulturist. This transition may seem difficult, but in actuality it is not. It is the curiosity, resolution, and willingness to try a new thing that sets you apart from those who only dabble in gardening.

The terms used in grafting and budding follow:

Stock (also called *rootstock* or *understock*) is the lower portion of the graft, which develops into the root system of the grafted plant. It may be a seedling, a rooted cutting, or a layered plant.

Scion (pronounced sigh-on) is the short piece of detached shoot containing one or several dormant buds, which, when united with the stock, becomes the upper portion of the graft, and from which will grow the stem and branches.

Cambium is a thin layer of cells of a

plant located between the bark (*phloem* - pronounced flo-em) and wood (*xylem* - pronounced zi-lem). Its cells are meristematic (capable of dividing). For a successful graft, it is essential that the cambium of the scion be placed in direct contact with the cambium of the stock.

Callus is a mass of leathery cells that develop from and around the wounded plant tissue. It occurs at the juncture of the graft union, arising from the living cells of both scion and stock. The production and the interlocking of these callus cells determine the success of the graft and begins the healing process.

The first step in budding is to become familiar with the meaning of the phrase "When the bark is slipping". If you are not of the Depression Era when children made their own whistle toys from small branches of willows, you are not familiar with bark that literally slips from the wood in late spring (south) or late summer (north). At the correct time of the season according to where you live, cut a small branch the diameter of your forefinger and attempt to peel the bark. If it slips off easily, the new growth is still active, and it's time to do some T-budding. If the bark adheres closely to the wood, budding time is past and you must wait till next season.

Step 1. Select plants of the same genus for budding. For example, a pear will not bud to a cherry, but a pear will bud to a pear, a cherry to a cherry, etc. There are some exceptions. These will be listed later. There are seven additional methods of budding. See references at the end of this chapter if you wish to investigate budding further.

Step 2. Prepare the stock first by locating a smooth section of bark on wood that is between one-quarter inch and one inch in diameter.

Step 3. Cut a "T"on the stock by first making a horizontal cut about 3/4 inch long through the bark; then complete the "T" by connecting a vertical cut about 1 1/2 inch long to the center of the "T."

Step 4. Select a leaf bud from the tree you wish to T-bud onto the stock. This bud is the scion. Cut off the leaf at the point where it connects to its stem; the leafstem will serve as a handle. The bud is in the cradle of the leafstem. It is doubtful that you would inadvertently select a flower bud, but check the bud to make sure it is an oval shaped leaf bud. Flower buds are round.

Step 5. Cut a portion of the wood surrounding the bud and leafstem to resemble a tiny shield with a square top and rounded bottom.

Step 6. Open the flaps of the "T" and slip the bud shield down inside the "T" until the horizontal cuts of the shield and the stock are evenly aligned.

Step 7. The bud union is then tightly tied with the wrapping material of your choice. Do not cover the bud. You can purchase budding rubber or raffia or cut a wide rubber band to wrap and tie around the union. Snip the binding material within a week or two after you are sure the union is complete because it will quickly choke a bud if left for too long.

If the union is successful, the leafstalk will drop away within about two weeks.

186

spring T-bud grafts will begin to grow quickly, while fall T-buds will grow the following spring. At the time growth begins for either, cut back the stock to just above the graft when the growth from the bud is about a foot long. The bud will become a new limb of the wanted variety. Rub off all buds on the stock below the bud and remove all suckers from the stock, should they occur.

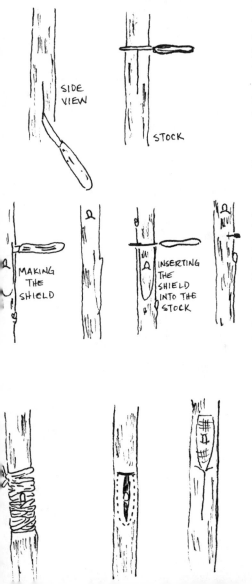

SIDE VIEW

STOCK

MAKING THE SHIELD

INSERTING THE SHIELD INTO THE STOCK

Double-Working

There are some rootstocks, ancient in use in fruit tree culture, that have the ability to accept a graft of a different genus. These are the exceptions mentioned earlier. Of these, quince(*Chaenomeles*) and privet (*Ligustrum*) are the more notable and most often used. Both of these genera are strong as well as disease and insect resistant. Incompatibility of these to some cultivars of desirable fruits creates a dilemma solved only by using an interstock that is compatible as a scion to the root as well as compatible as a stock to the desired scion. This is double-working, and it can be accomplished in one year, which is a cost-saving feat for the nurseryman.

For example, the flavorful 'Bartlett' pear is notorious for a weak root system. Quince roots are vigorous and cold hardy, but 'Bartlett' is incompatible with Quince. The 'Old Home' pear is compatible with Quince and 'Bartlett, although unflavorful and has a weak root. Quince is grown from seed one year. The following spring, a budless shield of the interstock cultivar 'Old Home' is inserted on the Quince. A standard shield of 'Bartlett' is inserted on the Quince just above the 'Old Home' shield. The Quince stock is removed above the 'Bartlett' bud as soon as the it has 'taken' and growth is about one foot long. If your previous attempts to update an an old orchard with new varieties, it usually means the scions are incompatible with your orchard stocks. Use the double-working method to overcome incompatibility.

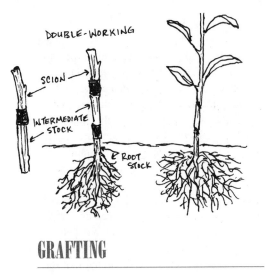

DOUBLE-WORKING

SCION

INTERMEDIATE STOCK

ROOT STOCK

GRAFTING

Grafting of plants can be traced back to the Chinese as early as 1000 B.C. Aristotle was familiar with the process, as were the early Romans. Paul the Apostle wrote of grafting the "good" and "wild" olive trees in Romans ll:17-24. As the Renaissance (1300-1500 A.D.) bloomed, plant explorers found large numbers of plants new to cultivation. Grafting was often a means of keeping them in good vigor. By the sixteenth century the cleft, whip, and approach grafts were in widespread use among gardeners in England. However, the reasons for the success of a graft union were not to be unravelled until early in the twentieth century.

There are five important requirements for a successful graft:

1. The stock and the scion must be compatible. Generally, the two must be closely related taxonomically.

2. The cambium of the scion must be in intimate contact with that of the stock. They can be held closely by wrapping, nailing, or the application of grafting wax.

3. The grafting operation must be done at a time when the stock and the scion are actively growing.

4. After the graft is made, all cut surfaces must be protected from dessication.

5. Care must be given the grafts until they can resume their former growth pattern.

Tools for grafting are simple and easily obtained. A thin-bladed, very sharp knife is the only blade necessary, but tool catalogs will show you many more types, few of which are useful. A single-edge razor blade, such as those used in beauty salons is an excellent substitute. Budding rubber, raffia, and grafting wax or asphalt wound compound are also useful.

Splice Graft

This graft is the simplest. Its only difficulty is in finding rootstock and scion that are almost identical in circumference so that the cambium of each will join perfectly.

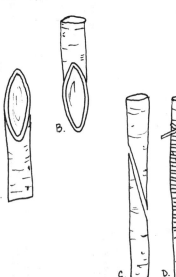

Splice Graft

Whip Graft

This graft is useful for small branches 1/4 to 1/2 inch in diameter. The cuts made at the top of the stock must match the cuts made in the scion.

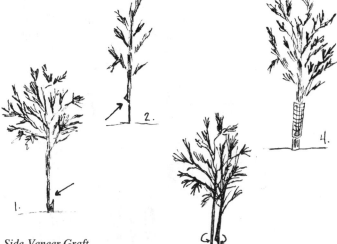

Approach Graft

Side-Veneer Graft

This graft is widely used to propagate narrow-leaf evergreen species that are difficult to start by cuttings. Rocky Mountain Juniper, which grows readily from seed, is most often used in the Mountain West as a rootstock for the exotic juniper species now being selected from Great Britain and Europe.

Whip Graft

Approach Graft

This graft is useful when two species are difficult to graft by other means. Two independently growing plants, usually in pots and standing side by side, are wounded so that cambium matches cambium. The two are tied with adhesive tape, and the whole union is sealed with grafting wax. After the graft union has healed, the stock plant is cut off *above* the graft, and the scion is severed from the parent plant just *below* the graft union.

Side-Veneer Graft

Bridge Graft

This graft is especially useful in the Mountain West for country dwellers who have damage by rabbits, porcupines, voles, elk, to the trunks of valuable trees. When trees are girdled, they are doomed to a slow death. Before undertaking what appears to be a difficult grafting procedure, be aware that your tree has a big root system waiting to grow and push up nutrients to the top. The only thing hindering this process is an ugly girdle. It's up to you to become the facilitator, to provide the bridge, to give your tree a new chance at life. The bridge graft is not nearly as difficult to perform as the drawing suggests. The work is most successful if performed in early spring just as you see buds swelling on your tree. If damage occurs in winter, keep the site of the girdle protected with aluminum foil, secured with electrical tape to keep the wound as moist as possible. As spring approaches, select scions from one-year old growth on the same tree or another that is of the same species and actively growing. The scions should be 1/4 to 1/2 inch in diameter. If necessary, wrap in moist paper towel; slip into a plastic bag and refrigerate until your tree is beginning to show swelling of buds. See illustration for the next steps in making the bridge graft.

Cleft Graft

This graft is the oldest known and has been pictured in ancient writings. It is useful in topworking (see below) and for smaller plants, such as grape vines, wisteria vines that are reluctant to bloom, and potted indoor plants.

Chances of success are best if cleft grafting is done in early spring just as the buds of the stock are beginning to swell, but before leaf break and active growth have started. One precaution is necessary before you start. The saw cuts you make must be at a *right angle* with the axis of the branch you are grafting. Slanting cuts will cause the scion to topple. If you do not own a steel wedge, remember that a wedge can be anything that will hold the cut open while to insert the scions. Improvise.

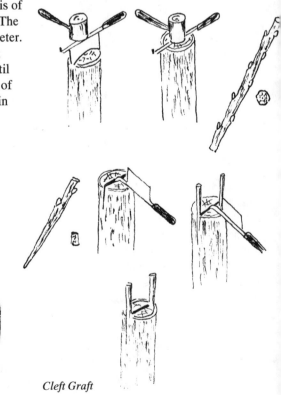

Bridge Graft   *Cleft Graft*

190

Topworking

Topworking is cleft grafting to change the top of an existing tree that is young and in good vigor. Apples, pears, and other flowering trees are good candidates. It is done in the spring when trees are dormant or shortly after buds swell. Three to five scaffold branches are chosen that are about 4 inches in diameter and close to the ground for convenience in making and checking the graft. Choose a cool, calm day when drying of the wounds will be minimal. The scions to be inserted on each branch should be less than 6 inches long. Nail a short piece of lath to the existing tree limb that is being grafted. When the scions begin to grow, tie them loosely to the lath to keep them from being whipped about in the wind.

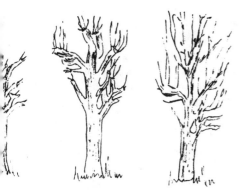

A mature pear has been topworked. One year later; six years later.

Checking Back

Budding and grafting take a considerable amount of time and thought. Keep copious records in a notebook. Don't walk away after the job is completed. Check back the following day to make sure the sealant has covered the surface. Check back in a week to see if the leaf stem of your T-bud efforts has fallen away. Check back within a month to slit the wrapping material so that it will fall away naturally. The following year the rootstock may put up suckers or shoots of its own. Remove these immediately. Budding and grafting is not for everyone, but if you try it, you'll soon be satisfied with your progress as a gardener.

Tissue Culture

(Also Called Micro-Propagation)

Tissue propagation is rapidly taking over the commercial production of new plants. Twyford Plant Laboratories, Inc., produces twenty-five million plants a year, and there are many more laboratories similarly engaged. It is not to be construed, however, that the hobby gardener should not have a tissue culture laboratory in the basement as a means of augmenting his/her income. A laboratory can be set up for about five thousand dollars. The output would be minimal but lucrative if the propagator concentrated on rare or difficult-to-propagate plants.

Tissue culture is the growth of a new plant from a single meristem in a test tube under very strictly sterile environs. For most species, the actively growing shoot tip is the source of tissue, but other tissues, such as bulb scale, leaf, root, stem, seedling, cotyledon, hypocotyl, rhizome tip, and flower bud can be used. Whatever plant part is used, it is called the *explant*.

Tissue culture provides two major benefits: a rapid clonal propagation, and the development, maintenance, and distribution of pathogen-free plantlets.

This section is not intended to give direction in tissue culture, which is at least a book-length topic. There are many readers who are completely familiar with the world of test tubes, petri dishes, sterile procedure, and laboratory equipment in general. If the possibilities entice you, consult the references at the end of the chapter for specifics in tissue culture.

The majority of readers will buy the results of tissue culture, which are called *propagules*. You will grow them like any rooted cutting. It is suggested that you plant them at first in a light, peat-based mix, either in a greenhouse or in sheltered rooting frames. Add a controlled-release fertilizer, such as Ozmacote, to provide continuous nutrition. Mist the propagules often for the first week. After establishment, the medium must be kept continuously damp. Transplant outdoors in their permanent location after hardening off.

Suggested Reading:

Plants From Test Tubes
1983, Lydiane Kyte,
Timber Press,
P.O. Box 1631,
Beaverton OR 97075.

The Reference Manual of Woody Plant Propagation
1987, Michael Dirr and Charles Heuser, Jr.,
Varsity Press, Inc.
P.O. Box 6301, Athens GA 30604.

Plant Propagation, Principles and Practices, 4th edition, 1989;
Hudson T. Hartmann and Dale E. Kester,
Prentice-Hall, Inc.,
Englewood Cliffs NJ.

Seeds of Woody Plants in the United States
Forest Service,
U.S. Department of Agriculture,
Agriculture Handbook No. 450,
available from Superintendent of Documents, U.S. Government Printing Office,
Washington DC 20402;
(price approx. $40.00)

Bulbs, Corms, Rhizomes and Tubers

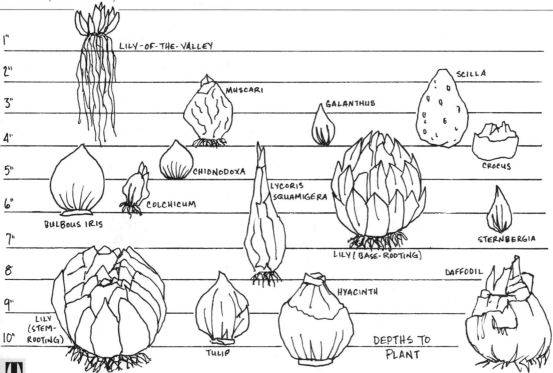

Labels in illustration: LILY-OF-THE-VALLEY · MUSCARI · SCILLA · GALANTHUS · CHIONODOXA · CROCUS · COLCHICUM · LYCORIS SQUAMIGERA · BULBOUS IRIS · STERNBERGIA · LILY (BASE-ROOTING) · DAFFODIL · HYACINTH · LILY (STEM-ROOTING) · TULIP · DEPTHS TO PLANT

Measurements on left axis: 1", 2", 3", 4", 5", 6", 7", 8", 9", 10"

The sale of bulbous plants has increased year by year until surely there is not a garden in which at least one species or another is represented. Where formerly all plants of this sort were imported from Holland, Belgium, France, or Japan, now the United States is a competitor to be reckoned with. With supermarket ease we use bulbs, corms, rhizomes, and tubers to complete or accent the main features of our garden. Before we begin the study of bulbous plants, a routine once-over of their anatomy is in order.

Bulbs, corms, and tubers are alike in one respect. They are all in reality *buds* or underground roots or stems bearing buds. They are in a state of dormancy waiting for the right season, the right temperature, the right amount of moisture to resume growth. They are self-contained: that is, each is the nucleus of an entire plant, not just part of a plant. They are constructed to serve as storehouses of food so as to support the plant as it begins a new season and until it can support itself. Hence, this explains how hyacinths can grow and bloom with roots in water and why the bare bulbs of *Colchicums* (fall-blooming crocus) are seen blooming atop the garden center counter or pinned to the kitchen curtain.

Unlike the buds of a tree or shrub which have a trunk or stem and connecting roots where food is stored, a bulb produces a new set of roots each year. Without getting into botanical technicalities, it may be explained that the food stored in any underground root, stem, or bud, to be carried over the dormant period as a reserve supply, is first taken up by the feeding roots, carried to the leaves to be elaborately processed, and then

■ *They are self-contained, that is, each is the nucleus of an entire plant, not just part of a plant.*

returned to dormant-season storage quarters. The foliage plays a very vital part in preparing the reserve food supply through photosynthesis.

The most important point for the gardener to remember is that the bulb, corm, or tuber cannot develop normally to its full size, or its maximum flower capacity, unless the leaves of the plant are allowed to complete their full growth under favorable conditions.Therefore, the leaves should not be cut off immediately after flowering.

Bulbs

An onion is the most familiar bulb. It is an underground stem, with a growing point surrounded by layers of stored food. These layers are held together by a base plate of hardened stem tissue. New roots develop around the base plate. During the growing season miniature bulbs or bulblets form around the base of the main bulb. *Bulbils* are tiny aerial bulbs which form along the stems or in the leaf axils of some species or varieties of species. *Lilium tigrinum* (tiger lily) regularly produces bulbils, as does the species tulip *Tulipa tarda*.

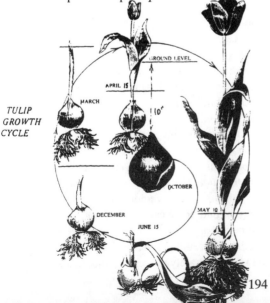

TULIP GROWTH CYCLE

Corms

A corm is a solid mass of fleshy tissue with buds showing up on top indicating where new growth will start. Unlike the bulb, the corm is only a temporary storehouse of food and withers and disintegrates as this food is used up. A new corm, sometimes 2 or more, forms on top of the old one. Gladiolus and crocus are typical corms. During the growing season, miniature corms called *cormels* form around the main corm's base.

CROCUS

Corm

GLADIOLUS

Tubers

A tuber is similar to a corm, but does not have a basal plate. It is a modified stem. The "eyes" of a tuber can be seen as the points where new growth will begin. Some tubers, such as potato, shrivel and disintegrate as the new plant matures. Typical tubers are caladium and tuberous begonia.

194

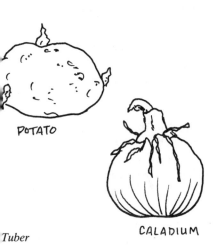

POTATO

Tuber

CALADIUM

Rhizomes

The rhizome is a half-way link between tubers and herbaceous perennial roots. It is a stem of solid tissue, but unlike bulbs and corms, it is elongated and sometimes branching. Roots develop along the lower surface, while leaves and flower stalks rise from buds (eyes) on the upper surface. Typical rhizomes are bearded iris, calla-lily, or the Rex begonia.

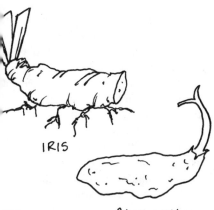

IRIS

Rhizome   CALLA-LILY·

WHERE WILD BULBS GROW

The majority of bulbs come from the 5 Mediterranean climates of the world:

coastal Chile, South Africa, coastal California and the lower portion of the Central Valley, the countries bordering the Mediterranean Sea, and portions of coastal Australia together with New Zealand. Add to that the famous English bluebells (*Hyacinthoides non-scriptus*) and you can find almost every genera in those areas.

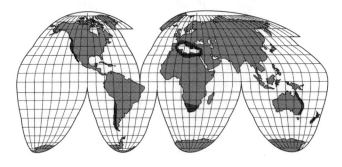

World map showing five Mediterranean climates.

Areas of lesser importance include New England for its trilliums and Japan and China for rare lilies. Mountain ranges the Alps, the Caucasus, the Tauros, the Hindu Kush, and the Tien Shan of Central Asia are also sites of our most exquisite bulbs growing wild.

Surviving the rigors of climate is only part of the game for bulbs growing wild. Grazing by animals and collecting by humans are the greatest threats. Grazing is very ancient; collecting is very recent and has by far the greater impact on world bulb populations. Make certain when buying bulbs that you buy from a reputable dealer who buys from a grower, not a collector.

Cultural Procedures for the Outdoor Culture of Bulbs, Corms, Tubers and Rhizomes*

Soil

The physical texure of soil is of far less importance for bulbs than for any other plant. With few exceptions, they will do well in heavy clay, loam, or sandy loam, provided the required nutrients are present. The medium sandy loam is ideal, and good drainage is required for all. A pH of 7.0 or more is their prime range, which is almost universal throughout the Mountain West.

Although poor drainage is not tolerated, water at the root level is. The bulb fields of Holland are maintained with a fixed water level at the root zone of the bulbs. For drainage problems, see Vol. I, Chapter 7, Plant Protection, Flood.

Exposure

The spring-flowering bulbs prefer full sun. The angle of the sun in late March, however, is still low on the horizon and not as strong as July sun. Deciduous trees are still bare and sunlight under them abounds so that bulbs planted here will prosper. Foliage and flowers will be strong if the trees are pruned up high enough for there to be strong light underneath. The bulb foliage will continue to function even when there is shade from the trees' new clothes.

Protection Techniques

It's not unusual to find Snowdrops blooming in January, or Daffodils weathering an April blizzard, but ice and wind cannot be tolerated. Protection by a low hedge, a solid fence, or a group of shrubs will often keep the bulbs from harm. There is no substitute, however, for the cardboard box, lightweight basket, or upturned flowerpot over the bulb plantings when severe weather threatens. Weights to hold these in place will be necessary also.

Groundcovers and mulches at least 6 inches deep are called for when you have planted a grouping of bulbs of doubtful hardiness or on the edge of the hardiness zone in which you live.

One of the most tolerant ground covers for bulb planting is *Lamium maculatum 'Silver Beacon' or 'White Nancy'*. The silver leaves and lavender or white blooms provide a background for the bulbs, but the protection from deep freezing of the soil is far more important. Mulches, such as pole peelings or shredded bark, will also prevent deep freezing, set off the blooms, and prevent spattering of mud from wind-driven rain.

Start With Good Bulbs

There are bargain bulbs and there are bulb bargains. The difference lies in how you percieve the result. If you will rise to the bait of "100 bulbs for $5" and be satisfied with scrawny foliage and here-and-there blooms, this bargain is for you. If, on the other hand, you are willing to wait till the end of the bulb-planting season when a garden center may have a surplus sale wherein you will be allowed to pick through the pile, risk unnamed or misnamed bulbs, and risk again getting them into the ground before the snow flies, then these bulb bargains are for you.

The one risk neither risk-taker should make is that of mail ordering bulbs. Until such time as bulb dealers understand the growing conditions of the Mountain West, the results of mail orders are too often too late for the price you pay. The increased costs of shipping add to the folly of mail

* The culture of forcing bulbs will be found in Chapter 16 "Indoor Plants".

order bulbs. Your local garden center or nursery will begin flying the familiar red and white Holland-Bulbs-Are-Here banner in early September. Buy then, if possible, for daffodils benefit greatly from a September planting and all will do better if planted then. When buying bulbs, qualities to look for are: size indicated is correct, firm, weight according to size, and appearance unblemished as to gouges and bruises.

Mail order bulbs seldom arrive until late October, and no amount of shouting over the phone, veiled and not-so-veiled threats of refusal of the shipment does any good. Apparently, the mail order nurseries are too large to cater to the whims of Mountain West gardeners. Your selection will be equally good at your local garden center or nursery. If you have need of a very rare bulb that your nursery does not handle, order from a mail-order source with the admonition "Will not be accepted if this order arrives later than _____."

Many bulbs will lose their skin, called the *tunic*, in shipping, but there should be no corky spots or fungus growths on the sides or on the base plate.

Planting

Soil preparation for bulb plantings is no different from that for vegetables or perennials. There are two precautions, however, regarding manure and compost. To bulbs, manure is an absolute abomination. It carries botrytis blight, which can wipe out a planting and walk over the fence to wipe out your neighbor's planting as well. Do not incrporate the soil with too much compost. One shovelful at the bottom of the planting hole may not seem like much, but it is best incoroporated into the backfill rather than risk the sogginess of the water-holding capacity of compost.

Instead, mix a few grains (about a teaspoon) of bulb fertilizer with the soil in the bottom of the hole. This is generally recognized as an analysis of 7-8-5 for the Dutch brand, and 4-12-8 for an American brand. Bone meal or wood ashes are not recommended. Bone meal is not what it used to be. Long ago it contained the nutrients of the entire animal carcass as it came from the rendering plant, but nowadays separate by-products are sold until the remaining bone meal is greatly diminished in value. Wood ashes are extremely alkaline, and though they are often a recommended addition of garden books written in the East, they are harmful to the soils of the Mountain West where alkalinity already abounds.

Planting depth is greater in the Mountain West than in other areas. For the major bulbs, hyacinths, daffodils, and tulips, the recommended depth of soil measured from the nose (tip) of the bulb to the soil surface is 10 inches! Add another inch for super large bulbs. For small bulbs, measure their diameter at their greatest girth and multiply by 4. For distance apart, 1 1/2 times the greatest girth will be sufficient. For the most natural effect, group a number of bulbs in each planting hole instead of single bulbs in rows. Watering-in[1] is imperative in the Mountain West. A long, dry autumn is not unusual, and the bulbs must have enough moisture to begin root growth immediately.

[1] *See Glossary.*

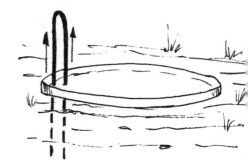

Bulb planting with a coffe can lid secured with a U-shaped pin.

The last operation in bulb planting is marking the site. If you have planted an entire bed of bulbs, you know where they are. But if you've planted groupings in between clumps of perennials, you are likely to step on the spot or accidentally dig into the group when you divide or cultivate the perennials. One solution is to use the pliable clear plastic top that comes with cans of coffee as a marker and label. The tops allow enough light to come through to keep the bulb tips growing, and give enough protection to the bulbs in the event of a deep freeze that would damage the growth tip. Label the planting by writing the name on the plastic lid with nursery pen marker. Secure the lids with a U-shaped pin that is normally used for pinning bed edging, or make your own from bending a coat hanger. Make the hole in the lid large enough so that the lid moves freely up and down the pin. You are assured that the growth strength of the bulbs will be strong enough to move the lid upward on the pin.

Bulbs Planted in Turf

The picturesque scene of flowering cherry trees with naturalized blooming bulbs in the grass beneath is in everyone's mind when we think of bulb planting. Many species succeed well in this setting. The most famous and most recorded is the bulb planting of Sandy Snyder of Littleton, Colorado, whose succesion of bloom of minor bulbs planted in a buffalo grass (*Buchloe dactyloides*) turf make a stunning display every spring[1]. By tossing bulbs onto the turf, you can locate the planting site for each. Use a long broad bulb-planting bit on your electric drill to plant the thousand or so bulbs necessary to make a showing of this type. Plan for a succession of bloom and for color coordination to set off each species. Take care to keep each species together for the best effect. Since Buffalo Grass does not green-up until after the bulbs bloom, and seldom attains a height higher than 4 inches, bulb foliage will mature without danger of being moved off.

[1] *"Splendor in the Grass" by Sandy Snyder, Fine Gardening Magazine May/June 1990.*

These minor bulbs will increase mightily as the years go by. The Buffalo grass is very drought-tolerant, which is an added benefit for these miniature bulbs, for almost all come from the Mediterranean climates where summer baking is the norm. They prosper under this regimen.

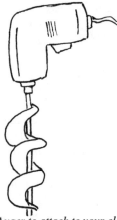

Bulb Planting Auger to attach to your electric drill.

Bulbs blooming in grass.

The First Spring

As spring approaches, the gardener is out there checking for the first pale yellow-green sprouts. Before they appear, remove large evergreen branches, but leave other mulches against the spring blizzard that inevitably blows in. Leave the plastic lid marker/labels until weather is more settled; then move the lid to the outside so that bulbs make normal growth and bloom. It stays in this place until after the foliage has ripened and been removed; then it is moved back to its former position of marking the bulbs below.

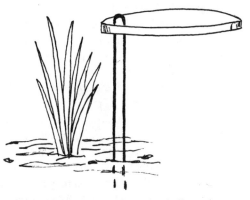

Move label lid to the outside so that bulbs make normal growth and bloom.

As the bulb foliage is emerging in spring, pour approximately a quart of liquid fertilizer over each planting. This can be any soluble fertilizer (such as RaPidGro or Miracle-Gro) that is higher in phosphorous (the middle number) than in nitrogen (the first number). This feeding is immediately available to each bulb. The bulbs you planted last fall have built-in blooms carefully cultivated by the grower and will put forth those blooms this spring, but you are fertilizing now to encourage the foliage to manufacture the food necessary for next years's blooms. Leave the mulch in place unless it is more than four inches deep; if so, thin it to four inches. It will conserve moisture and keep the soil cool, thus holding back the bulb growth until frost danger is lessened.

Gather A Bouquet

Cutting flowers for a bouquet requires some competence in judging when. Too often you prefer to enjoy the blooms from the dining room window before sallying forth to cut a few for the table. They are past their prime, quickly collapse and drop petals on the tablecloth during dinner. Cut when the buds are just beyond the tight bud stage, and when color is showing. Plunge immediately into deep, lukewarm fresh water and leave them for at least four hours in a very cool (40F.) dark place before arranging. If straight stems are imperative, stand them upright in the container and hold with crumpled wads of plastic; otherwise, they will curve gracefully, turning up at the bloom, a quality many arrangers want.

Blooms that are left in the garden to finish their alloted span must be snapped off as soon as they fade. You may also wish to cut the stem back to the first leaf for a neater look. Allowing spent blooms to form seed saps the strength of the bulb and many will not bloom next year. A few exceptions are: Blackberry lilies (*Belamcanda chinensis*), which form attractive, long-lasting black seed heads, and bearded iris stalks with seed heads that open to form a perfect "Star of Bethlehem" for your Christmas arrangement.

Care of Foliage

As stated previously, the foliage of all bulbous plants must be encouraged and maintained until it ripens and falls away naturally. All but daffodils are fairly swift in their departure, but the dafs become irksome in their durability. There are several ploys available. Plant groups of daffodils in front of daylilies. The strappy daylily foliage will blend with and cover that of the daffodils. Or plant the daffodils among the billowy types of perennials, such as Baby's Breath (*Gypsophila paniculata*) or Goatsbeard (*Aruncus dioicus*). Plant fast-growing annuals around the daffodil planting. Zinnias, petunias, annual dahlias, nicotiana, dusty miller, or cleome will quickly hide the ripening daffodil foliage. When the foliage has become lax and lays down on the ground, bundle it with a rubber band until it drops away.

Lifting and Replanting

Normal increase eventually creates an overcrowded planting that must be lifted and replanted. Some daffodils will increase outwardly in the planting hole so that they never need lifting. Tulips, hyacinths, and many others will crowd themselves into oblivion quickly. Hardy Amaryllis (*Lycoris squamigera*) and the *Colchicums* never need lifting or replanting.

Use the dying foliage of the spring-flowering bulbs to signal that the time has come. Dig straight down, beginning at a point 6 inches beyond the outermost dying foliage. Lift the clump to a waiting tarp and sit down to sort out the various sizes within the clump. Plant the prime-size bulbs back in the same location, but select a vegetable garden site for planting the smaller sizes that are the progeny of the prime-size. Keeping them separate as to species and color, plant them closely in close-together rows with a drip irrigation1 line running between. Plant them about the same depth as peas. They will be as big as onion sets by fall. Turn them out of the soil with a shovel and replant, deeper this time. By the third year they can be replanted in the garden. This is a good way to increase your bulb plantings two- or three-fold.

You may wish to plant tender bulbs among those that are hardy. A new device on the market, "Bulb Saver," is a mesh bag* in which you plant the tender bulbs. A permanent marker shows you where to pull the bag from the soil in fall without disturbing the hardy bulbs.

Pests and Diseases
See Chapters 4, and 5.

Precautions Against Pests and Diseases
Bulb plantings in the Mountain West endure the usual insects but, by and large, bulbous plants are less troubled by insects than are other plant groups. As with all pathological conditions, Mountain West plantings have almost no incidence of disease among bulbs. The dry air, good air circulation, species diversity, and overall thin plant cover in the wild are responsible.

Sanitation is just good housekeeping. Weeds are host to many insects and a few diseases. Keeping dead foliage and flowers removed and weeds under control will suffice to keep most pests, both plant and animal, at bay. Rodents in the Mountain West seldom bother bulb plantings, but if your bulbs are suspected victims, replant in cages made of hardware cloth or chicken wire.

* Bulb Savers, P.O. Box 3024, Princeton NY 08543

Observation is *seeing what you're looking at.* A stroll through the garden at evensong is a sedative toward composure after a hectic day. But take another walk at sunup or late afternoon when light rays are slanting into foliage and flower to illuminate bugs and bother. Your hands should be constantly busy turning over leaves, pushing aside foliage for a better look — in general, searching, searching. One swipe of your thumb over an insect population on the underside of a leaf may wipe out a potential problem later on. If this is the initial population cell of aphids, for example, you have then eliminated a whole host of time-consuming treatments in the future. Most diseases are well ensconced before their symptoms become apparent. Learn the look of each healthy leaf. Remove the entire plant if there is a suspicion. We have very few effective disease controls. Don't take a chance.

Application of the proper control for an out-of-hand problem is fast and easy if you have the equipment. Skimping on purchasing a good duster and quality insecticide sprayer will lead to an inordinate amount of time getting the job done and more expense in the long run.

Description And Culture of Bulbs, Corms, Rhizomes and Tubers

■ *Acidanthera bicolor*
PEACOCK ORCHID
A half-hardy, summer-flowering corm blooming white with dark markings on a 2 foot stem. Probably hardy in New Mexico and Southern Utah. Plant it with Delphinium 'Dwarf Blue Butterfly'.

■ *Allium spp.*
ORNAMENTAL ONION
The ornamental onions deserve more attention than they get. All are true bulbs that demand full sun, but are unfussy about soil and fertilization. Foliage is short-lived on most; so plant them where blooms with bare stems are masked with plants below. All should be deadheaded as they fade, for they seed around. A few of the most

attractive of the more than 600 species are:

A. acuminatum - 3-6 inches tall with deep pink flowers. For the rockery near *Dianthus* of complimentary shades of pink.

A. aflatuense - 3 feet. 4 to 5 inch globes of purple fade to mauve as these flowers last a month. Attractive planted among a creeping juniper groundcover.

A. christophii - fat 10 inch umbels of purple stars. The balloon-like flower heads are ethereal floating above early daylily foliage in May and June. Not reliably hardy. Mulch deeply.

A. moly - only 6-8 inches high, the yellow blooms are a loose umbel in late spring.

A. sphaerocephalum - 3 feet. The drumstick allium known for its deep purple, oval clusters in late June and early July. It combines well with Valerian (*Centranthus ruber)*, Catmint (Nepeta mussini) and *Erigeron* 'Pink Jewel'.

A. tuberosum - a rhizomatous East Asian native known to the herb garden as GARLIC CHIVES. The lacy white umbels on 3 foot stalks are long-lasting with the blue, white, and yellow border. Foliage is edible.

Oval clusters of the drumstick allium (A. sphaerocephalum) *rise above catmint, valerian, and* Erigeron *'Pink Jewel'.*

■ *Anemone blanda*
GRECIAN WIND FLOWER

These small tubers are hardy if planted in a sandy, humus-rich, well-drained soil in full sun or light shade. The 4 inch daisy flowers are more effective if planted in drifts of single colors rather than mixed.

Cultivars

'Blue Shades' - from pale to marine blue, these bloom at the same time as the miniature daffodils.

'Pink Star' - a lavender pink attractive with a deep purple early tulip.

'White Splendor' - the best of the lot, exquisite planted in masses with *Muscari* 'Blue Spike' or with red species tulips. Very strong grower.

A. sylvestris - An Old World species of glistening white fragrant cups on thin 1 foot stems in the moist woodland in a sunny spot. It blooms in spring and again in fall as weather cools. Expensive, but it spreads with moderate speed.

■ *Arisaema triphyllum*
JACK-IN-THE-PULPIT

A familiar tuberous woodland plant in the East, it can be naturalized in a moist western woodland if care is taken with deep incorporation of leaf mold and compost. An arum-type green bloom becomes bright red berries in fall. Buy a nursery propagated plant.

■ *Arum italicum*
WILD GINGER

Another showy tuberous woodland plant in a protected place. The broad white-marked leaves are followed by creamy-white jack-in-the-pulpit flowers. A string of bright red berries appears in fall.

■ *Begonia x Tuberhybrida*
BEGONIA, TUBEROUS

Tuberous begonias are included here because they are most often grown outdoors, though they are a tender tuber that requires digging and storage in winter.

The family *Begoniaceae* contains over a thousand species, none more tangled than the rhizomes, tubers, and bulbs. We deal here with the tubers for the most arbitrary of reasons — they are the most spectacular, most grown and most loved. Plant them indoors in March concave (indented) side up in a moist mixture of half sand, half sphagnum peatmoss at a very warm temperature (80°F). Plant them outdoors in mid-June when weather is settled. Grow them in bright shade in the ground in rich, moist soil, or in hanging baskets, window boxes, or patio pots where they are less likely to be attacked by slugs. Feed very sparingly with fish emulsion[1] because over-feeding will cause stem rot. Mist daily when Mountain West humidity drops below 20%. Let the first frost touch them; the foliage will fall away. Store in vermiculite as close to 50° as possible.

■ *B. x T. x camilliiflora*
BEGONIA, CAMELIA FLOWERED

Flowers of this begonia are double, petals are smooth-edged. Colors are delicate pastels to vibrant reds and yellows.

■ *B. x T.x crispa marginata*
BEGONIA, CRESTED

Flowers are single, white with a red border or gold with red border. Petals are ruffled, crested at the margins.

■ *B. x T.x fimbriata*
BEGONIA, CARNATION FLOWERED

Large double flowers with fringed petals that resemble a carnation. Colors as above.

■ *B. x T. x pendula*
CASCADE BEGONIA

These large pendulous begonias are suitable for hanging baskets hung high, for their flowers cannot be appreciated except when viewed from below. Size of flowers is slightly smaller than carnation flowered cultivars. Colors as above.

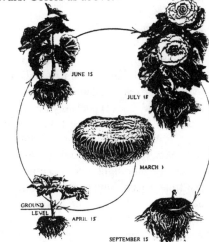

Life Cyle of Tuberous Begonia

■ *Belamcanda chinensis*
BLACKBERRY LILY

Red-spotted orange flowers brighten this lily's place in the bright sun of the perennial border. The flowers that resemble gladiolus are followed by shiny black seed heads prized for fall arrangements.

■ *Brodiaea sp.* See *Triteleia laxa*

These native American corms are growing throughout the Mountain West despite their tenderness reported in cata-

---

[1] *Recommendation of Gayle Zweck, Longmont CO, who is an expert with tuberous begonias.*

logs. The starry blue flowers are borne in umbels in June.

Cultivar

'Queen Fabiola' - violet-blue umbels in June.

'Lactea' - white

■ *Bulbocodium vernum*
SPRING MEADOW SAFFRON

A strange woolly corm of the Lily family that produces lavender-pink blooms in very early spring. Especially effective in the rock garden nestled in a pocket between rocks.

■ *Caladium x hortulanum*
ANGEL WINGS

Tender tubers grown for their colorful elephant-ear foliage. In March place tubers in waxed boxes (available at supermarkets as "chicken" boxes) packed with sphagnum peatmoss. Place in very warm environment to 85°F. When roots appear, pot them up in rich loam, one to each 6 inch plastic pot. Give very good light indoors until danger of last frost is past. Sink pots in the shade garden so that the rims are above the soil surface. Keep the soil moist; mist in hot weather; mulch the tops of the pots with pole peelings to thwart slugs. In fall, reduce water to force dormancy; cut them back BEFORE frost and store them in their pots in a warm place above 55°. If the tubers are chilled, they will not grow the following season.

■ *Calochortus Nuttallii*
SEGO LILY, MARIPOSA LILY

A corm that forms hillsides of bloom in early summer throughout the Mountain West. The delicate waving cups of white or pale lavender with a yellow throat seem too frail to survive their rugged environment, yet they appear each summer, multiplying

rapidly. Never try to dig these in the wild. It is unlawful and you won't be successful anyway. The tiny corm can be as much as 6 feet below the soil surface. If you must have this plant, collect a *few* seeds with permission of the land owner in late July, sowing immediately 2 inches deep in your favorite seed media. Allow the seed pot to stratify by remaining outdoors. It may be a year before germination takes place, and three or four years to achieve a corm large enough to plant in its permanent location.

■ *Camassia Quamash*
CAMASS, QUAMASH

This native of Oregon, Montana, Idaho, and British Columbia is a good bridge of bloom between tulips and the early perennials. It needs a deep, rich soil in sun or part shade. Strappy foliage, 3 foot stems bearing long-lasting China-blue racemes. Take care not to disturb it, and don't be too quick to deadhead. It will seed around.

■ *C. leichtlinii*
Cultivar

'Caerulea' - soft rich blue.

■ *Canna x generalis*
GARDEN CANNA

A thick, branching, tender rhizome enjoying new popularity after its decline from the days early in the century when their predictable planting made them known as "railroad station orchids." Now that stiff, round flower beds embellished with an iron deer are banished, Cannas have taken their place in groups in the middle of the border. Blazing red is not the only color choice offered. Pale salmon, gold, pink and white are available, some with bronzy leaves. See culture as for Tuberous Begonias. Set started rhizomes 3 to 4 inches deep in rich

oil in full sun when weather is reliably
warm. Fertilize once during the growing
season with 5-10-5. After first frost, cut
stems to within 6 inches of the root; store
pot clumps *upside down* at 50°to 60° in a
place where there is some light. In March,
divide the rhizomes, leaving several eyes on
each and start in flats as before.

Chionodoxa luciliae
GLORY-OF-THE-SNOW

An indispensible minor bulb with 6 inch
starry blue flowers shading to white at the
center. Planted in fall at 3 to 4 inches deep,
they will colonize to form wide permanent
swaths. Combines well with yellow
Doronicum cordatum. See Vol. 1, p. 174.

Colchicum autumnale
MEADOW SAFFRON

A charming little bulb with lavender blue
flowers that appear bare-stemmed in
September. The strappy foliage appears in
spring and disappears quickly. Plant with
purple mums.

Colocasia esculenta
ELEPHANT EAR

An ornamental form of the food *taro* in
the tropics. The enormous deep green
leaves with purple veins and midrib are
decorative in a bog or as a focal point of a
garden pool. Full shade needed. Culture as
for Tuberous Begonia.

Convallaria majalis
LILY OF THE VALLEY

A rhizome with buds on the top called
"pips." Wide very dark green basal foliage
with 6 inch bare stems of one-sided
racemes of white (or sometimes pink) bells
of delicious fragrance. To some, spring
doesn't start till a tiny nosegay of Lily of
the Valley graces the breakfast table. Plant
rhizomes in fall in rich, damp soil in partial
shade. Leave undisturbed, but give an
annual application of weathered manure.

■ *Crocosmia x crocosmiiflora*
MONTEBRETIA

A small corm with brilliant red gladiolus-
like funnel flowers that is enjoying unex-
pected hardiness in the Mountain West.
Culture is that of gladiolus, except that
lifting seems unnecessary. The corms
multiply quickly to give a colorful blaze of
red in August. Give protection of rockery
plus evergreen boughs in winter.

■ *Crocus spp.*
CROCUS, SPRING FLOWERING

The traditional harbinger of spring that
newspaper photographer interns are sent to
shoot. Familiarity does not breed contempt,
however. The welcome 4 inch clusters of
flower spathes begin with early species in
February and continue through April with
Dutch species. The tunicate corms are
planted 3 to 4 inches deep in fall in full sun.
Especially important is selection of a spot
of sandy soil protected from wind. Sandy
soil is their preference. Fertilization is not.
Keep them on the lean side. House finches
will attack crocus, especially the early-
blooming yellow species.

C. biflorus alexandri - white with purple
feathering.

C. corsicus - lilac striped with purple.

■ *C. chrysanthus*
SNOW CROCUS (very early)
Cultivars

'Advance' - peachy yellow or blue/
violet.

'Blue Peter' - soft blue with gold throat.

'Eyecatcher' - white with purple.

'Lady Killer' - pointed petals of deep purple, edged white

C. etruscus 'Zwannenburg' - lilac.

C. imperati - 'DeJager' - amber yellow, purple marks.

C. korolkowii - bronze speckled brown.

C. susianus - 'Cloth of Gold' - yellow/mahogany.

C. tomasinianus ''Roseus' -rosy lilac to silver gray.

C. vernus - good for naturalizing in the grass.

DUTCH CROCUS
Cultivars

'Enchantress' - light purple.

'Haarlem Gem - violet with gray.

'Paulus Potter' - deep pink.

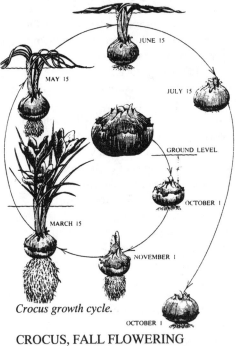

Crocus growth cycle.

CROCUS, FALL FLOWERING
Fall Flowering

C. asturicus - dark violet blooms in October.

C. cancellatus albus - pure white bloom in September.

C. sativus - the saffron crocus grown for the stigma, which is pulled for use as food coloring and flavoring. Should be lifted and divided every three years. Not easy.

■ *Cyclamen spp.*
PERSIAN VIOLET

The tiny, hardy rock garden *Cyclamen* is a miniature of the florist gift plant. Choose a site that has morning sun or day-long dappled shade. Soil is humus-rich, but well-drained. The reniform, marbled leaves appear in late summer, followed by flowers that twist and arch their petals backward in shades of carmine and dark to light pink. Set out growing plants in spring or fall. Plant dormant tubers in July or August so that the tops are about 2 inches underground. *Cyclamen* has an annoying habit of remaining dormant for a year, sometimes more. If you cannot distinguish top from bottom of the tuber, take a stab at it and wish yourself luck. Often there is not a vestige of a root hair to give you a clue.

C. ciliclium - deep pink to white flowers in late autumn. Prefers autumn sun.

C. hederifolium (neopolitanum) - pink or white flower in autumn.

C. purpurascens - fragrant rose flowers in late summer; leaves green or variegated; plant is never dormant. Prefers full shade.

■ DAFFODIL
See *Narcissus*

■ *Dahlia spp.*
DAHLIA

Dahlias are tubers of the *Helianthus* tribe of composites native to the New World. They come to us from the mountains of Mexico, Central America, and

Columbia. If you visit these regions, you will find them growing on volcanic soils amid the sprawl of other thick vegetation at the edge of the forest or in a clearing where there is sunlight.

The American Dahlia Society recognizes 17 groups of cultivars, based on the morphology of the head and the flowers. If you delve for long into growing these flowers of brilliant colors and fanciful shapes, you will eventually want to show them at flower shows. Avail yourself of the educational booklets of the American Dahlia Society to learn which classes to enter.

Dahlia Classes
Formal Decorative
Informal Decorative
Semi-Cactus
Straight Cactus
Lacinated
Ball
Miniature Ball
Pompon
Waterlily

Other Types:
Anemone Flowering
Collarette
Mignon Single
Novelty Types
Orchid Flowering
Peony Flowering
Single Types

Growing Dahlias

The first rule in dahlia growing is to give them full sun. Of all bulbous plants, they are the least tolerant of shade. Soil can be variable, with the ideal being a sandy clay loam, with a pH of 6.5.

Except for the low-growing species, Dahlias require staking, the least visible the better. Don and Carroll McAllister have come up with an ideal method of support. Using a medium-size tomato cage, Don cuts off the leg prongs with a heavy-duty wire-cutting tool. He places them in a vice and bends one end of each into a hook which will act as anchors for the cage.

Tubers are planted 4 to 6 inches deep with a tablespoon of triple superphosphate mixed with the soil at the bottom of the hole. Place 1 or 2 tubers in the hole, making sure that the neck of the tuber is pointing upward. Cover with 2 to 3 inches of soil and water lightly to settle. Keep soil slightly moist. As the shoots grow, gradually add soil until the hole is nearly filled, leaving a shallow "dish" to hold water for the thirsty dahlia.

Limit each plant to a single main shoot!

The cage is set over the planted tuber at planting time with the top circle of wire directly on the soil and circling the tuber. The hooks secure the cage strongly into the soil. Slip one of the plastic sleeves over the tomato cage. These are sold separately at garden centers and manufactured specifically to fit the cages. Leave it on until the second week of June. They protect the plant from hail, wind, and frost up until May or June. This method of dahlia caging is a giant step forward in plant support. It eliminates tying, becomes invisible, and supports the plant WITHOUT FAIL. the dahlia now becomes a civilized candidate for inclusion in the perennial border.

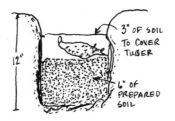

Tuber in planting hole.

About mid-June when the tubers will be about 1 foot tall, pinch out the central shoot at a node. For beginners this is a psychological barrier, but just DO IT! The plants will encourage side shoote and promote more and larger blooms.

The Dahlia staked with a now invisible tomato cage.

SUMMER CULTURAL PROCEDURES

A period of hot, dry weather in summer seems to occur throughout the Mountain West, with varying degrees of length. As experienced gardeners know, hot weather and mites go hand in hand, and nothing is as devastating to dahlias as red spider mite. Don and Carroll have found that overhead sprinkler irrigation every 7-10 days usually conquers the mite problem. However, this method ceases just as soon as the blooms begin to open, and they switch to drip irrigation. If the mite problem or any other insect problem continues, they use a mixture of Orthonix, malathion and half-strength Diazinon as a spray program. If you use Diazinon in tablet form, 1/2 tablet is sufficient for 50-75 plants. More will burn leaves.

When the plants are 8 to 10 Inches tall, Don tills in a 5-10-10 or 10-20-20 fertilizer and again when first buds appear. The drip irrigation system can also deliver nutrients, using 20-20-20 soluble formula, followed by a high phosphorous root-and-bloom formula. Dahlias also respond well to foliar feeding.

WINTER STORAGE

Don and Carroll leave the tubers in the ground as long as possible after frost has blackened the foliage, for this is the time when the eyes are developing. Then they cut down the foliage to about 8 inches and dig the clumps, being careful to dig 1 foot away and in a circle around the clump. They wash the soil off the tubers with a strong stream of water from the hose.

A warm day is chosen for the task of cutting the tubers from the main stem. The most important part of this task is to make sure that a portion of the neck stem is included in the cut. Next year's growth will come from the eyes on the neck of the tuber. The tuber is only a storage unit.The neck determines the strength of the growth for next season, not the size of the tuber.

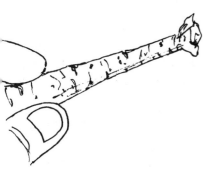

Cut tuber showing neck portion.

Write the name of the variety on the tuber with a nursery pen.

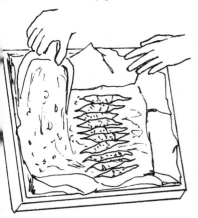

Getting Dahlias Ready for Winter.

STORAGE OF TUBERS

Don and Carroll store their tubers in dry sphagnum peatmoss or vermiculite to which they add a few shakes of bulb and gladiolus dust. The storage unit they use is the waxed cardboard box in which chickens are

delivered to the supermarket. The boxes cannot be used again for the same purpose, and recycling them is an added life to their indestructibility. Styrofoam picnic hampers with a few drilled holes for air circulation are also ideal containers. The tubers give their moisture to the media; then the media gives it back in January as the tubers dry.

Place the boxes in an area as close to 40°-42°F. as you can find. Crawl spaces where forced air furnaces are installed will guarantee failure. Unheated garages where temperatures don't drop to freezing are tops on the list. Check the containers monthly. Mist if shriveling. Discard if rotting.

■ *Eranthis hyemalis*
WINTER ACONITE

Northern gardeners appreciate these minor bulbs more than other gardeners because they are usually first to bloom after a long winter and as the snow melts, often blooming at the same time as Snow Drops.

Plant the tiny raisin-like tubers as soon as you find them in garden centers, for their shelf-life is not long. Plant them in drifts under deciduous trees where their bright yellow blooms and ruff of decorative foliage will poke out of fallen leaves. Dappled shade in summer suits them best.

■ *Eremerus spp.*
DESERT CANDLE, FOXTAIL LILY

The striking wands of midsummer bloom on the desert candle come from thick, fibrous roots, but are included here because the gardening public has accorded them rhizome status. Perhaps in an eon or two they will be. They will almost always achieve a height of 5 to 6 feet. Give them a site against a dark background, such as evergreens. They need the evergreens for wind protection, as well. The problem then

209

becomes one of carving a small space for them among the evergreen roots. Use a small pruning saw or heavy loppers. Fill an eight-inch plastic pot with rich soil and place the thick rhizome just below the surface. Cover and water well. Lower the container into the hole you have created among the evergreen roots. Fill in around it with good soil. Mark it well, for it will need extra water and an application every spring of a slow-release fertilizer such as Osmacote 14-14-14. Mulch heavily with evergreen boughs in winter, uncovering only very slowly as spring advances. Be ready to protect against late frosts.

E. bungei - 30 inches with primrose yellow flowers in midsummer.

E. himalaecus - Pure white spires

E. rubustus - Tallest and most spectacular. Early June bloom in pink.

E. Ruiter-hybrid 'Bird of Paradise' - Rose-pink blooms with orange and yellow highlights. 6 feet.

E. x Shelford - Available in separate colors, red, pink, orange, yellow, and white. 3 to 4 feet.

■ *Erythronium grandiflorum*
DOGTOOTH VIOLET, TROUT LILY

Natives of the Mountain West, these delicate, recurved petal flowers are sought after on spring and summer wild flower hikes. Never dig them from the wild, but collect a seed or two if you see the seeds forming in July. Plant the resultant tiny corms by fall in their permanent place in a shaded woodland garden or at waterside.

■ *Fritillaria spp.*
GUINEA HEN FLOWER, MISSION BELLS, CHECKERBOARD LILY

These appealing minor bulbs range from 3 inches to 3 feet in height. Six species are small; only *F. imperialis* stands alone in the giant category.

F. acmopetala - Purple and olive green bells; 18 inches.

F. affinis - Greenish with yellow and purple checks. 18 inches.

F. assyrica - Lime green with violet checks. 18 inches.

F. biflora - MISSION BELLS - native of Montana, Colorado, Wyoming; one to six nodding bells on 15 inch stems. Brownish orange with a white patch at the throat. They like clay soil, summer baking (withhold water).

F. imperialis - CROWN IMPERIAL - The prestige addition to any garden with very good drainage. First introduced by Clusius to the imperial court of 16th century Europe, this plant is sensational. Each 3 foot stem supports a leafy crown from which brilliantly colored bells hang. Golden stamens protrude to complete the image of bells.

Cultivars

'Aurora' - Deep reddish orange.

'Lutea Maxima' - Lemon yellow.

'Premier' - Soft orange; the largest of all.

'Rubra Maxima' - Rich burnt-orange with a purple stripe.

F. meleagris - Nodding bells in shades of purple and white checks; 10 inches.

■ *Galanthus nivalis*
SNOWDROP

An unbeatable herald of approaching spring, the snowdrop's nodding white bells have a green dot at the tip of each petal. They can withstand numerous snows; prefer a heavy soil in part shade. Your planting will spread gradually by seeding around.

G. elwesii - Giant Snowdrop that is the first to bloom.

G. nivalis - Plant generously with Winter Aconites.

■ *Gladiolus x hortulanus*
GLADIOLUS

A corm universally grown in the floriculture industry. Though gladiolus are usually grown in rows in the vegetable garden, a few gardeners have grown them in groups where they become accents of color for 3 or more months in the perennial border. They prefer a deep, sandy loam where drip or furrow irrigation is available, as overhead watering destroys the blooms. Hill them up as you would corn to keep the bloom stalks straight. Their greatest need for nutrients is during the flowering period and afterward when they are forming new corms.

In purchasing "Glad" corms, very large, flat corms with a concave upper surface are inferior to much smaller ones with a greater vertical diameter. These are termed "high-crowned." Corms of 1 1/2 inches and 1 1/4 inches will produce satisfactory flower spikes. Smaller corms will require another growing season to become a size that will bloom. In planting, cover with 3 to 4 inches of soil. If foliage appears diseased during the growing season, rogue these corms at once. Experience in growing will determine your need to control thrips. See Chapter 4, Insects.

Dig the corms after the first frost, leaving foliage attached. Place them in a cool, dry place to dry off. The foliage will drop away. Discard the old shriveled corm. Drop each variety of the new corms into a wide-meshed nylon bag such as those in which grapes are sold; then drop this bag into a paper bag of bulb dust. Shake a few times, and remove the nylon bag; remove the bulbs to storage bags of mesh, old nylon hosiery, or cheesecloth. Hang the bags where the temperature is as near 40°F as possible and where air circulates freely. Dust again in the same manner as above at planting time.

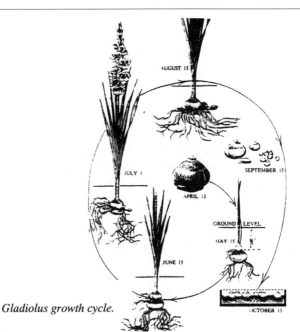

Gladiolus growth cycle.

■ *Hyacinthus amethystinus*
ALPINE HYACINTH

The alpine hyacinth of the Spanish Pyrenees has lavender-blue flowers on 6 inch arched stems in late spring. Plant in gritty soil in the rockery. Naturalizes.

■ *H. orientalis*
DUTCH HYACINTH

The familiar, sweet-scented club-like blooms often seen in formal plantings. Give them a chance in groups of 5 in the front of the south-facing shrub border.
Cultivars
'City of Haarlem' - Soft primrose yellow
'Delft Blue' - Large spike of soft lilac-blue.
'Pink Pearl' - Deep rose pink.

■ *Hyacinthoides hispanica*
SPANISH BLUEBELLS

The stout 12 inch stems produce scentless blue bells in woodland gardens in late May right after the late tulips.

211

■ *H. non-scriptus*
ENGLISH BLUEBELLS
   Similar to above, graceful, arching;
excellent under flowering crabapple trees.

■ *Ipheion uniflorum*
SPRING STAR FLOWER
   This tough little bulb produces delicate
China-blue star flowers in very early spring
on 8 inch stems above onion-scented blue-
green foliage. Plant it in the rock garden, at
the front of the border or under trees. Set 3
inches deep in any soil, for it is not fussy. It
is completely dormant in summer. Plant
annuals over it, but try not to disturb it.

■ *Iris spp., bulbous*
   After the Dutch iris, which are of recent
origin, iris are separated into four groups of
smooth bulbs: Juno (*I.bucharica*), English
(*I. Xiphioides*), and Spanish (*I. xiphium),*
and the reticulate bulbs which are typically
netted[1.] .
   Plant all of them in well-drained sandy
soil in full sun and leave undisturbed.
Mulch with evergreen boughs after the first
frost.

■ *Iris x hybrida*
DUTCH IRIS
   Recently hybridized by breeding Spanish
iris with many other species. Delight in a
soil that becomes dry in summer, known as
"summer baking." Bloom in early summer.
Cultivars
   'Imperator' - Indigo blue with golden
blotch.
   'Lemon Queen' - Sulphur-yellow.
   'White Superior' - Snowy white with
yellow stripe.

■ *I. bucharica*
JUNO IRIS
   Five to seven flowers of creamy white
with patches of yellow on the falls on each
stem in May. Prefers dry soil.

■ *I. xiphioides*
ENGLISH IRIS
   Probably imported by Portuguese
seamen; the mid-summer blooms are large
and substantial. They prefer a damp, semi-
shaded location in acid soil.
Cultivars
   'Isabella' - Lilac rose.
   'Mont Blanc' - White.
   'Queen of the Blues' - Indigo blue.

■ *I. xiphium*
SPANISH IRIS
   Bloom at midsummer in shades of
yellow, bronze and purple. Mulch heavily
in winter.

■ *IRIS, RHIZOMATOUS*

■ *I. brevicaulis*
LOUSIANA IRIS
   The use of iris in the garden was
considered strictly a Northern delight until
the 1920's when three multi-colored species
of iris were discovered in the Louisiana Delta
country. It was assumed these would be
tender, but they have been grown successfully all over the Northern Hemisphere. Give
them bog conditions with rich soil in full sun
and three inches of mulch in winter. Fertilize
annually with acid fertilizer.
Cultivars
   'Black Gamecock' - Velvety blue-black.
   'Dixie Deb' - Sulphur yellow; prolific.

[1] *See Glossary.*

I. x germanica
BEARDED IRIS

The most widely planted of all iris, the German Bearded Iris rhizomes represent the late spring garden more than any other. Because they are easily hybridized and propagated, there are thousands from which to choose. For planting direction, see Vol. I, p. 53. The rhizomes multiply so freely that division will be necessary about every four years. Give them full sun, fertilization with 10-10-10 and copious water at the beginning of the growing season. Then slack off on the water after buds are formed. Daily deadheading will keep the stalks in bloom for nearly four weeks. They prefer dryer feet for the remainder of the growing season. After the bloom season or at the end of the growing season, do not cut the foliage down or cut in any way. It remains over winter looking tatty, but necessary for the health and vigor of the rhizomes. Cut back browned foliage in spring.

The most prestigious award for Bearded Iris is the Dykes Medal. The following are a few of the most popular iris that have won the Dykes Medal:

> Beverly Sills
> Bride's Halo
> Dusky Challenger
> Jesse's Song
> Kilt Lilt
> Pink Taffeta
> Raspberry Ripples
> Song of Norway
> Stepping Out
> Victoria Falls

I. pallida
ORRIS

Fragrant lavender-blue blooms above stout foliage. Grown for the production of orris, used in perfumery. Moist site.

Cultivar

'Variegata' - Leaves of brilliant yellow, green, and white. Stunning at stream or poolside.

I. Pseudocorus
WATER FLAG

Sword-shaped leaves rise strongly from rhizomes planted in mud at the bottom of a pool. If in full sun they produce flat yellow flags for a month in June. Multiply rapidly.

Ixiolirion tataricum
SIBERIAN BLUEBELL

For the rock garden in a protected place. The true-blue lily-like flowers on a 6 inch stalk will come back year after year.

Leucojum vernum
SNOWFLAKE

A must for following Snowdrops, which are similar. These have a nodding bell tipped with green. Same culture.

L. aestivum
SUMMER SNOWFLAKE

Taller at 18 inches, this white nodding bell blooms in late May and complements late-flowering tulips or Camassia.

Lilium spp.
LILY

No other flower has enjoyed such rise in popularity as the lily. The exquisite form and color, coupled with their long-lasting characteristic have sensationalized the cut-flower trade and made them a house and garden necessity.

At peril of being boresome, the matter of drainage is even more imperative with the planting of lilies than with other bulbs. Soil type or texture is not as vital. Any good garden soil that has grown vegetables and common flowers will do. The old saying, "The best time to plant a lily is 15 minutes after it is dug" remains good advice. Suffice it to state, plant as soon as received. Soil should be rich with compost and minerals because this will be the last time you will invest time on it. As you plant, give each bulb a pad of sand under the base plate. This is a sanitation measure to keep it clean from organisms that may invade.

A good rule in planting is to plant at 3 times the vertical diameter of the bulb EXCEPT for *Lilium, candidum,* the beautiful Madonna Lily. It wants only an inch or so of gritty soil over it. If mice, gophers, or voles have been known in your area, surround a lily bulb in pea gravel so that at least 2 inches pad it on all sides. This will destroy the scent of the bulb so that the critter can't find it. Feed with 5-10-5 after danger of last frost and again in September. Lilies are not drought-tolerant. Allow the top soil to dry, but keep soil at root depth moist. If you cut a stem for display in the house, leave at least a third of the foliage to grow on through the summer. Mulch with evergreen boughs in winter. When shoots first appear in spring, keep cardboard boxes, pots, etc., handy to put over the foliage if there is danger of a frosty night.

LILY TYPES

Division	Example
Asiatic Hybrids	
(upfacing)	'Enchantment'
(outfacing)	'Connecticut'
	'Lemonglow'
(downfacing)	'Red Knight'
	Trumpet
Hybrids	
trumpet shaped	'Black Dragon'
bowl shaped	'Heart's Desire'
sunburst	'Thunderbolt'
Oriental Hybrids	
bowl shaped	'Empress of India'
flat flowers	'Stargazer'
recurved flowers	'Journey's End'

There are six more lily divisions: Martagon lilies, also known as Turk's Cap, which have tiers of pendant blooms; *L. longiflorum,* the Easter lily, which is beginning to be explored by hybridists; the little *L. pumilum,* formerly *L. tenuifolium,* charming in a rock garden or at the front of the border; the Regal,(*L. regale);* and the Madonna lily (*L. candidum).*

Types of Lily Flowers

LILY
GROWTH CYCLE

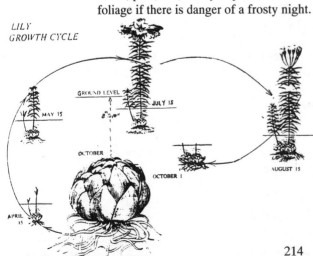

■ *Lycoris squamigera*
MAGIC LILY, NAKED LILY

A fascinating old garden favorite in the Mountain West, the *Lycoris* bulbs are usually sold in August, and should be planted immediately. The flower stems will appear quickly, bare of foliage, with a scape of baby pink, long-lasting flowers. The foliage will appear next spring as straps of dark green, dying back in early June. These bulbs are attractive when planted among the Hostas that can withstand some sun. The naked flowering stems appear to have leaves at the base, but they are, in fact, the Hosta leaves.

■ *Muscari spp.*
GRAPE HYACINTH

M. botryoides - The species first cultivated in Europe in 1576. Sky-blue flowers on 6 inch stems; fragrance of plums.
Cultivar

M. b. album

'Italian Grape Hyacinth' - A white form that does not spread. Bulbs should be planted shoulder-to-shoulder for good effect. Effective planted beneath groundcover *Lamium* 'White Nancy.'

■ *M. armeniacum*
Cultivar

'Blue Spike' - An azure blue 3 inch sterile flower that makes this cultivar more welcome. It does spread moderately by bulb division. Good combined with white Wind Flower (*Anemone blanda*).

■ *M. plumosum*
FEATHER HYACINTH

4 inch florets of lilac on slender filaments make this cockade-shaped flower an addition to the spring garden. Good combined with Daffodil 'Ice Follies.'

■ *Narcissus pseudonarcissus* hereinafter referred to as __
DAFFODIL

No other flower in the world is quite so universally associated with spring as the daffodil. The essence of the season is embodied in the flare of the cup, the curve of the petals. Not all the hybridizers in the world have been able change this ages-old form and fresh scent. Your landscape will shine with half a hundred or just half a dozen. Daffs thrive in a lean sandy soil; too rich a soil can curtail flower production. Do not add compost or manure to the planting hole. Fertilize with soluble solution every 3 years as the foliage is poking through the soil.

Types of Daffodils

Daffodils are divided into 11 divisions, with the miniatures coming from many divisions but generally grouped in a class by themselves. Listed below are only 3 from each division, and each of those has at least a 4-star performance as rated by the American Daffodil Society.

215

TRUMPET DAFFODILS
DIV. I
Cultivars

'Ballade' - Yellow petal and cup, early to midseason; 18 inches.

'Epitome' - Yellow petals, white cup has a yellow rim; midseason; 18 inches.

'Mrs. E. H. Krelage' - White petals yellow cup with white rim; early to midseason; 16 inches.

LARGE CUPPED DAFFODILS
DIV. II

'Avalon' - White petals, yellow cup; midseason to late; 16 inches.

'Carlton' - Yellow petals, yellow cup; vanilla fragrance; midseason; 16 inches. Best for naturalizing.

'Cloud Nine' - White petals, yellow cup; midseason to late; 12 inches; fragrant.

SHORT CUPPED DAFFODILS
DIV. III

'Barri Conspicuous' - Yellow petals, yellow cup with yellow to red inner cup; midseason; 16 inches.

'Queen of the North' - White petals, yellow cup; midseason; 16 inches.

'White Lady' - White petals, white cup; midseason; 16 inches.

DOUBLE DAFFODILS
DIV. IV

'Anne Frank' - White petals, orange cup; midseason to late; 16 inches.

'Cheerfulness' - White petals and cup; late; 18 inches.

'Pink Paradise' - White petals, pink cup; midseason to late; 16 inches.

TRIANDRUS DAFFODILS (two or three nodding blooms per stem).
DIV. V

'Hawera' - Miniature with yellow petals and cup hanging pendant on the stem; midseason to late; 8 inches.

'Honey Guide' - Yellow petals, yellow cup; midseason; 12 inches.

'Thalia' - White petals, white reflexed cup; midseason; 16 inches.

CYCLAMINEUS DAFFODILS (flared back petals)
DIV. VI

'February Gold' - Yellow petals, yellow cup; early, 8 inches.

'Little Witch' - Yellow petals, yellow cup; midseason; 8 inches.

'Tete-a-tete' - Yellow petals, orange cup; early; 5 inches.

JONQUILLA DAFFODILS
DIV. VII

'Bunting' - Yellow petals, orange cup; late; 12 inches.

'Buffawn' - Yellow petals, yellow cup; midseason; 12 inches.

'Curlew' - White petals; yellow cup; midseason to late; 14 inches.

TAZETTA DAFFODILS -The forcing bulb for Holidays (multi-flowers of pungent scent per stem). Also known as "Paper White Narcissus." Not hardy.
DIV. VIII

'Canarybird' - Yellow petals, yellow flare; midseason to late; 14 inches.

'Grand Soleil d'Or' - Yellow petals, orange flare; early; 12 inches.

'Silver Chimes' - White petals, white flare; midseason to late; 15 inches.

POETICUS DAFFODILS (simple white fragrant blooms, red-rimmed). DIV. IX

'Actaea' - White petals, red cup; midseason; 18 inches.

'Felindre' - White petals, yellow reflexed cup; late; 16 inches.

'Milan' - White petals, yellow reflexed cup; late; 16 inches.

SPECIES AND WILD FORMS DIV. X

N.bulbocodium conspicuus - A miniature; also known as 'Yellow Hoop Petticoat.'

N. jonquilla - The true jonquil; a miniature; 2 or 3 deep yellow blooms per stem; very late; very fragrant; native of Spain and Portugal.

N. x odorus - The Campernelle of poetry and song; yellow petals, yellow cup; early; 10 inches.

N. pumilus plenus - Yellow petals, yellow cup; early to midseason; 6 inches.

SPLIT CORONA DAFFODILS DIV. XI

'Canasta' - White petals; yellow cup; midseason; 18 inches.

'Changing Colors' - White petals; white cup, inner pink; late to midseason; 18 inches.

'Space Shuttle' - White petals, yellow cup; midseason. 16 inches.

■ *Ornithogalum umbellatum*
STAR OF BETHLEHEM, SUMMER SNOWFLAKE

Easily grown little bulb, 1 foot in height, with flowers like white stars with a green rib on the outside. They close at night to protect the pollen. Keep deadheaded as it can become a little too much at home.

■ *Oxalis adenophylla*
SHAMROCK

Small bulb-like tuber with crinkled blue-gray shamrock 1 inch foliage and large pink flowers lined with rose-purple. Not really hardy, but easily scooped up to winter over in the coldframe.

■ *Puschkinia scilloides*
STRIPED SQUILL

Milky blue flowers on 3 inch stems in very early spring. Plant in very well-drained soil in masses for good effect.

■ *Rhodohypoxis baurii*

A native of the higher elevations of Nepal and Lesotho. Hairy 3 inch leaves in which are nestled star-shaped flowers of pink. Long blooming. Protect with evergreen boughs in winter.

■ *Scilla spp.*
SPRING BEAUTY, SIBERIAN SQUILL

■ *S. bifolia*

The 4 inch Delft-blue harbinger of the spring season with broad strappy foliage. Good combined with the miniature daffodils.

■ *S. pratensis*
MEADOW SQUILL

A later blooming species of brilliant blue with dark purple stamens. A good transition bloomer between spring and summer.

■ *S. siberica*
SIBERIAN SQUILL

The familiar carpeting squill of early spring. Prussian-blue flowers that quickly seed around. Often planted in lawns where its foliage will mature before mowing time.

■ *Sternbergia lutea*
WINTER DAFFODIL, LILY-OF-THE-FIELD

A butter-yellow crocus blooming in fall, surrounded by glossy foliage. Long-lasting and weather resistant. Closes during inclement weather. Plant in very light shade, 4 inches deep. They fend for themselves.

■ *Tricyrtis hirta*
TOAD LILY

An ugly name for a beautiful fall-bloomer from Japan. Produces many creamy flowers splotched with purple on 2 to 3 foot stems. Plant in rich humus in part shade. Pile straw around the stems as they appear to keep stems upright and protected from wind and frost.

■ *Trillium grandiflorum*
WAKE ROBIN

The showiest of the species to which the common name is loosely attached. Three-petaled white flowers and three-whorled leaves greet spring. Great sentimentality is attached to this plant by Easterners transplanted to the Mountain West. Rich woodland soil in part shade.

■ *Tulipa spp.*
TULIP

The Tulip reigns supreme when spring has definitely arrived and settled down to stay. Their brilliant hues and large-size blooms can more than hold their own against all the other emerging spring foliage in the garden. From delicate pinks to somber violet-purple to screaming orange and red, there will always be a tulip to fit the scheme of the scene.

Of all the tulips, the lily-flowering are most suited to the Mountain West. It is the only one known to multiply freely in our soils. Plant them so that the nose is 8 to 10 inches beneath the surface, and you will soon have 100. Tulips, of all the bulbs, are the only ones that will wait. Plant them as late as January, if you can get a spade into the soil then, and they will bloom their hearts out. The only precautions are deep planting, for shallowly planted bulbs quickly "run out."

The Dutch government regulates bulb export to the United States, and only three sizes of tulip bulbs are allowed to be exported. All three are of blooming size. The U.S. bulb growers follow the same size stipulations.

The following are only 3 examples of each tulip type. New introductions each year assure a wide variety.

Types of Tulips

EARLY FLOWERING
APRIL TO MAY
Double Early
   'Carlton' - Deep blood-red.
   'Monte Carlo' - Sulphur yellow.

'Queen of Marvel' - Bright pink with rose edge.
'Kaufmanniana' - The waterlily tulips
'Pink Dwarf' - Scarlet/purple flame.
'Scarlet Baby' - Deep pink with red.
'Shakespeare' - Carmine red edged with salmon.

Single Early
'Apricot Beauty' - Delicate salmon-rose.
'Beauty Queen' - Rose feathered on salmon.
'Yokohoma' - Bright yellow.

EARLY MIDSEASON
'Fosteriana' - The Emporer tulips
'Flaming Emporer' - strawberry red.
'Golden Emporer' - Pure golden yellow
'Pink Emporer' - Soft pink
'Purissima' - Snow white.
'Greigei Tulips' - Leaves mottled purple.
'Cape Cod' - Apricot-edged yellow.
'Perlina' - Lemon-yellow.
'Red Riding Hood' - Scarlet

Multiflowering Tulips - Three or more flowers per stem.
'Orange Bouquet' -Brownish orange.
'Red Georgette' - Deep red.
'Weisse Berliner' - Ivory white, yellow flame.

PARROT TULIPS
'Bird of Paradise' - Deep red edged orange.
'Green Wave' - Pink flamed green and white.
'Yellow Parrot' - Yellow edged green.

MIDSEASON
Darwin Hybrid Tulip
'Apeldoorn Elite' - Red-orange feathered yellow.

'Burning Heart' - Ivory flamed red.
'My Lady' - Salmon orange.

Lily Flowering Tulip
'Ballade' - Pink purple with white edge.
'Mariette' Satin rose with white base.
'May Time' - Violet with white edge.
'Picotee' - White with pink edge.
Multiplies prolifically.

LATE TULIPS
Double Late Tulips
'Allegretto' - Red edged yellow.
'Uncle Tom' - Dark maroon.
'Wirosa' - Wine edged with white.

Fringed Tulips
'Canova' - Strong purple fringed white.
'Fancy Frills' - White with rose interior and fringe.
'Swan Wings' - Pure white with long curly fringe.

Tetraploid Tulips (extra vigor)
'Ernesto Cardenal - Bright pink.
'Muscadet' - Yellow.
'Pomarel' - Lilac.

VIRIDIFLORA TULIPS
'Esperanto' - Bold green and red with cream edge.
'Greenland' - Green edged with rose.
'Spring Green' - Ivory-white with green flame.

Wild Tulips
Many of the bizarre, miniature, and unusual species fit in this category. They sometimes resemble insects more than flowers, but each has a place in the rockery where summer baking will make them prosper. Consult a reputable catalog with good delivery policies and try a few more

each year. A few of the more reliable follow:

T. biflora Turkistanica - white with yellow center on 8 inch stem.

T. chrysantha - Yellow.

T. clusiana - White with crimson and purple center.

T. praestans - A scarlet cup on low foliage.

T. tarda - The easiest of all; yellow and white.

■ *Zedphyranthes candida* [spelling error]
RAIN LILY

Planted 2 inches apart in the gritty soil of the rock garden. These small rosy lilies will pop up with the first deep watering; then dry off for 8 weeks and bloom again. A third flowering is possible. Mulch deeply in winter.

Suggested catalogs

Dutch Gardens, P.O. Box 200, Adelphia NJ 07710

The Daffodil Mart, Rt. 3, Box 794, Glouster VA 23061

McClure & Zimmerman, 108 W. Winnebago, P.O. Box 368, Friesland WI 53935.

Plant Societies

American Daffodil Society, ATT: Mary Lou Gripshover, 1686 Grey Fox Trails, Milford OH 45150

American Dahlia Society, Michael Martinolich 159 Pine St., New Hyde Park NY 11040

Vines

More species of vines are available for the use of Mountain West gardeners today than ever before in the history of the area or, indeed, of the country. Coincidentally, Mountain West gardens are shrinking as land becomes more dear. We have mountains within our views, but often our gardens are all on the same plane with no vertical interest or changes of contour to lift the eyes of the viewer upward. Vines relieve the monotony, the sameness of the horizontal. Creating garden rooms within a garden with vines trained on an upright surface has gained renewed popularity as we roam about the globe and consider the walled gardens of England, the secluded courtyard gardens of Spain and China, or the perpendicular surfaces where the Swiss create a garden.

Walls, hedges, treillage, and fences give us the means of screening unsightly views and adding privacy to gardens, but it is the plants themselves that adorn and soften hard surfaces, provide seasonal color, and add changes of texture to bring the fillip to the composition.

The avid gardener who must have one of everything looks upon a vertical surface with joy and eye-squinting cunning. Here, then, is another site to add a coveted plant or two. A vine with its head in the sun, its feet in the shade has the best of both worlds. The gardener, with full knowledge of this cultural quirk, can spend an entire winter season in happy search of the right plant to fit the site.

Assessment of the Site

Put on your critical eye and adjust your most scoffing of attitudes before making a

■ . . .
consider the walled gardens of England, the secluded courtyard gardens of Spain and China. . .

final decision for the site of a permanent planting of a vine. Look first to the drainage. Only poison ivy can withstand wet feet. If water stands on the site for more than 1/2 hour, begin soil amendments with sphagnum peatmoss, and try the standing water test again after you have finished. If you have prepared the entire site as prescribed in Vol. I, Chapter 4, further amendments will not be necessary.

The next site requirements are aspect and light. Aspect has to do with the direction in which the planting will face. A north-facing planting must be extremely hardy in northern Montana, for example. Even in Colorado or New Mexico a north-facing planting must withstand the north winds that come upon occasion with a sagging weather front from the Arctic. A vine, for the most part, is only one-dimensional. Light requirements will vary with each species. A few we will consider can withstand full shade, but the greatest number require at least 4 hours of sunlight a day.

How Will It Climb?

Most of the plants that are called vines have special adaptations to accomodate their climbing habit. The strongest and most noticeable are called *hold-fasts*. These resemble a root or a pudgy little sea urchin that cements itself to a wall, a tree, or any object it comes upon as it grows. It makes the vine cling tightly — so much so that it requires strength and determination to loosen its grip. The hold-fast is also the nemesis of mortar between bricks. The hold-fasts can actually penetrate the mortar and pry it apart. We see ivy-covered cottages in the movies, but in actuality those cottages (if they were real) are in danger of slow demolition. Examples are

English ivy (*Hedera helix sp*) and climbing hydrangea (*Hydrangea anomala*).

The next climbing device of a vine is the tendril that grabs and wraps around whatever it touches with amazing speed. Unequal cell growth on the side that is touching the support and the side that is not causes it to spirally circle the support with amazing speed. Tendril coiling and tightening has been clocked at less than half an hour. The tendril can be a specialized leaf (pea vines) or a specialized stem (grape). Tendrils can remain a single structure or fork as they reach out to grab a wire, a lattice, or a limb. They develop the strength they need to carry the load of supporting the species they represent. You will see this as you compare the tendrils of squash and peas, for example. Clematis is also a grabber, but the device it uses is the *petiole*, which is the stem of the leaf. As Clematis begins growth in spring, it demands some attention to prevent the new leaves from twining around and suffocating each other. It takes a little time to persuade them to grow upward to cling to the trellis instead.

Boston ivy (*Parthenocissus tricuspidata*), Virginia Creeper (*P. quinquefolia*) and Trumpet Vine (*Campsis radicans*) have non-coiling, clinging tendril devices of a different style called an *adherent pad*. Like dots of glue attached to strong stems, they suck up to a rough surface without remorse. Be wary of the adherent pads' indestructibility. Even sand-blasting is not completely effective in removing them when the vine dies or is removed from a brick wall.

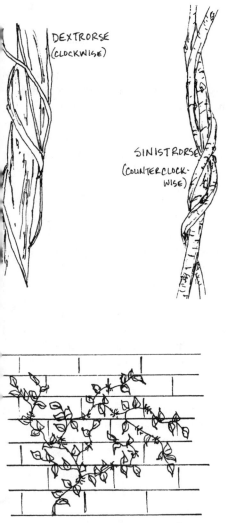

DEXTRORSE
(CLOCKWISE)

SINISTRORSE
(COUNTERCLOCK-
WISE)

How vines climb.

ROOTLIKE HOLDFASTS

motion called *circumnutation,* which increases its chances of contact with something to climb upon. *Geotropism* is the gravity-induced force that causes roots to grow in a permanent circle toward the earth by means of unequal cell growth on either side of the plant structure. With vines, there is a different type of *tropism,* known as *thigmotropism,* which is response to contact with the support. As soon as contact is made, the twining vine, with dextrorsity or sinistrorsity, grows rapidly and spirally upward on the support. Always allow the *twiner* to do its own twining, either to right or left, as this trait is hereditary and you can't change it.

Another class of vines might be better considered in the shrub category, for they have no structural parts to assist them in climbing. These are the sprawlers. They sprawl or lean over the support, and it is necessary to tie them as inconspicuously as possible. Roses and jasmine are examples.

What Will It Climb?

Matching the vine to the support is essential for success. For example, you are not likely to persuade a twiner to climb a brick wall, and you can't ask ivy to climb a wire.

There is difference of opinion regarding clematis. Supposedly, it gets its name from the word *lattice,* but some species are reluctant to twine around lattice. Tack a network of wire to the lattice to give the plants the slender supports they want. Clematis also are at their best climbing through shrubs. The variegated green and white foliage of a shrub dogwood, for example, can light up with *C. montana* that has hundreds of light pink blooms, each with fuzzy yellow stamens. Prune it back lightly after flowering.

■ . . .

twining is hereditary and you can't change it.

By far the greatest majority of vines climb by twining. They twist around any convenient object either clockwise (to the right) or counterclockwise (to the left). The growth is regulated by dextrorse for the right-handed twining vine, and by sinistrorse for the left-handed. A vine does not grow at an even rate upward as a sapling does, but in a rhythmic circular

223

Trellises are suited to twining vines. They twist themselves to the top, then branch to drape gracefully downward. Twining vines are also good candidates to make a chain-link fence invisible. Encourage your neighbor on the other side to 'plant out' the fence and you'll both be happy.

A single post of juniper or black locust (*Robinia Pseudoacacia*) adds a vertical interest to the perennial border. You can add a temporary vine such as blue morning glory, or the ultimate in elegance, *Ampelopsis brevipedunculata* — the Turquoise Berry Vine. These vines will twine upward to the top, then droop gracefully to bloom in late summer.

A vine on a grid against your home, garage, barn, or garden shed can give added insulation in both summer and winter. If the structure is wood, use hinges at the bottom of the trellis so that the whole grid can be laid down when there is need to paint. Use spacers made of 2-inch blocks of wood nailed to the wall; then nail the grid to the spacer to give air circulation to the vine.

Sprawlers, such as the climbing rose, can be very attractive against a length of a Western cedar stake-and-rider fence. Small hooks screwed into the lengths of cedar serve as anchors and a place to tie the rose stems.

Protection

Most of the vines listed below will be hardy. For the few that are of doubtful hardiness, new devices come on the market daily that will allow you to plant a tender vine so that it will make it through the winter. Keep in mind, however, that these devices require that *you* remember to put them into place. It's so easy to bask in the sunlight of an October afternoon, forgetting that Mountain West weather can drop the temperature 50 degrees overnight. Begin in early fall withholding water to harden off the plant that is growing strongly. Pull off leaves, if necessary, to force a plant into dormancy. Protect the top growth of a tender vine first with an insulated blanket; then look to the roots by placing evergreen boughs and dry leaves over the root run. Beginning in November water the planting monthly that snow is not present until March next year. In March we usually get enough natural precipitation to suffice.

Planting a Vine

Spring is the best planting time, beginning as soon as the frost is out of the ground and plants are available at your nursery. Roots can become established in cool soil, but you may have to protect the

GRIDS

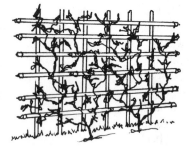

FENCES

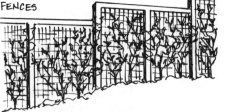

TRELLISES

Grids, fences, trellises.

top if killing frosts can be expected through April.

If the plant is bare-root, soak the roots in a bucket of warm water for an hour before planting. Clip each root slightly so that fresh tissue will be exposed and new roots will form immediately.

Dig a hole at least 2 feet wide and 18 inches deep. Mix 1/3 of the excavated soil with wet sphagnum peatmoss, compost, or weathered manure . Stir in a half-cup of 10-10-10 fertilizer. Next, set a stake deeply into the hole. This will be removed later after the vine has begun to climb the fence, wall, or lattice you have provided. Fill the planting hole 1/2 full. Hold the plant in the hole so that the crown will be covered by about 2 inches of soil. The crown is the point at which the stem meets the roots. Fill in with the soil mixture around the roots and crown to the top of the hole. Water gently but do not press down on the topsoil with feet or trowel. Mulch with river biscuits (smooth cobbles) to prevent loss of moisture, to insulate the soil, and to keep the plant in place. Tie stems and tendrils loosly to the stake. The planting will not need watering again until a finger pressed to the surface tells you that the soil is *almost* dry.

The supports for vines may be fences or buildings, fancy arches or plain lath, but the vines they hold can enliven the garden with color and texture, scent and creature food, and a shady nook for humans on a stifling day.

Perennial Vines for the Mountain West

■ *Actinidia kolomikta*
KIWI

This vine is covered in Chapter 2 Fruits, p. 81 but it is also an ornamental with pink, white, and green foliage. Small, thumb-nail size fruits appear in the third or fourth year if both male and female plants are planted on the same trellis. It is a twiner and needs a strong trellis.

■ *Ampelopsis brevipedunculata*
PORCELAIN BERRY VINE

A relative of grape, this much-sought-after vine is difficult to locate in local nurseries. As those who behold it spread the word, hopefully, it will become more available.. It climbs to about 20 feet on a grid of plastic wire that will not burn its tendrils. The grid should be south-facing because it needs heat to form its undistinguished blooms. The berry clusters change from greenish ivory to porcelain blue to deep metallic blue with each color in the cluster at the same time. It is long-lived and prolific, but slow to establish and bloom.

■ *Aristolochia durior*
DUTCHMAN'S PIPE VINE

As its name implies, it is an aristocrat among vines. On an arbor or pergola, its velvety, deep green, heart-shaped leaves overlap to provide dense shade. Its flowers are shaped like the white clay pipes of America's early Dutch settlers.

■ *Campsis radicans*
TRUMPET VINE

Also known as Cross Vine because of the cross that is visible when the wood is cut.

The vine needs heavy, moisture-retentive soil and a protected eastern exposure. Its orange trumpet-shaped flowers bloom from midsummer till frost. It climbs by hold-fasts and is attractive to hummingbirds.

■ *Celastrus scandens*
BITTERSWEET

A twiner suitable for a chain link fence. Dark green foliage; greenish-yellow flowers followed by orange berry clusters. At first frost the berries break open to reveal a bright red bract. There is a dubious tale going around that 2 are needed for cross-pollination. The author has only 1 and none others have been noticed in the neighborhood; yet it flowers and fruits with abandon. Attractive to Townsend's Solitaire who will fight off other birds to claim all the berries.

■ *Clematis sp.*
VIRGIN'S BOWER

Creative breeding has produced hundreds of cultivars with flowers of exquisite color and form. The British, to whom we are supposed to defer, pronounce it CLEM-atis. La-de-da. Pronounce it however you feel that day. It prefers its head in the sun, feet in the shade. Give it a mulch of river biscuits to keep the soil cool. Prepare the soil as illustrated for the best success. Choose a container-grown plant with stems as large as baling wire, not spindly weak sprouts. Give each plant or your collection of clematis a lattice to climb with its twisting petioles, paying attention in early spring to guide them upward. Pruning for each cultivar is different, according to the time of bloom. For your sanity's sake, give each plant a tag with pruning instructions in indelible nursery pen. Deadhead regularly unless you want the mop-head seed clusters

for fall flower arrangements. This chapter will not address the shrub clematis.

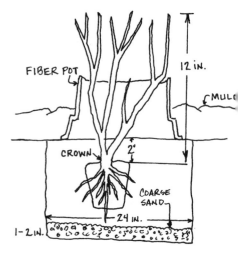

To Plant a Clematis

C. alpina 'Pamela Jackman' - A small vine with bell- shaped flowers of rich deep purple, each with a white "clapper" of stamens. Prune lightly in very early spring.

The Florida Group. Flowering on old wood in summer; should be pruned lightly and infrequently.

C. x hybrida

'Dr. Ruppel'- Large flowered clear pink, edged white. No pruning required.

'Ernest Markham'- Deep clear red, very large flowers.

'Nelly Moser' - Light shade preferred; white blooms with pink center stripe.

The Patens Group. Flowering on old wood in spring or summer. Should be pruned lightly and infrequently.

'Barbara Jackman' - Pale lavender blooms deepening toward center in late summer. Plant in light shade.

'Margaret Hunt' - Clear light pink blooms in midsummer.

'The President' - Large deep claret-purple blooms in midsummer; bronzy foliage in spring. Still popular after 100 years.

The Jackmanii Group. Flowering on wood of the current season. Should be pruned to the ground during the dormant period.

'Comtesse de Bouchard' - Covers itself with small pink blooms in early summer.

C.x hybrida jackmanii (pronounced jackman-eye). The most famous and free-flowering. Small deep purple blooms. Superb with a climbing pink rose or scrambling up a Cornelian Cherry tree (*Cornus mas)*.

'Ramona' - Light lavender-blue with dark stamens on 16 foot vine; good for lamp posts.

C. ligusticifolia - A native Colorado vine with flowers similar to *C. paniculata* (see below) but with larger seed heads and no fragrance. This species blooms in August, a month earlier than *C. paniculata*. It is also more tolerant of alkaline soil and winter sun.

C. montana rubens - The traditional wall and lampost clematis of the U.K. Small pink single blooms cover it so that foliage is obscured. It needs the protection of a shrub to scramble over.

C. maximowicziana, formerly *paniculata*. SWEET AUTUMN CLEMATIS - It should not take more than a few years to lose the latest species name for this lovely Clematis. Your nursery will still, thankfully, provide it with the **C. paniculata** moniker. The tiny fragrant white stars open in September. It will climb a tree with abandon, but try to keep its tendrils trained so that the blooms will face you at eye and nose level. In areas of Zone 4 and above, prune it only lightly. In Zone 5, cut it back sharply in early spring. Old wood will split with winter temperaure fluctuation. Avoid a south-facing planting site.

C. tangutica. RUSSIAN VIRGIN'S BOWER - Glowing yellow lanterns wih brown stamens. Vigorously growing 10 to 20 feet. Blooms from July through October. Cut back by half in late fall or very early spring.

The famed Steffen Clematis nursery in Fairport NY has introduced 5 new cultivars of small-flowered clematis that show great promise, but at this writing they have not been tested for hardiness in the Mountain West.

■ *Euonymus Fortunei 'Gracilis'*
CLIMBING EUONYMUS

Variegated foliage makes this aerial evergreen offering of the *Euonymus* genus more than welcome. Climbs by hold-fasts; its blooms are nothings, but are followed by tiny, bright pink seed pods which break open to reveal red seeds.

■ *Hedera helix*
IVY

The evergreen vine of centuries. We are fortunate to have a cultivar 'Thorndale' that is completely hardy throughout the Mountain West. Climbs by hold-fasts. In a very cold winter it will die back, but can be depended upon to return from the root. With age it has white bloom clusters, followed by clusters of blue berries attractive to birds.

H.h. 'Buttercup'- A half-hardy bright yellow-green cultivar that brightens shade or a container grown pink rose. Give it cold-frame treatment in winter until it puts on some years; then plant it on the east side of a deciduous tree.

227

■ *Humulus lupulus 'Aureus'*
GOLDEN HOPS

A vine for the warm valleys and southern sections of the Mountain West. Hops are used to flavor beer, but this cultivar is ornamental as well with bright yellow-green leaves that can lighten a mature specimen (40 feet) of the somber foliage of Douglas Fir, Ponderosa Pine, or a green Colorado spruce.

■ *Hydrangea anomala petiolaris*
CLIMBING HYDRANGEA

A hardy vine from the moist forests of Japan and China. If it finds the humidity it needs against a north wall or in a tree, it climbs quickly with holdfasts. Leaves are long petioled, broad-ovate, with serrated edges. No autumnal color, but blooms are lacy caps 10 inches across and creamy white in spring. Slow to establish.

■ *Lonicera sp.*
HONEYSUCKLE

Nostalgia for the scent of honeysuckle around the homestead brings back many wanderers — at least in the song. In reality this is a vine to plant for its prolific long, tubular, nectar-producing blooms. Only a few species are fragrant.

■ *L. heckrotii*
FLAME HONEYSUCKLE

Flushes of red bloom tipped with yellow stamens throughout the summer keep this vine popular. Mulch with compost; feed very seldom. Not fragrant.

■ *L. japonica*
JAPANESE HONEYSUCKLE

A rampant grower not for the southern reaches of this volume. In Wyoming, Idaho, Montana, and at higher altitudes, this plant is just barely hardy, which keeps it in bounds. In the east and south it is a thug to be grubbed out at every opportunity. Delightfully fragrant yellow-tinged-with-orange blooms from May to October.

■ *L. sempervirens*
CORAL OR TRUMPET HONEYSUCKLE

A hardy native that forms a discreet network on wire supports. The predominent color of bloom is coral. In areas of cool summer nights it will flush several times. Plant it with a yellow rose. Not fragrant.

■ *Parthenocissus quinquefolia*
WOODBINE

Climbing by tendrils as well as by adherent pads, this vigorous vine is often the "halls of ivy" of American univerisites and not the real ivy. Botanic correctness apparently is not the forte of "alma mater" song writers. Also known as **Virginia Creeper**, its compound leaves of 5 leaflets will turn brilliant wine in a mild autumn. Undistinguished flower clusters are followed by blue berries attractive to birds.

■ *P. tricuspidata*
BOSTON IVY

Another high climber with disk-tipped tendrils, this vine of doubtful hardiness has glossy, 3 lobed leaves. Fruit is blue-black, and fall color is also brilliant red in a mild fall. The cultivar 'Lowii' has very small purplish foliage.

■ *Passiflora incarnata*
PASSION FLOWER VINE

Though it will be an indoor plant in northern areas, this vine can be counted upon to be hardy if planted on a south-facing wall where it can get its roots beneath the foundation and into the crawl-space of a home without a basement. The flowers are said to contain the stations of the cross; hence, the name. Extemely sensitive to dessication, give it a rich, moisture-retentive soil. If it's happy, it will send up suckers (worse luck!), but be watchful and root them out. Be aware that this plant is regarded as a pernicious weed in Zones 8, 9 and 10.

■ *Polygonum auberti*
SILVER LACE VINE

We still have outhouses, or at least out-buildings, in the Mountain West, and they will still benefit from an enveloping vine. Silver Lace erupts with fluffy white flowers from August till October. Can withstand poor soil and drought, but treat it nicely for best effect.

■ *Rosa sp.*
ROSES

Roses may not have a place in a vine chapter because they have no vining characteristics whatsoever. Essentially, they are leaners. Nevertheless, we go to great lengths to fasten long, branching canes to supports and call them "climbing roses."

'Blaze' - This is touted as America's most popular climbing rose. In Western Colorado the red blooms are so numerous they hide the foliage.

'Climbing Peace' - Many hybrid teas have a climbing form. This is the best. Creamy peach blooms are large and fragrant.

'Dorothy Perkins' - A shower of small pink blooms in early summer and intermit-tently throughout the summer. Very hardy. Can probably withstand high country temperatures.

'Golden Showers' - Daffodil-yellow buds opening to deep gold.

■*Vitis vinifera* ''Purpurea'
PURPLE GRAPE

The lobes of grape foliage are familiar, but the dusky purple color is new. Scramble it with the pink, white, and green foliage of Kiwi.

■ *Wisteria sinensis*
WISTERIA

This member of the legume family is the vine of romance and poetry. The drooping panicles of lavender or white appear in spring, usually May, before the leaves unfurl. It is a twiner of great strength. Give it a very sturdy pipe support. Arbors or pergolas in full sun are excellent sites to show it off. Easy to establish, but not easy to induce bloom. Keep it on a lean regime, but make sure the deep roots are thoroughly soaked when watering.

Annual Vines
■ *Asarina barclaiana*
CHICKABIDDY

Resembling a climbing snapdragon, this vine of only 6 feet will decorate a small trellis in a patio pot with rich red, yellow, or blue and white flowers from late spring till frost. Start seeds indoors in March.

■ *Ipomoea alba*
MOON FLOWER

Fragrant white flowers fully 4 to 6 inches in diameter open at dusk with a swift unfurling, then close before noon the next day. Can be cut for evening table arrange-ments. Start scarified seeds indoors in March.

I. battata 'Blackie' - A sweet-potato relative that produces sharply lobed leaves of purple-black. Very attractive when grown with plants with yellow-green foliage. Use it as an indoor plant in winter and take cuttings in spring.

229

■ *I. tricolor*
MORNING GLORY

The old familiar 'Heavenly Blue' is still the best cultivar for covering trellis, or wire grid, or draped over a post. Does not come into full bloom until the heat of summer. Also available in mauve, pink, and red.

■ *Lathyrus odoratus*
SWEET PEA

The ever-popular climbing vine for a grid of strong twine or wire. For an unusual climbing device, erect several peeled trunks a Corkscrew Willow (*Salix matsudana*) in a half-barrel or large patio pot. There are many colors available. Mix them or grow them separately.

■ *Petunia integrifolia cv. integrifolia*
VIOLET-FLOWERING PETUNIA

A little known annual vine from Argentina. It is weather-resistant and forms a spreading mat with ceaseless progression of violet blooms, each with darkened throat. Combine it with *Cleome* 'Violet Queen' and *Artemisia* ''Powis Castle.'

■ *Phaseolus coccineus*
SCARLET RUNNER BEAN

A useful climber to conceal an unpainted fence or poor view. The coarse, hairy leaves as well as the bean pods are large and attractive. Available with scarlet or white flowers.

■ *Rhodochiton atrosanguineium*
PURPLE BELL VINE

An annual demanding heat but part shade to bring forth its parasoled flowers of rich fuchsia-purple. Let it ramble through a purple-leaved *Cotinus* or a patch of tall pink zinnias. Collect seed in fall, for it is hard to come by.

■ *Thunbergia alata*
BLACK-EYED SUSAN VINE

A 4-to-6 foot vine with black-centered flowers of white, gold, or orange. Good in hanging baskets.

■ *Tropaeolum peregrinum*
NASTURTIUM

The vining types of this old familiar trumpet-shaped flower are good scramblers over and through plants with contrasting foliage. This one is stunning combined with the lacy blue foliage of Rue 'Blue Mound.' Plant the large seeds direct when weather warms. Available in variegated foliage as well.

Suggested Reading
'Vertical Gardening' Caroline Boisset, Weidenfeld & Nicolson, New York NY, 1988.
'Shrubs and Vines for American Gardens' by Donald Wyman, Macmillan Company, New York NY 1961.

Roses

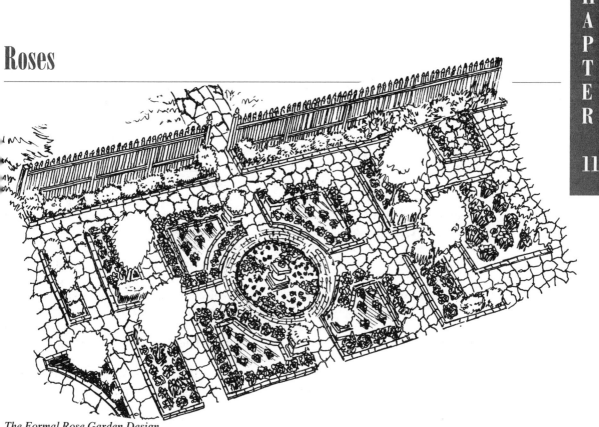

The Formal Rose Garden Design.

There is a fossil imprint of a rose in the Smithsonian Institution. It is 40 million years old and was unearthed in Colorado. It is believed that roses evolved 60 million years ago, probably in Asia, and spread over the Northern Hemisphere, but inexplicably never crossed the Equator. No other plant figures so prominently in history, whether pre-history through pictographs or through recorded history. The rose was avoided by early Christians who linked it with the excesses of pagan Rome, but by the Middle Ages the rose had undergone a transformation in the eyes of Christendom. It became the symbol of the purity of the Virgin and the inspiration for the magnificence in stained glass known as the rose window of the Gothic cathedrals of Europe.

While the history of rose growing in the Mountain West cannot match the antiquity of the rose, there is, nevertheless, a unique quality of high elevation color that cannot be matched elsewhere, and rose growing in the Mountain West is easier than it once was. Breeders are paying attention to growers' demands for a vigorous plant with disease-resistant foliage, though we aren't as plagued by rose diseases as Easterners are. Better coloring is now ours, especially for a red rose that does not *blue-out* under Mountain West sunlight. Fragrance is returning in new cultivars, having been cast aside by geneticists for years as a desired quality to breed toward. More rigorous testing for adaptability to our forgotten climate is now possible. Hardiness is tops in the breeding programs of all the famous

■ *Our own enthusiasm for growing roses can become a nemesis.*

rose houses. With all this going for us, how can we lose? Well, there is one limitation. Our own enthusiasm for growing roses can become our undoing. If you are unrealistic in your estimate of the amount of work involved in growing roses, you will plant too many. A dozen plants well cared for can give you pleasure and satisfaction. Two dozen poorly cared for will be a disappointment, with the blame seldom placed where it belongs. Begin with the number you can care for properly. You can always EX-PAND!

Where will Roses Grow for You?

The cultivars available to gardeners, plus the new devices for winter protection now on the market make it possible for roses to be grown at ALL altitudes and latitudes of the Mountain West. There are some restrictions regarding the choice of site for the rose garden, however.

A hillside site is a difficult one for roses. Though they need good drainage, sharp drainage is a drawback. Drought produces bushes that are small and that have weak and unproductive canes. To provide the extra water required to keep them productive in such locations is a waste of the West's most precious resource. Choose a site that is almost level.

A shady site is equally difficult for roses. Though they appreciate a little respite from the blazing sun of the Mountain West from 11 A.M. until 3 P.M., the blooms will not be initiated without sun, or, if they are, there will be wide internodes between blooms. After observing the best in rose growing over the years, the east exposure is a winner. If the site is offered protection from the wind direction that is most damaging, but at a distance safe from root competition, so much the better. This will vary with each locality.

The worst possible site is one that is wet and boggy. Be watchful for possible drainage, perhaps over which you have no control, from a neighboring property. See Vol. I, Chapter 7. "Dealing with Drainage from a Neighboring Property" for possible solutions. Under the eaves is another poor choice for a site. There should be nothing growing under the eaves. Sunlight and natural precipitation are limited. Watering plants growing there will eventually damage the foundation of your home.

This leaves the aesthetic considerations of choosing a site and the accompanying choice of design. Where do you spend the most leisure time in your garden? Roses should be seen often if we are to appreciate the different stages of each bloom. The patio is probably the answer, yet restricting the patio with roses planted all around is not the answer either. An area adjoining the patio is the ideal. You can see and smell them while enjoying the leisure of the patio, and they are quickly accessible for care and gathering of blooms.

The design of a rose garden is very personal, but one that should be agreed upon by all members of the family. Roses are now being incorporated into the perennial border. Rose hedges are seen along the perimeter of the property or as thorny barriers against intruders in front of windows in the foundation planting. A design that should be considered strongly is the formal rose garden, a design that goes back to the Middle Ages, cloistered walls, and palace gardens. The formal beds are surrounded on all sides by a grassed or paved surface, an amenity much appreciated when caring for the plants. Each color of bloom can be concentrated in the formal beds for a lush color effect. The perimeter enclosure can be lattice or any type of fencing that provides the surface for the display as well as protection of climbing roses. Climbers aren't always easy to grow in all areas of the Mountain West.

Another design consideration is that of a bed backed by shrub and tall grandiflora roses, with each plant grown to perfection in a pleasing design.

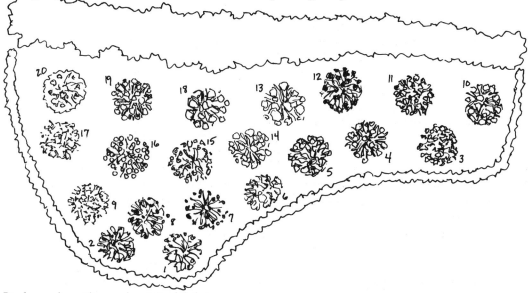

Border garden with named varieties labeled.

BORDER
(*Miniature Roses*)
1. Debut — Red blend
2. New Beginning — Orange/red/ yellow blend

MID GROUND
(*First row - Floribundas*)
3. Class Act — White
4. Amber Queen — Amber yellow
5. Sun Flame — Bright yellow
6. Pleasure — Coral pink
7. Intrigue — Deep plum
8. Showbiz — Brilliant scarlet
(*Shrub*)
9. Carefree Wonder — Pink/creamy pink reverse

(*Second row - Hybrid Teas*)
10. Sheer elegance — Soft pink/ salmon edge
11. Perfect Moment — Yellow/red tips
12. Mikado — Scarlet/yellow blend
13. Touch of Class — Pink with coral and cream
14. Voodoo — Yellow/peach/orange
15. Broadway — Reddish pink/yellow
16. Sheer Bliss — Near white
(*Shrub*)
17. Bonica — Light pink

BACKGROUND
(*Grandifloras*)
18. Shining Hour — Yellow
19. Tournament of Roses — Coral pink/pale pink
20. Prima Donna — Deep pink

The addition of elements of foliage contrast is important to design. Korean Boxwood (*Buxus microphylla koreana),* hardy in Zone 4, lends itself to shearing to become a dark green globe of foliage to set off rose blooms. The traditional privet hedge (*Ligustrum amurense)* is of doubtful hardiness throughout the western range, but a walk-through of the nursery will give you ideas about shrubs with small, dark green leaves that will complement roses. Yellow-green foliage is fashionable right now, but make sure it is acceptable to your own aesthetic sense. An edging for a rose bed is not necessary, but, for some, a cover for bare soil is a necessity. Pole peelings weather to a nondescript shade of brown, giving an advantage of conserving moisture, concealing a drip system, preventing weed growth and keeping the soil temperature even. An edging of a gray-foliage plant, such as Lamb's Ears (*Stachys lanata)* appeals to some, while white annual Sweet Alyssum is favored by many more. English lavender (*Lavandula angustifolia purpurea nana*) is also a good choice with a scent that complements the scent of the rose. Your choice should be limited to plants that do not compete with either the roots of your roses or the beauty of the roses.

Do You Offer A Rose Your Best Soil?

The answer is no. Heavy clay soils are paramount in the Mountain West, which is by no means a negative. They contain the mineral nutrients necessary for strong plant growth, whether rose, tree, or minuscule flower. They are also efficient in holding water. Only organic matter is limited in our native soils, an element easily remedied by the addition of sphagnum peatmoss, compost, or weathered manure. Rose roots are exceedingly strong. They have no trouble penetrating heavy clay, but are

happier if there is also organic matter present in moderation. If, on the other hand, your soil is light and sandy, you will need a soil amendment of 1/3 heavy clay as well as 1/3 by proportion of organic matter.

How Will Water Be Delivered To Your Roses?

Roses need considerable water at all times, including winter watering, if they are to grow and bloom well, but they must have it on their own terms. Sprinkler irrigation is out! It spreads disease spores from plant to plant, ruins blooms, and seldom penetrates the soil deep enough for benefit of deep-growing, wide spreading rose roots. The best of all rose growers use a drip irrigation system topped by a fabric weed barrier, which is, in turn, topped by pole peelings. The usual rule-of-thumb for watering is 1 inch of water per week, but any good gardener knows this is a rule easily modified. Double the amount in a hot July or if soil is light and sandy. Cut it by half in spring and fall. If you can't afford a drip system the first season, use a deep-root watering device, also known as a root feeder or soil needle to attach to your garden hose so that you can deep-water each individual plant weekly without getting water on the foliage or blooms.

Roses under drip irrigation or porous hose, fabric weed barrier, and pole peeling mulch.

Buying a Rose

It is doubtful that any Mountain West rose grower lives near a growing nursery for roses. The climate is not suited to bringing a plant to salable size in the shortest possible time. The climate in which a rose is grown has no bearing on its inherent hardiness. Most of our roses are grown in California or Texas. Your local nursery or garden center stocks roses that are the top grade, while discount houses will often carry several grades, often not the top grade. Your nursery is knowledgeable in caring for roses during shipment and while they are in the sales area, while the discount house often falls down in this category. Mail order nurseries that specialize in roses offer a wider variety of cultivars than your local nursery. With improved packing methods, these can be delivered in good shape. You pay dearly in shipping costs, however. There is one situation in which Mountain West gardeners should stick to northern-grown plants. This is in fall planting, which is a risk in any part of the Mountain West. If you wish to take this risk, buy northern-grown stock to plant in the fall, but be sure you have 6 weeks of establishment time before full freeze-up. Don't ask how you can determine this date — that's why fall planting is a risk.

The top grade in a rose is #1, 2 year old field grown. It will have at least 3 canes[2], 18-inches long before pruning for shipping. If your budget cannot stand the price of these plants, look for the older roses that have won awards and for which the patent has run out.[1] Many roses are not patented; the best ones are. You will find many of these fine old, previously patented, roses in the gardens of true rosarians.

Bare-Root, Potted, or Plastic Wrapped, Waxed or Unwaxed?

As with woody plants, the best roses are bare root and completely dormant. When planting must be delayed, such as in the high country, the potted stock is best. Sometimes when planting, however, you will find that roots have been drastically pruned to make them fit the pot, or the roots have been wound around the inside of the pot to make them fit. The root-pruned plant will be set back some, but not fatally. The plant with coiled roots will need a little surgical procedure known as *scoring* to persuade its roots to stop growing in the circular direction. Use a sharp knife or new razor blade to make slits at 3-inch intervals across the roots. Use stones to hold the roots straight and outward-pointing in the planting hole. As you pack soil lightly around each root, remove the stones, and, as always, KEEP YOUR FEET OUT OF THE HOLE.

Think carefully before buying the plastic-wrapped rose at the supermarket or discount house that will be in full leaf and drenched with moisture or the opposite — dried out and brittle. Remove it from the bag, shake out the tangled roots and plant immediately. Prune back the dried out specimen. Leave the wet and soggy specimen unpruned until next spring. If the growing season is well along, cover the planting with a basket or well-ventilated cardboard box until the leaves harden enough not to sunburn. If it is still early spring, prune and mound up as directed under "Planting A Rose."

If you are buying your first rose at a nursery, you will notice a thick white film of wax covering the canes of the roses, especially those that are potted. This is a barely warm wax in which a dormant rose plant is

[1] *See Glossary*
[2] *Order the current Handbook for Selecting Roses from American Rose Society, Handbook Editorial Department, P.O. Box 30,000, Shreveport LA 71130-0030.*

dipped before it is potted or shipped bareroot. The idea is that the plant will be saved from transpiring too much during the sales period before it is planted. It is then supposed to green up and the wax slough away without harm to the plant. This is generally true, but rosarians seldom ascribe to the waxing of roses and seldom buy these plants. For the general public, however, a waxed rose is a good buy, for it has a better chance at surviving the unskilled handling of a novice gardener.

Planting A Rose

The timing of planting a rose is the same as for woody plants — SPRING! Just as soon as the soil is workable is the rule because the plants will have time to generate a fine mesh of nutrient-absorbing root hairs before they must take up the task of supporting leaves.

The holes should be 18-inches wide and 12-inches deep. Don't crowd the roots. If a plant doesn't fit, dig the hole larger. Set the backfill aside on a tarp to be mixed with a handful of triple-superphosphate (0-45-0) and organic matter. Replace some of the backfill to build a hill within the hole. Place the rose on top the hill, directing the roots outward and with the bulge that denotes the graft union about one and 1 1/2 to 2 inches below the finished soil surface in the coldest areas, and just even with the finished soil surface for the southern areas of the Mountain West. Pack soil on top of and around the roots until the hole is 1/2 full. Use the hose to fill the hole to the brim, allowing the water to seep away before filling in with the remaining backfill. Water again to push soil into possible air pockets.

Keep your feet out of the planting hole. The water will settle the soil sufficiently. Continue adding backfill to mound up around the canes until only the tips are showing. As the season progresses you will see leaf buds swelling and leaves unfurling. At this time pull down the cone of soil until the bed is level, and the drip system, fabric weed barrier and bark mulch can be set in place.

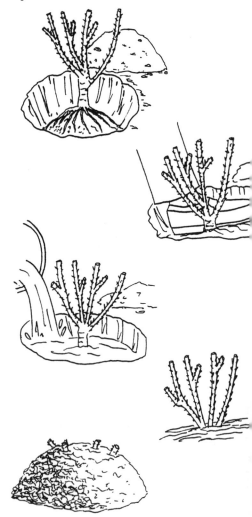

Planting a Rose .

Planting a Miniature Rose

The drying winds of spring in the Mountain West bring special problems to the tender little canes of a newly arrived miniature rose. Give them protection after planting with a 3-pound coffee can with both ends cut out. Shove the can down deeply into the soil around the newly planted mini, and replace the clear plastic lid over the top of the can. Water well and keep the soil moist, but don't open the lid until a day arrives that is 75°F.; then leave it ajar.[1] Watering is more imperative with miniature roses than with others because the roots are very close to the soil surface.

What Kind and How Much Fertilizer?

Wind is an early spring problem in many areas of the Mountain West. Roses that have been fertilized early will have a soft cane attachment that is often snapped off in a brisk wind. Replace the soil mound that you removed earlier so that it covers the cane attachment point until after the windy season. If this is too much work — you really have to be dedicated to go to this much trouble — read on.

After 6 weeks of growth has been attained, give each plant a feeding according to direction on the package. Fertilizer formulas are closely guarded by rose societies throughout the Mountain West. They shield their secret formulas from neighboring societies with whom they compete at rose shows, and they use the fertilizer as a fund raising activity. They buy each ingredient in bulk and members mix their own. If you are not yet a member of one of these rose societies, a tried-and-true formula to purchase is 15-30-15.

After the initial fertilization, you may wish to add the same fertilizer formula monthly until August l5, or you may wish to change formulas to a slow-release, such as Osmocote 14-14-14. An easy way is to add the correct formulation to your drip irrigation system. You can also use a foliar application, which can be applied much later in the season (after August 15) without danger of creating soft, watery growth which would be winter killed. The popular deep-root watering device or soil needle also has a cup where soluble rose fertilizer tablets can be added to fertilize the plants at the same time water is administered.

Pest Control

See Chapters 4,5 and 6

Propagation

See Chapter 7, Propagation, Roses

Pruning

In most areas of the Mountain West the climate is not The Grim Reaper, it is The Grim Pruner. Too often we uncover our roses gradually in spring only to find that The Pruner has killed them back to only a few inches from the soil surface. In the areas where rose growers are more fortunate, the greenish canes will be untouched by winter all the way to the tip. At this point the grower must decide the goal of the pruning — is it for competition in rose shows or for color, fragrance, and beauty? Pruning for the latter is called *high pruning*.

TIMING

The most acceptable time to prune is early spring in the areas where rose canes

---

[1] *Alice Sampson of Jack's Mini Roses, Albuquerque, New Mexico, from The Rose Window, a publication of the Denver Rose Society.*

are not winter damaged, and late spring where canes are almost always killed to within a few inches of the ground. You will sometimes see advertisements in newspapers for fall pruning of roses. This practice is self-defeating. If you prune in fall, winter will, almost without exception, cut further into the plant. The only exception is the shortening of long canes after the leaves have fallen. Wind is a given in winter in the Mountain West (except for the San Luis Valley of Colorado). Rose canes being blown about will snap or rub together, destroying the cambium tissue. Shorten them to 18 inches and tie them together with soft twine or cut bands of nylon hosiery.

TECHNIQUE

The complexity of pruning vanishes when the operation is broken down into steps. **The first step** is to remove all dead and diseased wood. When it is not necessary to remove all of the cane to cut out the dead or diseased part, make your cut just above an *outward facing bud*.

Where a whole cane is taken, make your cut just beyond the flare of the point where the cane meets supporting wood. Leave no stubs, but neither leave flush cuts. **The second step** is to remove any weak or crossing wood and the slender twiggy growth common to all roses, especially miniatures, floribundas, and polyanthas. Remove it flush with the base. The center is now open to sunlight and air circulation. **The final step** depends upon the vigor of all roses in your area, the class of the rose, and the inherited growth characteristics of the cultivar you are pruning. A stout old *Queen Elizabeth* in the Grand Valley of Western Colorado or Southern Utah will be 5 feet high with canes the diameter of a thick thumb. The same *Queen Elizabeth* growing in a less charitable climate will have canes of lesser diameter, but will, nevertheless, be vigorous. For both, look closely at the remaining canes and **remove only those that are sure to grow into the path of another.** Examine the direction of the topmost bud to determine the direction it will grow. That's it, you're done.

Too close.

Too Long.

Just right.

Ways to prune roses.

are single or may have 2 rows of petals, bluish red, and totally of no value. Another, Dr. Huey, has double red blooms with gold stamens. Multiflora rose root stocks produce small white blooms. None of these is the rose you bought. Cut them back to the point of origin. If there are no other desirable canes left living above the graft, it's time to bid goodbye to that rose.

PRUNING CUT TREATMENT

White glue is the standard now for dabbing on pruning cuts. The squeeze-bottle top is easily manipulated, and the non-leaking bottle is convenient to carry in a pocket as you are pruning.

DEADHEADING & CUTTING BLOOMS

The necessity for deadheading roses is the same as removing spent blooms from perennials or annuals — to prevent seed formation which would reduce bloom later on. When gathering blooms for bouquets or deadheading, the cuts should not be deep. The cut made just above the first (or second, if you want a very long stem) 5 leaflet leaf will give you the best results. The stems of roses gathered for the home should be plunged immediately into a pitcher of very hot water that you have carried to the garden with you. They are then placed in a cool room in dim light to harden. When the water has cooled, the roses should be ready to arrange and will last several days. If you wish to prolong their life, remove each stem and re-cut it **under water each day** and rearrange the stems. Floralife or another preservative added to the water will also add to the life of the blooms.

Roses that are winter-killed below the graft will send up shoots arising from the root stock to which the scion was grafted. Pull away the soil to make sure the offending canes are rising from below the graft union. If they are, they are often from an old Italian rose, Manetti, known for its strong, hardy roots. The blooms, however,

For arranging in the home cut blooms just below a 3 or 5 leaf leaflet.

THE CANDELABRA

For unknown reasons a cultivar will suddenly throw a very long strong cane with an arrangement of budded shoots at the tip that resembles the arms of a candelabra. This gift is a wonder to behold. The blooms often open simultaneously and can be cut for a show or for display in the home. Often, more buds will form, and, indeed, candelabras have been known to live 3 years or more, at which time the cane dies and is removed.

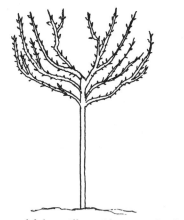

The candelabra will provide top quality for up to 3 years. Some cultivars put up candelabras annually.

CLIMBERS

Before we think about pruning, let's consider training. The canes want to grow straight up. Persuade them, instead, to grow outward, with canes alternating between right and left of the trunk. Tie the canes to their support and soon little lateral shoots will be seen growing along the cane. These are the stems that will bloom. Climbing hybrid teas and floribunda roses bloom on wood produced in the current season. They are pruned as above directed. The large-flowered climbers and ramblers bloom on laterals from old wood. A lateral is a side shoot, not the terminal growth at the tip. These are pruned just after blooms fade, for they bloom only once. Cut back the lateral cane to 6 to 10 inches. Two or 3 of the oldest canes should be removed at the base. This is renewal pruning as described in Vol. I, Pruning Shrubs, p. 90. If the plant throws more new canes than were removed, select the best of these and remove the rest. For all cultivars with continuous or fall bloom periods, deadheading is imperative to improve the next bloom period.

Climbing roses trained over wire or lattice arches are charming, but there is another method of training that should be used more often. This is the growing of a climbing rose as a pillar. In Great Britain hybrid poplar trees are grown quickly to a height of 8 to 10 feet; then the tree is dug in spring when the bark is slipping and the bark peeled from trunk and major limbs. The shallow roots are trimmed back to form a plate-like base. Several of these are positioned at strategic points around the rose garden to form a needed vertical design element. Concrete is poured around the plate of roots to keep them in place and prevent rot. Climbing roses (usually 2) are planted at

he base of these pillars and trained to grow
p and over. In bloom they are a stunning
ight. Even when not in bloom the foliage
orms an attractive column of green. You
vill find the hybrid poplars listed in Sources
t the end of this chapter.

MINIATURE ROSES

Little pruning is necessary except for the
wiggy growth attached to slim canes.
Remove at the point of attachment to
upporting wood. Once in awhile a mini
vill put up a cane the size of a hybrid tea
ane. Remove it at once.

SHRUB ROSES

The popularity of shrub roses is increas-
ng with each year. One reason may be that
he pruning is minimal. They are allowed to
each their normal height without heading-
ack. Only dead wood or weak and/or
rossing branches are removed. As they
loom, deadhead as usual, but for the last
lush of bloom, do not remove the flowers
nd they will produce a crop of bright red
ips for winter color and for bird food.

At this writing there is no firm
ommittment among rosarians as to the new
David Austin shrub roses from England.
Though they are rated in the catalogs as
ardy from Zones 4-9, the tests thus far are
ot showing them to be as hardy in Zone 4
s we would like them to be. They grow
bout 4 feet high and 4 feet in diameter,
vith mildly thorny canes covered with
mall, cup-shaped blooms in June and
ntermittently throughout the summer. The
ragrance is strong with a sweetness and
emony overtone. Wayside Gardens of
Hodges, South Carolina, has the exclusive
ight of introduction of these roses into the
United States.

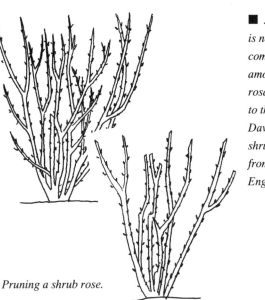

Pruning a shrub rose.

■ . . . *there
is no firm
committment
among
rosarians as
to the new
David Austin
shrub roses
from
England.*

TREE ROSES

The tree rose is a hybrid tea grafted to a
Japanese rootstock. A second graft of IXL
forms the stem. It may produce some non-
blooming suckers along the trunk that
should be cut out *flush* with the trunk. The
top is pruned in the same manner as a
hybrid tea, cutting out diseased, dead, and
weak and/or crossing wood. Trim canes
back to a symmetrical shape so that the
leafed-out top will become a luxuriant,
globe-shaped crown of foliage and blooms
that provides a vertical accent in the rose
garden or in a container.

Winter Protection

In areas of the Mountain West where the
temperature seldom drops below 0° F.,
there is no need for winter protection of
roses. They are better off with sunlight and
air circulating on all sides. If you are in
doubt about whether to protect, leave some
unprotected and next spring compare their
degree of survival.

If your wintertime low is much below -10° F, avoid the classes of roses noted for tenderness: the Noisettes, and the famed 'Lady Banksia.' However, if 'Banksia' is a must for you, consider a frame of lath built to fit over this climber; then cover the frame with an insulated, weatherproof blanket that fits snugly around the base. Insulate the soil around the root run with styrofoam.

HARDENING-OFF

Growing a rose to perfection is the ultimate in preparing it for winter, but this isn't always possible despite your skill and experience. During a long cool fall we are often fooled into thinking that winter won't really come, but it always does. In early August give a no-nitrogen feeding such as 0-10-10 to encourage fall buds but not to encourage any more new shoot growth. Look for this fertilizer at a farm supply store where it is sold as a fertilizer for small grain. As soon as fall buds have formed, begin to decrease water each week. Never allow plants to dry out to the point of wilting, but keep them on the dry side.

Serious rose protection does not begin until just before the soil freezes in your area. Ask around if you don't know when that is. It varies with every valley or hilltop.

The second best protection, after a structure, is the soil mound. Pour soil over the center of the plant until the angle of repose is reached at about 10 inches. Do not scrape the soil needed from between the plants. The roots would be seriously exposed to freezing. Instead, gather this soil from the vegetable or cutting garden. It can be returned next spring. The best device to keep the mound in place is a rose collar of white corrugated fiberglass. These are constructed to snap together. Don't be tempted to use dried leaves or bark chips as

a mound over your roses. The mice and voles will find cozy comfort and a winter source of rose canes for food! In areas where temperatures may drop to -20° F, place an additional insurance of evergreen boughs over the collars and soil mounds. A cheap source is the lopped branches from your Christmas tree and other holiday evergreens.

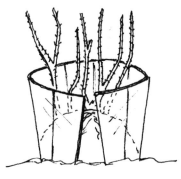

Rose collar with soil mound to protect a rose.

New on the market are weather-resistant cloth blankets insulated with foam. They fasten around each plant by means of velcro binding. They are available in various heights and lengths. For a large plant, the velcro can fasten 2 or more of the blankets together to achieve the desired girth.

Rose shelters designed to resemble a cold frame are needed in Zones 2 and 3 of the Mountain West. They are used in Boerner Botanical Gardens, Minnesota with good results. The shelter shown below will cover 6 roses. A good shelter must be portable, and have ventilation and a light-transmitting roof. A roof constructed of clear corrugated fiberglass is excellent, for the corrugation provides the needed continuous ventilation and allows light penetration. Use a door hinge with a removable pin. Close the roof only when the temperature drops below 20°F. and raise it above 32°F. If the plants inside exceed the height of the shelter, bend them over or cut them back. Drop tree roses to their sides by digging a rootball that is wrapped in burlap; then mound the entire plant with soil before positioning the shelter over it. Add a container of warfarin mouse poison before closing the lid

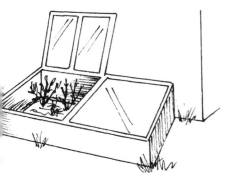

A serious rose shelter for high country and those roses growing in Zones 2 and 3 of the Mountain West.

REMOVING THE PROTECTION

If shelter, collars, and mounds are left too long as the season advances, soft new shoots will grow that will break off or wither when the protection is removed. Pull down and remove the soil mounds gradually, starting in March. Remove the shelters when snow has melted from the top and the temperature rises daily above freezing. Close the lid at night until frost is no longer a danger.

WINTER WATERING

After the plants are well-hardened and bloom is finished, water each plant well on a mild day. As winter advances, water monthly on mild days when there is no snow cover. Even though the soil is frozen, it can accept water.

The Major Classes of Roses and Prize Winning Examples

Hybrid Tea

Hybrid Tea roses resulted in crosses made with Hybrid Perpetuals and the true Tea roses. As time went on, other lines were brought in to improve growth and bloom characteristics. The most important cross was made with Austrian Copper, the beloved old homestead shrub rose of the Mountain West. This cross broke out the pink, white, and crimson-with-a-bluish-cast mode so that clear reds, yellows, and orange could be bred with ease. Hybrid Teas grow about 3 to 5 feet in height; buds are long and pointed, generally 1 to a stem.

'Blanche Malerin' - A scarce good white with long, urn-shaped buds. Fragrant.

'Charlotte Armstrong' - Many deep rose-pink fragrant blooms. Much used in breeding.

'Chicago Peace' - As strong a grower as its parent, but has richer flush of pink over coppery-yellow base color.

'Chrysler Imperial' - Heavy bloomer in crimson. Fragrant.

'Dainty Bess' - A light pink single undaunted by heat.

'Double Delight' - A red blend with outstanding fragrance.

'First Prize' - Pink blend of good substance.

'Garden Party' - White with faint pink overtones.

'Helen Traubel' - Not a good rose for show, but neverending supply of apricot pink blooms of delightful fragrance.

'Mr. Lincoln' - Sturdy plants with plenty of deep red, somewhat flattened blooms

'Oregold' - Deep yellow blooms, long-lasting.

'Peace' - The rose of the century; pink, yellow over cream; very large size.

'Touch of Class' - Many flowers of deep pink blend.

'Tropicana' - A red with orange over-tones.

Floribunda

The Floribunda class came along as a hybrid between Polyanthas and Hybrid Teas. They are hardy, vigorous , and seldom without bloom. The flowers are borne singly or in clusters and the color range is excellent.

'Betty Prior' - A very old, tall, vigorous plant bearing hundreds of single carmine-pink flowers.

'Fashion' - beautifully formed salmon.

'First Edition' - An orange blend of good substance.

'Ivory Fashion' - Creamy version of Fashion.

'Little Darling' - Well-shaped small blooms of soft pink with apricot flush.

'Sarabande' - Single to semi-double flowers in dazzling crimson.

'Simplicity' - Covered with small pink flowers all summer.

Grandiflora

A blurring of the line between hybrid tea and floribunda gave us the grandiflora, which is vigorous, usually over 6 feet in good rose-growing country. It may have flowers that are one to a stem, or clusters.

'Carrousel' - Deep red flowers with fewer petals, some in clusters, some single stemmed; nice fragrance.

'John S. Armstrong' - Dark red clusters of bloom.

'Montezuma' - Pink and salmon blended in a short, high- centered bud. Plant is very tall; give it room.

'Ole'- Very free flowering vermilion red with ruffled petals. Very short, seldom over 2 feet.

'Pink Parfait' - clusters of pink flowers with a pale yellow base.

'Queen Elizabeth' - Vigorous, tall, disease resistant, many pearly pink blooms of lasting quality. The best grandiflora.

Climbing Roses

A rose cane never develops any hold-fasts; therefore, actually there are no true climbing roses. For more than a century, however, there have been plants with canes that are 8 feet long that can be trained up; thus the eventuation of the term. A few are climbing sports (mutations), such as Climbing Dainty Bess.

'America' - an orange blend flower in smothering clusters.

'Blaze' - A vigrous dark red, a favorite throughout the West.

'Don Juan' - Deep red fully double blooms on drought resistant vine. Also spider mite resistant.

'Golden Showers' - A medium yellow bloom that accents many other colors. Suggest growing it with *Clematis jackmani.*

'New Dawn' - A delicate pink shading to white.

Rosa banksiae lutea - An English

designation for a plant called 'Lady Banksia' in America. This vigorous, thornless, very fragrant climber can smother a New Mexican hacienda with tiny yellow flowers over a period of 2 months. Hardy to zero degrees and maybe more. Totally impossible to prune. Cut out the dead as best you can in February. See above for method of protection for this rose in other aeas.

Climbing Hybrid Tea

'Cl. Dainty Bess' - Single, salmon-pink flowers with a silvery sheen.

'Cl. Peace' - Very hardy duplicate of its bush form of cream, overlaid with yellow and pink.

Rambler

Ramblers are mentioned here only to include 2 that are often found at the site of old homesteads and country homes where they often covered the pergola that housed the cistern.

'American Pillar' - Late blooming pink on vigorous vine.

'Dorothy Perkins' - A very old cluster-flowered pink with canes of 20 feet or more. Can withstand minus 25°F. or more.

Creeper

The creeper is not a recognized group or classification. There are 2 cultivars that are useful in some parts of the Mountain West, especially planted at the top of a slope in a deep depression to catch natural precipitation. Allow to spill downward where they will sometimes root at nodes.They form excellent ground covers against erosion. The bloom stems stand up straight about 8 inches. The bright red hips are a colorful sight and attractive to wild life.

Rosa wichuriana - Single white blooms

R. 'Max Graf' - a cross between *R.*

rugosa and *R. wichuriana*. Very hardy; useful in sandy soil; pink flowers; orange hips.

Polyantha

Many blurred lines in breeding make it difficult to designate this class. They generally have dense twiggy growth with many small fragrant flowers.

'Cecil Brunner' - Perfectly formed buds of pink, often used as a boutonniere.

'Mothers Day' - A vermilion red cluster of blooms will appear all summer, beginning at Mother's Day. Good for containers.

'Margot Koster' - Bred for the rough Danish climate; large salmon clusters of bloom all summer. Only 18-24 inches tall.

'The Fairy' - One of the most famous, sometimes placed with the floribundas. Big mounds with continuous supply of small, light pink blooms. Give it your best soil and at least 4 feet of space.

Miniature

The leaves, canes, and flowers of miniature roses are elfin copies of their larger cousins, and, despite their size, hardy without exception.

'Cuddles' - Deep pink.

'Dreamglo' - A red blend with pale

yellow.

'Magic Carrousel' - A red blend highly rated.

'Yellow Doll' - Well-formed medium yellow buds.

Tree Rose

See above for the parentage of these single stem globe-shaped heads of foliage and flowers. They make striking accents in the formal rose garden, and are also good container subjects. There are miniature tree roses as well as weeping tree roses.

Cultivars are counterparts of the hybrid tea and grandiflora and climber cultivars listed above.

Shrub and Species Roses

'Austrian Copper' - A chance mutation of an all yellow rose originally brought to Europe before the 13th century by the Moors who invaded Spain from Africa. Also classified as *Rosa foetida bicolor*.

'Bonica' - An All-America winner with continuous pink blooms, orange hips. Good as a hedge.

'Champlain'[1] - Dark red flowers; hardy without protection across Canada. Susceptible to blackspot.

'David Thompson'[1] - medium red flowers all summer; resistant to mildew and blackspot; hardy without protection across Canada. 4 feet.

R. eglanteria - The Sweet Brier rose of song and poetry with foliage that smells like apples, more intense when wet; small blush pink flowers. 6 feet.

If interested in obtaining a list of nurseries that sell plants of the new Canadian cultivars (those listed above as "hardy across Canada"), send query to Public Inquiries, Agriculture Canada, Central Experimental Farm, Ottawa, Ontario K1A 0C5.

'Harrison's Yellow' - Also known as the Memorial Day Rose; small semidouble blooms of bright yellow at the end of May. Strong fragrance. Suckers at the base; 5 feet x 5 feet. Introduced in 1830.

'Henry Hudson'[1] - Clouds of fragrant white flowers in repeated flushes. Resistant to mildew and blackspot. Hardy without protection across Canada. A dwarf at 18 inches.

R. rubrifolia - As the name suggests, the foliage is a smoky purple-red; highly prized by arrangers for the foliage alone, but it produces charming single pink flowers as well. Hardy thru Zone 2 (minus 50° F.), yet can withstand the heat of New Mexico. Hip crop is large and decorative. Does not sucker.

R. rugosa - The grandaddy of all the best shrub roses. Use it as a hedge or a barrier, to beautify utility buildings, and in the shrub border. Heavy textured pleated leaves.

'Frau Dagmar Hastrup' - Continuous single pink flowers with satiny texture, good fragrance.

'F. J. Grootendorst' - Small bright red fringed flowers followed by good hips. Others available: 'Pink Grootendorst' and 'Grootendorst Supreme'. All top out at about 6 feet.

'Sarah Van Fleet' - Fragrant, rose-red blooms produced over a long period. 8 feet.

'Sir Thomas Lipton' - Double white flowers on a 6 foot plant with good dark green foliage.

R. spinosissima altaica - One for the outhouse. This species and cultivar from Siberia is ideally suited to cover the outbuildings on the sandy soils of Eastern Colorado, Eastern Nevada, Northern Idaho and Eastern Montana. It can withstand the savage winds, drought, and lack of care, and still produce

widespread canes bearing large creamy yellow flowers. The Scotch rose.

Antique Roses

Marie Antoinette, the ill-fated queen of France during the French Revolution, was known to be a rose fancier, but we owe the Empress Josephine the greatest debt of gratitude for her devotion to her rose garden. Equally important is the homage paid to the rose by her flower painter, Pierre-Joseph Redouté. Her dedication to roses and her famous rose garden are shown in the painting *La Rose de la Malmaison* that hangs in the Louvre. It portrays Napolean offering a rose to his Empress as she languishes among her ladies in waiting. Until her death in 1814, one of history's greatest rose collections was gathered in one place at Malmaison. The garden was soon to be destroyed, but the Redouté paintings give us today the correct labelling of the genus and species of each, the exact leaf placement on the stem, the exact form of the thorns for each species, the exact petal arrangement, the exact placement of subtending buds, and most importantly, the exquisite colors of the old roses. You can almost smell them.

The Cabbage Roses

R. centifolia - a 100 or more petals overlap as in a cabbage, hence the name. The blush pink deepens in the center. Important in the breeding of hybrid perpetuals and, eventually, the hybrid teas. Try *R.c.* 'Red Provence' or 'de Meaux.'

The Moss Roses

The true moss rose has hairy sepals that envelop the bud and resemble soft, moss-like growths. Generally the moss is green, but it can also be red. The moss roses are mutations of the cabbage roses.

R. centifolia muscosa - grows 6 feet high with large, double, cupped, very fragrant blooms in pink, once only in June. There is

The Gallicas

Rosa gallica - a vigorous, fragrant red rose hardy throughout the Mountain West. It was probably transported to England from the Roman Empire about A.D.1100 and became "The Rose of Lancaster," the symbolic red rose the House of Lancaster of Britain's civil War of the Roses. Better known and more available is the Apothecary rose, *Rosa gallica officinalis*, which can still be found in old gardens, near deserted cellar holes, and along roadsides. The petals hold their fragrance, making it much sought after for potpourri. It is semi-double and deep red. Try 'Cardinal Richelieu.'

also a white form.

The Damask Roses

R. damascena - the summer damasks bloom once with double blooms; the autumn damasks bloom in summer and autumn. They have yellow-green leaves. Try 'Celsiana' - blush pink, 'Madame Hardy' - clear white. Both very fragrant.

The Musk Roses

A diverse group ranging from 4 foot shrubs to climbers 40 feet tall that are glorious if they have a dead tree to clamber over. Some bloom only once, others continuously. They result from a cross between *R. moschata* and the Noisette ''Reve d'Or'. All bloom in trusses; most are fragrant and have attractive hips in the fall. Try 'Buff Beauty', 'Cornelia' or 'Nastarana.'

The Albas

R. alba semiplena - the symbol of the House of York, this is the white rose of the War of Roses, England's civil war. Grown especially for its very large urn-shaped hips. Try 'Maiden's Blush' *or* 'Felicity Parmentier.'

The China Roses

It is from China roses that the Hybrid Tea, the Grandiflora, and Floribunda got their free-flowering habit. They are not as hardy as the groups described earlier, seldom withstanding more than 0°F. There are red and white forms. The red has a few nasty thorns and the wood is dark. The white form has green wood and almost no thorns.

The Tea Roses

Not hardy in any part of the Mountain West, with careful protection tea roses are, nevertheless, worth growing in the antique rose garden. They bloom and bloom and bloom, with a very fragrant, fragile charm. Try "Catherine Mermet,' 'Duchess de Brabent' or 'Madam Cochet.'

The Bourbon Roses

Named for the Bourbon monarchs of France, this species is seldom seen today, but should be because the Bourbons are vigorous, hardy shrubs with glossy, bright green foliage. Most repeat, and fall blooms are of best quality. Try 'Hermosa,' 'Madame Isaac Pereire,' or the most famous Bourbon of all, 'Souvenir de la Malmaison.'

Growing Roses for Show[1]

For those who would like to enter the competition in showing roses there are some definite do's and don'ts.

Proper culture before the show is of utmost importance, and your roses will tell you by their performance whether they merit an outing at a show. As buds form on hybrid teas, carefully snip off the buds below the terminal bud.

The stem must be strong enough to hold up the bloom, and the flower must have substance so that it will last. The substance, or starch or vitality, is easy to detect. A many-petalled rose needs more stem for support and balance, but you will be marked down if it looks as though you have cut half the bush.

Cut the blooms for the show and place them immediately in very hot water. Evening seems best. Make sure you have a

[1] From an article by Marie Shields in the Utah Rose Society publication of May, 1979. Reprinted in The Rose Window, 1979.

name tag for each rose as you cut, for no matter how well you know your roses, in this last minute rush and poor light, you may be fooled. Cut the bloom when the sepals are down and the outer petals just beginning to open. Keep blooms separate if in a large container, so there will be no damage from a neighbor's thorns. If you are unable to place all of your roses in a refrigerator, or if they are red or white (which don't refrigerate well), then place in a cool, dark place out of any breezes. Shop yard sales for a wooden cola/soda case holding 12 bottles. It is un-tippable for travel to the show. Use a cone of heavy butcher paper stuck into the top of the bottle for each rose. Clean up the foliage and petals. No dust, white streaks, no split or confused center. The flower should be in its most perfect form, from 1/2 to 3/4 open, depending on its petallage. Thorns may be removed below the water line. If you feel a rose may open before the show does, tie the flower with white yarn, then slip it off as you place your exhibit on the entry table. Do not travel with your roses in the back of an open pick-up, for they will open wide before you get there.

The Baker's Dozen Best Roses

Asking the local rose societies to arrive at a concensus as to the best roses is, apparently, similar to asking the members to experience the same nightmare. Nevertheless, they have been good sports to offer the following 13 as the best of the best. Though no explanation was given as to the order ascribed, author hesitated to aggravate them further by inquiring.

The Baker's Dozen
Touch of Class
Tiffany
Pristine
Oregold
Peace
Pascali
Miss All American Beauty
Heirloom
Granada
Keepsake

Grandiflora
Aquarius
Gold Medal
Queen Elizabeth

American Rose Society Ratings
10	perfect
9.9-9.0	superior
8.9-8.0	very good
7.9-7.0	good
6.9-6.0	average
5.9-5.0	poor
4.9 or below	very poor

Roses Susceptible to Powdery Mildew
American Spirit	Midas Touch
Apricot Nectar	Neon Lights
Betty Prior	Oklahoma
Caribbean	Prima Donn
Dolly Parton	Red Cascade
First Prize	Royal Highness
Fragrant Cloud	Sheer Bliss
Granada	Sundowner
Holy Toledo	Tropicana
Joseph's Coat	Unforgettable

Roses suscaptible to Black Spot
Chicago Peace
Dynasty
First Prize
Gold Medal
Peace
Prima Donna
Simplicity

Suggested Sources:

High Country Rosarium
1717 Downing St.
Denver CO 80218
Catalog $1.

Historical Roses
1657 W. Jackson St.
Painsville OH 44077
Free list for long SASE

Heirloom Roses
14062 Riverside Dr. N.E.
St. Paul OR 97137
Free list.

Pickering Nurseries, Inc.
670 Kingston Rd.
Pickering, Ontario
L1V 1A6, Canada
Catalog $2.

Roses of Yesterday and Today
802 Brown's Valley Road
Watsonville CA 95076-0398
Catalog $3

Source for hybrid poplar:
Gurney's
110 Capitol Street,
Yankton SD 57079

Ornamental Grasses

Next in importance to the divine profusion of water, light and air, those three physical facts which render existence possible, may be reckoned the universal beneficence of grass. Lying in the sunshine among the buttercups and dandelions in May, scarcely higher in intelligence than the minute tenants of that mimic wilderness, our earliest recollections are of grass; and when the fitful fever is ended and the foolish wrangle of the market and the forum is closed, grass heals over the scar which our descent into the bosom of the earth has made, and the carpet of the infant becomes the blanket of the dead.

Grass is the foregiveness of Nature - her constant benediction. Fields trampled with battle, saturated with blood, torn with ruts of cannon, grow green again with grass, and carnage is forgotten. Streets abandoned by traffic become grass grown, like rural lanes, and are obliterated. Forests decay, harvests perish, flowers vanish, but grass is immortal. Beleaguered by the sullen hosts of winter, it withdraws into the impregnable fortress of its subter-ranean vitality and emerges upon the solicitation of spring. Sown by the winds, by wandering birds, propagated by the subtle horticulture of the elements which are its ministers and servants, it softens the rude outlines of the world. It invades the solitude of deserts, climbs the inaccessible slopes and pinnacles of mountains and modifies the history, character, and the destiny of nations.

Unobtrusive and patient, it has immortal vigor and agression. Banished from the thoroughfares and fields, it bides its time to return, and when vigilance is relaxed or the dynasty has perished, it silently resumes the throne from which it has been expelled, but which it never abdicates. It bears no blazonry of bloom to charm the senses with frangrances or splendor, but its homely hue is more enchanting than the lily or the rose. It yields no fruits in earth or air, yet should the harvest fail for a single year, famine would depopulate the world. - "Grass" by John James Ingalls, American Forests, September, 1969, p. 36.

Design Qualities and Possibilities

The English perennial border has held our attention for as long as anything holds the attention of North American gardeners, and we are ready to make it our own by incorporating into it the ornamental grasses. No longer do the words "ornamental grass" mean bluegrass turf. Many exotics have joined the native sod and bunch grasses to be included in the term. If we listen, we can hear the whisper of the shortgrass and tallgrass prairies as they call us back to a time where first early fur trappers and then pioneer wagon trains crossed 800 miles of grassland to reach the Mountain West. Many exotics have joined the native sod and bunch grasses to be included in the term "ornamental grass." Mountain Westerners are urged not to lose sight of the natives that sustained our ancestors. Take care not to allow your

■ *Ornamental grasses have a tremendous scene softening property.*

¹ See Glossary

255

■ *If left standing in winter the stalks present a golden warmth in an otherwise shivery landscape.*

ornamental grasses to escape into forest land, or even into a vacant lot in the city. We can never know when we are unleashing a lamb that may become a monster. See **Species to Avoid.**

Boundary lines of shortgrass and tallgrass prairie.

Ornamental grasses offer a scene-softening strength. Just a few plants can soften the look of concrete, such as near a swimming pool parapet, and they don't drop leaves in the pool. Tall single plants become sculptural accents. Medium varieties can meander down a slope where a breeze sets them waving in swirls that mime the drama and movement of water. Low species can trail languidly into a pool, while others brighten shade with variegated leaves.

Grasses are generous with 4-season good looks. Spring finds them putting forth delicate tender shoots, matching the spring green of perennials and groundcovers, yet adding the vertical dimension often absent. The arching form of summer growth soars to heights tall enough to qualify as "bones"[1] of the perennial border. Fall is their shining best season when colorful seed heads develop. If left standing in winter the stalks present a golden warmth in an otherwise shivery landscape. Heavy snow will pack

them down, but if it is removed quickly, they spring back without harm. Only late winter finds them without appeal, for they must be shorn to about 4 inches to allow spring sunlight to stimulate the crown.

Site Preparation

Many of the ornamental grasses are related to prairie grasses, and, therefore, do not require a rich soil. Average soil is all that is needed. If soil is too rich in organic matter, growth will be soft, watery, and weak-stemmed. The drainage must be sharp for most varieties; the exceptions are swamp dwellers, such as the variegated sweet flag, *Acorus calamus.*

Planting and Care

The seed of native species is viable and available. It may take 3 years of growing in a nursery bed to grow to a size suitable for transplanting. Planting from 1-gallon containers is easier and the plants are not expensive. Compost and fertilizer in the planting hole are not encouraged, but a drip emitter nearby and a reasonably thick mulch of pole peelings or bark will assure a carefree summer. Each spring, give each clump a miserly helping of a slow-release fertilizer, such as Osmacote 14-14-14.

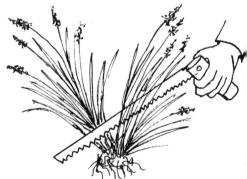

Use a small tree saw or a chain saw to divide a clump of ornamental grass.

Dividing a clump of ornamental grass is not an easy undertaking. About every 3 years lift the entire clump to a nearby plastic tarp. Use a small tree saw or chain saw to saw through the tough roots and strands. Discard the woody center portion. When resetting divisions, take care not to set too deep, or the crown will be smothered. Water well. There is no need for fertilizer until active growth resumes.

Insects are almost unknown, but a few green aphids may invade the tender spring foliage. Washing with a strong stream of water from the hose will usually dispatch them.

Diseases are equally unknown as none of the major turf diseases that may invade your nearby lawn are likely to spread to the ornamental grass. *Stripe Smut* (*Ustilago striiformae*) has been seen. Leaves develop gray or black stripes which break open to become somewhat moist and drippy. The affected leaves turn light brown, wither and die. The only treatment is to remove affected leaves as soon as they are observed.

In areas of heavy snow, the clumps of ornamental grass can be tied unobtrusively midway up the stalks to assist them in remaining upright under heavy snow loads. Almost all cultivars are hybrids. The seeds, therefore, are sterile and they will not invade other areas with seedlings. The annual grasses, however, are shorn for gifts and used in dried arrangements because their seedlings can become a nuisance.

Cutting and Preserving

Grasses can be cut and dried in almost any stage of development. Cutting when leaf stems are green gives you a fresh fountain of color to combine with tulips or iris for an Ikebana arrangement. Cutting further into the growing season adds a graceful arch to a summer bouquet. Cutting in fall gives you ideal material to combine with cattails, everlastings, mullein stalks, black-eyed Susan seed heads and a myriad of other fall dried materials.

When you sally forth to cut roadside grasses, take along a ball of twine. Cut lengths 18 inches long and place them on the deck of the trunk of your car. Cut swatches of grass as large in diameter as your thumb and fingers can encircle, cutting at ground level. Lay a swatch across a length of string, tying immediately with enough tail of the twine to hang the bundle in a warm, dry place when you return home.

Dried grasses do not collect dust when displayed in the home like many other materials. They are, however, attractive to spiders. If you notice one day that your grasses are enveloped in spider webs, hasten them outside or to the shower for a bath.

Winter Protection

Many of the most decorative genera of ornamental grasses are not hardy in all areas of the Mountain West. In November before the soil freezes give the soil a deep mulch (6 inches) of dried leaves. Hold this mulch with a few evergreen boughs. Don't cut the foliage until spring. The existing foliage, though dead, will afford some protection.

Using Ornamental Grass to Convert the Intermittent Stream to a Grassy Waterway

For country dwellers the occasional downpour brings an environmental problem that is now controlled by law. It pays to keep as much renegade water as possible right where it has fallen. One inch of rainfall over an acre of land amounts to 3,630 cubic feet of water. That is slightly more than 27,152 gallons of water. And

■ It pays to keep as much renegade water as possible right where it has fallen.

that is a lot of water, any way you figure it, when it is roaring down an unprotected gully. The main ditch will be deeply eroded and side runnels will develop as rain continues to fall. Tons of soil will be washed away, clogging storm sewers and muddying streams. Eventually, authorities will come looking for the culprit who is responsible for the problem. And the enemy is you.

The root systems of ornamental grasses, slow the water so that it does not erode the soil. When slowed sufficiently, more of the water sinks downward, easing the volume of runoff. Environmental Protection Agency regulations are stringent about runoff.

Your first line of defense against erosion is the deepening and widening of the intermittent stream into a series of depressions that will become pools. Each pool becomes a basin that, when full, overflows into the next basin. Planted to a mixture of grasses, the intermittent stream becomes a meadow. Soil preparation and establishment water are the same as found in Volume I, Chapter 4, "Soil," and Chapter 21 "Turf," pp. 262-264. If you want the look of turf, plant Buffalo grass, which can withstand inundation, or plant bunch grasses and cut your grassy waterway twice a summer at a 5-inch height. Leaving your grasses uncut will see them form tall stems that will wave down the hillside with still a different look.

A blend of Switch Grass (*Panicum virgatum*) Smooth Brome, (*Bromus inermis)* and Reed Canary Grass (*Phalaris arundinacea*) will present the best appearance and effectively slow down an intermittent stream. These grasses are invasive. Cutting them down before seed heads drop will prevent invasion. Keep a sharp shovel handy if the roots spread out of bounds.

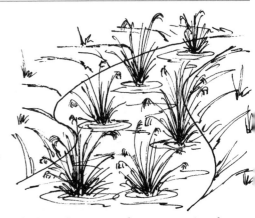

An intermittent stream becomes a series of grassy pools instead of a roaring torrent.

Revegetation of Disturbed Land

If you have an irrigation canal or natural stream running through your property, plant the bank to *Agropyron trachycaulum,* Slender Wheatgrass. 'Streambank' is a good cultivar with roots that will not invade the waterway and that will establish itself without irrigation.

If you have an acid soil on mine spoil resulting from surface coal extraction, Switchgrass (*Panicum virgatum)* , Deertongue Grass (*Rhexia mariana),* and Weeping Lovegrass (*Eragrostis curvula)* will grow well with establishment water.

The cultivar 'Montane' of Curleaf Mahogany (*Cercoparpus montanus)* is an excellent choice for planting on rocky or disturbed ground. It is a shrub growing to 6 or 7 feet. It is good browse for deer, a good windbreak, and will hold the soil against wind and water erosion. Its altitude limit is 7,000 feet.

For grass revegetation, use grass species such as Indian Rice Grass 'Nezpar' (*Oryzopsis hymenoides*) on high altitude roadside areas. Drill seeding is far superior to hydro-seeding. Jute mesh pegged down over the seeding is superior to the material now being sold as "erosion net."

Species to Avoid

An exotic plant is an alien, non-native species. With the tendency of perennial grasses to spread by underground stolons and rhizomes, and the same tendency of annual grass seed to be spread by the wind, we must be ever mindful of planting exotic species that can crowd out native species.

■ *Agropyron cristatum*
CRESTED WHEAT
You may have a situation where a mixture of grasses would revegetate a vacant city lot or a disturbed area that is presently ugly with weeds. Examine the label of the grass mixture carefully to be certain that it does not contain Crested Wheat. This successful grass from the Russian steppes is extremely tolerant of drought, wind, and cold winters. That is why it is widely planted in the Midwest and Mountain West. Where ornament is desired in a grass mixture, however, it will soon become the only species growing. Crested Wheat has the allelopathic characteristic that causes it to exude a toxic substance from the roots that prevents the germination of other seeds nearby. It is the eventual winner in the survival battle within a grass mixture.

Crested Wheat

■ *Bromopsis inermis*
SMOOTH BROME
This grass is the hill-holder and roadside erosion prevention of the Mountain West. It is beautiful in all stages of development. But take care not to plant it in an ornamental planting of grasses for it will be the eventual winner, driving out all others.

Smooth Brome

Planting exotic species poses a dilemma for the high country stockman, who, understandably, wants no part of growing grass for ornament. Native grasses predominate in the high country, but do not provide the nutrition for cattle, sheep, and horses as does non-native Timothy (*Phleum praetense*), which is an escapee from Eurasia via Alaska. The voices of environmentalists are loud against Timothy, but, clearly, there can be a middle road. Watchfulness is a part of every gardener's curriculum. Stewardship of the land is foremost in our minds as we plant each seed.

■ *Stipa tennuifolia*
THREAD GRASS
This non-native is invasive and quick to take over pastures as well as ornamental plantings.

■ *Dactylis glomerata*
ORCHARD GRASS
This beautiful grass has a thick seed head that is very nutritious to cattle, sheep, and horses. It is often included in seed mixes with alfalfa as a pasture. Not overly invasive, it must be watched with care.

Species to Choose

Note: Growing ornamental grasses is a relatively new endeavor for gardeners everywhere. Hardiness ratings are not fixed rules. Be willing to experiment and let others know your findings.

■ *Acorus gramineus variegatus*
VARIEGATED SWEET FLAG
This pot plant is included here because its yellow striped green grass-like leaves are a welcome addition to pools, ponds, and bog gardens. Native of India and Sri Lanka, it can be potted up in fall and wintered over in the greenhouse or sunroom.

■ *A. g.* var. 'Ogon'
Same as above, but with a clear yellow variegation.

■ *Agrostis nebulosa*
CLOUD GRASS
This annual grows only 8 to 20 inches high and is one of the few to tolerate light shade. It is beautiful in a border, with panicles that hover cloud-like above the leaves.

■ *Schizachyrium scoparium*
(formerly *Andropogon scoparius*)
LITTLE BLUE STEM
A famed native of story and legend. Little Bluestem will grow 1 1/2 feet to 4 feet in height, depending on conditions. Orange-red seeds heads with bluish stems for good fall color. Extremely durable, it takes dry conditions well. Zone 4.

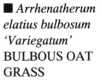

■ *Arrhenatherum elatius bulbosum* 'Variegatum'
BULBOUS OAT GRASS
At 1 to 2 feet this soft white and bluegreen striped grass is effective in the rock garden in sun or light shade. If it burns in summer, cut it back for attractive fall appearence. Zone 4.

■ *Avena sterilis*
ANIMATED OATS
This annual is grown in the cutting garden for its 1 foot golden panicles used in indoor arrangements. Its common name comes from its ability to move as moisture levels in the stem change.

■ *Bouteloua curtipendula*
SIDE OATS GRAMA
A native warm-season clump grass effective in naturalized areas. Sun, dry soil, 2 to 3 feet. Zone 4

■ *B. gracilis*
BLUE GRAMA
   A native of the shortgrass prairie Blue Grama can be used as mowed or unmowed turf, in masses, or as a single plant. Sun, dry soil, 1 to 2 feet, Zone 4.

■ *Briza maxima*
QUAKING GRASS
   An annual 2 to 3 feet tall with nodding bronze fruit clusters that noisily tremble in the slightest breeze. Also called Rattlesnake Grass, for the sound is not unlike that of the warning of a rattler.

■ *Calamgrostis acutiflora*
FEATHER REED GRASS
Cultivar
   'KARL FORSTER' - At 4+ feet this grass has pink flower heads in May, changing to purple in summer, and finally to gold by season's end. Its durable, narrow, upright form is best in large drifts or as a background accent. Needs full sun to light shade. Zone 4.

■ *C. stricta*
   Same height and foliage, but blooms 2 weeks later than 'Karl Forster.'

■ *Carex conica marginata*
MINIATURE JAPANESE SEDGE
   At 8 inches, this perennial evergreen has green leaves with a silver margin. It tolerates drier conditions than most sedges. Good for camouflaging the ripening leaves of daffodils and tulips.

■ *C. morrowii*
JAPANESE SEDGE
   A perennial neat mound 12 to 18 inches tall. It seldom blooms. Needs a cool soil and can withstand shade. Zone 4.
Cultivar
   C. m. variegata - Foliage is green with a silver edge.

■ *C. muskingumensis*
PALM SEDGE
   Leaves radiate from a center growing tip like a palm. Good as a groundcover. Seeds around. 1 to 3 feet, Zone 4-9.

■ *Coix lacryma-jobi*
JOB'S TEARS
   This annual has hard, shiny 1/4 inch seeds, white streaked with gray, borne above narrow 2 foot stems. The seeds are used as beads in jewelry and crafts. This grass tolerates part shade and dampness.

■ *Cortaderia selloana*
PAMPAS GRASS
   A giant among ornamental grasses grows to 12 feet in Zone 7 or Zone 8. The showy silkywhite or pink plumes are themselves 3 feet long. The roots of this grass can be dug and stored over winter in a cool dry place in colder areas. Zone 7.

■ *Cymbopogon citratus*
LEMON GRASS
   The herb you pay dearly for in the Asian marketplace can be grown a for accent flavoring in well-drained soil in sun. It's not hardy, so pot up a clump and grow indoors in winter.

■ *Deschampsia caespitosa*
TUFTED HAIR GRASS

A semi-evergreen perennial 2 feet high with a delicate, airy inflorescence. Sun or part shade. Zone 4.

■ *D. c.* 'Bronzeschleier'

Bronzy yellow long-lasting bloom. Will remain attractive from July to September.

■ *Erianthus ravennae*
PLUME GRASS

This perennial look-alike for pampas grass, grows to 14 feet and has tall, silvery-beige plumes 3 feet long that turn golden brown after frost. This grass is hardier than Pampas Grass. Zone 5.

■ *Festuca* ovina glauca
BLUE FESCUE

A 12 inch densely tufted perennial of rigid habit with leaf blades of blue. Does best in dry soil, and withstands partial shade. Seeds around profusely. Cut back to 2 inches in autumn. Zone 3.

Cultivar

'Elijah Blue' - A recent introduction that keeps its mound of steely blue foliage and pale seed heads in good condition through-out the winter despite repeated snows.

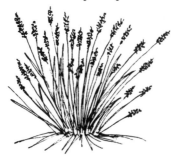

'Elijah Blue' fescue (Festuca ovina glauca).

'April Gruen' - a drought-and-wind tolerant green species good for a windy deck or roof garden.

■*Glyceria maxima*
MANNA GRASS

At 2 1/2 feet this perennial showy grass can stabilize the bank of a large pond or lighten dark shade. Its brilliant white to yellow variegated leaves turn green in too much shade, however. Zone 5.

■ *Helictotrichon sempervirens*
BLUE OAT GRASS

A 2 foot perennial with good steel-blue foliage in early spring. Graceful seed heads rise to 3 feet above leaves. Soil must be well drained. Zone 5.

■ *Hordeum jubatum*
SQUIRREL'S TAIL GRASS

A perennial to be kept confined in a sunken wash tub in the cutting garden. Green, silky plumes 4 inches long in late spring and early summer. Very invasive. 18 to 24 inches tall. Zone 4.

■ *Imperata cylindrina*
JAPANESE BLOOD GRASS

The crimson leaves of this 2 foot perennial are oustanding when backlit by the sun. Plant it at the top of a west-facing hill, but make sure soil is kept moist. Hardiness is in question. Mulch heavily in winter, just in case. Zone 5.

■ *Lagurus ovatus*
HARE'S TAIL
GRASS

An annual with light green leaves followed by dense wooly heads like a rabbit's puffy tail. The tails are ideal in fall arrangements and do not shatter. 12 to 24 inches.

■ *Luzula nivea*
SNOWY WOOD RUSH

From a grass-like plant family, this 1 foot plant looks best in a mass planting in moist shade or as an accent in the woodland garden. Its spring-blooming, white flower heads are silky, but strong throughout summer.

■ *Miscanthus sinensis*
EULALIA GRASS

An arching perennial clump 4 to 6 feet will accent any area; a mass will wave throughout winter. Blooming in October, the pink flowers explode into fluffy masses for indoor arrangements. Zone 5.

Cultivars

'Gracilimus' - MAIDEN GRASS; graceful, with very narrow leaves. The coppery flowers in September turn to fluffy tan.

'Morning Light' - a silver-edged variety 4 to 5 feet tall. Full sun.

■ *M. s. zebrinus*
ZEBRA GRASS

This perennial plant has spectacular gold and green banded leaves, plus large, showy feathery plumes of beige-pink. It will tolerate some shade and does well in damp soil beside pools or streams. 4 feet. Zone 5.

■ *Molinia caerulea*
MOOR GRASS, PURPLE MOOR GRASS

Early to midsummer flowers of yellow and purple fade to tan. Full sun, moist, fertile soil. 3 feet. Zone 4-9.

■ *M. c.* subsp. *arundinacea*
'Bergfreund'- purple flowers turn bright yellow by fall.

■ *Oryzopsis hymenoides*
INDIAN RICE GRASS

A light, airy native perennial grass worthy of substituting for Baby's Breath. Pale tan seed heads adorn a perfectly rounded specimen. Ideal for creating importance, without visual weight, to either side of a pathway entry or step. Grows to 5 feet high in New Mexico and 2 feet high in Montana. Attractive to birds. The cultivar most suited for higher altitude is 'Nezpar.' Zone 3.

■ *Panicum virgatum*
SWITCH GRASS

This 4 to 6 foot perennial plant has pink open panicles attractive to American Gold-finch. Particularly good for mass planting as a screen. It withstands poor drainage and wet feet. Zone 4.

■ *P. v.* 'Rotstrahlbusch'
RED SWITCH GRASS

More compact than above; green foliage with red leaf tips, changing to red fall foliage; interesting winter silhouette of dark reddish brown.

■ *Pennisetum alopecuroides*
FOUNTAIN GRASS

The height is 3 to 4 feet for this graceful perennial. The brightly colored pink or purple spikes are long and arching, appearing in late summer after most perennials have gone by. Rated at Zone 7, it needs moist soil; protect it heavily in colder areas or lift the clumps to overwinter in the coldframe.

Cultivars

'Hamelin' - a dwarf form of the above at 1 1/2 feet high, 2 feet across. Blooms in July; lasts longer and is more scaled to the small garden. Short stems make it wind resistant. Zone 5

'National Arboretum' - outstanding black foxtail flowers; fall color is almond to yellow.

■ *Sorghastrum avenaceum*
INDIAN GRASS

A tall drought tolerant native prairie grass useful in restoration, naturalizing and highway plantings, and on slopes. Stunning accent as a single plant in the border. 4 to 9 feet; Zone 4 and Zone 3 if snow cover is present in winter.

■ *Spodiopogon sibiricus*
FROST GRASS

For a sunny, moist site, the bamboo-like bright green fuzzy leaves give way to airy panicles of purple/brown. Very dramatic. Grows slowly in heat. 4 to 5 feet. Zone 5-9.

■ *Sporobolus heterolepsis*
PRAIRIE DROPSEED

At 1 to 3 feet, this native perennial grass has graceful golden foliage and blooms in July and August. Drought and heat resistant; it tolerates rocky soil. Zone 4.

■ *Stipa comata*
NEEDLE AND THREAD GRASS

A native cool season bunchgrass with thread-like awns 4- to 6 inches long said to be used by Native Americans as thread and needle. Injurious to livestock. Zone 3.

■ *Stipa pennata*
FEATHER GRASS

All members of this genus are wispy, with graceful spikes of bloom from 3 to 4 feet in height. Massed down a hillside, this one is outstanding. Zone 4.

USDA HARDINESS ZONES		
Zone Number	Average Annual Minimum Temperature	
1	below	-50°F
2	-50° to	-40°
3	-40° to	-30°
4	-30° to	-20°
5	-20° to	-10°
6	-10° to	0°
7	0° to	10°
8	10° to	20°
9	20° to	30°
10	30° to	40°
11	above	40°

USDA Hardiness Zones

Suggested Reading:
"Ornamental Grasses" John Greenlee;
Rodale Press, 1991.

Suggested Sources for Grasses:

PLANTS
John Greelee & Associates
301 E. Franklin Ave. • Pomona CA 91766

Kurt Bluemel, Inc.
2740 Greene Lane
 Baldwin MD 21013-9523, catalog $3.

Limerock Ornamental Grasses, Inc.
R.D. 1, Box 111-C
 Port Matilda PA 16870, catalog $2

Prairie Nursery
 P.O. Box 306
Westfield WI 53964, catalog $3.

SEEDS
Park Seed Company
Cokesbury Rd. • Greenwood SC 29647

Sharp Bros. Seed Co.
P.O. Box 665 • Clinton MO 64735
Native grasses of the Mountain West.
l-800-421-4234

Stock Seed Co.
Rt. 1, Box 112 • Murdock NE 68407

Container Growing

A new wave in gardening is growing plants in containers. We are a mobile society, whether spurred by itchy feet or job-related necessity. The same attachment to plants as for pets gives us reason to take the plants along on the move. Even if we are not moving, nothing can be more cheering than an assemblage of pots planted with textured foliage and brightly blooming flowers. They can be planted to suit the site or moved to create a picture for a special occasion. Any number of planters on wheels can be moved daily to follow the sun, a tortuous task. We go all out in our devotion. Window boxes and hanging baskets are once again in vogue, with every conceivable variation giving us the pleasure of an extension of color, texture, and fragrance to enhance our world.

Container Engineering

The frustration of failed eye-bolts, wobbly window boxes, or hangers that break away from their moorings may make you want to give up a container. Before you do, give a thought to the pitfalls and how they might be avoided so that you can select the right size or shape of container.

Weight Is The First Consideration

The condominium or apartment balcony, as well as porch railings, window sills, and the roof are all likely sites for the container garden. Before you place a weighty tub or window box, consider that a cubic foot of dry soil weighs approximately 50 pounds!

To find the capacity of a cylindrical container, square the diameter in inches, multiply by the height in inches, and multiply this product by the decimal .34. Point off 4 decimals and you have the capacity in gallons.

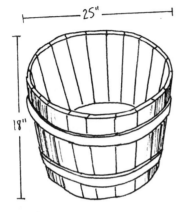

Whiskey barrel measurements.

A cubic foot of water weighs 62 1/2 pounds and contains 7 1/2 gallons. A water-soaked cubic foot of sandy loam soil can weigh 80 to 90 pounds. From this calculation you can see how quickly the pounds add up. Your porch, balcony floor or flimsy porch rail may not be strong enough to hold all the plants you want to grow. Changing the groups of pots will distribute weight, but it may be still too much for a floor. Ask your building superintendent for the plans of the building or check with a builder for a stress determination.

Window Box Attachment

Window boxes are best kept at 4 feet or less in length to keep them manageable at put-up and take-down time. However, if the site calls for a longer box, see illustrations for anchoring methods. Window boxes are positioned so that the top of the box is even with the sill. There is a

tendency to rest the box on top of the sill, especially with a brick home, but think again. Your inside view of the box would be more box than blossoms. **A word of caution - all window boxes should be at least 6 inches wide. In the Mountain West the strength of sunlight on containers raises soil temperatures above levels required for good growth. Using a 6 inch width gives needed bulk and insulation.**

Various methods of attachment for window boxes are available with strong and secure anchorage. One method is the use of steel or wrought iron brackets plus strong but decorative wood brackets (see illustration). Steel brackets are available with a pre-formed hole. Nail the bracket through the pre-formed hole to each side of the wood sill. Expansion bolts are used for a home of brick construction. If desired, the head of the nail or bolt may be removed to make removal of the entire unit easier for winter storage. The wood brackets are attached to the house wall with lag screws and expansion shields or by bolting to studs.

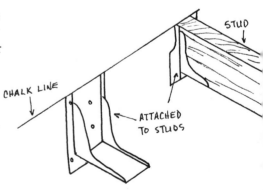

The brackets help in distributing the

weight against the wall. The box is separate and rests on the steel brackets. The wood brackets provide secondary support. Safety chains on either end of the box are attached to the window frame.

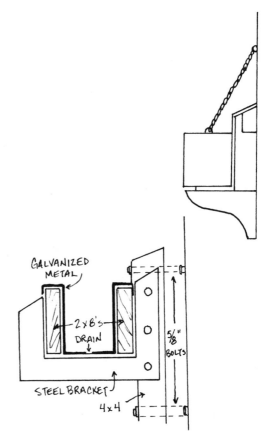

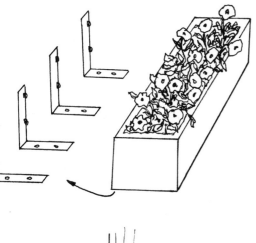

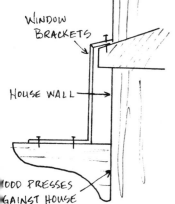

For long boxes attached to porch rails or house walls, three methods are suggested.

Custom made iron brackets and custom formed galvanized metal boxes will ease the headaches of engineering as well as care. Look for Metal Fabricators in the Yellow Pages. Wood boxes warp even if made of redwood or cedar. Use the decorative wood as a container for a galvanized metal liner. Both must have drainage holes.

Window-Box Wicking
The self-watering, wicked window box is the ultimate in easy care. The biggest bugaboo with container-grown plants is the problem of their drying-out too quickly. Using wicks in a custom-made galvanized pan beneath the window box, concealed by

the outer decorative box will give you the freedom of a vacation without the worry of coming home to dead window-box plants.

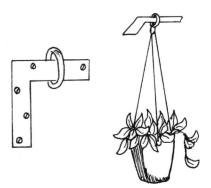

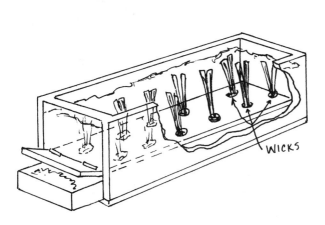

This window box is custom-made of redwood. A custom-made galvanized tray fits loosely under a custom-made galvanized liner. Fiberglass, cotton string, or nylon stocking strands serve as wicks to be pulled up through drainages holes and laid over the soil mix before planting. Allow 5 inches of wick in the water and 4 inches into the box above. Wet the wicks before inserting them and do not allow to dry out. A hinged door at one side of the box allows refilling the tray. Water-soluble fertilizer can be added to the tray.

Hanging Plants

From ceilings to soffits, some builder's trademark today is a flimsy material that won't support a heavy hanging plant. Use of lag screws helps, or you can use the method illustrated below to distribute weight when the soffit or ceiling is a thin plywood.

To distribute weight for a hanger in thin plywood, intall an L-brace (also known as a corner brace) with wood screws. Position a D-ring around one of the arms before anchoring; then hang the plant with an S-hook through the ring.

Plants hanging in high places are impossible to care for unless they are hung with a pulley to lower them. If these will be subject to high winds, secure them at the bottom with a side wire to the house that can be unhooked like an old-fashioned screen door hook.

To Prevent a Theft

Thievery is a growing problem. To thwart the theft of a hanging plant, screw an eye-bolt into the wood of the soffit or overhead grid of a patio. Use the the loop of a sturdy steel padlock to hold the hanging chains that cradle the basket. Using a multi-strand wire, circle the top of the basket. Twist it securely to the chain. The thief might still steal the basket, but not easily or quickly, and most of the hardware would remain. For standing containers, thread multi-strand wire through the drainage hole before adding the planting mix. After planting is complete, attach the wire to a stationary object, such as the porch rail. Some owners have successfully attached hidden bells to containers.

Beware of using knotted fiber or macramé slings for outdoor plants. They quickly deteriorate in the strength of western sun and wind, and are easily cut by a thief.

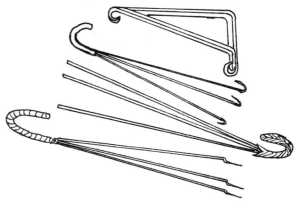

Basic wall brackets and wire hangers.

Basket hung from a high entry may be lowered for watering.

Wall Hangers

Plants hanging from walls provide the vertical interest needed for a flat, uninteresting site. Wall hanger hardware is handsome and easily available. Match the pieces — either all those of brass or all of wrought iron. The metal wire hangers are functional, but certainly not beautiful. Shop around for black or *verdigris* chains. Hanging a stone or concrete lavabo from a garden wall is no job for amateurs. Call a professional and be assured of a guarantee of their work before they begin.

Pots on Wheels and Skids

Planters placed on the floor of your patio or around your entry will invariably need to be moved from time to time. A wheeled device for each will make moving your containers infinitely easier. One device easily available is a "creeper" from an auto supply store. It can move a bevy of pots.

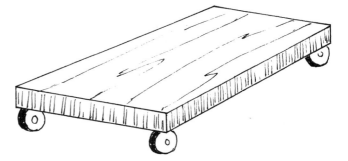

"Creeper" from an auto supply store moves a bevy of pots.

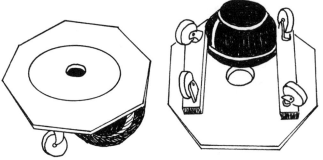

A platform on casters makes a heavy pot movable. Dish fits underneath to catch drips.

Dragging a heavy pot up or down steps or a grade can present formidible problems. Use your garage creeper or ask your plumber for 2 short lengths of metal pipe to use as "wheels" for a board platform. Tip the creeper or platform so that you can slide the heavy pot onto it. Attach a rope with an eye-bolt to the front or back edge of your makeshift platform. Pull it to its new location gradually by pulling the length of the board, leaving the back "wheel" behind. The front "wheel" then becomes the back wheel as you move forward, replacing the "wheel" at the front end of each board-length move.

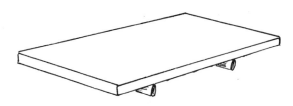

A makeshift platform uses lengths of pipe for wheels.

Shifting a heavy pot down a slope or steps is not difficult if you are reasonably strong. Use 2 boards that reach from top to bottom of the incline. Ease the pot onto the

boards. The boards will stand straight out at this point. Secure a strong rope around the pot. Brace your feet and slowly play out the rope until the pot begins to slide and the boards point downhill. The pot may arrive at the bottom more quickly than you planned if you are not strong enough to hold back the pot.

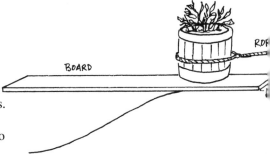

BOARD   RDP

Moving a pot down steps or a slope calls for strength (or 2 persons).

Sizes and Shapes

The Convenient Half-Barrel

Since America cut back on its consumption of hard liquor, the oaken barrel has been available on the market to become a convenient container for growing plants. Thankfully, they are sawn in half elsewhere before being shipped to the garden centers and hardware stores. The boozy smell is easily overcome by filling with soil. Their bulk when filled, is formidable. They are neither stolen nor moved easily. Drill 3 holes in the bottom for drainage.

Container growing is a good way to introduce children to gardening because the height of a half-barrel is right for them. The space is large enough for most things they might want to grow, except the Halloween pumpkin.

Those who cannot bend or stoop enjoy gardening in the half-barrel; the height is the same as that of a wheelchair armrest. It can hold enough vegetables or flowers to keep those less ambulatory interested in gardening.

Pots, Plain and Decorated

The standard clay pot, or its more expensive counterpart, terracotta, or fake look-alike of plastic is still the most functional of containers. The plants, after all, are the main attraction, so the container should not detract from the plants. Nevertheless, a pleasing color, a twist of decoration, a curving handle won't hurt the total composition. The size of the container is paramount to the health of the plants. Skimping leads to plant failure. In the Mountain West the strength of sunlight dooms many plants growing in pots that are too small. A dainty Lobelia will thrive in a six-inch wood tub, but burn up in a 4 inch plastic pot. Larger pots provide insulation and bulk. Alas, another tragedy of the MW — the charming crusty-with-lichen, mossy old clay pot familiar in the East just isn't going to happen. No amount of painting with buttermilk (the current prescription) will cause lichen or moss to appear.

Painting a clay pot with paint is acceptable. Make up for the newness or lack of crustiness of a pot with a little enamel paint in a shade called *celedon,* is a mingling of gray and celery green. In many pot plant combinations, it will set off the plants far better than all the crustiness.

Pot saucers are a must in the Mountain West. Easteners go on about the clay pot allowing evaporation of moisture, while in the West we must go to great lengths to overcome this trait. Use a matching saucer at least one size larger than the pot.

The Ali Baba jar, the earthenware urn, the rope of clay pot, and even the porcelain jar are all just pots to the plants that occupy them. Try many combinations before settling on the perfect container. While the plants will grow to almost cover the container, there is still a need to make groups of containers compatible, but don't be afraid to add a quirky element now and then. An old blue enamel teakettle filled with pink geraniums; a copper washboiler overflowing with signet marigolds, a piece of weathered wood brought home from a mountain hike will all add spice to the composition.

Plant Pillows

The English have perfected the art of growing plants in plastic or art paper bags on top of the garden soil. Large plastic bags, such as fertilizer or garbage bags are filled with a soilless or potting media of your choice and stapled shut. Add slits on the side that will become the bottom. Crosses are cut on the top and plants are planted in the media. The bag is set upon a wide board or directly on garden soil and cared for in the same manner as any container plant. Its advantage is growing colorful annuals to be moved to become a display where other plants have gone out of bloom. It is also a convenient way of growing annuals over an area that is heavily planted with spring-flowering bulbs.

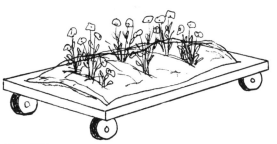

Plant Pillows rest on a garage creeper or directly on garden soil.

273

The contained garden can be functional or highly decorative, with a variety of styles.

Planting and Care Techniques

Preparing the Pot

A layer of gravel or stones in the bottom of a pot is the worst possible practice. The change in the soil column, from a finer (soil) to a coarser (gravel) texture, will cause water to collect above that gravel layer, making it become a giant bucket holding water. Drainage will be excellent if only one stone or a pot shard is placed over a drainage hole. This will prevent soil from washing through the hole. Even better is a piece of window screen or fabric weed barrier.

Spacing

When we plant annuals and perennials in open ground, we emphasize giving them room to expand and grow, but when planting in containers, we cram as many plants as possible into the space, laying the root ball on its side for those that are intended to drape gracefully over the edge. Careful attention to watering and feeding will keep containerized plants growing and blooming for a season.

There is a strong temptation to plant spring-flowering bulbs in planters and permanently placed half-tubs and pots. These are seldom successful because the soil becomes too cold. Clay pots crack in winter temeratures. You can try insulating each planted container with one of the new foam wrap-around plant insulators or fashion your own from foam insulation or burlap and fabric hook fasteners. Bulbs planted in pots and stored over the winter in the coldframe are the safest bet for a good display. (See Chapter 9 Bulbs). Begin checking on their growth in early March. Leave the frame open on sunny days when the temperature is well above freezing, closing and insulating at night.

Soil Mixes

Beware of commercial potting mixes that originate in the Mountain West because they may contain mountain peat. As seen in Volume I, p. 33, mountain peat is alkaline in reaction, and disturbing our peat bogs is ecologically unwise. Soilless mixes are a safe bet. You can provide constant nutrients, but you can't provide the minerals often lacking from the mix. Making your own mix with these standard proportions and ingredients will assure the best quality of growth and bloom.

Potting Mix

1 part heavy clay loam
1 part good garden loam
1 part homemade compost or sphagnum peatmoss
1/2 part perlite
1/2 part vermiculite

The heavy clay and garden loam will supply needed minerals that are easily leached away in container growing. Two other ingredients are essential: Perlite sheds water, vermiculite holds water both are needed for balance. Your nursery will supply all of the materials except the heavy clay loam, and it shouldn't be too hard to find a clay soil anywhere in the Mountain West. At the end of the season it is not necessary to discard the soil of containers. Soil does not wear out as some merchants would have you believe. With the addition of organic matter next season, the soil will be restored to fertility.

Use of Polymer Gels

A revolution in soil amendments occurred in about 1985. The super-absorbent polymers came to the gardening marketplace to give us still another tool to prevent drying of soils in containers, bog gardens, putting greens, and many other gardening uses.

The polymer gel resembles the clear gelatin granules we use to make gelatin salads and desserts. It is mixed at a rate of only 1 rounded teaspoonful per gallon of soil. Mix 5 gallons at a batch on a plastic tarp, using a 5 gallon bucket as your measure. The soil must be absolutely bone-dry! You won't see anything happen until you have planted the plants in the container and watered them in. Then you will notice a drastic decrease in the number of times you will have to water the containerized plant. The gel retains water that normally drains from the soil so that plant roots still have a source of moisture when the soil appears dry. More than one gardener has noted that the gel's water-holding capacity begins to wane toward the end of the growing season. It breaks down to carbon dioxide, a small amount of nitrogen, and water. Next season as you replace organic matter in the potting mix, replace also the polymer gel.

Growing in Foam Blocks

Florist foam, often known as *Oasis,* has been in the trade for years as a medium for holding cut flowers in place. The water-holding capacity of this material is surpris-ingly huge. Always use new foam. Use a carving knife to cut blocks to the size of the container in which you wish to grow the plant. Wash the foam in cool, soapy water. Rinse, then weigh down the block in a bucket of water with a heavy object. When bubbling ceases, remove the heavy object. The foam should be floating with only the topside visible above water. Line the container with foil to catch leaks, and place the foam block on the foil. Insert stems stripped of foliage into pencil-drilled holes in the foam. The stems quickly root and will often survive for years on a modest

fertilization program and the occasional addition of water. Candidates for foam growing are ivies and other foliage plants, zonal geraniums, and tip cuttings of annuals brought in before frost in the fall.

Methyl Bromide As A Soil Fumigant

A soil fumigant is a chemical that will destroy a wide variety of pests. When applied to slightly moist soil, fumigants quickly form a gas and diffuse through the soil, destroying harmful insects, fungi, bacteria, and some viruses. Control is best in a light, sandy soil. Methyl bromide is one fumigant that may have a place in container growing if you have suspicions that there may be harmful pests in the soil, and if you have expensive plants that must have every precaution taken to avoid loss. Methyl bromide comes in a pressurized cannister. The slightly moist soil pile is covered with a plastic tarp and secured tightly around the edges. The cannister is opened and placed under the tarp and the tarp secured quickly once again. The gas will diffuse upward through the soil. Methyl bromide has an agreeable odor that dissipates within 24 hours. Nevertheless, it is a potentially harmful chemical if directions are not followed, and you must have a license to buy it. Most states conduct testing of gardeners and commerical operators before a license is issued.

Deadheading

Removing spent flowers is as important with container plants as it is with borders and beds. A plant's objective in life is to re-create itself. Flowers pollinate themselves to become seeds or insects do it for them. When seed is formed, the plant's objective is accomplished and it no longer blooms. We deadhead to prevent seed. The plant will keep on trying to recreate itself by continuing to bloom. Daily deadheading is not difficult. Cut the spent bloom back to the nearest leaf or flower bud. With window boxes, it's a different matter, for they are difficult to deadhead. Plant those high boxes with plenty of ivy geraniums (*Pelargonium x peltatum*) which are "self-cleaners." This means the spent flowers drop away on their own and before setting seed. In addition, these geraniums will drape down the side of the box with dramatic abandon. See Chapter 16 for handling ivy geraniums indoors in winter.

Deadheading is a daily, puttering type of job that most gardeners enjoy.

Watering Techniques

With the polymer gel in place in your potting mix, you won't have trouble keeping your container plants moist and growing well. After a container is planted, move it to its permanent place and water slowly until the water runs through the drainage hole. You are then assured that the entire soil mass is wet and there are no air pockets.

A drip irrigation system is the ultimate in carefree growing. The head hose is easily snaked through a group of containers and the emitter hoses secured to the sides of each pot. Using a head hose attached to an overhead grid (see Vol. I, p.8) makes it possible for emitters to be placed in each basket hanging from the grid high above the patio floor.

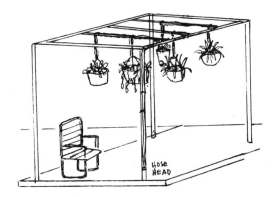

Head hose is attached to an overhead grid, with emitter hoses leading to each basket hanging from the grid.

Wick watering is possible for a group of pots also. A large container of water can be concealed within or behind a group of pots with wicks leading to the bottom of each container and up into the soil mass for at least 5 inches. See the previous paragraph on window box construction for wick watering of window boxes.

Wick watering assures pots will receive the correct among of water while you are on vacation.

Mulching

With the watering system in place, it's time to mulch the surface if the season is far enough advanced. A mulch conserves moisture, prevents weeds, and keeps the soil at an even temperature. At altitudes above 7,000 feet in the Mountain West mulches may not be needed at all. The full effect of the sun's rays will be needed to warm the soil enough for good root growth. A soil thermometer will give you the answer. When the soil temperature is above 72° F. a light mulch is in order. Dried grass clippings, pole peelings, pebbles, or Spanish moss are all possibilities. Sphagnum peatmoss is not recommended because it hogs the moisture, leaving none for the plants. When using sphagnum, always incorporate it into the soil.

Treillage

Creating a vertical element in a planter is often desirable for one container within a group. Make a lath trellis with green plastic poultry wire or an arch made of # 9 wire. The plastic wire will resist heating, but wrap the # 9 wire with plastic tape to prevent burning the climbers' tendrils. Twiggy, curved, peeled branches, such as those of Corkscrew Willow (*Salix matsudana*), make a charming trellis for climbing sweet peas. Keep them picked to keep them flowering all summer.

Vines such as morning glory, black-eyed Susan vine (Thunbergia alata) add importance to a planted pot.

A twiggy branch becomes a sculpted trellis for sweet peas.

Winter Care

Very few perennials can be left outdoors in containers over the winter. Soil in containers will freeze to the bottom or the pot may crack if the soil is wet. Clay pots flake off gradually. The plants, if they survive the freezing, cannot withstand the deep fluctuations of temperature as spring comes on. Set aside time on a sunny fall day after the first heavy frost to dispose of the annuals and store the pots planted with perennials in the cold frame. You will be amazed at the growth they will make during the winter and spring, even in the dark when the frame lid is covered with heavy carpet.

Moving Time

Some moving companies will take potted plants along with the load, but most will not. You are stuck with a car or van full of potted plants. To make it as easy as possible:
1. Water them well the day *before* the journey
2. Lay out layers of newspaper in overlapping sheets beside the plant to be wrapped.

3. Tip the pot over onto the newspapers and roll it up in a cornucopia with newpaper covering it from tip to pot bottom. Staple loosely.
4. Trundle them off to the waiting car or van in a cart or wheelbarrow, trying not to disturb the newspaper covering as you lay them on their sides to forestall tipping.
5. They can be counted on to survive a week-long trip without light or further watering, PROVIDED they are travelling in an air-conditioned or warmed vehicle, depending upon the season. Sunlight should not reach the paper wrappings, for it will heat up the air inside and dessicate the plant. Make sure when you stop for the night in winter that the temperature in your vehicle will not be below freezing. Treat your journeying plants as you would a child or a dog and they will make the trip in good health.

Plant Combos for Short-Term or Long-Term Good Looks

For some gardeners the esthetics of plant combinations come naturally. For others the "red-and-yeller-catch-a-feller" penchant runs at a feverish pitch. Author feels the same about plant combinations as with turfgrass decorated with plastic pink flamingos. If it pleases you, that's all that is important.

Short Term Flowering Plant Combinations

Spring: daffodils 'King Alfred'(yellow), *Iris reticulata histrioides major* (clear blue), *Iris danfordiae* (yellow). Suggested pot, 10 inch clay.

Tulip 'Halcro'(crushed raspberry red), *Oxalis adenophylla* (gray foliage, pink bloom), grape hyacinth 'Blue Spike'. Suggested pot, 10 inch clay.

Tulipa tarda (very early dwarf yellow species), 12 bulbs alone in a shallow 8 inch clay bulb pan.

Tulip 'Toronto' (deep red), blue *Myosotis alpestris* (forget-me-not), *Ibiris sempervirens* (white candytuft). Suggested pot, 12 inch buff clay.

For Late Summer: blue morning glories climbing a poultry wire trellis, black-eyed Susan (*Rudbeckia hirta*), *Nicotiana* 'Metro Lime', Nasturtium 'Alaska' (has variegated foliage). Suggested pot, 12 inch pale blue plastic with matching saucer.

Helenium 'Bruno' (deep red), *Sedum* 'Autumn Joy', Zinnia 'Torch' (brilliant orange), curly dwarf parsley. Suggested pot, 12 inch maroon pottery.

Chrysanthemum 'Lavender Lady', *Setcreasea pallida* 'Purple Heart' (deep maroon foliage), *Silene* 'Peach Blossom'. Suggested pot, 12 inch gray-brown pottery.

Plants for Long-Term Good Looks - Full Sun

Pink *Coreopsis rosea*, blue morning glories on a wire arch, pink Canterbury bells, *Sedum Middiflorum* (lavender), white alyssum 'New Carpet of Snow'. Suggested pot, 22 inch wood tub.

Artemisia 'Silver King', *Veronica* 'Sunny Border Blue', *Chrysanthemum* 'Clara Curtis' (pink), *Coreopsis* 'Moonbeam', (pale yellow), *Alyssum* 'New Carpet of Snow', curly dwarf parsley. Suggested pot, 20 inch clay painted celedon.

Artemisia 'Silver King', Rose 'The Fairy' (pink), double multiflora petunias 'Delight Mixed' (mixed colors). Suggested pot, half barrel on wheels.

Ipomoea 'Cardinal Climber'(maroon) climbing on a bamboo pole, *Helichrysum petiolare* (lime green fuzzy foliage), *Salvia* 'Blue Victory.' Suggested pot, classic urn.

Torenia 'Clown Mix' massed in a shallow five-parted clay container that surrounds the center pole of a patio umbrella.

Cosmos 'Purity' (tall white), Cosmos 'Sonata' (dwarf white), blue salvia 'Victoria', tall marigolds 'First Lady,(yellow), trailing Lobelia 'Mixed'. Suggested pot, half barrel.

Cosmos 'Sonata' (white dwarf), *Celosia* 'Pink Castle', Petunia 'Hot Pink", Petunia white multiflora, *Heliotrope* 'Dwarf Marine (purple), Ivy 'Buttercup' (yellow-green). *Celosia* requires soil that is allowed to dry between waterings. Plant in 4 inch pots so that pot rims are above the soil surface. Water as needed. Suggested pot, 14 inch wood tub.

Petunia 'Hot Pink', *Heliotrope* 'Dwarf Marine', *Artemisia* 'Silver King' pinched at 6 inches and again at 12 inches. Suggested pot, 12 inch clay pot painted celedon.

Heuchera 'Palace Purple' (bronze foliage, white blooms), Lamb's Ears (*Stachys Olympica*) (fuzzy gray). Suggested pot, 12 inch clay potted painted pale pink.

Ruta 'Blue Mound', fibrous begonia 'Gin' (pink), 1 tuber of Begonia *Crispa marginata* (pink or red), *Salvia farinacea* 'White Porcelain',* Dahlberg Daisy (*Dyssodia tenulobi*a) (yellow), a few *Nasturtium* seeds. Suggested pot, blue-gray 20 inch plastic tub.

Bells of Ireland (lime green spires), *Cosmos* 'Purity' (tall white), fall aster "Wonder of Staffa" (lavender-blue), *Achillea* 'Red Beauty', Snow-in-Summer (*Cerastium tomentosum*), salmon ivy geranium, white grandiflora petunia . Suggested pot, window box.

Container Combinations for Shade

Ipomoea battata 'Blackie' (black sweet-potato vine), *Lychnis nummularia aurea* (yellow-green). Suggested pot, hanging clay pot, part shade.

Tuberous begonias, all species, colors and sizes. Suggested pot, hanging baskets or window boxes (where slugs can't get at them).

Astilbe 'Fanal' (bronze foliage, red flowers), Hosta 'So Sweet' (variegated foliage, white flowers). Suggested pots, matching porcelain jars.

Athyrium Filix-femina Lady Fern, *Caladium* bulbs, mixed colors, *Convallaria majalis* Lily of the Valley. Suggested pot, plastic tub color coordinated with patio furniture.

■ *Agapanthus*

When touring grand estate gardens, you may have been floored by great tubs and urns of beautiful blue flowers held in stately mass above cascading vivid green foliage. You have been privileged to come upon *Agapanthus,* Blue Lily of the Nile. This strong grower comes from a rhizome, with thick cords of roots. It will break a pot quickly if it becomes pot-bound. Grow it in a large, deep pot, dividing every March. It is a gross feeder. Give it a constant fertilization program of 1/4 teaspoon of houseplant fertilizer dissolved in 1 gallon of water each time it is watered. Bloom is regulated by warmth, not day-length. In the Mountain West *Agapanthus* should be shaded from mid-day sun between 11 A.M. and 3 P.M. In New Mexico, Nevada, and at high altitude, give it dappled shade. To force it to produce more blooms, put it into a "panic" by easing off on the watering in

April. When buds begin to form, stop watering altogether unless it wilts. If it wilts, mist and give it a little water. As soon as 70% of the buds are open, resume watering to make the blooms last longer. Cease feeding and cut back on watering a month before the average killing frost date. When growth ceases, bring it into a cool sunporch or greenhouse to spend the winter in poor light on the floor or under a bench.

■ *Aerial Azaleas*

Hanging baskets or tubs of azaleas make stunning displays for the latticed summer house or the overhead grid of your patio. If tubs are hung from big beams by sturdy chains and eye bolts, turnbuckles allow plants to be easily turned for even growth and light. Pruning to force each plant to cascade over the edge is less work if you choose a pendant variety.

Azaleas in tubs for a shaded open porch.

■ *Fussy Fuchsia*

In early summer fuchsias are hard to resist, yet they are one of the most difficult of hanging displays in the Mountain West. Our low humidity is not to their liking. Hang them from a low limb over the lily pool and they love it, reflecting their tear-drop blooms in the water. They prosper from the same nutrient solution at each watering as above. In fall allow a light frost

to touch them. This will nip back tender foliage. Prune the strongest branches to 8 to 10 inches, removing all others, and treat as an indoor plant. See Chapter 15 Indoor Plants. Or store the plants in a box filled with damp insulating material such as peat moss, sawdust, or vermiculite. Make sure there is at least 8 inches of insulation between the plants and the sides of the box. Store the box in a cool (40° to 50°F) frost-free location. Next March or early April, remove the plant, repot if necessary, and keep it in a bright, protected area until danger of frost is past. Move once again to a partly shaded, high humidity location outdoors (or indoors) and begin feeding and watering.

■ *Humungus Hibiscus*

For a big show there is nothing to compare to *Hibiscus manihot* or *H. hoscheutos*. The big single hollyhock-like flowers in outstanding colors come on in August when other container plants may be waning from the heat. Don't skimp on the pot. They demand space to perform well. The best varieties are propagated by cuttings because varieties do not come true from seed. However, you can buy 6 seeds for less than 2 dollars and take your chances. Soak seed in very hot water for 1 hour before sowing; germination will be from 10-30 days.

Hibiscus has a place on the large, sunny patio.

■ *Datura*

Angel's Trumpet (*Datura metaloides*) will wow you with its exotic scent on a warm evening on the terrace. The white trumpets are shown off against blue-green foliage. It will grow to a height of 8 feet if given a big pot and a warm location. This is an extremely poisonous plant, not recommended if children are in the household or expected visitors.

■ *Oleander*

You have admired the ever-blooming, softly waving wands of dark green foliage along the highways of Arizona, California, and Nevada. Think of it also as a patio plant. *Oleander indicum* 'Petite Salmon' will give you an very drought tolerant tall shrub for a big pot on a sunny patio. At the first hint of cool weather, cut it back sharply and rest it until late spring; then repot in a mix of loam and weathered manure. This, too, is a very poisonous plant; even the smoke of a burning leaf is poisonous.

■ *Bougainvillea*

This well-known colorful vine has been bred in bush form. A big round pot of 'Crimson Jewel', 'Rosenka', or 'Hawaii' will give you an all-summer show. It will attain a height of about 2 feet, with a 3 foot width. At the first hint of cool nights, it will sulk and may drop leaves. Bring it in to spend the winter in a greenhouse or sunporch with bright winter sun. See Chapter 16 Indoor Plants.

■ Trailing Miniature Crape Myrtle (*Lagerstroemia indica*)

A true genetic miniature of the famous June- to August-blooming small tree much admired in Williamsburg, Virginia, and points south can be blooming in a large

hanging basket on your patio. Like its tree species cousin of the same name, it likes heat and can tolerate some drought. It becomes dormant in winter, losing its leaves. Store it on the floor of the basement or a frost-free garage, watering occasionally. Under greenhouse conditions, it will remain in leaf, but of no account. Give it a rest.

Crepe Myrtle in trailing form becomes more full and floriferous every year.

■ Dahlia

Single tubers or clumps of tubers will give you color and close-viewing grandeur when grown in containers. Give the single tuber a 22 inch pot and the same staking and cultural treatment as found in Chapter 9 BULBS. It will fill the pot with tubers by fall. Let the first frost touch the foliage; then move the pots to a frost-free place where the foliage will fall away. Throw an old quilt or styrofoam tarp over the pots for the winter. In March, check for new growth, repotting if necessary. Bring them to a sunny porch or greenhouse to begin growth and a repeat performance.

■ *Rhododendrons*

There is one rare rhododendron that is ideal for container growing. Plant explorers first discovered Vireya (pronounced Vee-RAY-a) rhododendrons 140 years ago in the Malay-Indonesia archipelago. They took them to England where the famed Veitch & Sons Nursery hybridized the vivid reds, pure whites, and blends of orange and yellow. The flowers are tubular and many are fragrant. They enjoy the cooler growing conditions of high country gardens in the Mountain West, but the entire 8-state area is suitable. Care must be taken to protect them from a summer frost, but they enjoy the nightime temperature drop of the MW. Containers can be of wood, clay or fiber, but not plastic. Use a potting mix of equal parts of orchid bark, *coarse* peat moss and *coarse* perlite. Avoid a continuously soggy mix. Fertilize sparingly 3 times in spring, again in summer, and again after buds appear. If your local nurseryman cannot supply these beauties, try The Bovees Nursery 1737 SW Coronado, Portland OR 97219, or Vireya Specialties Nursery, 2701 Malcolm Ave., Los Angeles CA 90064.

The Vireya rhododendron makes an exotic container plant for the cool, partly shaded patio.

CHINESE POT GARDENING

Continuous color in the garden is seldom achieved; yet gardeners long ago devised methods of keeping color always in view in small, highly organized areas. Oriental walled gardens are older than the atriums of the Roman Empire. The traditional chrysan-

themum makes a late appearence in the season, however. It's not unusual to see a small area of color that precedes the chrysanthemum display. A closer look reveals the blooms are in pots set into pots permanently installed deeply in the soil.

8 inch slip pots are permanently installed, ready for seasonal displays of flowers.

In this country a typical area of display of seasonally blooming pots is around the entry. Though the plan seems simple enough, be advised that an area for growing the potted plants up to their showy season is much greater than the area needed for display.

How-To

Install the slip-pots as illustrated. Then trench a row or two in your vegetable garden by tilling deeply so that the soil is easily lifted into a cart or wheel barrow to be used later in filling pots. In the fall plant spring-flowering bulbs in 12 pots, which are then sunk 5 inches deep into the trench, covered and mulched deeply with straw and evergreen boughs. This is now called a "grow-row." The following spring, these 12 are trucked to the slip-pots to await their spring flowering season. If you have the space, use 2 sets of 12 pots each, one for mixed daffodils and *Iris reticulata* and one for tulips and forget-me-nots. As soon as the frost-free date arrives and the tulips have finished blooming, summer-flowering annuals are planted in a second set of 12 pots, and the bulb pots are rested in the grow-row to allow their foliage to mature. Also in spring, the fall display pots are filled with mums, asters, and frost-hardy edgers, such as alyssum. These pots are also sunk rim-deep in the grow-rows. Care during the summer is minimal if a drip emitter is located for each sunken pot and the tops of the pots are mulched to preserve moisture and prevent weeds. The total number of pots needed for a 3-season display in an area of 42 inches x 36 inches is a whopping 36. This is a good project for a gardening zealot with little else to do.

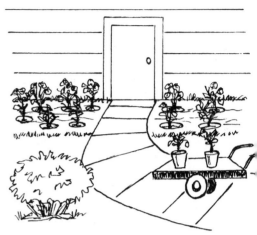

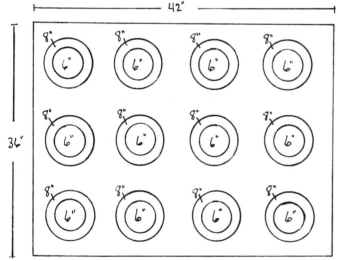

Topo drawing of bed and the circles representing 8" slip pots, 6" grow-pots, with 2" between them in 3 rows; six inches between rows. 36" x 42" total.

Displaying A Collection

Indoor plants, as well as your hobby collection of bonsai, ferns, cacti and succulents, or any other plant fancy are difficult to stage without a plan. Juggling them around on ledges, flat rocks, or rickety tables is not the answer. The side yard, that difficult space relegated usually to a means of getting from the backyard to the frontyard, is a possibility for display space if there is sufficient sun for your sun-loving species. In the Mountain West, we can count on 4 hours of sunlight equaling 7 hours of flatland sun.

A side yard is the site for a tiered display bench.

A single post on the patio anchors a stage for display as well as good growing conditions for bonsai, herbs, or for sunning indoor plants in summer.

The new alpine ivy geraniums become members of the family. Mass them all together in a new version of the wine or whiskey barrel.

Vertical Gardens

When space is minimal and the only place to go is up, the vertical garden, though time-consuming to create, compensates for your trouble by by giving you easy maintenance. A vertical garden is available commercially and is marketed as Living Wall. To make your own cage-like structure at least 3 feet high and 6 inches thick, use a #6 sturdy but not too sturdy grade of wire. Weight is of some importance. Line the wire structure with a plastic bag, and fill with a soilless media that is suitable for growing annual plants, for this is not a structure for perennials. Build the structure of redwood lath to hold the grow-media, making sure your design is battered, meaning wider at the bottom than at the top. This assures stability and gives the bottom plants as much sun as those on the top row.

The media, despite how tightly you pack it into the bag, will continue to slip and slide downward with repeated waterings. To counter this move, use the following planting ploy: Cut an x through the wire and plastic large enough to accomodate the root ball of the plant; push the top flap of the plastic x inward. Gather the remaining plastic flaps into a jutting lip with an inch or 2 of electrical tape. Push a little soil mix around the roots and water carefully, a drip at a time. Use the wire flaps as a support for the plastic flaps, which now form a cup similar to the cups of a strawberry jar. Purchase a drip-tray of plastic or galvanized metal for your creation. If you make it a *deep* drip tray, it can become the receptacle for wick-watering. See above p. 271). Add anti-algae tablets to the drip-tray. They can be purchased from an aquarium supply store. They are harmless to plants. Wheels are a possibility if you wish to plant both sides of the grow-bag; then turning each side to face the sun is a necessity. The most stable vertical garden, however, is 1-sided and bolted securely the the house wall.

A vertical wall garden

Choice of Plants

Multi-flora petunias are recommended over grandifloras. They have small flowers, but they number in thousands, as compared to the grandifloras which have larger flowers but tumble and break off easily. Fibrous begonias, especially those with dark foliage, are stunning combined with petunias and light ('Cambridge Blue') and dark blue (Blue Moon') lobelia. Don't forget to add white flowers. They add the fillip to a color scheme. Avoid purple because it shows up as a black hole at dusk and dawn or on cloudy days. Vegetables are a natural for the vertical garden, as are 'Quinalt' strawberries. See Chapter 1 Vegetables and Chapter 2 Fruits.

Roof Gardens

Gardeners perplexed about lack of gardening space would do well to glance upward. A whole new world of potential outdoor living atop the family garage or apartment roof awaits. Rooftop gardens make particularly good sense if your lot size is small, if you have a steep hillside site, or if the lot is in dense shade and you have a hankering to grow sun-loving plants.

First, the negative aspects. The planting and maintenance of a roof garden requires intense dedication. All vagaries of climate, all attacks of insects and disease, all problems of litter removal and water drainage, heavy lifting, winter kill and heat scorch intensify rather than dissipate. Yet, when there is no place else to garden, these tests and tasks disappear with the satisfaction of creating something from nothing.

Weight Load of Flooring

Your local building inspector must become heavily involved in your project right at the start. Consult this department of your government for regulations as well as guidance. Even a modest roof planting with a pathway requires 2- by 16-inch rafters set 15 inches apart and reinforced at 2-foot intervals with cross bracing. The material of the roof itself is of consequence. If it is rough cedar-shake shingles, a layer of sand will be required to make it smooth enough to prevent puncture of the 20 mil poly-vinyl-chloride (PVC) that will be your roof garden floor. A pathway or small patio is a possibility, but, once again, weight is the dominant factor. Brick in a warm color is ideal because it gives the garden color during the winter months. A structure strong enough to support brick, however, is best made of concrete. A parquet of redwood 2x4's at 3/8-inch spacing is of much lesser weight and remains attractive for years. Each parquet can be constructed elsewhere and laid in place later. This parquet allows also plastic drain piping to run unobtrusively underneath.

Parquet floor of roof garden allows plastic drain piping underneath to lead from planter boxes to existing gutter and downspout.

Design of Containers

Containers for a roof garden look like the raised beds of some vegetable gardens. Weathered railroad ties are ideal, but weight load is your guiding factor. If they prove too heavy, use the light-weight and smaller landscape timbers available now at any lumber yard or garden center. The depth for the largest plants is 18 inches. For lower edging plants, the depth is shallower. Keep the design long and low, but narrow. A planting around the edge of the roof may be in order if the view directly below is unsightly, but if it is beautiful, keep the edge free of planting, using only a decorative wrought-iron rail to prevent falls.

Rooftop decks.

Planting, Fertilization, and Watering

A soilless mix is ideal for rooftop planting. Spread roots of deciduous plants as you would in any planting. Keep evergreens contained within the burlap root ball until the plant is positioned; then remove the top half of the burlap and all of the ropes or wires. If the planting mix is soilless, it is sterile, yet it holds water and drains well. Nutrients, both macro and micro, must be given at each watering to both deciduous and evergreen plants, which is not as tiresome as one might think if a cannister for holding nutrient tablets is attached to the hose. A drip irrigation system, strangely enough, is not recommended for a roof garden. It is too difficult to monitor the needs of each plant. Poking a finger into the soilless media will still be the best way to determine the each plant's need for water. Continuous fertilization is necessary. Once deficiency symptoms

occur, the damage is done, for the plants are then predisposed to physiological problems, possible insect attack and a less than satisfactory appearance. Ask your county extension office for colored sheets that show deficiency symptoms in leaves. Avoid fertilizer tablet formations that carry non-essential or salt-forming ions. Potassium chloride, for example, contains the non-essential salt-forming chloride ion. Aluminum sulfate contains aluminum ions which can become toxic in amount should the pH drop below 5.5. Different plant species have differing tolerances to salt concentrations, so avoid excess fertilization. A symptom of salt build-up is scorched edges of leaves and a white crust along edges of containers. Should salts build up, add enough water to thoroughly leach salts from the media.

To Lighten the Load

To mix a soilless growing media for a large container that is more thrifty of the expensive soilless mixes on the market today, place a layer of fabric weed barrier over the bottom of the container; fill to half full with perlite; then mix 1/2 perlite and 1/2 soilless mix to further fill 1/4 of the container; and end with 1/4 pure soilless mix. You are cautioned that this media is devoid of any nutrients. Plants growing here will need a small amount of all-purpose fertilizer added to the water to each watering, or a monthly fertilization at the rate suggested on the fertlizer container.

Troughs

Since prehistoric man scraped out soft stone to form a basin, the gardening world has hankered after that basin. There is a fascination with the look of ancient age. It sets off a rare little rock/alpine plant like no other element. In this country we have little access to the stone troughs of England, but we've come up with a good imitation - fibermesh hypertufa, which is actually stronger and lighter than any old stone trough found in an English farmyard. Yankee ingenuity wins again!

The following directions are from Ernie Whitford of Colorado Springs. His troughs are for sale at Birdsall & Co, 1540 South Broadway in Denver, or at Kenny's Nursery in Colorado Springs.

The molds to hold the mixture of concrete and other ingredients (see below) are made of wood. Geometric shapes are the easiest to make and to unmold.

Dry Ingredients

1 part cement
1 part perlite
1 part sphagnum peatmoss
1 ounce of dye per one gallon of dry cement: yellow dye for buff trough, red for reddish, black for gray.
1/8 to 1/4 ounce of Fibermesh per gallon of dry mix - or one big fluffy handfull.**
WEAR A DUST MASK AND RUBBER GLOVES WHEN MIXING THIS MATERIAL.

Measure the dry cement by placing a 1 gallon bucket in a metal wash tub; pour the dry cement into the bucket; dump the bucketful into the tub. Add the dye by sifting it through a tea strainer and mixing with the dry cement. Pour this mix into a cement mixer.

Add the perlite and sphagnum moss and blend the mixture It may be necessary to pre-grind the moss if it is coarse. Cover the mixer's opening with plastic secured with a cord to keep down dust. Store the dry mix in a 30-gallon trash can until you're ready to use it.

To Make a Trough

The form you choose can be configured to many shapes. Ernie Whitford prefers geometric shapes — square, rectangular — but freeform shapes can be achieved by making a trough over a mound of wet sand. For a permanent form — one you will reuse many times — make 1 box with a bottom as illustrated, and one 1 1/2 inches smaller without a bottom. Ernie says the sharp corners tend to break off. He rounds them off within the mold with a dab of putty. After the putty dries, coat the inside of the mold with linseed oil. Use lightweight plastic to separate the form from the hypertufa to assure an easy release when the trough is finished. For a one-time form, rummage through the box pile at the supermarket for the waxed chicken boxes of different sizes.

** *If you can't find Fibermesh at your local cement supply warehouse, contact the manufacturer for the dealer nearest you at: Fibermesh Company, 4019 Industry Drive, Chattanooga, TN 37416, Phone: 615-892-7243.*

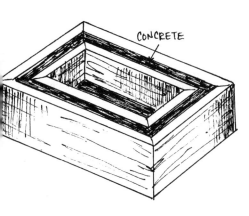

CONCRETE

Cover your work table with a piece of plastic long enough to reach the ground. You'll see why later.

Lubricate the mold(s) with linseed oil. Pour one part of the dry mix (cement plus dye) into a mixing tub, such as a wash tub. Add the Fibermesh at the same time you are adding enough water to barely wet the mixture. It should be on the dry side, about the consistency of cottage cheese. Pack the bottom first; wait about 10 minutes for it to set up, poke the drain hole all the way through, and then use the inner mold to form the sides. After you are finished, draw the plastic drape over the trough and <u>don't touch</u> for 48 hours! After this period, turn the mold over and run the blade of a screwdriver around the edge. Gently tap the mold with a hammer to loosen it until it emerges from the mold.

Brush the sides of the trough briskly with a wire brush to get the texture you want. You may have to spray it with water if it is too dry. Then turn it over and brush the top edge and corners. Does it look as if it were covered with cat hair? Good. It's supposed to. You'll deal with the cathair effect later. But for now, move the trough to a safe place and cover securely with plastic again. *Be sure to lift it up by the bottom.* Lifting up by the sides causes internal cracks that

seriously damage it. Let the trough cure for another 2weeks. Keep damp while the curing process is in progress. The slower the cure, the stronger the trough. After it has cured well, hose it off with water to remove the dry dust and let dry again for about an hour. The Fibermesh 'cat hair' is easily removed with a propane torch. Don't hold the torch in one place for more than a second or two. The torch is a rental item if you don't own one.

Planting and Displaying Troughs

Troughs need not contain a miniature boulder, but until you find the perfect one, skip it. You then have a quest for the rest of your life. Perfect little boulders are usually of conglomerate of no particular color, shaped like a cone that collapsed under pressure - flatish on top with a couple of undefined ledges. It should take up no more than 1/8 to 1/4 of the space in the trough. Fill the trough with a standard rock garden soil mix (see Vol I, Chapter 17), and place your mini-boulder, if you have found one, off-center. Then begin planting the tallest or most sprawling plant near it. Continue planting your rarest and most difficult to grow, keeping in mind their bloom season and bloom color. Leave at least one to drape charmingly over the side.

To display a trough you don't need an English trough yard like those at Kew, Wisley, or Edinburgh. You do need a nearby water source, sun or shade according to the needs of each trough. And you need some supports, such as blocks of wood, to bring them into viewing range. Try to keep them congregated together, with a variety of shapes in each group.

In winter lower them to the protection of contact with the soil under a tree and covered with evergreen boughs. Water monthly.

289

An English trough yard is not difficult to duplicate.

Bonsai Care

The art of forcing trees and shrubs to grow in shallow containers or trays originated in China and Japan centuries ago. It is called *bonsai* (pronounced bone-sigh), and it is an exacting art that requires skill and dedication. No attempt will be made here to give direction for forming a bonsai, only in caring for the finished product because it is highly probable that a good gardener will receive a bonsai as a gift. Everyone knows you are a gardener. Friends and relatives are sure you will appreciate a gift of one of these rare, perfectly dwarfed little gems. Whether you will appreciate it will depend whether you can keep it alive long enough to understand its needs.

1. In the Mountain West only tropical plants trained as bonsai are grown indoors. Bonsai juniper, pine, maple, etc., are not houseplants.
2. If the plant has been growing in a greenhouse nursery, expose it to full sun gradually over a period of 2 to 3 weeks. Grow it on a bench or bracket so that it can be turned weekly to promote growth on all sides.
3. Water daily, sometimes 3-4 times daily, to keep the soil barely moist at all times. Bonsai dries out at warp speed.

Deep water weekly by placing the container in a basin of water to soak for 30 minutes. A weak nutrient solution added to the water monthly will keep them fed. The soil (what little there is of it) is leached of nutrients quickly.

4. Rub off any developing sprouts as they appear on either evergreen or deciduous specimens. You own a finished bonsai and additional branches will detract from the asymmetry of the piece.
5. At any hint of rain or hail, bring them under cover. If you live in Hail Alley (Colorado's Front Range), keep a bonnet of chicken wire over the bonsai. It will slice most of the hail pellets into small pieces.
6. As winter approaches, give it cold-frame protection. If you don't own a frame, a basement window well serves, but each plant must be wrapped in insulating styrofoam. Unwrap and water monthly with warm water in the middle of the day. Check cold frame plants for moisture monthly.
7. As spring approaches, buds on your plants will swell. If you are not hooked on these miniscule temptresses by now, it is best to find a new home for them. If you are hopelessly trapped, enroll in a class and welcome a new plant hobby into your life.

Vegetables in Containers

The apartment dweller with a balcony, courtyard, or lanai is not forgotten in the vegetable section. At first thought it would seem that not enough vegetables could be grown in containers to fill a family bowl of stir-fry or soup. Big 12 inch clay or plastic pots, redwood tubs, 5 gallon buckets (white is preferred), and half-barrels are all good candidates for container culture. All should have a saucer beneath so that water will percolate upward to keep the soil ball from shrinking, as well as to prevent spills and drips onto your own patio or onto your neighbor's below.

Seed Growing

Almost all vegetables are grown from seed sown directly into containers. Exceptions are tomatoes, peppers, and melons.

Lettuce is a favorite crop for a half-barrel, for a crop can be harvested every 26 days. Mix the seeds of such varieties as Mesclun, Black Seeded Simpson, and Grand Rapids. As soon as 4 leaves have formed, harvest 2 of them. Reluctance to harvest seems to be the handicap of the new gardener. Cut the leaves with scissors and you will have fresh leaves forming quickly from the center whorl. Depending on heat build-up during the summer, you should be able to harvest lettuce and other greens for 2 months.

Spinach is another favored container-grown vegetable. Make successive sowings about 2 weeks apart of Melody, Dixie Market, or your own favorite variety.

Radishes and the small, finger-type carrots grow well together, with radishes maturing in 30 days or less. Carrots can be harvested throughout the summer or left to develop sweetness into the fall. Be sure to thin to the proper distance apart or these plants will fail to make edible roots.

Onions grow readily from seed. Onions sets, however, can be tucked into odd places, such as in the corners of flower boxes.

Tomatoes, Peppers, Cucumbers, Squash, and Melons

Undoubtedly, the most satisfying plant for Mountain West gardeners is the tomato. Only the lower altitudes and latitudes are real tomato country; nevertheless, we all try to grow them each year. The reason container-grown tomatoes fail is lack of water throughout the entire root ball. Their roots are extensive and demanding. Use a root watering device for watering; water slowly until you are sure the root ball is wet. Nutrients are quickly leached. Fertilize weekly at 1/4 strength. Side shoots are called "suckers" by some gardeners who are determined to remove them in the name of increased production. Research at Colorado State University and many other research institutions has proved "suckering" is not a prudent practice. Pruning limits growth, which limits production. Simple as that. You can train the vines upward or let them sprawl to the ground to travel around. Since space is usually at a premium, a grid attached to the container keeps the fruit clean, warm, and with good air ciruclation for the prevention of powdery mildew and other diseases.

For high country gardeners, tomato growing containers need wheels so that the entire unit can be wheeled into the living room that adjoins that patio at night. Night temperatures below 50°F will cause the plants to vegetate rather than produce fruit.

Tomatoes grow spread on a grid attached to the tub.

Peppers demand heat, which is usually abundant on the sunny patio, but 6 hours of sunlight daily may not be as easy to come by. Set up an aluminum foil reflector to increase the foot candles of light reaching your plants.

Squash varieties are now availble that are bushes rather than ramblers. Keep in mind they are also heat lovers and will fail to bloom if sunlight is scarce.

Melon varieties are available in miniatures, but standard varieties produce as well when grown in containers as when grown in the garden plot. Give them a sturdy trellis and give the fruits a panty-hose sling to take the weight off the vine stem.

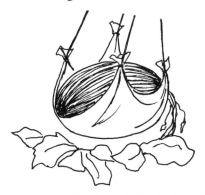

A panty-hose sling for each developing melon will take the weight off the vine stem and keep it from breaking.

Peas, Beans, and Corn

The pole and string trellises available at garden centers and through national catalogs is the ideal way to grow peas and beans in containers. A central aluminum pole is attached to a small wheel at the top and a larger one at the bottom. Strong twine is strung between the wheels. When stuck firmly into the soil of a large wood tub, the pole is very steady and able to carry the weight of pea and bean vines.

Sugar Snap peas are planted in March to germinate quickly in the warm soil of the container. They will bear heavily until late May, at which time the bean seeds are planted beside them. The pole varieties will bear successively all summer after the pea vines are carefully pulled.

Corn is largely an ornamental curiosity in containers, for not enough can be grown to make much of a showing. Grow it for its educational value in watching the open-pollination process. Buy corn from farmer's markets, roadside stands or the supermarket.

Your success with vegetables in containers will depend, as in all gardening, with your location and with the amount of time and space you can devote to the project. At first, stick to fewer plants of fewer species to do a superior job with each. Branch out as you become more proficient.

The Display: Spring, Summer, Fall and Winter

There are almost no constraints on sites for containers. Sunny sites, shady sites, sloping sites, even "out-of sight" for those with only an ephemeral period of bloom. The possibility of season-of-bloom display within the perennial border adds the dimension of the container for its sculptural quality and the plants in the container as added color and texture. Lumber scraps, together with pointed stakes, become plant stands that can be thrust into the soil of the border. Lifting a pot of gloriously blooming marigolds above the mundane out-of-bloom foliage of a patch of chrysanthmums will light it up with new focus. A pot of blooming lobelia or pansies tucked into the foliage of the border can be removed when blooms fade. A creeping juniper groundcover can suddenly come alive with a three-dimensional display of daffodils, followed by tulips. The possibilities are endless.

Whatever effect you wish, with patience and planning, you can achieve it with container gardeing.

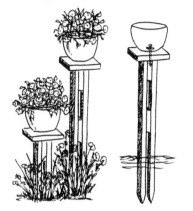

Pots can be lifted for display among the out-of-bloom areas of the perennial border.

Suggested Reading:

"Bonsai for Americans", George F. Hull, Doubleday & Co., 1964.

"Handbook on Dwarfed Potted Trees", Brooklyn Botanic Garden, 1000 Washington Ave., Brooklyn NY 11225

"The Contained Garden", Beckett, Carr, Stevens, Viking Press, 1993.

Product Sources:

Polymer gel: "Hydrosource", Western Pennsylvania Inc., P.O. Box 790, Castle Rock CO 80104.

Attracting Birds and Butterflies to the Garden

The making of a garden is an absorbing task that, once begun, denies all distractions. Your focus is on "garden" in all its stages — design, soil preparation, plant selection, planting, and maintenance. It seldom occurs to you to think of the birds and butterflies that will appreciate your efforts as much as you do. If you were a "birder" or butterfly enthusiast before you became a gardener, your planning stage included careful selection of garden accessories and plant species that will satisfy the needs of both. Let's examine what research efforts have found to enhance your garden toward attracting birds and butterflies, and give you the pleasure of wings, song, and color, and the fascination of life forms beyond your own.

Birds

The Layered Look

Mountain Westerners dress in layers to meet the challenges of changing weather, but often we are not aware that we can dress our landscapes in layers to attracts birds.

DECIDUOUS TREES

The tall shade trees, the highest layer, provide shelter during migration as well as summer nesting sites. Leafiness means a hiding place for many securely placed nests that are anchored against wind. Larvae that feed on trees, as well as their pupa hidden in bark crevices, are food sources for birds.

■ . . . *the pleasure of wings, song, and color, and the fascination of life forms beyond your own.*

Sit down
on a knoll
overlooking a
hackberry and
enjoy the
show!

■ *Acer spp.*
MAPLE

The protecting arms of the thousands of soft maples (*Acer saccharinum*) in the Mountain West provide nesting cavities for owls[1] and nesting sites for many species. This tree species is susceptible to various insects that, in turn, feed many bird species: the 3 nuthatch species (Pygmy, White Breasted, and Red Breasted), Brown Creeper, House Finch, American Robin, Song Sparrow, Pine Siskin, Evening Grosbeak, Black-capped Chickadee, Junco, 2 bluejay species and others. The seed clusters produced in summer hang on to feed them during winter as well. Look for nests of Merlin, American Kestrel, and Eastern and Western Kingbird high in the tops of these trees. Dead branches make good surveying-of-territory posts.

■ *Celtis occidentalis*
HACKBERRY

A hardwood native to the Mountain West, the hackberry was used by early settlers for wagon wheels and furniture. It is the unhappy circumstance that a psyllid invades its leaves, which causes the leaf to swell into a nipple-like gall. The flying stage of the psyllid is almost too small to be seen by the human eye, but birds, especially migrating warblers in spring, will see the swarms of psyllids around a hackberry. Sit down on a knoll overlooking a hackberry and enjoy the show!

■ *Fraxinus spp.*
ASH

From the familiar Green Ash to the exquisite 'Autumn Purple,' the genus *Fraxinus* plays host to many birds. The seed clusters in late fall are raided by Purple Finch, House Finch, Evening Grosbeak, and Bobwhite.

■ *Populus sargentii*
PLAINS COTTONWOOD

The thick, wide-spreading limbs of the cottonwood along rivers and streams are roosting and nesting places for birds of prey, such as the Bald and Golden Eagles, both buteo and accipiter hawk[2], and the Great Blue Heron, as well as the cavity - nesting birds such as the flicker and owl[1]. Bald eagles and Great Blue Heron, because of their wingspan, cannot alight on a nest among leafy branches; therefore, you will see them nesting high in the limbs of dead cottonwoods near water. The birds of prey will seldom be found nesting in backyards, but they are gaining some confidence in cohabiting with mankind from time to time where the housecat becomes their prey. This situation is regarded as a mixed blessing among birders who are also cat lovers, since housecats are the single largest destroyer species of songbirds.

■ *Tilia americana*
AMERICAN LINDEN

Tallest of the lindens, the American Linden lends leafage to nesting birds. From August to October the nutlike fruit is eaten by Common Redpoll, Bobwhite, and Blue Grouse.

■ *Ulmus americana*
AMERICAN ELM

A few are left throughout the Mountain West where they remain the premier tree for the swinging nest of the oriole. The samara seed, present early in the season when birds are especially hungry, is eaten

[1] *Owls: Western Screech, Great Horned, Long eared.*
[2] *Accipiter hawks: Sharp-shinned, Cooper's: buteo hawks: red-tailed, Swainson's and ferruginous.*

by American Goldfinch, Pine Siskin, and House Finch. The Elm Bark Beetle that carries the dreaded Dutch Elm Disease is relished by the vireos, warblers, and nuthatches. Black-Capped Chickadees are seen picking at Elm Leaf Beetles, but they seldom eat them.

EVERGREEN TREES

We find that evergreens — tall, medium, and low — provide shelter from wind and cold winter temperatures, as well as providing insect and seed sources for food.

■ *Pinus spp.*

The pines, especially the *Piñon,* are attractive to the seed-eating birds. The piñon-juniper forests occupy a niche in the ecology of the foothills zone of Colorado, Utah, and New Mexico, and other scattered areas of the Mountain West. These forests provide a distinct set of living conditions for birds as well as plants. The dry, sparsely vegetated land is home to Brown Creeper, Clark's Nutcracker, White-Winged Cross-bills, Pine Grosbeak, Gray Jay, Nuthatches, Piñon Jay, Road Runner, and Phainopepla (New Mexico). These species are casual in other parts of the Mountain West. Blue Grouse feeds almost exclusively on conifer needles in winter. In towns and suburbs where Rocky Mountain Juniper and Red Cedar (*Juniperus scopulorum* and *J. virginiana*) are planted in landscapes, Townsend's Solitaire is attracted in fall and winter, as well as both species of waxwing, Bohemian and Cedar.

FRUITING TREES AND SHRUBS

Trees and shrubs with soft fruits form the understory and still another layer, offering the greatest attraction of all trees for their fruits, for the insects that attack the fruits, and for their ideal nesting sites and shelter.

■ *Amelanchier alnifolia*
SERVICEBERRY

Native to a wide area of the Mountain West, this suckering small tree or tall shrub holds bird populations captive because of its sweet blue fruits in late summer. American Robin, Bullock's Oriole, Mountain Bluebird, many species of warbler, Bohemian and Cedar waxwing, Mockingbird, and Townsend's Solitaire will wait patiently, checking every day, until these berries ripen. Fortunately for the birds, these berries are not palatable to the human population.

■ *Berberis spp.*
BARBERRY

The small fruits would not seem to offer much nourishment, but birds will spot them, especially in winter, to clean this shrub of its fruits.

■ *Cotoneaster spp.*

All forms of this shrub and prostrate creeper are covered with berries that are attractive to birds.

■ *Crataegus douglasii*
BLACK HAWTHORN

This hedge or barrier plant has the most formidable of thorns. It makes good songbird habitat at the edge of a corn field where the warblers will range forth to eat the corn earworms, and where American Robin will pull corn rootworms to the surface. The winter berries further feed the avian population.

■ *C. rivularis*
RIVER HAWTHORN

A native of streamside and river bottom land, this thicket forming small tree or tall shrub produces quantities of nutritious berries in fall and is responsible for

■ *American Robin will pull corn rootworms to the surface.*

297

■ *This native roadside thicket plant is attractive to all fruit/ insect-eating birds.*

successful overwintering of many of the fruit/insect eating birds. If you plant hawthorne seeds, expect them to put down a root the 1st year and to put up a shoot the 2nd year. Make a small backyard nursery for these shrubs that are so valuable to bird habitat. As each reaches transplantable age, plant them in a suitable site in the wild.

■ *Elaeagnus angustifolia*
RUSSIAN OLIVE

It is unfortunate that this tree has escaped cultivation to become wild and crowd out more desirable species. The soft bitter fruits are attractive to Evening Grosbeaks, species of woodpecker, Red-Shafted Flicker, and other fruit and seed eaters. The hot ailimentary tract of a bird enhances the germination rate upon being expelled in feces. The tree, therefore, is deemed a nuisance and we are encouraged to destroy it when found and to cease and desist from planting it.

■ *Euonymus alata*
WINGED EUONYMUS

The tiny red berries produced by this attractive landscape shrub are often so numerous as to give the entire shrub a red winter color. The berries are evidently not very palatable to birds, for they leave them till they are almost starving in late winter before they attack and clean them.

■ *Lonicera tatarica*
TATARIAN HONEYSUCKLE

The value of the red summer berries of this shrub is controversial. Young American Robins eating them have been known to die, apparently from acute diarrhea. When the berries dry in winter, however, they seem not to harm the many birds that flock to them.

■ *Malus spp.*
APPLE, CRABAPPLE

Non-birders curse marauding birds and put up netting and scare devices that are only partially successful. In actuality, the birds eat far more than their weight in harmful insects that attack apples and crabapples than they eat of the fruit itself.

■ *Moras alba*
RUSSIAN MULBERRY—attractive to 14 species.

Many cherry orchardists plant the mulberry on an outfacing row with the hope that birds flying in to raid the cherries will be distracted and, finding the mulberries more tasty, will stay to dine. This, too, is only partially successful, although the mulberries are more nutritious than the cherries for the birds.

■ *Prunus spp.*
P. americana
AMERICAN PLUM

This native roadside thicket plant is attractive to all fruit/insect-eating birds, including American Robin, many warblers, Townsend's Solitaire, Mountain Bluebird, Swainson's Thrush, Bullock's Oriole, Western Tanager, and many species of flycatcher.

■ *P. virginiana*
WESTERN CHOKECHERRY

Another thicket shrub of moist places. The chokecherry is attacked frequently by tent and fall webworm caterpillers, which are difficult for birds to feed upon because the web is somewhat sticky and hard to penetrate. Nevertheless, birds feed upon the small clusters of black stone fruits, as well as the aphids that are abundant in number.

■ *Rhus spp.*
R. glabra
SMOOTH SUMAC

The cockade shapes of sumac fruit are attractive to returning Western and Mountain Bluebirds in spring, as well as to the American Robin, Common Redpoll, Redstarts, and several species of finches.

■ *R. trilobata*
LEMONADE SUMAC

This native shrub that is often used in home landscapes, produces a fuzzy cluster of berries in late summer. The berries are also sticky and attract dust. Birds are wary of dust-covered fruits, but if you give your sumacs a washing now and then, you'll find that Western Tanagers, Bullock's Orioles, American Robin, and many other fruit-eaters will be attracted. This trait was discovered, of course, when an afternoon shower washed the dust away and birds came from near and far to feast.

■ *Ribes spp.*
R. aureum
GOLDEN CURRANT

A dense and impenetrable native shrub, this currant produces yellow or reddish berries that are eaten voraciously by birds. The crossing growth is also attractive as nesting sites by warblers.

■ *Sambucus canadensis*
AMERICAN ELDER

This is not the native roadside plant of distrubed ground in the high country, but an immense shrub of 10 foot height and girth, often planted in home landscapes, that produces plates of edible berries, attractive to both birds and humans.

■ *Sorbus aucuparia*
EUROPEAN MOUNTAIN ASH

Overall, for the Mountain West the mountain ash is the premier tree for hardiness at all elevations (except the sub-alpine and alpine zones) for attracting birds. The clusters of orange berries attract fruit-eating fall migrants. It is not unusual to see Eastern Bluejay, Gray Jay, Steller's Jay, Cedar Waxwing, American Robin, House Finch, and Evening Grosbeak in the tree at the same time. The fruit-bearing twigs are thin and flexible, and the birds must be acrobats to get them. Though waxwings seldom touch the ground, they will forage on the ground for berries that have dropped in early spring when they are very hungry. Cooper's and Sharp-shinned Hawks are well aware of the attraction of this tree. They will pick a secluded viewing post nearby from which they swoop in to take a bird about every 3 days.

■ *Symphoricarpos albus*
SNOWBERRY

The white berries of this small, shade-loving shrub are seldom allowed to hang more than a week before the birds have eaten them all. The berries of the red cultivar *S. orbiculatus,* on the other hand, are left till spring before being consumed.

■ *Viburnum spp.*
V. opulus
CRANBERRY BUSH

Plate-like clusters of red, then black berries decorate this shrub in fall. Birds will leave a few for winter.

■ *V. prunifolium*
BLACK HAW

The haws, as the berries of this species

■ *. . . when an afternoon shower washed the dust away and birds came from near and far to feast.*

are called, are more palatable to birds than the cranberry, and are almost all consumed before the red autumn foliage drops.

EDGE OF THE FOREST

If yours is a country property, you may have planted a windbreak (see Vol. I pp. 103-108) which, to a bird, is the transition between forest and plain. It attracts more species of birds than the remainder of your property. If you live in the high country, you probably have a natural forest that melds into a meadow where high country grasses are harvested in summer. Two very different plant communities come together in these areas, with many species of birds attracted to each.

SHRUBS

Both deciduous fruiting and evergreen shrubs will keep birds happy in both summer and winter. Bird species that are able to change feeding habits from hard seeds in winter to soft fruits and insects in summer are *euryophagous.* They are morphologically advanced to be tolerant of a wide variety of food in both summer and winter. For example, crows and gulls with their straight, simple beaks and strong digestive system can eat fish, small birds, eggs, invertebrates such as snakes, fruits, vegetables, seeds, and carrion. On the other hand, hummingbirds with their long, probing tubular tongues, are closely restricted to drinking only nectar from flowers or sugar water from feeders, though if they come upon a large soft-bodied insect population, such as a cluster of aphids, they manage to lick them up like popsicles.

VINES AND GROUNDCOVERS

As we explore the bottom layer, the floor of a dense Mountain West forest is barren except for ferns, shade-tolerant weeds, and a few species of ground covers that can withstand the lack of light and the competition for nutrients and moisture. Therefore, we look for vines and creeping groundcovers at the edge of the forest or as planted features in home landscapes that are bird attractants. Fruiting vines, such as Bittersweet (*Celastrus scandens)* are useful to birds as a winter food source, shelter, and nesting sites. Virginia Creeper (*Parthenocissus quinquefolia*) is equally attractive to birds with black fruits from July to September, or as long as the birds allow them to hang. The groundcovers, such as the berry-producing creeping juniper (*Juniperus horizontalis*) is also the hiding place for ground-nesters, such as Dark-Eyed Junco, while alfalfa fields host the Western Meadowlark nests.

The flowering perennials and ornamental grass plants in the home landscape can further the last of the layered look for attracting birds. Among them are Globe Thistle (*Echinops spp.*), Mexican Sunflower (*Tithonia rotundifolia)*, Ornamental Grasses (*Pennisetum* spp.), Purple Coneflower (*Echinacea purpurea*), Rudbeckia (*Rudbeckia spp.)*, Salvia (*Salvia spp.)*, and Tickseed (*Coreopsis spp.*).

SHORE AND WATER HABITAT

Water gardening becomes more popular each year in the arid Mountain West. Bird baths are now an integral part of the home landscape, not only to provide water for birds, but also for their sculptural interest. Almost all species of birds are attracted to water by sight and sound for drinking as well as bathing. Some, however, use water only in the juvenile stage of their lives. Owls, for example, are birds of prey that, as adults, do not need water because they rely on the blood of their victims for nutrients and water. Owlets, however, will play in a birdbath, much as children everywhere, while their parents look on in disgust. The Goatsucker family, which includes Poorwill and Night Hawk of the West, are also known to dabble in water when young.

Keeping water in a birdbath during spring migration is especially important. If you've ever watched a dust-covered, mite-infested robin who has just come in from a long migration, you will see your birdbath water turn to murky brown with a scum of drowning mites. The robin, refreshed and clean, will sing you a song as a thank-you.

Water features in your garden should include flat stones or boards at the water line that project into the water or are half submerged. The water over them will warm with the sun and provide a welcome warm bath on a chilly day, and provide a perch from which to drink. Recirculating pumps in a lily pool should be set to recirculate very slowly, for birds, except for the American Dipper, are fearful of a roaring torrent. On the other hand, they are attracted by a steady drip or a tinkling trickle of water.

If yours is a country property, your pond will be attractive until it freezes over for swallows, fly-catchers, gulls, and terns swooping over the surface for insects; ducks (both dabblers and divers) for the underwater plants, fresh water crustaceans, fish, crayfish, frogs, snakes, mosquitos, and other insects; for shorebirds of all sorts[1] for Belted Kingfisher who will use the muddy bank for scooping out a nesting site and perch on overhanging tree limbs to watch for prey in the water.

Nesting sites in and near the country pond are many and varied. Your objective will be to provide as many safe-from-predator areas as possible. The cattail swamp need not be large to house the hidden nests of ducks and the floating nests of American coot. An island in the center will keep goslings of Canada Goose safe from coyotes at night. Give the geese a standard pole nest near the shore of the island planted with willow species, such as Sandbar Willow[2] (*Salix exigua*). Only one island will be needed unless you have a large lake. Geese are not anxious to nest near others of their own kind.

Wood fence posts mounted in your man-made or natural swamp will attract many water birds for use as viewing or singing posts. It's only natural for a fine fellow to want to show off for his lady, and to properly show himself, he needs a post.

Devices to heat water prevent bird baths from freezing in winter and are standard equipment for the serious birder. Stock tank heaters are probably the most economical to use for the large water feature. It won't prevent the water in a large pond from freezing, but will keep enough open water that birds and animals will come from miles around to drink.

For the bird bath there are small heaters that are easily attached to an outdoor extension cord and plugged into a grounded electrical outlet. The number of birds

■ *Owlets, however, will play in a birdbath, much as children everywhere, while their parents look on in disgust.*

---

[1] *The term* Shorebird *is used to include a very large group of birds that get their food from wading in the shallow waters of the shore. Their feet are usually only half-webbed, and, though some can swim, they are not adept swimmers. Examples are herons, avocets, ibis, rails, sora, sandpipers, curlew, yellowlegs, etc.*

[2] *You cannot buy this species. It is the common gray-leaved, single-stem willow, pioneer low-altitude willow-carr species along streambanks throughout the West and Mountain West. Dig a small plant from the wild and it will spread gradually.*

attracted to a winter water feature will amaze you. They queue up like children at a swimming pool. Also like children, there will be a few pushy individuals who misbehave.

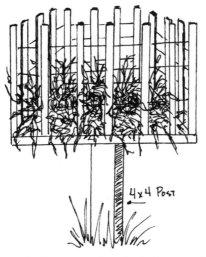

A standard goose nest box of a 4x4 post, and a platform with snow-fence section rail. Excelsior makes a good nesting material.

If you are fortunate to have a stream running through your property, you have the opportunity to build an island to attract such wonders of nature as the Sandhill Crane. They flock at dusk to an island where they noisily settle down to stand, shoulder to shoulder, and sleep all night, safe from predators. Take care to keep their island free of vegetation. They do not feed on watery vegetation, but on the grain stubble left in farmer's fields in fall or on new grass and insects in spring. The nesting area of these stately birds lies mostly in Canada and Alaska, but is also within the Mountain West in Idaho, Montana, Wyoming, Utah, Nevada, and a casual nest in northern Colorado.

Attracting Gallinaceous or Fowl-like Birds

When you live in a mountain community, on a ranch, or in the country near a small town, you expect to see a pheasant, grouse, or quail now and then. Unfortunately, such sightings don't happen often. The proliferation of predators (coyotes, housecats, dogs, and most of all *people*) has cut the natural population to the point that big business has moved in to raise the *Gallinaceous* birds in a domestic setting, to be released for the purpose of hunting. Gun clubs pay very well for large numbers of these birds to be released on private property. Hunters pay very well also for memberships to these clubs and the privilege of hunting.

Your chance of attracting these birds from a natural population is very slim. You can, however, raise a few yourself to release into suitable habitat, with the hope they will stay and successfully raise young of their own.

Newly hatched chicks of quail, Chukar partridge, and Blue Grouse are available by mail. You will find them advertised in the back pages of sports magazines and farm journals. The Extension Office in your county can refer you to the wildlife service of your state university that will give you information on raising the chicks. Plan on providing such paraphernalia as brooder lamps, special water troughs, and special food for their downy stage. Keep them in a pen with high, stout sides and a wire netting cover, for hawks and owls consider these captive chicks a tasty morsel. At night they will need a small, secure house with roosting rails. If their pen can be located at the edge of the area where they are to be released, so much the better, for the transition between the open pen door and the wide open spaces will be difficult for them. Sadly, don't count on a high success rate for this project.

Raising crops that are attractive to the pheasants, quail, and grouse is very successful. Even a small patch of corn, sorghum, wheat, or barley will be spotted by the gallinaceous birds. Wild Turkeys have mysteriously appeared among the standing stalks of these crops in late fall and early winter.

Of Dust Baths and Brush Piles

To make your property attractive to birds, you must tolerate a moderate amount of disarray. The secretive, furtive bird species love a pile of brush in which to hide from predators, as well as for nesting and shelter. They won't notice if you pile up dead logs and tree branches in a pattern that is more neat and pleasing to YOU, but give it a location away from bothersome human noise and presence.

Some bird species, notably sparrows and the gallinaceous birds, prefer to bathe in fine dust rather than water. Try to locate a source for a heavy clay. Grind a bucketful to dust with a makeshift mortar and pestle. Then locate a level sunlit area. Dig oval-shaped depressions in the soil about 5 inches deep and 12 inches long. Fill with a quart or two of the dust. Wait and watch as many birds come to fluff their feathers to allow penetration of the dust, which apparently kills mites and well as cleans oil and debris from the feathers. They will appreciate a nearby perch of a dead tree cemented upright into the soil, for, as you may surmise, they must sit for a long period cleaning the dust away with their beaks.

Crop Stones

You will also need an area close to at least one of your feeders to set aside for coarse sand and pea-sized gravel. You have seen birds picking over a stony area, then choosing one or two stones to swallow before flying away. These are the stones for their crop which are necessary for digestion. You can also purchase a mixture of chicken grit, granite dust, ground oyster shell and limestone as well. Ground charcoal from your outdoor grill is welcome, provided it is not impregnated with a flammulant. Gravel or sand between stepping stones is often sufficient. Keeping the area free of snow and ice in winter is a courtesy.

Locating Birdbaths

Birdbaths located near overhanging branches of trees will lure birds that want to check out the situation before flying in, but placing birdbaths near low shrubs or perennials is tatamount to luring them to their death. Cats are very quick to learn that the bath is the ideal place to catch a bird unaware. They hide in the shrubbery and pounce before the bird can react. Place the bath in open lawn so that the bird can check on all sides before hopping down to the bath. Hanging birdbaths are ideal if the branch they hang from will support the bath, but not a cat.

Tree Collars

Contact a sheet metal shop to make collars to fit your trees that will prevent a cat from climbing up to kill nesting birds and their young. The collars can be painted to make them less noticeable, but, sadly, the paint doesn't stay on long and must be renewed every spring.

■ ... *you must tolerate a moderate amount of disarray.*

Tree collar

Feeders

Catalog mail will inundate you with feeders you can purchase, but often the best ones are those you make yourself. The south or east side of your home or of any structure is the most ideal location for a bird feeder. Filling a feeder when snow is deep in winter or you are suffering from some malaise requires ingenuity. If you have eaves on your home, and if you have windows that afford easy access to the eaves, remove the window screen; attach a hook to the underside of the eave directly at the window you will open. Hanging your feeders in this area of the eave also thwarts Fox Squirrels and other squirrel species. These little animals make quick work of finding a way to bypass all other squirrel deflectors, but they cannot climb or swing down to a feeder attached to the underside of eaves. To prevent birds from flying into your windows, make an "X" of masking tape on the window.

Feeding platforms are merely flat boards with an edge of molding to prevent wind from blowing away the food. They are usually mounted on a post near enough to a tree branch that a bird can land on the branch to check the situation, but far enough away from the branch to prevent a squirrel from jumping from the branch to the platform. The platform is for the birds that cannot or will not approach a covered or hanging feeder. Scatter a variety of foods on the platform, with emphasis on the dried fruits for the fruit/insect eating species.

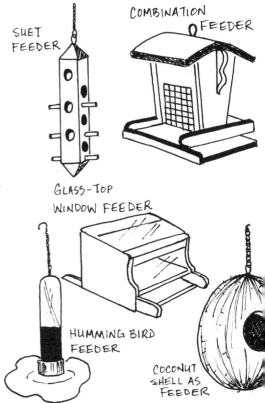

Feeders, homemade and store bought.

FEEDING THE BIRDS

The centers that specialize in selling wild bird food mixes will provide you with every conceivable type of food for the seed-eating birds: thistle seed for American Gold Finch; pine nuts for Pine Siskin, Pine Grosbreak, Piñon Jay; black oil sunflower seed for House Finch, Blackcapped and Mountain Chickadee, Titmouse, and Rose-breasted, White-Breasted, and Pygmy Nuthatch; cracked corn for the upland game (Gallinaceous) birds and jays; white millet, peanut and sunflower hearts for the gourmet fare for all. Safflower seed might lure in a Northern Cardinal, which is now only a casual migrant in the Mountain

West, but which may become a resident within the next 50 years.

What You Can Do in Early Spring to Feed and Shelter Migrants and Returning Resident Birds

Birds winging back to the Mountain West in great numbers in early spring are heralded by the Mountain Bluebird, which usually makes its appearance in early March. These birds fly in migration in flocks, staying a few days here and there before beginning their upward migration, following the snowline as it melts in the foothills, then nesting in the Montane zone from 8,000 feet to 10,000 feet. Bluebirds are especially vulnerable during their migration because they often follow a southwest wind to aid them in flying their long journey. It is this same southwest wind that brings our most disastrous storm fronts in the Mountain West. You can save the lives of countless Mountain Bluebirds during one of these storms if you have an open, but covered, patio, or if you have an unheated garage or barn. Keep on hand a long length of wire and some cuphooks. If a storm is eminent, screw the cuphooks into the walls of your patio, garage, or barn, and string the wire so that it is at least 12 inches from the ceiling. Place shallow pans of water on the floor, as well as trays of chopped apples, raisins, oranges, banana, or any other fruit you have on hand.

Leave the light on all night each night of the storm and during the day if the sky is exceptionally dark or the snowfall heavy. Bluebirds will often fly at night during migration and will seek out a lighted shelter. They *must* have the wire upon which to perch. If a flock should come, take care not to open the door or disturb them in any way. If you hear a large number of birds arriving, wait about 30 minutes; then turn out the light. They must have total darkness in which to rest. If you open the door or disturb them in any way, they will fly out into the night — often to die in the cold and snow.

How much do you relegate to the garbage disposer that could keep a bird alive during the harsh winter and early spring season? Most of us have bird feeders and supply them with wild bird seed mixtures, which is good for seed-eating birds, but what about the soft-billed birds that cannot eat seeds? They depend on insects and soft fruits for their subsistence.

During the harvest season you are often discarding many pounds of possible bird food. This includes wind-fall apples, crabapples, plums, and other fruits, or pieces of fruits that you have purchased for preserving. A bird doesn't care if there is a rotten place in a piece of fruit; in fact, a wormy apple is extra delicious and nutritious.

Take time at harvest season to chop up some of those fruits - cores, seeds, skins and all. Spread them out directly on the roof of your garage or porch or any out-of-the-way sunny place. They will dry within a few days. In the regions where mulberry (*Moras alba)* trees are hardy, these berries are particularly relished by the fruit-eating birds[1] If you have a rack upon which to place all the fruits, they will dry faster. You can leave the fruits there all winter unless wind will scatter the pieces all over the yard. You can gather them up and keep them in open jars. Use the mixture to stock platform feeders and to place on the ground

[1] *Mulberries are often grown along with cherry orchards, hoping to attract the birds to the mulberries, forsaking the cherries. They fall from the trees quickly. Rake the berries in piles, or, if the trees are planted in lawn, move the berries into windrows with a strong stream of water from the hose.*

or back on the roof for birds too shy to come to a feeder. Hawks and owls have been seen taking this type of food. Take along a jar of the mix on winter hikes to scatter along a trail.

In this age of awareness about the necessity of recycling EVERYTHING, we must take time to recycle discarded fruit for the benefit of birds.

Suet — the Real Thing, and Other Foods

We often read that we must supply suet for the birds in winter. Very few know that suet is not just any animal fat, but is only the fat around the kidney of a slaughter animal. It is extremely valuable as bird food because it is high in calories and never becomes rancid. The bacon fat mixtures in "seed bell" and seed cakes will quickly become rancid in weather much above freezing and thus, unpalatable to birds.

However, there are many mixtures that will attract birds and may be made from foods from the kitchen cupboard.

Fill cupcake tins with mixtures of bread or pancake crumbs, sunflower seeds, white millet, rice, wheat, old breakfast cereal, cracked corn, salt-free nuts, oatmeal, and peanut butter. Melt bacon fat to pour over. Refrigerate and serve to birds on the platform or in nets hung from a tree branch.

Cooked noodles with a tiny bit of salt are relished by almost all species. Ground dog biscuits mixed with a liberal portion of chicken grit will disgust the dog, but attract a bird. Chicken grit may be purchased at a farm supply store.

What Not to Feed

Garbage will attract starlings and the Blackbilled Magpie. Though it is comical to watch a Magpie try to down a frozen noodle, it will stay around to raid the nests

of more desirable birds in summer. They are also quarrelsome and noisy.

Hummingbirds can have only sugar and water mixes, usually three parts water to one part sugar, boiled and cooled. Honey is not recommended and is, in fact, harmful.

Red millet is disdained by birds, no matter how hungry they are. It is often included in cheap mixes.

Bird Houses

The bird houses available on the market today are of immense variety. Incredible craftsmanship and exquisite design make these small sculptures worthy as garden art. Yet the birds are not always appreciative of them. An old tomato can opened with a hunting knife and strapped to a branch with two shoe laces is home-sweet-home to a chickadee.

Tomato can birdhouse.

Scrap pieces from a sawmill will often have missed the de-barking machine. Strangely, cavity nesting birds are fooled by the bark covered lumber when it is made into an unassuming house. Presumably, the

306

striations on the bark and the pre-drilled hole translate into "This tree is made for ME."

Houses made of sawmill scrap slab lumber appeal to many cavity nesters.

House Finches are willing nesters in the middle of your favorite hanging basket. Rather than interrupt their nesting, carefully water the plants, and they won't mind your presence, and the moisture will not rot the bottom of the nest. To prevent this procedure next year, give them a two-board shelf up under the eaves. This shelf is inaccessible to grackles and other nest raiders because they are too tall to alight on the shelf.

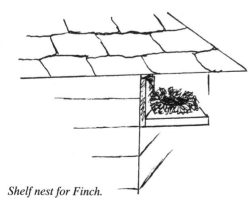

Shelf nest for Finch.

Robins build beautiful nests, but will not nest in enclosed houses. Give them a small shelf up under the eaves, as well. They need a little more headroom than the finch.

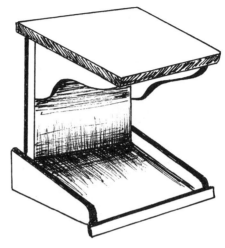

Shelf for robin nest.

Swallows can be a serious problem when they decide to cement their nests to the top of your porch light or the wall outside your kitchen door. Give them a more inviting place by building a swallow box in a place protected from wind. If you live on a ranch, you might attract Say's Phoebe, a real treat to watch.

Swallow box.

Birds most often roost at night in conifers, but during a severe storm, many die from exposure. Give them a protective box where many, often of different species, will seek shelter. Wood shavings on the bottom will make it more inviting and add insulation.

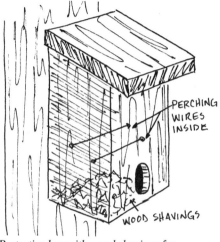

Protective box with wood shavings for insulation.

Every year advertisements for the multiple-apartment Martin houses appear in garden magazines. Sadly, the Martin does not frequent the Mountain West. If a gift of a Martin house shows up, put it up, but don't expect more than one Tree Swallow family to move in. House Sparrows will nest in winter.

Mountain and Western Bluebirds may never again nest on the Plains or near cities and towns. The crush of human population is too great for their liking. If you live in a mountain community, or on a high country ranch, however, Bluebirds will become very tame, helping themselves to every civilized amenity, including the TV aerial, the outdoor wash rack basins, your clothespin bag, and a tasty dish of pasta. Give them a box to their specifications

because they are very precise in their requirements. If we make sure that every measurement is correct, we might enlarge the Bluebird range. Mount it on a fencepost facing southeast at eye level. To discourage predators such as snakes, raccoon, or field mice, wrap the post with aluminum roof flashing and double the thickness (not the diameter) of the entrance hole. **This admonishment is good for all bird houses**. It prevents the predator birds from reaching down into the hole to kill the nestlings. These are sold as "predator extensions" or you can make one yourself from a scrap of wood. Other improvements are screened one-quarter inch vent holes beneath the overhanging roof on the sides. Also add horizontal grooves on the inside front of the box to give the baby birds traction in their first steps up toward the exit hole.

Bluebird house with predator extension.

Longspurs and many other species of ground nesters will nest near a cow chip in a pasture. Is this because the heat of decomposition is welcome in a cold spring? Is it because they use it as a landmark to find their nest from the aerial view? Is it because the cow chip becomes a source of food with kernels of grain as well as tasty dung beetles? We may never learn the answers. Birders never tire of surmise and theory.

Townsend's Solitaire nests under ledges. It may also take a shelf nest of larger proportion than the finch nest pictured.

Brown Creeper nests where bark is pulled away on a tree from a frost crack. This is another reason not to be too quick to pull loose bark from a tree.

Despite your efforts at providing bird housing, the majority of species will not come to it. Concentrate, instead, on providing materials they can use to entice them to nest nearby. **None of the material should be more than 4 inches long.** Robins will search for a piece of white string to start their nest. All species will take lengths of rough twine, shreds of bark, and clumps of excelsior and dried grass. Short twigs are needed to make the framework when beginning a nest. Hummingbirds will welcome a cattail. Pull a little of the down out, and they will get the idea. Every time you comb the dog or cat, save the combings for the birds. Contrary to popular belief, they are not the least repulsed that this material comes from an enemy. Birds do not have a well-developed sense of smell. As a container for all of these small items, use the small wire cage you used last winter as a suet feeder. Attach it to a tree limb in a prominent flyway through your yard; then watch it disappear!

Butterflies

Watching butterflies may one day become as popular as birdwatching, but at present only a few are dedicated to this endeavor. The intriguing part of butterfly watching is that it requires no equipment. You might want a binocular, but it isn't required, for the best way to observe their beauty is close up. You can't really take in their beauty with a binocular.

In review, the butterfly is the adult stage of the *Lepidoptera* order. With complete metamorphosis, the female adult mates and lays eggs which hatch into tiny larvae with chewing mouthparts that voraciously eat their way through the leaves and stems of the plants they prefer. They grow many times the size they were upon hatching from the egg. After molting several times, they spin a chrysalis, attaching it by a thread in a protected place where their life form changes (metamorphoses) in a time period specific to the species, and they emerge an adult butterfly. Like all insects, butterflies have 3 main body parts, head, thorax, and abdomen, 3 pairs of jointed legs, and 1 pair of clubbed antennae. Most have 2 pairs of scaled wings. Their scaled wings distinguish them from all other insects. The scales, unlike fish scales, are powdery and overlapping in rows that are invisible without magnification.

Lepidoptera is the largest order of insects except for *Coleoptera*. Tropical regions have the greatest number of butterflies, but the Mountain West has its fair share.

To attract butterflies, plan your garden to include plants that produce nectar for the adults to sip, and food plants for the caterpillars to chew. Providing mud puddles and moist sand for the sipping pleasure of

■ *The best way to observe their beauty is close up.*

■ *Rotting fruit, bird dung, and honeydew produced by ahpids, are added attractions for butterflies.*

males is an added attraction. The attraction of these 'gentlemen's mud puddle clubs' is not fully understood. It may be for the dissolved minerals needed in their life processes, or it may be only a guy thing. Since this is the Mountain West, we are certain mail order catalogs will soon display butterfly brass rails.

Rotting fruit, bird dung, and honeydew produced by aphids, are added attractions for butterflies. However, their main source of food will be patches of flowers producing their favorite nectar. Patches of the same species of flower will be a greater attraction than spotty groups here and there. Choose species that will flower in sequence, such as lilacs in spring; geraniums, cosmos, marigold, verbena in summer; zinnias, asters, cinquefoil (*Potentilla fruticosa*) and Butterfly Bush (*Buddleia davidii*) in late summer; Gaillardia and Rabbitbrush in fall. Many of these flowers have light-colored lines leading to the throat where the nectar is stored. Butterflies use the nectar guides and pollinate the flower while sipping the nectar. The nectar guides of many species of flowers, once pollinated, will turn dark. The butterfly does not see the darkened lines; thus, does not waste time in trying to sip nectar that has been depleted, and moves on to a newly opened flower.

Many have observed butterflies hanging bravely on a flower during a wind strom or less than gentle breeze. Many floweres have adaptations to assist their friends, the butterflies. Pinks (*Dicentra sp.*) have lacinated edges on their petals; lilies and flowering tobacco have deep, sticky throats where small moths and butterflies can seek refuge during a strom.

Dill and parsley plants will be the place where the beautiful Swallow Tail types will lay their eggs. We have the Two-Tailed with double projections on the hind wing, the Western Tiger colored butter and black, and the Black swallowtail, a dramatic black with a touch of turquoise and gold. The fearsome caterpillers are sometimes caught by an early freeze. If one is predicted, hasten outdoors to gather them up for protection inside the house until the danger is over. Don't dump them all in a coffee can. Give each a separate drink cup with a sprig of parsley or dill to tide them over until you can place them on individual plants outdoors.

The beloved tawny orange and black Monarch butterfly overwinters along the West Coast, often populating a single tree like spangles. We can attract it here, however, by allowing milkweed to bloom in out-of-the-way places. Also, plants of the genus *Ruta* have been reported to attract it. The common Rue, *Ruta graveolens,* is well known in the herb garden as Herb of Grace. Neither *R. g.* 'Blue Mound' or 'Curly Girl' are reliably hardy in all parts of the Mountain West, but it can be lifted in fall to overwinter in the coldframe. The Monarch will lay eggs on the rue in spring and again in early fall.

Two woody plants and one herbaceous perennial are stand-out attractants to butterflies, the Butterfly Bush (*Buddleia davidii and B. alternifolia*) and Butterfly Weed (*Asclepias tuberosa*). Butterfly Bush almost always dies down to the ground in Mountain West winter, but comes up willingly in spring to bloom profusely. Pink, white, lavender, and purple cultivars are available. The bright orange Butterfly Weed is notorious for resenting transplanting. Grow it in a yard-wide patch from direct seeding and you will never regret it.

What You Give Up For Butterflies

If you persist as a butterfly enthusiast, you will soon sigh and give up your neat and tidy ways in keeping your garden weeded. Unfortunately, butterflies are attracted primarily to some of our most noxious weeds. Be a little tolerant of a few weeds. However, Canada thistle is almost universally prohibited by law throughout the Mountain West. Bull thistle is a biennial and if you are careful NEVER to allow seeds to scatter, your butterflies will find plenty of nectar to sip from this species.

You will also put away your spray materials, for butterflies are insects, and insecticides will quickly bring their presence to an end. You cannot use the organic pesticide sold as BT, Biocide, or Dipel because it is deadly to the larval forms of *Lepidoptera*. The *Bacillus thuringiensis* in these materials invades and blocks the mid-gut of the larvae. They discontinue feeding and die within about 3 days.

Bird and butterfly watching are part of the reward of gardening. As we get caught up in observing their daily lives, they become part of our family. Our gardening habits change to suit their needs, and we once again enjoy the benefits of "As you give, so shall you receive."

Table 1: Ten flowering plants useful for attracting butterflies in eastern Colorado.

Asters	Lilac
Butterfly bush	(Syringa vulgaris)
(Buddleia davidi)	Marigold
Butterfly plant	(Tagetes spp.)
(Asclepias tuberosa)	Rabbitbrush
Bush cinquefolia	(Chrysothamnus nauseosus)
(Potentilla fruticosa)	Verbena
Cosmos	(Verbena spp.)
(Cosmos spp.)	Zinnias

Common butterflies in eastern Colorado and the foods used by these insects are included in Table 2. By planning the yard or garden to include these food sources, a steady flow of butterfly visitors is encouraged.

Table 2: Food used by common eastern Colorado butterflies and skippers.

Butterfly	Flight period	Caterpillar food	Common nectar plants, adult food
Two-tailed swallowtail (Papilio multicaudatus)	April-August	Green ash, chokecherry	Geranium, thistle, milkweed
Western tiger swallowtail (Papilio rutulus)	May-July	Willow, cottonwood, chokecherry	Zinnia, lilac, butterflybush, thistle, milkweed
Black swallowtail (Papilio polyxenes)	April-September	Dill, parsley, fennel, carrot	Butterflyweed, alfalfa, thistle
Monarch (Danaus plexippus)	June-October	Milkweed	Cosmos, Canada thistle, rabbitbrush, etc.
Weidemeyer's Admiral (Limenitis weidemeyerii)	June-September	Willow, aspen, cottonwood	Sap flows, snowberry, dung
Hackberry butterfly (Asterocampa celtis)	May-September	Hackberry	Rotting fruit, sap flows
Painted Lady (Vanessa cardui)	April-October	Thistle, hollyhock, sunflower	Grape hyacinth, cosmos, zinnia, alfalfa, many flowers
European cabbage butterfly (Pieris rapae)	April-October	Broccoli, cabbage (mustard family)	Many
Checkered white (Pontia protodice)	April-November	Tumble mustard	Alfalfa, mustards, beeplant
Clouded sulfur (Colias philodice)	April-November	Alfalfa, clover	Alfalfa, phlox, rabbitbrush, aster, marigold
Orange sulfur (Colias eurytheme)	April-October	Alfalfa, vetch, pea	Alfalfa, marigold, zinnia
Melissa blue (Lycaeides melissa)	April-October	Wild licorice, alfalfa, etc.	Beeplant, sweet clover
Gray hairstreak (Strymon melinus)	May-October	Many	Many
Variegated fritillary (Euptoieta claudia)	April-October	Various, incl. pansy	Rabbitbrush, Canada Thistle
Edwards fritillary (Speyeria edwardsii)	June-September	Nuttall's violet	Rabbitbrush, Gaillardia, beeplant
Gorgone checkerspot (Charidryas gorgone)	May-September	Sunflowers	White clover, dandelion, Canada Thistle
Mourning cloak (Nymphalis antiopa)	February-November	Willow, aspen, cottonwood, elm	Rabbitbrush, mildweed, sap
Wood nymph (Cercyonis pegala)	June-August	Grasses	Rabbitbrush, clematis, Canada Thistle
Silver-spotted skipper (Epargyreus clarus)	May-July	Wild licorice, locust, etc.	Lilac, dogbane, zinnia, sweet pea, Canada Thistle
Checkered skipper (Pyrgus communis)	April-October	Mallow, hollyhock	Verbena, dandelion, Canada Thistle, aster

[1] From the Service in Action sheet of Colorado Cooperative Extension # 5.504 written by Dr. Paul A. Opler, chief editorial section, Office of Information Transfer, USDI-FW and Dr. Whitney S. Cranshaw, Colorado State University assistant professor of entomology, and Extension specialist in entomology.

Growing Wildflowers

The settlement of the Mountain West dates only to the post-Civil War era when mining, lumbering, and farming gradually gained a foothold. As with gardens throughout history, the first Mountain West gardens were planted with medicinal herbs. If a flower was planted, it was from seed from the home settlers had left back east, carefully saved and wrapped to preserve its viability during the long trek across the plains. Cuttings and scion wood of favored shrubs and especially fruit trees were stuck into the center of a potato where moisture sometimes preserved the viability until rooting occurred when the destination was reached. Though poetry preserved from that era extols the beauty of the fields of wildings blooming in the high country and on the plains, strangely, there is no evidence that seeds or plants were collected for planting around homesteads or in town yards. Even today when we spot a remnant of a tumbledown chimney marking a homesteader's cabin or a miner's shack beside his diggings, it is an ancient lilac or thorny rose from "back home" that marks the planting made by a lonely woman who brought nostalgic order to her wild surroundings.

The 1970's "back to nature" movement agrandized by the young people of the era known as "hippies" sent scurrying the professional horticulturists to meet their demand of how to grow the wildflowers of mountain and plain in their own gardens. Digging of plants in the wild was (and still is) frowned upon, but never actually forbidden until legislation passed in several Mountain West states in l978, long after hippie and non-hippie alike had discovered the plants they dug from the wild seldom

■ *. . . it is an ancient lilac or thorny rose from "back home" that marks the planting made by a lonely woman who brought nostalgic order to her wild surroundings.*

313

These predecessors, then, are spiritual kin to all today who set foot to spade, who aspire not to tame a wild thing, but to recreate the habitat that will see it flourish.

survived anyway. These predecessors, then, are spiritual kin to all today who set foot to spade, who aspire not to tame a wild thing, but to recreate the habitat that will see it flourish.

In the Mountain West a natural diversity of plants grow that are unlike any other area due, in part, to the interaction of latitude, longitude, topography, and the resultant weather patterns. We revel in high desert, low desert, forests, wetlands, prairies, tundra, roaring torrents, lazy rivers, and tinkling rivulets. The endemic plant and animal taxa and unique geologic formations that comprise our heritage give us an urge to preserve this diversity in havens within our home boundaries. The fact that many have failed before us seems not to daunt, but remains an unfinished business we still explore.

The strongest push toward gathering all information on the cultivation of wildflowers into one place began with the founding and funding of the National Wildflower Research Center in Texas by Mrs. Lyndon (Lady Bird) Johnson in 1982. She deeded a 60-acre tract of land and gave an initial $125,000 to launch the research program. The basic premise of the Center was prompted by the untimely mowing of roadsides where grew the famed Texas bluebonnets (*Lupinus subcarnosus*) before the seeds could ripen and scatter naturally. By substituting wildflowers for grass along highways, mowing is reduced to one mowing in late fall, and the bluebonnets have flourished to this day. The Center remains a repository for wildflower-growing information throughout the North American continent.

Adding to the wildflower preservation movement is Operation Wildflower sponsored by the National Council of State Garden Clubs. Its objective is to promote beautification of roadsides and other areas throughout the nation and to build public understanding and appreciation of native grasses and flowers.

What Are Your Goals?

The look of either a mountain meadow, acres wide, or a small backyard patch is attainable, but not without variables lurking in the wilderness of research in progress. Asking you to "start small" is not the answer because you may want to view a gentle slope of wildflowers some time before you die. Then again, there are questions of 4-season color if you live year-round at this site. Are you a purist who insists only upon native plants? For the Mountain West the number of natives is astounding, but does not include California Poppies or Batchelor's Button, 2 species that seem to dominate many wildflower seed mixes. Are you planting to attract butterflies and birds? A commendable reason, but neither cares a whit about whether a plant they feed upon is native or not. Are you planting wildflowers to save water? An illusion comes from the notion many gardeners have that all plants native of the Mountain West are xeriscape candidates. The truth is, though we have many plants that are chary of water, they all demand it at the time they are establishing and periodically after that. Natural precipitation in the Mountain West is not reliable.

Sun or Shade?

It is tempting to plant wildflowers where nothing else will grow. When you have considered why nothing grows there, you will be dissuaded. Planting on a steep slope in poor soil in deep shade is a regrettable folly. Full sun in reasonable soil on a well-drained site is the preference for the greatest number of species. However, a moist shady site with deep rich soil will give you a whole new realm of possibilities in plant species.

High Country Considerations

If you are attempting wildflower establishment at an elevation of 6,000 to 11,000 feet, there are special considerations: short growing season, cold rocky soil lacking organic matter, wind without ceasing in some areas, and wildlife grazing. There are a few moisture-retentive soils that are green throughout the summer. Look for these as the best sites for wildflower seed sowing if— and this is a big IF — there is enough sunlight. Some species that prefer full sun will establish in the shade, but bloom sparsely and be very slow to mature. Amend the poor soils with sphagnum peatmoss or compost, but not weathered manure unless it comes from animals that grazed on the local vegetation. We need not risk introducing the weeds of the Plains into the high country. If the site you choose is on a steep, rocky slope, cover the soil and fill in around the rocks with a fine pea gravel. Then sow the wildflower seed directly into the gravel. It will fall into crevices and cracks to the soil. If the site is kept moist, the seed will germinate quickly and the seedlings will make their way to the surface in and around the pebbles. Both the meadow and the rocky hillside in the high country will need fertilization 3 times annually — early spring, midsummer, and fall. Scattering a compost made with animal manure is excellent, or you may choose from 10-10-10 or 5-10-5 commercial fertilizer.

Design

The design of nature cannot be captured in a season or two of effort and enthusiasm. Be prepared for the long haul of gradually refining your design as you become more familiar with the wants and needs of each species. Plan for one or more paths to meander through the area. You can't enjoy the total picture or the smaller species without close examination. Also, the scent of the flowers will not come upon you unless you are among them. Two points to remember about paths: They create surprise and the illusion of space when one cannot see around the corner, and they are most successful when they begin or end at a point where there is a view beyond, a vista that invites further exploration. A path is also a maintenance feature, for you won't want to trample the flowers with a wheelbarrow load of stone mulch or a tarp-load of pulled weeds.

Soil Preparation

The knowledge gained thus far in creating a wildflower meadow begins with the soil. Unless what you have is pure sand, don't give amendments another thought. The directions above are for high country only. Your objective is to select plants that will *withstand*, grow and multiply with what's there. *If you have pure sand*, add clay soil and a small portion of organic matter, both of which will increase the water-holding capacity and add mineral nutrients to your sandy soil.

The biggest hurdle concerning soil is weed seeds. Some have lain near the surface for centuries. Still more are buried deeply. Those who first attempted wildflower growing ripped a grassy plain with a rotary tiller, raked off the stubble to make a smooth bed, then sowed by hand a wild flower mixture of seeds endemic of the area. They mulched with anything handy that they hoped had no weed seeds and watered during dry spells knowing that moisture is essential during the germination

■ *The biggest hurdle concerning soil is weed seeds.*

period. The results were a bumper crop of ragweed and almost no flowers. No ragweed was seen to grow on this ground prior to the tilling, but apparently, ragweed seeds had lain dormant in the soil depths since the ground had been graded years before, and the tilling brought them to the surface. An experiment with similar results was conducted by the American Horticulture Society on their wild flower meadow attempt at River Farm in Virginia. Their surprise crop was pokeweed.

Recent attempts have brought better results. If a lawn of turf grasses is to be converted to a wildflower meadow, tilling the turf is not recommended. Instead, the sod should be stripped off as thinly as possible with a power-driven sod cutter, or with a sharp flat spade if the area is small. Set aside the turf for later use piling it in blocks stacked upside down. With the subsoil exposed, and you can proceed to the next step.

If it is poor and rocky, remove surface rocks only and bring it up to the previous grade with hauled-in top soil which can be cultivated into the existing soil.

If the area is one of sparse weediness with grassy and broadleaf weeds, or the above exposed subsoil-plus-topsoil, consider waiting until midsummer to begin watering the area copiously to bring up weeds. When a good crop appears, spray them with the contact systemic herbicide glyphosate (often sold as Roundup). After 48 hours resume watering to bring up late-comers. Spray individual weeds again as needed until late September (in Montana) or late October (in New Mexico), according to your latitude. Then sow the wildflower seeds shortly before freezing weather. Rake in lightly to create small, shallow furrows, then smooth by using the back of the rake. Tamp down by walking over it. The seeds

will undergo chemical changes within (See Chapter 8, Propagation, Stratification) as the winter and spring progress, then germinate later in the spring without the usual flush of weeds.

If your seeding is planned for spring, you have 2 alternatives. You can spray each individual weed with glyphosate as it appears and then sow. Or you can water the area copiously, then spread sheets of black plastic over the entire area. The weed seeds will germinate in the hot darkness, but they will succumb quickly to heat and lack of light. The ground is then ready to sow. With either method there will be late-comers that must be routed out by hand. You will soon learn how to distinguish a weed seedling from that of a treasured flower. A good booklet that depicts weed seedlings in closeup colored photos is "Common Weed Seedlings of the United States and Canada", published by the Cooperative Extension Service, University of Georgia, College of Agriculture, Athens, Georgia.

Choosing the Seeds and Sowing

Just as a forest matures from single species to mixed species, a natural wild-flower meadow matures from its first emergence as a single patch of one species to patches of other species with no mixing of the species within patches. As wind, water, animals and birds scatter seed, the meadow matures and has many species growing side by side. The plant community becomes one of partitions or windows of bloom within the growing season. One species will bloom in spring before another has even emerged. The blooming plant then dies down and the newly emerged plant takes over. The shorter blooms are earlier; taller species come later. The result is an ever-changing succession of bloom throughout the growing season. Under the soil surface, fibrous roots are intertwined with tap-rooted species, some deep, some very shallow. When a wildflower meadow becomes established, there isn't room for weeds.

Yet there is something to be said about planting single species in patches. You may have seen many times breath-taking patches of Parry's Gentian (*Gentiana parryi*). It is then that we know to be true the saying, "There is no blue like Gentian blue." Yet a single plant of Parry's Gentian might be lost if were blooming amid plants of Gaillardia, Tansy Asters, and Mule's Ears, all of which bloom at the same time. A mature meadow is a horticultural zoo, yet it is as natural as the patches of single species. The choice is yours as to the look you want.

If your choice is one of the mature mixed species, use the directions above for sowing. If you want to have patches of single species, use the garden hose to outline areas you wish to plant with single species. Be aware that as your planting matures, the mixing of species will occur just as it does in nature.

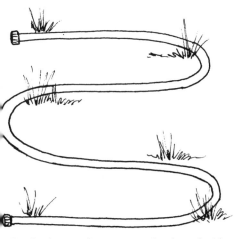

Garden hose outlines areas to be planted with single species.

Seeds of single species are available, but you may have to search. Seed mixes are much more available. In general, seed mixes of plants for a cold climate are the best choice throughout the Mountain West. Most mixes will have a combination of annuals and perennials, though there aren't many annual species native to the Mountain West. A wildflower meadow somewhere near Socorro, New Mexico, for example, might include some warm season flowers, but species able to withstand cold temperatures will survive there also.

Collecting seed is not easy. That's why wildflower seed is expensive. The seed laws have also changed recently, becoming more restrictive and further limiting the variety of species available. The few seed merchants who began by collecting seed from the wild quickly gave it up because it is a difficult timing problem to harvest an area at the moment the seed is ripe. Equipment for harvesting wildflower seed is almost non-existent. Growers now grow fields of single common species, such as *Penstemon stricta*, *Erigeron speciosus var. macranthus*, or *Aquilegia caerulea*.

If you want to harvest your own seed from the wild, be aware that harvesting is illegal in all national parks, most national forests, and many county open space areas. Never harvest any seed from plants on the Conservation List or the Endangered Species list. Harvest with permission on private land, and then harvest only a pinch from each plant, leaving plenty for it to reseed itself. Never harvest from a plant that is the lone example of a species in an area. When harvesting any of the Paintbrushes (*Castilleja sp.*), take a pinch of seed of nearby sage as well as a pinch of soil with the hope of satisfying the symbiosis of sage and *Castilleja*, thus overcoming the antipathy of this genus to germinate and grow.

Species To Avoid

California Poppies and Batchelor's Button have been mentioned previously as non-native species to avoid. Other species are:

Linaria vulgaris &	
L. dalmatica	Butter and Eggs
L. genistifolia	Dalmatian Toadflax
Saponaria officinalis	Bouncing Bet
Tithymalus Cyparissias	Cypress Spurge
Hesperis matronalis	Dame's or Sweet Rocket
Lythrum salicaria	Lythrum
Salvia aethiopis	Mediterranean Sage
Euphorbia myrsinites	Myrtle or Mercer's Spurge
Leucanthemum vulgare aka Chrysanthemum leucanthemum	Ox-Eye Daisy
Matricaria perforata	Feverfew or Scentless Chamomile

Transplanting and Thinning

Before beginning to thin seedlings whose only sin has been to come up too close to a neighbor, arm yourself with a British "dibbler." This is an instrument resembling a narrow shoehorn. You can fashion one by sharpening a grapefruit spoon or wooden chopstick. Mix a small carton of "transplant solution," which is 1/4 teaspoon of a soluble houseplant fertilizer in a pint of water. Native plants often have a taproot even when very young and with only 2 pairs of leaves. As you carefully dig deeply to remove a crowded seedling, lift it with crumbs of soil attached to the root and drop it into the solution. As you move about the plot (probably on your knees — this is a

task for the dedicated, remember), use your dibbler to dig holes to fit each seedling in bare areas where seeds failed to germinate. Transplant a thinned seedling from your carton and cover loosely with a pinch or two of dried grass clippings to shade it from cruel sun until it can recover from transplant shock. Water lightly. Since you will be encumbered with a number of objects, consolidate them on a tray that will slide along the soil as you move. Fill your knapsack sprayer with water for watering each transplanted seedling. **Water the entire area with a mist when the top half inch of soil dries.** You can expect a 75% "take" on your transplants, which makes the work worthwhile.

Use a dibbler to transplant seedlings thinned from a crowded area.

Transplanting from an area about to be destroyed is a common and worthwhile practice. Sometimes haste will dictate getting as many plants as possible out ahead of the bulldozer. If a plant has been roughly dug out of dry ground and soil falls away from the roots, plant it with a bonnet and a mini-drip system all its own for a few days. After transplanting, cover the plant with a basket, preferably an old, beat-up one with a few staves missing so that light, but not much light, will enter the enclosure. If

318

saving old baskets is not your thing, purchase roofing paper to make teepees. Then place beside it a water-filled gallon jug with a small hole punched in the bottom with an icepick. Constant moisture and darkness soon will make recovery from shock possible.

As establishment takes place, cut back the watering. However, **with any wild-flower planting in the Mountain West, you must supply 1/2 inch of water weekly during the growing season if that amount of natural precipitation does not fall**. For wildflowers sprinkler irrigation is easier than using a drip system unless the grade is steep. Keep a close watch on the watering process so that you can turn it off when puddling begins. Little puddles of water mean the water is being applied faster than it can be absorbed. Puddling brings the finest of soil particles to the surface, destroying soil structure. If puddling continues, rivulets soon form ravines and erosion beings on a massive scale. Until there are clumps of perennials growing vigorously, puddling will be a danger.

If the grade is steep, using lines of black porous hose straight across the slope will be the most efficient. Porous hose is not efficient unless it is level. It can be buried shallowly under a mulch to conceal the look of bull snakes sunning themselves.

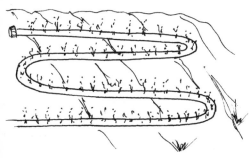

Porous hose will efficiently water a slope if placed at a right angle with the slope.

Seasonal Maintenance

Weeding will be your first consideration every spring. Try to disturb the topsoil as little as possible when weeding. The greatest number of weeds will be grassy. Keep in mind that many lower priced wildflower mixes have grass as a base. Grass seed and seeds of other weeds are often wind blown; therefore, it will be an annual problem. Where grass seed has been introduced with a seed mix, the grass will eventually drive out all other species. It is not by chance that all traces of blood-soaked battlefields are eventually soothed by gentle grass. Make no mistake, however, for under the benign blades lie fiercely competitive roots that will drive out the strongest wildflower. A practiced eye can quickly judge the stewardship of the owner of grazing rights in the high country. Discriminating bovine, ovine, and equine lips will selectively graze the grasses, leaving the flowers. Overgrazed land abounds in wildflowers.

Perennial weedy grasses can be eliminated by mixing a bowl of glyphosate (Roundup) and donning a pair of rubber gloves, then a pair of cotton gloves. Dip your hands in the solution, wringing your hands together slightly to prevent drip. Then stroke each grass blade from bottom to tip. This is a tiresome task, but it works. The grass will be dead within 3 weeks.

Bindweed (*Convolvulus arvensis*) and Canada Thistle (*Cirsium arvense*) are the most vexing. Place an open-ended box over the thistle just as the bloom buds are showing color and spray glyphosate down on the plant; wait until mist has settled, then remove the box, and move on to the next plant. For bindweed, spray with glyphosate in the late fall after frost has browned or blackened all other vegetation. Bindweed remains green until late in the year.

■ *Discriminating bovine, ovine, and equine lips will selectively graze the grasses, leaving the flowers. Overgrazed land abounds in wildflowers.*

■ *At the first*
hint of soil
thawing, put
on your
boots . . .

An early November mowing to a height of 4 to 6 inches is an annual maintenance chore. Your lawn mower may not have a setting that high. A string trimmer will give you the desired height. If there are no grass plants, leave the clippings to form a mulch to protect against winter drought, and to provide more flower seed to reach the soil's surface. If grass plants have invaded, dig them out one by one, if you have the strength, time, and inclination. If you have only time and inclination, keep each grass plant clipped very short to kill them gradually, or use the method above described for Canada Thistle.

Overseed bare spots in the fall also, using half the amount as originally seeded. Transplant little clumps of plants that have seeded around. After the fall mowing, winter watering will be essential in all of the Mountain West except those areas that are snow covered from October until May. Water monthly with sprinkler or hand-held hose to quench every plant even though they lie dormant and seemingly without life. Winter's freeze and thaw will dry out the soil's surface as well as heave plants out of the soil. At the first hint of soil thawing, put on your boots and walk back and forth across your wildflower planting, pressing your foot down on each clump to press it firmly into the soil. As establishment occurs, light fertilization with a soluble liquid, such as Miracle-Gro, in early spring at emergence and again in late summer will keep growth and flowering in good vigor.

Death by Choking

The contrived wildflower meadow on prepared soil will quietly choke itself to death if left untended. One or more of the planted species will dominate to overpower all others. Only your close examination every 2 or 3 weeks will give you a close acquaintence with the plants. You will quickly learn which ones must be dug out or reduced to half-volume before they crowd out a desirable neighbor. Deadheading the spent flowers of the dominant species as they occur all during the growing season may be sufficient to slow down the dominence of a single species, but don't spare the spade when your judgment decrees "Out!"

The Third Year Blues

Repeated trials of wildflower growing has brought to light an incontrovertible fact. There is a period — usually at the 3rd year— that causes an unexplained demise of many desirable species. Every conceivable method of growing has been tried to overcome this shortcoming. Thus far, to no avail. Be forewarned and be ready. Begin stratification of small amounts of seeds of desirable species during the winter of the 2nd year. Start a seedling nursery in your coldframe or some other protected place. In the spring of the 3rd year if you find that many species are missing, begin transplanting your seedlings to the bare areas. If you learn of a method to prevent "the 3rd year blues," be quick to publish your news.

Wildflower Carpets

Enterprising individuals have capitalized on our love of wildflowers. We sometimes see a sod of wildflowers for sale. It is grown in flats 19 inches x 38 inches on approximate 1 1/2 inches of soil, backed with netting. Each flat weighs approximately 15 pounds. Soil preparation is recommended so that it can be laid on loose, friable soil where it will knit quickly. It also can be cut into squares and installed as plugs where it purportedly will spread to fill in the bare spaces within a 1 to 2 year period. Regular watering and fertilization every 6 weeks is recommended also.

The sods vary in the species planted, but none thus far examined contain species exclusively native to the Mountain West. Species such as Johnny Jump-up, Shasta Daisy, Maiden Pinks, and Dame's Rocket (see **Species To Avoid** above) may be wild flowers *someplace*, but they will not satisfy the purist who wants a meadow of true Rocky Mountain wildflowers.

The list below is a few of those species that are desirable in your wildflower planting. Not all will be available for purchase. For some species, seed is almost non-extant: some species do not set seed every year, some never, and some spread only by underground stolons. Joining the North American Rock Garden Society will give you access to the seed exchange of members all over the world, thus eliminating for those who think it tiresome, the collecting of a tiny pinch of seed from our own Mountain West wildflowers. Your wildflower meadow may become a life-long project, albeit a labor of love of the Mountain West and a fascination with growing wild plants.

For a Meadow

Abronia micrantha	Sand-verbena
Aconitum columbianum	Monkshood
Agastache cana	Hummingbird Mint
Aster laevis	Smooth Aster
Aster porteri	Porter's Aster
Agrostemma gigatho	Corn Cockle
Anaphalis margaritacea	Pearly Everlasting
Anemone cylindrica	Windflower
Anemone patens ssp. *multifida*	Pasque Flower
Aquilegia caerulea and	
A. elegantula	Columbine
Arenaria fendleri	Fendler Sandwort
Argemone polyanthemos	Prickly poppy
Arnica cordifolia	Heart-Leaf Arnica
Asclepias tuberosa	Butterfly Weed

Astragalus shortianus	Early Purple Milkvetch
Castilleja linariaefolia	Wyoming Paintbrush
C. integra	Foothills Paintbrush
Campanula rotundifolia	Harebell
Claytonia megarhiza	Spring Beauty
Cleome serrulata	Rocky Mountain Bee Plant
Cryptantha virgata	Miner's Candle
Delphinium all species	Larkspur

If you live in a high country community or ranch on the Plains, do not grow this plant. Poisonous to livestock.

Dryas octopetala	Mountain Dryad
Erigeron macranthus	Showy Erigeron
Epilobium angustifolium	Fireweed
Erigeron melanocephalus	Black-headed Daisy
Eriogonum umbellatum var. aurea	Sulphur Flower
E. alatum	Winged Eriogonum
E. annuum	Annual Eriogonum
Gaillardia aristata	Blanket Flower
Gentiana dentosa elegans	Rocky Mountain Fringed Gentian
G. parryi	Parry's Gentian
Geranium fremontii	Fremont Geranium
Geum triflorum	Prairie Smoke, Pink Plumes
Heterotheca villosa	Golden Aster
Hymenopappus filifolius	Dusty Maiden
Ipomopsis spicata	Scarlet Gilia
Lewisia rediviva	Bitterroot
Liatris punctata	Kansas Gayfeather
Linum lewisii	Wild Blue Flax
Lupinus argenteus	Silvery Lupine
Machaeranthera coloradoensis	Tansy Aster
Mentzelia multiflora	Many- Flowered Evening Star
Mertensia ciliata	Chiming Bells
Mirabilis multiflora	Four o'clock
Oenothera brachycarpa	Stemless Evening Primrose

O. hookeri	Evening Primrose	Primula Parryi	Parry's Primrose
Penstemon ambiguus	Sand Penstemon .	Sidalcea candida	Modest Mallow
P. eatonii	Firecracker		or Checkermallow
	Penstemon	Thermopsis divaricarpa	Golden Banner
P. fruticosus	Bush Penstemon .	Viola nephrophylla	Northern Bog
P. secundiflorus	Side-bells		Violet
	Penstemon		
P. stricta	Rocky Mountain	**Conservation List**	
	Penstemon	Aquilegia caerulea	Blue Columbine
P. utahensis	Utah Penstemon	Aquilegia elegantula	Red Columbine
P. virens	Blue Mist	Aquilegia saximontana	Alpine Columbine
	Penstemon	Calypso bulbosa	Fairyslipper
P. whippleanus	Whipple's		Orchid
	Penstemon	Chimaphila umbellata	Pipsissewa
Pedicularis groenlandica	Elephantella	Clematis columbiana	Sugar Bowls or
Phacelia sericea	Purple Fringe		Leather Flower
Polemonium pulchellum	Jacob's Ladder	Clematis hirsutissima	Rocky Mountain
P. viscosum	Sky Pilot		Clematis
Polygonum bistortoides	American Bistort	Cornus canadensis	Bunchberry
Ranunculus glaberrimus,		Cypripedium calceolus	Yellow
var. ellipticus	Sage, Buttercup		Ladyslipper
Rumex venosus	Begonia Dock		Orchid
Saxifraga rhomboidea	Snowball	Erythronium grandiflorum	Snow Lily
	Saxifrage	Eustoma grandiflorum	Prairie Gentian
Sedum integrefolium	King's Crown	Gaultheria humifusa	Western Creep-
S. rhodanthum	Rose Crown		ing Wintergreen
Thalaspi montanum	Mountain Can-	Gentiana thermalis	Fringed Gentian
	dytuft	Gentianopsis microphylla	Bog Kalmia
Thalictrum fendleri	Meadow rue,	Lilium philadelphicum	Wood Lily
	Fendler's	Linnaea borealis	Twinflower
Trollius laxus	Globeflower,	Moneses uniflora	Woodnymph
Valerian occidentalis	Western Valerian	Primula parryi	Parry's Primrose
Viola sheltonii	Shelton's violet	Stanleya pinnata	Prince's Plume
V. biflora	Northern yellow	Telesonix jamesii	James Saxifrage
	violet	Viola pedatifida	Birdfoot Violet
		Viola selkerkii	Great-spurred
			Violet

Species for a Moist, Partly Shaded Or Sunny Site

Caltha leptosepela	Marsh Marigold
Dodocatheon pulchellum	Western Shoot-ing Star
Hydrophyllum fendleri	Fendler Water-leaf
Lobelia cardinalis	Cardinal Flower
L. siphilitica	Great Lobelia
Myosotis scorpioides	Mountain Forget-Me-Not
Osmorhiza depauperata	Sweet Cicely

All ferns except Bracken
All *Castilleja spp*
All ball Cacti All alpine plants
All Bog Orchids and Coral Root
Any other flower if rare where found. Authorities: H.D. Harrington, "Manual of Plants of Colorado", William A. Weber "Rocky Mountain Flora."

Suggested Reading
Handbook of Rocky Mountain Plants,
by Ruth Ashton Nelson,
revised 1992 by Roger L. Williams.

Suggested Sources
Alplains
32315 Pine Crest Ct. • Kiowa CO 80117
Catalog $1.00

Applewood Seed Co.
5380 Vivian St. • Arvada, CO 80002

Colorado Alpines, Inc.
P.O. Box 2708 • Avon CO 81620

Davenport Seed Corporation
P.O. Box 187 • Davenport WA 99122-0187
1-800-828-8873

Daybreak Alpines
P.O. Box 304 • Jamestown CO 80455

Habitat Plants Nursery
9730 Center Valley Road
Sandpoint ID 83864

High Altitude Gardens
P.O. Box 1048 • Hailey ID 83333

High Country Garden
2902 Rufina St. • Santa Fe NM 87501

J.L. Hudson Seedsmen
P.O. Box 1058 • Redwood City CA 94064
Catalog $1.00

Josef Halda Seeds
P.O. Box 514 • Englewood CO 80151-0514

North American Rock Garden Society
Executive Secretary,
NARGS PO Box 67 • Millwood NY 10546
(membership $25 annually)

Plants of the Southwest
Rt 6, Box 11A • Santa Fe NM 87501
Catalog $3.50

Rocky Mountain Rare Plants
P.O. Box 200483 • Denver CO 80220-0483
Catalog $1.00

Indoor Plants

If you are an average gardener, a tour around your home will find indoor plants flourishing (or surviving) under your care. The mania for houseplants during the 1960's was short-lived for those who did not readily succeed with them, but for others dogged persistence paid off with gradually understanding the why and how of growing them.

There are many lessons to be learned along the way to understanding indoor plants, but they are simple lessons, in no way as complex as maintaining a fruit orchard, a vegetable garden, or the care of an herbaceous border. Yet people who take on the care of an outdoor yard without a qualm still cringe at the idea of taking care of plants indoors and are willing to settle for dreary imitations in plastic or silk.

First, let us dispel the tiresome myth of the green thumb — the idea that you must possess some occult, mysterious power that is given only to a chosen few — before you can dare to take up indoor horticulture, or any form of horticulture, for that matter. All you need is an interest in plants! A gardener visiting your home will always be able to tell whether the plants are present only as a part of the decor (and probably replaced on a regular basis from the supermarket) or if you have a genuine interest in growing them.

Where Indoor Plants Come From

You will progress as a gardener if you are able to understand and care for your

■ . . . *let us dispel the tiresome myth of the green thumb.*

325

indoor plants by knowing the climates they call home. Tropical America is the home of more plants that have been brought into domestic culture than any other area on the planet. In motion pictures the tropical rain forest is lush and crowded with flowers and foliage, while in truth a mature tropical rain forest has a high (100 to 200 feet) canopy of foliage that allows only dim light to reach any plant that might take root below; therefore, the floor of the forest is a tangle of protruding roots and fallen trees from which grow only ferns and the high water requirement plants. These need very few nutrients. The frequent intense rains at the rate of 200 inches per year leach any minerals out of the soil. Organic matter is abundant, but it cannot make up for lack of minerals that plants need. *Epiphyllums, Bromeliads* and orchids and other epiphytes cling to the trunks of trees, surviving on rain, the nitrogen in the atmosphere, and bits of nutrient organic matter lodged in branch crotches. Of these, the best suited to the dry air of our homes are growing in the middle story.

Liana is the term used to designate the thick vines that strangle trees and hang draped from tree to tree. Looking through the canopy generates visions of Tarzan swinging through, using our old friend, the Split-Leaf *Philodendron*, as a means of transportation. The dreaded hurricane (Atlantic) and typhoon (Pacific) are not part of the usual weather patterns of Central America; therefore, forests do not evolve through destructive forces of weather. The friendly *Philodendron* is present, but it is the Strangler Fig (*Ficus aurea*) that fells immense specimen trees with regularity. Numerous insect species and high rainfall combined with heat complete the job of rendering them back to the earth. The

interdependence, specialization, and the extravagance of adaptation are just beginning to be understood. The greatest irony of our time may be that just as we begin to grasp the remarkable complexity of living systems and our dependence on them — the greatest profusion of life that has ever existed is slipping away forever. For example, in the tropics a single tree species has been found to support over a thousand species of beetles. Fifty bird species are entirely dependent on the wanderings of army ants through the forest. With the destruction of the rain forests we are losing thousands of undiscovered foods, medicines, and other valuable substances.

The transition area between the dense forest and the clearings created when a tree falls is the place where most of our houseplants grow. Those we consider "foliage plants" will be found nearest the shade of the forest. Those that bloom brightly and without difficulty in our homes are growing in full tropical sun, a punishing existence if it were not for abundant rain and a soil made rich by rotting vegetation. Vast areas are ideal in soil, temperature, and light requirements for growing multitudes of plants that could become indoor plants in this country.

The vegetation zones of Mexico have been mapped and are shown to outline the areas where various familiar plants come from, and to give you an example of Central American countries and their immense diversity of plants available to us as indoor plants.

As you descend from the U.S. border into Mexico, you encounter the pine/oak forest, the mesquite grasslands, and desert. As you descend further south in latitude, the tropical/deciduous and tropical/evergreen forests appear, high mountain cloud forests, interspersed with thorn forest and areas of arid tropical scrub. Each has made offerings in plants to our homes.

Vegetation Zones of Mexico

TEMPERATE
1. Pine - Oak Forest
2. Mesquite - Grassland
3. Desert

TROPICAL
4. Rainforest & Tropical Evergreen
5. Savanna
6. Tropical Deciduous
7. Thorn Forest
8. Arid Tropical Scrub

Vegetation Zones of Mexico.

Areas 1, 2, and 3 make up 70 to 80 percent of the whole area of Mexico. These are rich in the annual flowers that we grow, such as ageratum, cosmos, marigolds, and zinnias. *Agaves* are native in Area 2, while Area 3 is home to the lily family members: *Yucca, Beucarnea, Dasyliron, Sedum, Echeveria*, and the Bromeliads *Dykia* and *Hecktia*.

In Area 4, the home of tropical evergreens and true broadleaf evergreens, the leaves of the plants have adapted to the wet, hot climate by developing a hard, waxy coating to give protection from disease. The margins of the oblong leaves are entire with strongly indented veins and midribs to channel rain away, much like a river and its tributaries.

From There to Here

Plants are propagated or dug from the wild to be potted up in long open sheds near the point of their growth. It is not unusual to see a small coffee plantation, with the female side of the owner-family tending a shed of houseplants which will be sold to the big dealers or at the market in a nearby town. It is reminiscent of American farms in an earlier era when "mother and the girls" tended the flock of chickens and got to keep the egg money. The large operators, however, grow thousands of cuttings to maturity before they are shipped, bareroot to comply with laws regarding plants entering the United States to large points of sale, such as those in Apopka, Florida. Here still another middle-man buys the plants, pots them up and packs them into either refrigerated or heated trucks for shipment to the point of sale to the public. If it were not for the ineptitude of many plant enthusiasts in growing them, essentially killing the same plants over and over, the industry would die out, for there are not many new introductions each year. Natural selection in the tropics and breeding of plants in this country is the only hope to save the many species yet to be discovered from the well-publicized destruction of the tropical rainforest. To dispel any notion you might have that the rain forest is being destroyed by plant hunters, it takes only one plant, and often only one is taken, to propagate millions by means of tissue culture. These people are dedicated to bringing as many plants as possible into cultivation before destruction by lumbering and burning is complete.[1]

GENERAL CULTURE
Soil Mixes

There are many soil mixes on the market, but the best is one you make yourself. Too often soil mixes contain mountain peat, which not only destroys our valuable mountain fens, but is alkaline and poor in structure. Also, these mixes can contain pathogens that will cause plant diseases that are not normally present in the Mountain West. Long ago, soil mixes were pasteurized, but unless labeled, you can be assured that it is not.

All-Purpose Mix
1 part garden loam
1 part coarse vermiculite
1 part home-made maple
   or oak compost
1 part sphagnum
   peatmoss
1 part perlite

Succulent Mix
1 part All Purpose
   Mix
1 part perlite

Cacti Mix
4 parts commercial
   cacti
      mix
1 part sphagnum peat
1 part vermiculite

As to the "garden loam" listed above, fears that yours won't measure up may be quickly assuaged, because the reason for the listing is the mineral elements it contains. Mountain West soils are rich in minerals (see Vol. I, Soils), and a reasonably rich vegetable garden soil will do. As to the maple or oak compost, there are no worthy substitutes. Fortunately, it can be made in the fall and it will be ready for use by June of the next year, see Vol I, Composting.

Ideally, the entire batch that you mix is pasteurized, but you can also keep a large amount of the mix in a 40- gallon plastic trash can, to pasteurize as needed.

Soil Pasteurization

To pasteurize, place the slightly moistened soil mix in a metal container such as a roaster pan; place a meat thermometer in the center and heat in the oven of your stove with the control set at 300°. Watch the thermometer; when it reaches 140° to 180°, turn the stove down to 200° and continue the pasteurization process for 30 minutes. The odor emitted will fill your home with a somewhat earthy scent. To avoid this, you may use a second method. Place a 1 cup measure of water in your microwave oven. Set the control on high for any amount of time. Watch carefully through the window, stopping the heating as soon as you see the water come to a boil; then use this amount of time and a plastic container to heat the slightly moistened mix. With both procedures, allow the soil mix to cool before use.

Watering

Learning to water indoor plants is the most difficult part of their culture. There are no rules, except that artificially softened water is a death knell to all plants. You have to be tuned in with respect to the normal appearence of each plant, last watering day, the age of the plant, the last potting date, the humidity and cloud cover outdoors over the past few days, and the average humidity and light the plant has received indoors. If this isn't sufficiently intimidating, add the plant family to which it

[1] To aid in the classification of tropical plants, the compilation of native plant remedies, and to beat the pace of further destruction of the tropical rainforests worldwide, contribute to Conservation International, 1015 18th Street NW, Suite 1000, Washington D.C. 20036. This organization does NOT waste money in sending letters begging for funds.

belongs, for as you become more accustomed to using botanical plant names, the name will tell you a lot about its culture.

Your fingers will be your greatest asset in learning to water. Simply press 2 fingers on the soil surface. If it's moist, no need to water. Almost all plants profit from a dry soil surface for about 2 days before being watered.

The quantity of water is debatable. Evaporation and absorption of water into a soil is dependent on the type of pot, the environment of the plant in your home, and the type of root system the plant has. Some advice is to water till you see water running out of the drainage holes. This practice would quickly deplete the soil's minerals, but it is still good advice for an every-6-months routine. Salts from fertilizers build up in the soil, but can be leached away by 1 heavy watering.

If through your forgetfulness or an unforseen incident, your plants have not been watered and have wilted, don't despair. Water them only enough to soak down an inch or 2; then wait an hour and water a little more; wait another hour and water copiously until water runs through into the saucer. If water runs through immediately without seeming to soak up, this means the rootball has shrunk away from the sides of the pot. Fill the sink with tepid water and allow the pot to sit in it until the top of the soil is wet and the rootball is once again the normal size.

Misting

Misting is a term used to describe the mist-like droplets of water sprayed from a bottle. The practice restores humidity in the air that has been dried by artificial heat in a home in winter, or the hot, dry summer atmosphere in a non-air-conditioned or refrigerated air-conditioned home. Using tepid water for misting is a must, but misting itself is another debatable topic. In a cool atmosphere in winter, misting is not advised because it can spread disease organisms. Misting under hot, dry, conditions in either summer or winter is recommended.

Air Circulation

The forced air furnace brought about a revolution in home heating in the 1940's, but it also brought about more houseplant ills. Fanning hot, dry air about the room shut down the plant's respiration, causing brown leaf tips and edges. One of the most effective methods to keep a small amount of air moving in your home involves using 2 small electric fans at opposite ends of a room, but not opposite each other. It creates the same effect with moving air as the swirling of the bath water in your tub.

Roots need oxygen — that's why the light-weight materials are added to the soil mix. There is another way, however, to get oxygen directly to the soil ball. Using a dull knife, make 3 evenly-spaced slits in the soil in the top of a potted plant. Insert a common drinking straw into each of the slits. Cut off each straw slightly above the soil so that soil crumbs won't block the straws. The straws channel air leading to the roots. This method means that the plant will dry out faster. Be watchful.

The bathtub effect of using 2 fans to move air in the area where your plants are growing.

Humidity

Humidity is the one factor that is the most difficult to inject into the home environment in the Mountain West. Humidifiers attached to the forced air furnace will bring the humidity up to 35 to 50 percent. The small floor models or big cabinets will also help, but none are perfect. To supply constant moisture in the air, the pebble tray is still a good device and never-failing. Fill a tray, such as a cookie sheet, with pebbles; set pots directly on the pebbles; pour water into the tray so that no water percolates up through the drainage holes of the pots, but evaporates up into and around the foliage. A drop or 2 of bleach will prevent algae from forming on the pebbles.

If you have windowsills about 4 inches wide, the wallpaper paste trough is a means to corral 4 inch pots into a cohesive unit to give them the humidity they need. These light-weight plastic trays are sold at paint and wallpaper stores and are used to soak rolls of wallpaper in the paste. About 36 inches long and 6 inches deep, they can be sprayed any color and fitted out with water and pebbles as described above.

Pebble trays are still the most effective way of adding moisture to the air around indoor plants.

For the large decorative floor pot, a hidden source of humidity is in a moist pebble base beneath the plant, which is planted in a plastic inner pot, with the decorative pot at least 2 inches larger in diameter.

Double-potting a large plant in a decorative outer pot with source of humidity inside.

Light

In the indoor garden, light is measured in foot candles. A foot candle is the amount of light cast on a sheet of white paper by 1 candle 1 foot away. On a sunny day out-of-doors in the Mountain West, the number of foot candles is 25,000. Inside your sunny window, the number is only 10,000. A plant accustomed to 25,000 FC has some adjustments to make to survive with the mere 10,000 FC your window offers. We can acclimatize a plant gradually to accept this amount. We can choose plants that prefer 10,000 FC. We can cut back on fertilizer and water to force some plants to change metabolically.

We can also supply artificial light in the form of florescent tubes, Verilux Trubloom, and 160-watt Wonderlite mercury vapor lights. Mercury, sodium and metal halide lights are available in wattages as high as

1,000. By far the most popular and inexpensive are the florescent tubes, using 1 high-output deluxe cool white daylight florescent and 1 high-output deluxe warm white daylight florescent tube mounted in an ordinary "shop light" reflector, 6 to 8 inches above the plants for 16 hours daily. The amount of light is greater at the center of the tube than on the ends. The tubes should be replaced annually. Even though they seem to give off a good amount of light, it is considerably diminished after 1 year. Tubes 4 feet in length are standard, but consider 8 foot tubes if you have even a modest number of plants needing additional light.

Beware of the expensive light that changes the appearence of plants, making them look lush with brighter colored blooms. Look at the back of your own hand under this light. The age spots disappear and your hand looks 15 years old again! Nevertheless, the benefit to plants is not justified by the cost.

Light absorption is diminished if leaves are covered with dust. House dust also includes an oily substance. Monthly cleaning is a must if they are to remain healthy and able to absorb light. See *Grooming*.

Fertilization

Plants restricted in a pot eventually use the nutrients in the soil mix. There are choices in fertilizers and only a few rules.

Complete fertilizers have the 3 major elements, nitrogen, phosphorous, and potassium, in soluble form. Often trace minerals and iron are also added. Fish emulsions are made from an infusion of ground fish. They can be deodorized, but your cat can get the slightest whiff and investigate, often with disastrous results. The percentage of each nutrient is as important in houseplant fertilizers as it is in those used outdoors see Vol. I, Soils, p.34. For any type of fertilizer, follow the directions on the container.

Fertilizer is applied the day *after* a plant is watered to avoid burning dry roots. Fertilize foliage plants monthly from early spring through fall **when they are in their most active growth.** With the timed-release food, the capsules are sprinkled on the surface of the soil and the food is released gradually during the growing season. Timed-release pellets, fortunately, don't work well in the lower temperatures of winter. Flowering plants generally enjoy a period of rest after they have bloomed, so hold back on feeding for 2 months after blooming.

Transplanting

When you purchase a plant, it is wise to check the rootball after you get home. Knock the plant out of the pot; if you don't see any roots on the outside of the soil ball, you can assume the plant was sold with few or no roots. Treat it like any cutting, watering carefully, giving it the amount of light it requires, and fertilizing very minimally until it is showing good root structure.

How to knock out of the pot

If, on the other hand, you find the roots clotted and tangled or growing out of the drainage hole, some surgery is indicated. Use a sharp knife to score through the roots vertically very lightly, not severing any. This procedure will activate adventitious buds and new roots will venture outward into the new soil in the new pot. You can also tease a few roots out of the tangle, but you run the risk of their continuing to grow in a circle, a phenomenon known as *geotropism.*

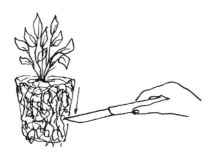

How to score vertically through tangled roots.

In transplanting a plant showing moderate root crowding, choose a pot only 1 inch in diameter larger than the previous pot. This is a procedure known throughout the horticultural world as *potting on.* Further on, we'll learn about *potting back.* Overpotting can cause the quick demise of some indoor plants; with others, failure to thrive can continue for years, long after you've forgotten that you transplanted it to a big pot, thinking to save time and trouble later on.

Clay pots allow more evaporation of water through the pores, are heavy, and break easily, while **plastic pots** have no

pores, tip easily, and crack eventually under our punishing sunlight. Both materials have their devotees, and author has no preference. Drainage holes and pot saucers, however, are imperative.

With either material "crock the pot"[1] and pack the slightly moistened soil mix 1 inch deep in the bottom and around the sides all the way to the top of the pot. Slip the plant from its existing pot and place it into the prepared pot. Use a chopstick or blunt knife to push new soil down around the sides of the pot. Complete by adding soil as needed, keeping 1 inch of space between the top of the soil and the top of the pot to leave room for watering. Fill the sink with water and allow the pot to soak until moisture shows on the top of the soil. Do not fertilize for at least 6 months after repotting. Dressing the topsoil is a nice touch. White seashells actually reflect some light upward into the foliage, but you can also use moss or pebbles.

Grooming

A great number of plants can be washed quickly when they are grouped on the floor of the shower or bottom of the bathtub. But first, eliminate the possibility of overwatering by cutting foil pie plates to the center and fitting the plate around the stem of the plant. Thus, the soil will be covered and very little water will penetrate.

Use a spray bottle to spray a diluted soap solution onto the leaves before rinsing with clear water from the shower head. If you have large plants that are too heavy to move, use the spray bottle of diluted soap and another spray bottle filled with clear water as a rinse. If you really want to spif up the smooth leaved plants, use 2 soft cloths to polish leaves, holding one under the leaf with one hand while polishing the

[1] *See Glossary*

top surface with the other.

Plants with hirsute foliage can also take the soap and water treatment. Let them dry in a warm room.

Pinching

Without judicious pinching, many plants can become leggy eyesores. Use thumb and forefinger to pinch off tip growth to encourage side branches to develop on such plants as *Acuba,* gardenias, *Impatiens,* wax begonias, and any other plant that branches. Single leader plants, such as *Dieffenbachia, Dracena,* or rubber tree should not be pinched.

Pruning

Often a major branch must be removed to resolve a symmetry problem. Choose a time when the plant is actively growing, usually in spring, or soon after it has bloomed. Study the plant carefully. Imagine how the plant will look before cutting off a major branch. Use sharp shears and make a smooth cut just above a growth bud. If you've made a mistake, take heart — a new branch will form to replace the lost one.

Trouble Signs and What To Do

- Wilting: Leaves drop from many sites throughout the plant. Leaf tips brown.
  The cause: Overwatering
- Wilting: Old leaves drop from lower points. New leaves at tip droop. Leaves yellowish, then browning before drying.
  The cause: Underwatering.
- Leaves look faded and are streaked with yellow or brown mottling.
  The cause: Too much light; also, could be spider mites. Examine with a flashlight to detect slight webbing dotted with mites that drop to a sheet of paper held beneath when the branch is tapped.
- New growth is elongated with long spaces between nodes. Leaves are pale and undersized.
  The cause: Not enough light.
- Leaves become yellowish, but veins are green. Lower leaves drop off and new growth is weak.
  The cause: Underfertilization.
- The plant puts on new growth rapidly, but often it is puckered. Stems are weak and streaked yellow.
  The cause: Overfertilization. Flush the build-up through the soil by watering the plant several times in a few hours. Pour collected water out of the saucer.
- Leaf edges curl under and dry out.
  The cause: Room temperature is too high.
- Sudden wilting and browning of tender plants, such as African Violet, Lipstick Plant, Maranta, Episcia, and other tropical plants.
  The cause: Temperature in the room is too low. Sudden wilting can also indicate larvae of various insects attacking the roots. Water in a weak solution of an insecticide for chewing insects.
- Failure to grow. Plant doesn't die, but doesn't grow either.
  The cause: Overpotting. Many people think "I won't have to do this again soon if I transplant to a BIG pot." Plant will sulk and fail to thrive.
- Bud and leaf drop.
  The cause: Hot dry air, excess fertilization, gas fumes and drafts; relocation shock (see list "Plants that like to stay put" below). Thrips can also cause bud drop. (See Chapter 4, Insects).
- White cottony masses in crevices between leaves and stems.
  The cause: Mealybugs. See Chapter 4, Insects. Dab each bug with a cotton

swab dipped in alcohol.

- Stems and leaves get tiny brown "warts." **The cause:** Scale. Flick it off with your fingernail or treat as above or use summer oil spray as directed.
- Leaves get a mottled dusty look, eventually have webs on the branches. **The cause:** Spider mites. Rinse foliage weekly with a strong stream of tepid water.
- Puckered leaves and sticky material around plants, sometimes turning black. **The cause:** The honeydew exuded by aphids, scale, and mealybugs attracts a fungus that causes the sooty appearence.

- Clouds of fast flying white insects emerge when plant is disturbed. **The cause:** Whitefly. Use a small hand-held vacuum cleaner to suck them up daily early in the morning when they are cold and sluggish.
- Holes in the leaves. **The cause:** A slug or cutworm has sneaked indoors after the plant has been growing outdoors in summer. Drive it from its hiding place by watering with soapy water. Watch the topsoil closely for the culprit to emerge.

Plants that move readily

Aglaonema
Araucaria heterophylla
Asparagus, ornamental
Archrontophoenix
    cunninghamiana
Aspidistra elatior
Asplenium
Begonia, all species
Chamaedorea
Chlorophytum
Cissus
Coleus
Cordyline
Crassula
Davallia
Dieffenbachia
Dracaena
Epipremnum aureum (pothos)
Fatshedera lizei
Ficus elastica
F. lyrata

Hedera helix
Howea
Maranta
Monstera
Nephrolepsis exalta
'Bostoniense'
Peperomia
Philodendron
Plectranthus
Polystichum
Pseudopanax lessonii
Rhapsis
Rhoeo spathacea
Sansevieria
Spathiphyllum
Streptocarpus
Syngonium podophyllum
Tradescantia

Plants that like to stay put

Acalypha hispida
Adiantum raddianum
Aeschynanthus
Anthurium
Aphelandra
Calathea
Caryota
Chrysalidocarpus lutescens
Dizygotheca
Episcia
Euphorbia pulcherrima
Fatsia
Ficus benjamina
F. diversifolia
Fittonia
Gynura
Hoya
Polyscias
Schefflera
Sedum morganianum
Schlumbergera
Sinningia speciosa
Tolmiea
Tupidanthus

A List of Fifty Indoor Plants

■ *Abutilon spp.*
FLOWERING MAPLE

A flowering plant reaching 20 inches with judicious pinching. Bell-shaped flowers produce nectar which can damage carpet. Five to 6 hours of full sun, night temperature 50°-60°F. Outdoor culture in summer is beneficial. Prune back by 1/3 when returning indoors.

A. hybridium
'Moonchimes' — Yellow flowers; attractive in a hanging basket.

A. pictum ''Thompsonii' — Green and yellow spotted leaves; apricot flowers.

■ *Aechmea Fosterana*
AIR PINE

The popular supermarket bromeliad with stiff blue-green leaves forming a rosette and a shaft of orange and blue flowers in the center. The center of the leaf whorl must be kept filled with water, but do not add fertilizer to this water. After flowering, this bromel is doomed to a long decline, during which it emits foul odors and becomes very unattractive. If you can stand it this long, it will eventually throw offsets at the base, which you can pot up and start all over again.

■ *Aglaonema modestum*
CHINESE EVERGREEN

The foliage plant indestructible. Attractive pewtered leaves unfold unfailingly, even when the plant is grown in water. Needs only 15 foot candles of light.

■ *Ananas comosus*
PINEAPPLE

An easy houseplant to grow. Choose a supermarket pineapple with a handsome, undamaged top. Cut the top along with a thin plate of the flesh. Place it on a bed of wet, coarse sand in a tray in a sunny window. Give light frequent watering. Within a month a root will begin. Pot it up in the succulent mix. As leaves elongate, they are very sharp. Place it in full sun where it will not damage passersby. To persuade it to bloom and fruit, enclose the entire plant in a plastic bag with an apple. As the apple ages, it emits a gas that will cause the bromeliad to initiate.

■ *Araucaria heterophylla*
NORFOLK ISLAND PINE

This evergreen coniferous tree of the Southern Hemisphere is often poorly grown and much maligned when grown indoors for its propensity to drop whole branches on the carpet without telling you why. Usually purchased as a 1 foot cutie at the supermarket, it grows (if it grows) to juvenility with moderate speed, and at that point it takes on intransigent obstinance which brings on dousings with fertilizer. A quick demise follows. If it is given indirect light in a cool room (never above 75°F), frequently misted to clean the foliage, almost never fertilized, and transplanted to a pot 1 size larger about every 5 years, it will give you years of graceful dark green foliage as it becomes a member of the family. When the top begins to brush the ceiling, you can cut it back several feet and train a new terminal shoot by wiring a nearby shoot upright with a chopstick. Expect the plant to have a somewhat decapitated look for several years, however.

■ *Arundinaria pygmaea*
PYGMY BAMBOO

A dwarf of only 14 inches with typical stalks and linear leaves of taller cultivars.

Bright light but no sun, drafts or temperatures lower than 50°. Fertilize in spring, midsummer, and fall. Warning! This plant is very invasive. Do not plant in open ground out-of-doors. *A. viridistriata* has velvety stems of green and gold 2 to 3 feet high.

■ *Aspidistra elatior*

Cast Iron Plant. Its name indicates its ability to withstand dim light, dusty leaves, lack of water and air circulation. The plant can be handsome when cared for. Use it in a mixed planting where its dark green leaves set off those of a plant with yellow-green or green and white variegated leaves.

■ *Begonia spp.*
BEGONIA

A genus of over a thousand species of vastly differing form native to the transition zone of the tropical rainforests of both hemispheres. They are ideally suited to the home because they like warmth. A few of the more choice are listed.

B. gigantea x B. metallica 'Alleryi' — To 6 feet or more, fibrous-rooted, white-hairy, toothed, bronzy leaves. Many rose-pink flowers August to October.

B. Logee's *cross* ''Muddy Waters' — A rhizomatous introduction by Logee's Greenhouse, 141 North St., Danielson, Connecticut 06329. Deep maroon oval crested leaves, each bearing a white eyelash. Pink flowers in late winter. Can be allowed the same pot for years where convolutions of the stem will curl downward into a cascade.

B. x Crestabruchii 'Lettuce Leaf' — broad oval leaves ruffled glossy green. Rhizomatous. Airy panicles of flowers in winter.

■ *Bougainvillea x Buttiana spp.*
PAPER FLOWER

The riotous blooms of the sun-baked Santa Fe patio can be yours if you grow this thorny vine in full sun under hot, dry conditions. Wait until it is slightly wilted before watering. Bring it to a warm sunny window in winter. Fertilize when in active growth. Prune immediately after flowering. Blooms on new wood. Available in many colors.

■ *Bromeliad spp.*

The thousands of plants of the middle story of the tropical rainforest that thrive on the low light and heat of that area, but must have very high humidity to do well. Many forms abound, with the pineapple being only one. Other cultivated forms include *Aechmea, Billbergia, Dyckia, Guzmania, Hechtia, Neoregelia, Pitcairnia, Puya, Tillandsia, Vriesea, and Witrockia*

■ *Brunfelsia australis*
YESTERDAY-TODAY-AND-TOMORROW

A tall, wide-spreading plant for the floor of the sunporch or conservatory. Requires part sun, warmth, constant moisture, and moderate humidity. In late winter deep purple buds appear; open to sky blue; the following day they are white The 3 colors appearing at once make this a unique plant.

■ BULBS, FORCING

The spring-flowering bulbs and the minor bulbs, as well as daffodils, hyacinths, and tulips, are easily forced into winter bloom after a cold period of only 6 weeks. Don't mix different species of bulbs in 1 container. They may bloom at the same time outdoors, but indoors is a different story. Using a bulb pan, which is a wide, shallow pot of either plastic or clay, fill half full with the standard soil mix; plant the bulbs so that the shoulders almost touch, leaving enough room for the bulbs to be barely covered. With hyacinths use stones to dress the top of the pot after foliage emerges. This will keep bulbs from pushing upward. Water the pots by placing them in a sink of water until moisture shows on the top of the pot. Wrap them in a plastic bag and place in the bottom of the refrigerator for 9 to 12 weeks. If you plan to plant a lot of pots, you will need a coldframe (see Vol.I, p. 243). With coldframe culture don't be in a hurry to plant until late October, for it won't be cold enough before then in the Mountain West to keep the bulbs dormant for the required cold period. Insulate the coldframe pots with 6 inches of bagged DRY leaves or a length of net-wrapped excelsior that you purchase where evaporative air coolers ("swamp coolers") are sold. The pots can be left longer in the refrigerator or cold frame if you want a succession of bloom in the house. After the cold period is completed, bring the bulbs to indirect light in a cool (50 F.) place. Bulbs can be forced under florescent lights if you have a hook and chain arrangement holding the fixture. The lights must be moved upward frequently so that they will not touch the growing foliage.

After growth begins, bulbs need a cool room and full sun because floppy weak foliage results from too much warmth. The bloom is "built-in," meaning that it was in place in embryo form before the bulbs left the bulb grower's farm. After blooms open, bring the pots to indirect light, and the blooms will last longer. After blooms fade, cut them off, leaving the foliage intact. Keep watering until the foliage drops naturally; then turn the bulbs out of the pots and plant in the garden. Daffodils will almost always bloom again within 3 years. Tulips are more iffy, but it doesn't hurt to try. The minor bulbs will all prosper within a year or 2 if planted in the garden after forcing.

Proven Cultivars for Forcing

Minor Bulbs	Common Name
Allium karataviense	Turkestan Onion
Chionodoxa Luciliae	Glory of the Snow
Crocus, all species	Crocus
Eranthis hyemalis	Winter Aconite
Galanthus nivalis	Snowdrop
Iris Danfordiae	Danford Iris
Iris reticulata	Dwarf Iris

Tulips
'Apricot Beauty'
'Bellona
'Christmas Marvel'
'Negrita'
Hyacinths
'Blue Jacket'
'Carnegie'
'Delft Blue'
'Pink Pearl'

Daffodils
'February Gold'
'Ice Follies'
'King Alfred'
'Peeping Tom'
'Téte-á-Téte'

Forcing *Freesias* and Paper-White Narcissus requires a slightly different procedure, for the fragrant *Freesias* should not be crowded in the pot. Two inches must stand between each corm because they form their flower buds as they grow and need extra nutrients. Use the standard mix once again, covering the pointed corm tips with an inch of soil. A temperature of no higher than 55° F. is needed for 45 days, but no light is needed until the first leaves show. At this stage, move them to a brightly lit location at 65°-70° F. Florescent tubes in a cool basement fill this requirement nicely. Keep them moist with a pinch of a complete houseplant fertilizer added to the water weekly. *Freesias* have notoriously weak stems and foliage. Stick 8 chopsticks into the soil on the outer rim of the pot and loop string around them to form a cage for the foliage. Or you may wish to use an embroidery hoop wired to the chopsticks. *Ornithogalum arabicum* Star of Bethlehem and *Sparaxis x hybrida* Wandflower can also be forced by this same method.

Paper-White Daffodils belong to the Tazetta Division 8 class of *Narcissus.* They do not require a cold period. They are easily grown in a low bowl filled with pretty pebbles. Anchor the bulbs leaving about 1/2 inch of the bulb uncovered. To encourage root growth, add water so that it is just barely beneath the bottom of the bulb. If the water level touches the basal plate of the bulb, it is likely to rot. Use the same arrangement of chopsticks and string described above to corral the foliage. Keep the bowl in a cool dark place until you see shoots forming; then bring it to bright light, and finally to full sun in a cool room as the chlorophyll begins to form in the leaves. Blooms will open in 5 to 7 weeks after planting. If you are planning to give pots of either *Freesias* or Paper Whites as gifts, time the blooms so that you deliver the pots when only buds are showing. The recipient will then have the pleasure of watching the blooms unfold. The gift card, of course, should have full directions for care.

■ *Calathea Makoyana* & *C. Warscewiczii*
PEACOCK PLANT

From the dense vegetation at the edge of the rainforest, both of these species take some pampering with high humidity, diffused light, and temperatures never below 60°F. Their common name describes the colors in the leaves — purple, yellow-green, and red.

■ *Citrus spp.*

All plants of this genus favor a very cool sunporch or window garden. Allow them to dry between waterings. Fertilize in March and again in midsummer. If you live at high altitude, they will appreciate summering outdoors where cool nights will bring on flowering of intense fragrance. They fruit and flower at the same time, but don't expect to be overwhelmed by fruit.

C. aurantiifolia 'Tahiti' KEY LIME Use the fruits in gin or vodka drinks and in Key Lime pie.

C. limon 'meyer' MEYER LEMON becomes a 10 foot tree bearing gigantic seedy lemons that make good lemonade and lemon meringue pie.

The little *C.x limonia* 'Otaheite' OTAHEITE ORANGE bears marble sized oranges.

C. Fortunella margarita KUMQUAT makes good marmalade, but connoisseurs prefer the Sour Orange (*C. Aurantium)* for marmalade. Citrus plants grown from seed seldom flower.

■ *Clivia miniata*
KAFFIR LILY

The dark green strappy foliage of this large plant is its main attraction, but it will throw a long-lasting flower stalk of apricot-pink after a period of 6 weeks cool rest in winter. Keep it closely potted. When it throws an offset, wait until it is as tall as the parent before cutting it loose and potting up. Keep evenly moist. Fertilize monthly March through October.

■ *Crassula aragentea*
JADE TREE

Many specimens are handed down through the generations. The 'Cookie Tree' cultivar has fat round leaves of blue-green. All species make heavy branches bearing fat succulent foliage. With cool winter temperatures, an old specimen will burst forth with sprays of white blooms. Prune regularly to maintain shape. Fertilize almost never. Water only when dry.

■ *Cycads*

These palm-like plants are ancient in the evolution of plants on the planet. Most often grown is *Cycas revoluta*, the SAGO PALM. To grow a symmetrical specimen, grow it in the succulent mix (see above) and begin fertilizing moderately in March through midsummer. Water before soil surface dries, but never let it be soggy. Soft new leaves will unfurl. If they are crowded, bump another plant, or have inadequate light, they will harden in a twisted, leaning unattractive position. Give them space until leaves harden. Summer outdoors in dappled shade.

■ *Cymbopogon citratus*
LEMONGRASS

Grow a pot of this for flavoring your Thai or other Oriental dishes. Put it out in the summer in full sun. Keep evenly moist.

■ *Cyperus papyrus*
EGYPTIAN PAPYRUS

Every indoor plant collection deserves one of these. Grow it in a bucket of water where the feather-topped stalks will reach 5 feet. Give it a summer outing in the lily pool. Easily divided. Full sun. Fertilize annually in early spring.

■ *Dizygotheca elegantissima*
FALSE ARALIA

Five-fingered, dark green leaves alarmingly resemble marijuana. Delicate foliage is attractive in the living room where it will grow for years in bright light, to become a ceiling-height decorator's dream. Keep evenly moist, above 60°F.

■ *Epiphyllum x hybridus*
ORCHID CACTUS

Flat, scalloped strappy foliage with startling spring flowers of giant proportions resembling water lilies, which gives rise to another of its common names — Pond Lily Cactus. Adaptable to 40°F., but prefers a range in the 70's. Water well during spring growth, but allow to go almost dry in winter. Fertilize monthly from April through September. Many colors available.

■ *Euphorbia pulcherrima*
POINSETTIA

The traditional plant of the winter holiday season makes a remarkable houseplant because its foliage resists the deposit of dust. This welcome repulse makes it a candidate as a tall foliage plant, whether it blooms or not. Being day-length sensitive, it won't bloom unless it has 14 continuous hours in complete darkness in each 24 hour period from late September to the middle of October. Situated in a west window in the living room, the foliage is yellow-green, a complement to most decors. Keep evenly moist; fertilize monthly.

■ *Ficus spp.*
FIG

The standard foliage plants of the home, sunporch, and conservatory. Often difficult because of they resent being moved. *Ficus benjamina* will often drop all of its leaves upon arriving at your home, a disconcerting event when it was purchased to impress expected guests. All species need moderate moisture, humidity, and warmth. Cleaning the leaves is a major task when the specimens reach ceiling height. Then it's time to give them to the library, hospital lobby, or courthouse foyer.

F. benjamina
LAUREL, JAVA, or WEEPING FIG

The small street tree pruned as a lollipop on the West Coast, it makes an attractive background and specimen tree for the large conservatory. Its familiarity in shopping malls breeds contempt, but it still holds a place as an indoor plant, whether with a braided trunk or caricatured top. If it drops it leaves upon arrival, keep the soil just barely moist and do not fertilize until leaves appear again. It needs bright light and moderate humidity.

F. elastica Rubber Tree. The old favorite with green oval leaves, tipped in maroon. Same culture as above.

F. lyrata FIDDLE-LEAF FIG. A species of wide-spread leaves of violin shape. Same culture as above.

F. pumila CREEPING FIG. An attractive self-clinging vine with small oval leaves. Should not be allowed to go dry. If it wilts and drops leaves from lack of water, it will re-leaf within a month with normal care.

FERNS

Davallia feejeensis
RABBIT'S FOOT FERN
Nephrolepsis exalta bostoniensis Dallas' DALLAS FERN, *Pteris cretica* Albolineata' VARIEGATED BRAKE FERN. Three of the hundreds of ferns available as indoor plants will be treated here. *Davallia* is the ideal of the 3, living under less than 'ferny' conditions. It can withstand some sun, some dryness, and without fail, will live to be handed down to your grandchildren. The fronds are medium green and very lacy, and the feet are described as furry claws, named for various furbearing animals — rabbit, hare, deer, and squirrel. Divide it only when it is very

crowded. The Boston Fern of finicky culture has been replaced with a cultivar named 'Dallas' for its ability to thrive in that hot dry climate. It was discovered at the edge of the rainforest, having adapted to dry air and sunny conditions. But give it indirect light, keep the stringy air roots pruned off, and feed only lightly every 3 months. It grows with prodigious speed and needs space to become symmetrical. Divide only when very crowded. Knock it out of the pot and split with a sharp butcher knife into as many sections as you need divisions. Pot up each without trying to tease out roots. The *Pteris* fern is the pretty little gray-green foliage plant that grew in a silver "fernery" in the middle of your grandmother's dining room table. It is popular once again, able to withstand moderately dry air and indirect light. All ferns should be kept constantly moist, but not soggy.

Fuchsia x hybrida
FUCHSIA, LADIES EARRINGS

There are hundreds of cultivars of this old Victorian houseplant. We in the Mountain West are victims of its beauty around Mother's Day when baskets of it drip with "ladies earrings" at the local florist, and a basket is often presented to Mother, who must then try to grow the thing the rest of the hot summer. It loves cool moist shade, which is why it flourishes in coastal areas. Fortunately, in the Mountain West we favor the evaporative "swamp cooler" type of air conditioning (not the refrigerated variety), which adds copious amounts of moist cool air to the home. Instead of hanging the fuchsia on the patio, keep it indoors summer and winter. It wilts if the temperature is above 75°F. Watering is tricky. Too much and roots rot, not enough, blooms and buds drop. Water at that indescribable point that is just slightly drier than moist and considerably wetter than bone-dry. If temperatures go above 75°F, misting is in order. If overwatered or under extremely humid conditions, fuchsia will go into *guttation*, a process whereby drops of moisture are exuded to hang on the tips of foliage — a pretty sight and thought to mean that it is a highly evolved plant species. Indirect light suits them, but direct air blowing from the cooler does not. In the late fall prune back to the rim of the basket, leaving branches 6 to 8 inches long. Keep them under high humidity and bright light. Pinch back shoots to form a compact plant or store as directed in Chapter 12 Container Plants. Begin feeding half strength in February and your plant should be in full bloom again by Mother's Day.

■ *Gardenia jasminoides*
'Fortuniana' GARDENIA
Chances are strong the first corsage you gave or received was a gardenia. Supermarket sales soar for this nostaligic, but difficult plant. Keep it moist, warm (60°F. to 85°F.), and in bright sun and high humidity. It will drop its buds IF ANY OF THE FOLLOWING CONDITIONS OCCUR: there is poor light, lack of humidity or moisture, low temperature. Fertilize monthly with Miracid when in active growth. Buds are initiated between 60°-65°F., a very narrow range. If you want winter flowers, pinch off bud growth until September.

■ *Gesneriads: Saintpaulia ionantha*
AFRICAN VIOLET and *Streptocarpus x hybridus* CAPE PRIMROSE. Two members of the *Gesneriaceae* that are most often grown in window gardens or under lights. Both do well in indirect light or under lights, but the *Streptocarpus* can withstand much colder temperatures. The hairy leaves of a well-grown African Violet rotate around the pot as a wheel, with a cluster of blooms rising from the center. The "Strep" leaves are long, hairy, thick and strappy. They lie in layers over the side of the pot with the blooms rising from the center. Wash the foliage of both frequently in tepid water and allow to dry in a warm room. Fertilize monthly. There are many other species of Gesneriads for the enthusiastic grower to investigate.

■ *Hedera helix*
ENGLISH IVY
Nostalgia and introduction of new cultivars keep ivy tops on the houseplant list. Baltic ivy (*H.h.* 'Baltica') is hardy and grown outdoors in the Mountain West, but English ivy is of doubtful hardiness except in the southern areas of the Mountain West. Let it dry between watering; fertilize monthly when in active growth. *H.h.* 'Buttercup' has yellow-green foliage which is very chic now. 'Curlylocks' has curled leaf margins; 'Irish Lace' is 5 pointed; 'Glacier' is variegated green and white; 'Fan' is fan-shaped; 'Goldheart' has a yellow area along the midrib.

■ *Helichrysum petiolare*
'Limelight' LICORICE PLANT
Soft velvety leaves the color of lime sherbet give this graceful, wide branching foliage plant its name. It is especially beautiful in combination with blue flowers, such as Salvia 'Blue Victory'. Easy to propagate from cuttings. Two hours of sun; can withstand heat; water moderately.

■ *Hippeastrum vittatum*
AMARYLLIS
A strappy-leaved evergreen bulb from

Chile which many think must be dried off and allowed to go dormant half the year. This is only a trick of the big growers to cut shipping costs. Keep it close-potted in a pot no larger than 2 inches in diameter more than the bulb with 1/3 the bulb above the soil. Keep it moist and in a place where a temperature of 70°F. can be maintained. When foliage appears, apply fertilizer monthly and give full sun with 50°F. nights and 70°F. days. After bloom, cut the bloom stalks. When all danger of frost is past, sink the pots rim deep outdoors in partial shade. Don't remove the bulbs from the pots. They shock and refuse to bloom. When bringing them indoors in the fall, scrape a little soil off the top of the pot and add new soil. Keep them cool, slightly drier and allow to rest. When you want them to bloom, bring them to a warm place and begin watering normally again. Amaryllis will often throw an offset. These should never be allowed to die down. Keep them growing until half the size of the parent, then cut away with a sharp knife and pot up.

■ *Hoya carnosa*
WAX PLANT

A vine that will twine counterclockwise around a wire strung around your sunporch or greenhouse window. With silver-speckled, deep green, thick leaves; clusters of sculpted florets that resemble cloth and emit a strong perfume at night. The nectar is very sticky. Fading flowers should be allowed to fall or you can pull them off by the stems. Never cut the peduncle — the new shoot and new buds grow from it. Prefers to be pot-bound. *H.c.* 'Variegata' has leaves of pink, cream, and green, but does not flower.

■ *Kalanchoe Blossfeldiana*
(pronounced kalan-KO-eh)
PALM BEACH BELLS

The pot plant of Christmas behind Poinsettia. A succulent of the *Crassula* family demanding full sun and succulent potting mix (see above) allowed to dry between waterings. They look best in a hanging basket where the orange-red flowers will last 6 weeks. Being day-length sensitive, they must remain in darkness for 15 continuous hours for 4 weeks prior to setting bud in November.

■ *Lagerstroemia indica*
MINIATURE CRAPE MYRTLE

A small version of the summer-flowering tree of the Southis now available for the indoor garden. Grow it from a plant or seed[1] as a shapely shrub to enjoy the small frilly flowers in the heat of summer. Easily moved to the patio in summer. Allow it to be lightly frosted so that it will go dormant and lose its leaves in late fall. Store in darkness and above freezing. Bring it into warmth and watering again in March.

■ *Mittriostigma axillare*
AFRICAN GARDENIA

The scent of the pink flowers of this plant makes it worth growing, for it's not much to look at otherwise. Smooth green leaves sometimes twist and curl. Very slow growth, eventually reaching 5 feet. Regular potting mix; moist, but not soggy; 4 hours of sun per day; temperature above 50°F.

■ ORCHIDS

Warm: *Phalaenopsis spp., Cattleya bowringiana, Dendrobium spp.* Cool: *Oncidium spp,* formerly *Cypripedium,*

[1] *Available from Park Seed Co., Cokebury Road, Greenwood SC 29647-0001. Listed as Crape Myrtlettes*

Paphiopedilum spp., Vanda. The temperature restrictions apply to both day and night. For warm varieties, 65°F. minimum night temperature; for cool, 60°F. or less at night. Humidity for all should approach 50%, which is possible with gravel trays beneath. For those in hanging containers, keep a portable humidifier within 4 feet of the container. Both the *Cattleya* and *Vanda* need full sun in winter in a south-facing window. The remaining species are happy with an east or west exposure. The *Oncidium* has a strange requirement, that of very cool night temperatures in autumn. Hang it from a tree limb for 3 weeks in September, being watchful for sudden frosts. Potting media fir bark, often called "orchid bark", is easily purchased at a nursery. As you progress, you will mix your own special potting media. Orchid-mania is contagious. Soon you will have a set of "orchid friends."

■ *Oxalis Regnellii*
OXALIS
Your grandmother had a pot of this bulbous plant in her kitchen window. So should you. The shamrock foliage, squared-off, droops daintily over the pot edge, with a cluster of delicate white flowers rising in the center. There is also a deep maroon foliage cultivar, *O. braziliensis.* Full sun or part shade; lighten the potting mix with a little sand. Divide and repot about every 2 years.

■ PALMS
The ultimate in sophisticated indoor plants — *Rhapsis excelsa* — the Lady Palm, has fronds of deep green that are fan-shaped, not pointed. It becomes a neat bush about 4 feet high and can live 100 years. Give it your most treasured cloisonné urn

and an elegant stand. Next in importance are the graceful, bold silhouettes of the major palms for indoor use: KENTIA PALM *(Howea forsteriana)* that we see in hotel lobbies. Withstanding more neglect than others, it takes even moisture and bright light, but not sun and it will reward you handsomely. PYGMY DATE PALM *(Phoenix roebelenii)* is a delicate 4 feet. It needs more light than Kentia; a few fronds will yellow and fall in autumn. FISHTAIL PALM *(Caryota urens)* has squared-off leaves on strong fronds and tops out at 6 feet. Hard to find. CHINESE FOUNTAIN PALM *(Livistona chinensis)* is a very short, neat fan-palm not easy to find. See sources at end of chapter. NEANTHE BELLA PARLOR PALM *(Chamaedorea elegans)* survived the Victorian image and is now given conservatory status. Tops out at 4 feet. Very tolerant of dark; too much light yellows the foliage. Watch for spider mites.

■ *Passiflora actinia*
PASSION FLOWER VINE
This vine rambles over fencerows in Arkansas, but in the Mountain West it can be grown in a window where it will receive full sun. The flowers are works of art, said to resemble the stations of the Cross and the Passion of Christ. The edible fruit is made into jam. Keep it evenly moist in temperatures above 55°F. Fertilize in summer, especially if you put it outdoors. Flowers develop on new growth; therefore, prune once a year in late winter while it is dormant, removing 1/3 of last year's growth. See Chapter 10, Vines, for outdoor culture.

■ *Pelargonium peltatum*
IVY-LEAF GERANIUM aka MARTHA WASHINGTON aka REGAL

Many families can count back generations to the ancestor who began handing down this treasured plant. However, intense hybridization has led to more than a thousand cultivars now available. Especially popular as window box plants in Europe, they are "self-cleaning" and do not require deadheading for continuous bloom. They have thick smooth glossy leaves shaped somewhat like ivy. Flower colors include red, salmon, pink, magenta, lavender, and white, as well as various white-eyed species. The Alpine Ivies of Europe are now available and are more heat tolerant than American Ivy Geraniums. The flush of spring flowers is followed by sporadic flowering all summer. Keep them in cool shade. Pot back in September by knocking the plant out, shaking soil off roots and pruning roots to fit into a pot 1 size smaller than previous. Then prune the top similarly; repot in standard mix; then place it in a cool place in good light, but not sun, and almost no water. By the first of the year new growth will begin. No pinching will be required and normal watering can begin. It will set bud and the cycle will begin again.

■ *Pentas lanceolata*
STAR CLUSTER or PENTAS
A continuously flowering small shrub for a warm location. Fertilize when in active growth; keep moist. Keep deadheaded. A good plant to decorate the patio in summer. Available in pink, white, lavender, and red.

■ *Rhododendron obtusum*
AZALEA, cv. KURUME
A popular gift plant for the hospital patient or at holiday time. Can be maintained to bloom again if transplanted into a standard mix into which extra sphagnum peatmoss has been added. Fertilize with Miracid monthly when it is making new growth in spring. Sink the pot in partial shade outdoors in summer; keep moist. Leave it outdoors until night temperatures drop to 40°F., when it will set its buds. Bring it to a very cool sunny window where its long-lasting flowers will brighten the winter.

■ *Ruta graveolens*
'Blue Mound' and *R.g.* 'Blue Curl.' RUE, aka HERB OF GRACE
Herbs indoors are more trouble than they are worth unless you have a greenhouse, but this herb is grown for its beautiful blue-green foliage toward the front of the perennial border or in a pot on the patio. It is borderline hardy in the Mountain West. It will live over but it will seldom bloom. The bloom is what you are after if you wish to attract butterflies; therefore, winter it over in a pot as a beautiful indoor plant in winter and in summer give it partial shade, plenty of water and warmth outdoors.

■ *Serissa foetida* 'Variegata'
YELLOW RIM SERISSA
A refined plant for your most treasured porcelain pot. Very small green leaves, rimmed in butter yellow, with dozens of small pink flowers. Lends itself to topiary or bonsai. Part shade, evenly moist. Fertilize when in active growth.

■ *Sparmannia africana*
AFRICAN HEMP
A flowering plant with soft 8 inch, leaves, angled and lobed with silky hairs. It will mature at ceiling height. In spring white umbels appear, each floret tipped in purple. Keep above 50°F. and evenly moist; full sun indoors, partial shade outdoors in summer.

■ *Stephanotis floribunda*
MADAGASCAR JASMINE

This fragrant white wedding flower is long-lived but difficult to establish. It will wind its way up a trellis or pole 15 feet or more in bright light, but not sun. Fertilize in spring and again lightly in midsummer. Flower production will be best if you watch for new growth and pinch tips to force blooming side growth. If your plant refuses to bloom, force dormancy by reducing water in fall. Resume regular watering when new growth begins and flowering should begin in about 6 weeks.

■ *Trachelospermum jasminoides*
CONFEDERATE JASMINE

This small-leaved vine will cover itself with fragrant white flowers in spring. Give it a trellis of string in full sun; then weave the growth back and forth as it climbs upward. Even moisture, high humidity, fertilize every 8 weeks.

Suggested Sources:

Altman Specialty Plants (succulents)
553 Buena Creek Rd.
San Maarcos CA 92069 • catalog $1

Arnold J. Klehm Grower, Inc.
44W637 Rt. 72 • Hampshire IL, 60140
catalog $1

Colorado Cuttings
wholesale only, contact your nursery

Fischer Greenhouses (Gesneriads)
Oak Ave • Linwood NJ 08221

Logee's Greenhouse • 55 North St.
Danielsonm CT 06239 • catalog $3.00

■ *Tupidanthus calyptratus*
MALLET FLOWER

A trendy plant now in favor by decorators for its handsome compound leaves, each more than a foot long. It tops out at 12 feet — perfect for stairwells lighted with a plant light to keep it going. Evenly moist; above 60°F. Fertilize when in active growth.

■ *Zantedeschia aethiopica*
CALLA LILY

This plant may become a good window garden subject for winter and outdoor water garden plant in summer if it can lose the "funeral flower" label. A strong rhizomatous plant that will break a pot without compunction. Peter Loewer in his book "The Indoor Window Garden" recommends growing it double potted, with the outer pot filled with water almost to the rim of the inner pot. Bloom is in January. After flowering it dies down. In summer place the pot at the edge of the water garden or in the bog garden where its feet are continually bathed, and it will flower once again. Heavy feeder, temperature no lower than 55°F., full sun.

Merry Gardens
P.O. Box 595 • Camden ME 04843

Rhapsis Gardens • P.O. Drawer 287
Gregory TX 78359 • catalog $1

Shady Hill Gardens (geraniums)
821 Walnut St. • Batavia Il 60510
catalog $1

Sunset Nursery (bamboos)
4007 Elrod Ave. • Tampa FL 33616
Send bus. envelope and 2, 1st class stamps.

Glossary of Horticultural Terms

Alternate host — one of the two plants required by certain insects or fungi to complete its life cycle.

Ascospores — the reproductive stage of fungi; also includes *basidiospores*.

Auricle — claw-like or ear-like projection at the base of the blade of grasses.

Axil — the upper angle where a leaf or a branch joins the stem.

Blade — the flat extended part of a leaf.

Blanch — to take the color out of by bleaching or to plunge into boiling water for a short period of time to stop enzyme action.

Bolt — the early production by a plant of a seed-stalk.

Bones—the basic structure of a landscape, usually formed by trees or shrubs placed strategically.

Bottom heat — heat source beneath a seedbed or propagation tray, usually from electric tape or fresh manure.

Bract — a reduced or modified leaf often surrounding the bae of a flower.

Calyx — the outer parts of a flower composed of leaf-like parts called *sepals*.

Canker — an erosive eruption on a stem or trunk, usually exuding a viscous liquid or the teliospore of the causal fungi.

Clasping — a term used when the blade of a leaf reaches partly or entirely around the stem.

Cole — term used to encompass plants of the cabbage family *Cruciferae*. Also called *crucifers*.

Crock the pot — a procedure to partially block the drainage hole of a planting pot. Broken clay pots are called *crock* and a piece of crock is used to block the hole before planting.

Crown — as in turnips, carrots and other root crops — the beginning of the formation of several stems of foliage and the swelling of the edible root.

Cucurbit— a member of the squash family *Cucurcitaceae*, including cucumbers, melons and squash.

Cytokinen — a hormone-like compound in plants that promotes cell division and cell differentiation into roots, and shoots. Also inhibits aging in plants.

Desert ephemeral — a opportunistic desert plant that takes advantage of rainfall to germinate, grow, bloom, and set seed within a short period of time before scorching weather arrives or resumes.

Dieback — the death of the terminal portion of limbs or stems of a plant.

Etiolation — blanching by excluding light from a plant.

Floating row cover — a spunbonded fabric sold by the yard or roll for the purpose of protecting plants from inclement weather, insects, or wind-borne diseases.

Forb — an herbaceous plant other than grass.

Gall — a swelling or growth produced by a plant in response to insects, eriophyid mite, fungi, or other organisms.

Girdled — the complete removal of bark and cambium in a ring around a trunk or limb.

Guttation — a process in a few advanced plants that allows them to get rid of excess moisture by exuding it through the edges of leaves.

Hardening off — exposing a plant gradually to lower or higher temperatures, thus hardening the cells and making them less vulnerable to low or high temperatures.

Herbaceous — a higher plant that does not produce woody tissues.

Inflorescence — the flower parts of a plant.

Initiate — the beginning of root, shoot, or flower buds.

Integrated pest management — **(IPM)** a philosophy of managing pests that involves use of all available control techniques in a coordinated and integratedmanner. Often implied in integratest pest management is the ideal that management will be accomplished in a way that minimizes undesirable effects on desirable species and retards development of pest resistance.

Involucre — a ring of small leaves or bracts at the base of a flower.

Jiffy-7 — a brand name of a compressed fiber pot used for seed starting or transplanting of young plants.

Knock out — a horticultural procedure in which a plant with root intact is quickly removed from a pot by holding the pot upside down and knocking the rim sharply against a stationary object.

Life cycle — a series of changes in form undergone by an organism in development from its earliest stage to the recurrence of the same stage in the next generation.

Lining out stock — saplings grown from seeds sold to be lined out in rows to grow to a larger transplantable tree.

Maggot — larval form of an insect, usually legless.

Metamorphosis — a change in form in a life form (e.g., egg, larva, pupa) before reaching the adult form characteristic of the species.

Molt — shedding of the exoskeleton by an arthropod.

Monoecious — a term describing the flower of a plant in which both male and female organs are produced within the same plant.

Necrosis — gradual decay of a plant.

Netted — a series of fine lines or symmetrical growths on a plant surface.

Node — that part of a stem from which a leaf starts to grow.

Peduncle — the stem of a flower.

Phenoxy — a category of herbicides containing 2,4 dichloro**phenoxy**acetic acid.

Pheromone — a chemical used to communicate by members of the same species, e.g. females of many insect species produce sex pheromones to attract male mates.

Phloem — the vascular plant tissue that transports nutrients.

Polarity — the inherent action of a plant in which the shoot grows upward and the root grows downward.

Potting back — a planting procedures in which a plants' roots are trimmed back; the top is pruned back moderately, and the plant is re-potted in a smaller pot than that in which it was previously growing.

Potting on — a planting procedure in which a plant is transplanted to a pot one size larger than that in which it was previously growing.

Radicle — the emerging root of a seedling.

Rhizome — a subterranean, thickened plant stem.

Riparian — that area adjoining a stream or river.

Rogue — a horticultural term meaning to destroy.

Sclerotia — the masses of reproductive cells of fungi that are enclosed in a dark, hardened covering so as to resist unfavorable environmental conditions.

Seeded — a horticultural term meaning seeds have been planted.

Sessile — plants without a stalk or stem.

Sheath — the lower part of the leaf which surrounds a stem.

Side dressing — an application of fertilizer scattered on either side of a plant or row of plants.

Sink the pot — to lower a planted pot into the soil to the rim of the pot.

Spike — an inflorescence of one or many florets that is upright, narrow, and pointed at the tip.

Stick or sticking — the process of placing plant cuttings into the soil.

Strike — a term used to designate the beginning of the rooting of a cutting.

Subtending buds — buds located below the terminal bud on a stem.

Summer baking — the requirement of some plants, notably certain species of bulbs, that require a dry soil at high temperature in summer.

Teliospore — a thick-walled, elongated structure that is the final stage of the rust fungus.

Terminal — the topmost area of a plant.

Topping — the detrimental practice of lopping off a tree at random locations on limbs and branches.

Watering up — to apply water to soil to induce the germination of seed.

Watering-in — to apply water to a plant after planting so as to settle the soil and eliminate air pockets.

Winter annual — a plant that has the ability to germinate and grow in early fall; withstand the winter and to bloom and set seed in the following spring. Winter wheat is a winer annual.

Woody — a plant that has hardened woody tissue; trees and shrubs are termed "woodies."

Reference Data

METRIC EQUIVALENT CHART

1 acre = 4,047 square meters = 0.405 hectare

1 yard = 0.914 meters

1 foot = 30.48 centimeters

1 inch = 25.4 millimeters = 2.54 centimeters

1 square foot = 0.09 square meters

1 square yard = 0.8 square meters

1 pound = 453.6 grams = 0.454 kilograms or kilos

1 ounce = 28.35 grams

1 gallon = 3.785 liters

1 quart = 0.95 liters

1 teaspoon = 5 milliliters or cubic centimeters

1 tablespoon = 15 milliliters or cubic centimeters

1 cup = 236.6 milliliters or cubic centimeters

Metric Multipliers

APPROXIMATE CONVERSION FACTORS

Symbol	When You Know	Multiply by	To Find	Symbol
		LENGTH		
in	inches	2.54	centimeters	cm
ft	feet	30	centimeters	cm
yd	yards	0.9	meters	m
		AREA		
in_2	square inches	6.5	square centimeters	cm2
ft_2	square feet	0.09	square meters	m2
yd_2	square yards	0.08	square meters	m2
		MASS OR WEIGHT		
oz	ounces	28	grams	g
lb	pounds	0.45	kilograms	kg
		VOLUME		
tsp	teaspoons	5	milliliters	ml
tbsp or T	tablespoons	15	milliliters	ml
fl oz	fluid ounces	30	milliliters	ml
c	cups	0.24	liters	l
pt	pints	0.47	liters	l
qt	quarts	0.95	liters	l
gal	gallons	3.8	liters	l
ft_3	cubic feet	0.03	cubic meters	m3
yd_3	cubic yards	0.76	cubic meters	m3
		TEMPERATURE (exact)		
°F	Fahrenheit	5/9 after subtracting 32	Celsius	°C

Bibliography

Beckett, Carr, Stevens, *The Contained Garden*, Viking, 1993

Hull, George F., *Bonsai For Americans*, Doubleday, 1964.

Lane Books, *Sunset Garden Patio and Building Book*, Menlo Park CA 1966.

Saximontana, Rocky Mountain Chapter, American Rock Garden Society, Vol. XIII, No. 9, October, 1990.

Rockwell, F. F. & Esther Grayson, *The Complete Book of Bulbs*, Doubleday, Inc. 1951

Johnson, Mary, *Tub Farming*, Mary Johnson, Garden Way Publishing, 1978.

Nisbet, Fred J., *Growing Better Roses*, Alfred A. Knoph NY 1973

Crockett, James, *Underwood Roses, The Time-Life Encyclopedia of Gardening*, Time-Life Books, Alexandria, VA 1975.

Lima, Patrick, *Herbs, The Harrowsmsith Illustrated Book of*, Camden House, Camden East, Ontario Canada 1986

Riggs, Carol, *Herbs, Leaves of Magic*, Sycamore Island Books, Boulder CO 1979

Lust, John, *The Herb Book*, Bantam Books NY 1974

Crawford, Stanley, *A Garlic Testament, Season on a Small New Mexico Farm*, Harper Perennial, 1992

Jacobs, Betty E.M., *Growing and Using Herbs Successfully*, by Garden Way,Charlotte VT 1981

Cranshaw, Whitney, *Pests of the West*, Fulcrum Publishing, Golden CO 1992.

Leatherman et al, *Aspen, a Guide to Common Problems in Colorado*, Colorado State University, Colorado State Forest Service, 1986

Pierce, John H., *Greenhouse Grow-How*, Plants Alive Books, Seattle WA 1977.

Hill, Lewis, *Fruits and Berries for the Home Garden*, Garden Way Publishing, Charlotte VT 05445 1980

Schutz Walter, *How To Attract, House and Feed Birds*, Collier-MacMillian, London 1970.

Wyman, Donald, *Shrubs and Vines for American Gardens*, Macmillan, 1961.

Welty, John Carl, *The Life of Birds*, W.B. Saunders, Company, Philadelphia PA 1964.

Craighead, Craighead, and Davis, *A Field Guide to Rocky Mountain Wildflowers*, Houghton Mifflin, Boston, MA 1963.

Cruso, Thalassa, *Making Things Grow*, Lyons and Burford, 1970.

Pesman, Walter M., *Meet the Natives*, 9th edition, Denver Botanic Gardens, Roberts Rinehart 1988.

Carleton, R. Milton, *Your Lawn, How To Make It and Keep It*, Van Nostrand, 1959.

Raymond, Dick, *Dick Raymond's Gardening Year*, Simon & Schuster, 1984.

Westcott, Cynthia, *Are You Your Garden's Worst Pest?*, Doubleday, 1961.

Westcott, Cynthia, *The Gardener's Bug Book*, 4th edition, Doubleday, 1973.

Dirr, Michael A. and Charles W. Heuser, Jr., *The Reference Manual of Woody Plant Propagation*, Varsity Press, Inc., Athens GA, 1987.

Burpee, Lois, *Lois Burpee's Gardener's Companion and Cookbook*, Harper & Row, 1983.

Borror & White, *A Field Guide to the Insects*, Houghton Mifflin, 1970.

Zimdahl, Robert, *Weeds of Colorado*, Cooperative Extension Service, Colorado State University, Fort Collins CO 80523 1983.

Whitson, et al *Weeds of the West*, Western Society of Weed Science, Univ. of Wyoming, 1992.

Hartman & Kester, *Plant Propagation Principles and Practices*, Second Edition, Prentice-Hall Inc., Englewood Cliffs NJ

Harrington, H.D., *How to Identify Plants,* The Swallow Press Inc., Chicago, 1957.

Metcalf, C.L., Flint W.P., *Destructive and Useful Insects, Their Habits and Control,* McGraw-Hill Book Company, NY.

Index

3187